THE CENTENNIAL HISTORY OF THE UNITED STATES SAILING ASSOCIATION

Formed in 1897

Reformed in 1925

Transformed in 1975 into USYRU

Renamed in 1991 as US SAILING

FROM THE PRESIDENT

The history of the organization of sailing in North America is an integral and significant part of the Centennial celebration of the North American Yacht Racing Union and the United States Sailing Association. We owe a debt of gratitude to Harry Anderson and the late Rob MacArthur for researching and composing the story and for supplying so much color and recollection from their own rich memories. We also appreciate the generous support of Rolex Watch U.S.A. which has been vital in permitting the high production standard and timely presentation of this book. On behalf of all US SAILING members, I extend heartfelt thanks to Harry, to Rob's memory and to Rolex.

At times we may become so wrapped up in our day to day lives and pursuit of our sport that we do not consider the past, but it is beneficial for each of us to revisit our history and traditions. There is a great deal we can learn from the glorious history of Yachting, as told in these pages, that will provide guidance and inspiration to all of us who sail as we take the sport boldly into the 21st Century.

David Irish

US SAILING.

ISBN: 1-882502-51-5

Sponsored by

ROLEX

IN CELEBRATION

Rolex is pleased to join in the Centennial celebration of US SAILING and its accomplishments. Throughout 100 years of service, US SAILING and its dedicated volunteers have not only developed a national community for sailors, but also set and maintained the standard of excellence by which that community pursues the sport it loves.

Rolex's rewarding relationship with US SAILING began in 1980 with the first Rolex Yachtsman and Yachtswoman of the Year Awards. It has continued through a 13-year partnership with the US Sailing Team; six runnings – and soon to be a seventh – of the Rolex International Women's Keelboat Cham-pionship; eight years of the US SAILING/Rolex Junior Sailing program; and our sponsorship, new this year, of US SAILING's Adult Championships.

Without US SAILING and its dedicated constituency, these events and programs would not be possible. We salute your first 100 years and look forward to sailing with you through the end of this century and into the next.

Cordially,

R. Puton.

Roland Puton
President and CEO
Rolex Watch U.S.A.
August 1997

CONTENTS

CHAPTER IV - REVIVAL OF NAYRU IN 1925

CHAPTER V - INTERCOLLEGIATE YACHT RACING

CHAPTER VI - INTERSCHOLASTIC SAILING ASSOCIATION

CHAPTER VII - YACHT CLUBS

CHAPTER VIII - CLASSES AND ONE-DESIGNS

PREFACE

This history chronicles the first one hundred years of the United States Sailing Association in four stages: yachting on the continent prior to 1897; the birth of NAYRU in 1897 as a multi-national authority and the evolution of the sport during the quarter of a century after its lapse; its revival in 1925 and influence on yachting until World War II; and its role after the War, culminating in NAYRU's metamorphosis into the US Yacht Racing Union, and later the United States Sailing Association, as a National Authority in consort with the Canadian Yachting Association. Sources for the most part are Yacht Club histories, those of a limited number of Yacht Racing Associations fortunate to have had their story recorded, those of some of the Classes and publications of such titans of yachting history as:

> *William P. Stephens – a chronicler in depth on design and measurement rules and most noted for his work of epic proportions* Traditions and Memories of American Yachting;
>
> *Arthur H. Clark who covered the period 1600-1815 in* The History of Yachting in Europe and the Colonies;
>
> *Edwin J. Schoettle whose* Sailing Craft *recounts the development of open, restricted and one-design classes constituting a sequel to Clark's work;*
>
> *Charles Lane Poor's analysis in depth of rating rules in* Men Against the Rule;

and the more recent works of:

> *John Parkinson, Jr., historian for the New York Yacht Club, Seawanhaka Corinthian Yacht Club and Cruising Club of America;*
>
> *Diana Eames Esterly's treatment of the history of one-design classes in* Early One-Design Sailboats;
>
> *Robert C. MacArthur's* Room at the Mark *the research for which provided much of the source material for this history;*

and countless other publications many of which are out of print.

For those who have not read Room at the Mark – A history of the development of yachts, yacht clubs, yacht racing and the racing rules *it is beyond doubt the most comprehensive account of the racing rules related against a background of* the highlights of the history of yachting in North America and the British Isles. MacArthur was a Senior U.S. judge, International Judge, past Chairman of the Inter-Collegiate Yacht Racing Association Appeals Committee, member of the US SAILING Racing Rules Committee and a yachtsman who has been instrumental in serving as a judge and recruiting and training others to do so, especially for college sailing meets.

Additional sources for the Centennial History include: research in public and private libraries stretching geographically from the Maritime Museum in San Diego to the Boston Public Library, oral histories at Mystic Seaport Museum, verbal and written recollections of yachtsmen, the library of the New York Yacht Club (by far the most comprehensive collection of yachting history) and last, but not least, records at the US SAILING headquarters. An attempt has been made to identify sources in footnotes as an aid to anyone seeking further information on a subject and, also, to recognize the publications of yacht clubs, classes and individuals. As above-mentioned, the preponderance of the material drawn from various publications is not 'original' in the true sense of the word, inasmuch as it has been cited in other publications over the past century and a half.

The concept of a centennial history arose from the appointment of the U. S. Yacht Racing Union Centennial Committee, chaired by Richard H. Roberts, for the purpose of planning ways by which to celebrate the centennial. A member of the Committee, Henry H. Anderson, Jr., who served as Executive Director of NAYRU from 1968 - 1977 and on its Appeals Committee for 20 years, suggested that publication of a history of NAYRU should be one of the features. Next he co-opted Robert C. MacArthur as editor who, by reason of his book, Room at the Mark, already had a leg up on the project and gratuitously offered to tackle the task. To the great loss of the yachting community, especially inter-collegiate racing, he passed away on the eve of bringing this History to completion. The publication constitutes a major contribution by him to the lore of the sport; likewise, his work with the US SAILING Racing Rules Committee and with the Rules of the Inter-Collegiate Yacht Racing Association constitute a major contribution to the law of the sport.

To Anderson went the task of collecting materials about clubs, classes, yacht racing associations, etc. sleuthing in libraries, soliciting copies of yacht club and yacht racing association histories and persuading past officials of National Authorities in the United States, Canada and the United Kingdom to exhume their files and revive their memories. After the loss of the editor, his final task was preparing the work for publication with the able and indispensable assistance of the US SAILING staff.

Many hands had a part in this publication; many sources contributed to it; and recognition thereof is attempted by way of attributions in the footnotes.

As a caveat, reliance on archivist material in the marine field begs the question of whether an author is an historian or story-teller – too often a case of history making history. As was observed in Room at the Mark, original sources are slim pickings in the field of yachting history, since very few chroniclers cite their sources, and successive writers tend to rely on what their predecessors wrote, thereby perpetuating errors or making deductions on unsound premises. Another pitfall of relying on the works of earlier historians is their lack of access to records that have become available to later generations. For example, not until the recent publication of Sailing at the U.S. Naval Academy by RADM Robert W. McNitt, USN (Ret.) has it been verified that the Midshipmen Boat Club formed in 1847 started as purely a rowing club thereby putting paid to the claim of its being one of the oldest sailing clubs in North America.

It is not the aim of this History to serve in the role of being the ultimate, or finite, authority for settling claims of being the 'oldest' club or class or yacht in North America. The subject of 'firsts' is a 'slippery elm to climb' inasmuch as it is contingent on whether the parameter, for example, for determining the original date of a yacht club is the gathering at which the project was proposed, the meeting at which a resolution to launch the project was adopted, or the date of incorporation or the date of the first regatta. To boot, all these elements are rarely a matter of record. Rather, the aim is to paint with a broad brush the yachting activity, recreational and competitive, during the periods above-mentioned. Coverage after World War II is selective because constraints of time and space make it infeasible to attempt to encompass the dynamic escalation that has occurred in the sport since then.

The one lament is the lack of time and space to include all the organizations for which material has been offered and/or been the subject of research. Some of the smaller clubs have provided sailors who have performed outstandingly at the international level, spawned leaders in the sport at home and abroad and pioneered new classes. An example is the Noroton Yacht Club located in Connecticut on Long Island Sound whose members are legendary for their exploits: Susan W. Sinclair, U.S. Woman's Sailing Championship, William S. Cox, U.S. Men's Sailing Championship, U.S. Match Racing Championship and America's Cup Trials helmsman; Robert N. Bavier, Jr., President of NAYRU, IYRU delegate, American's Cup helmsman; Paul H. and Hilary H. Smart, Olympic Gold Medalists; Glen S. Foster, Olympic Silver Medalist; Emil Mosbacher, Jr., America's Cup defender; three winners of the Herreshoff Trophy: (P.H. Smart, W.S.Cox and R.N. Bavier, Jr); and Bruce Kirby, noted naval architect. The contents of the History are kaleidoscopic in an attempt to present as broad a timespan and as wide a geographical spread as possible.

Henry H. Anderson, Jr.
Coordinating Editor
August 1997

DEDICATION

It is the exploits of generations of sailors who have provided the substance of this History and to whom it should rightfully be dedicated. In 'parens,' as it were, and in recognition of their pioneering exploits, this History, therefore, is dedicated to the memory of two singular leaders among them:

Clifford D. Mallory of New York City who, if there was a 'father' of organized yachting in North America, is the obvious choice;

and

Æmilius Jarvis of Toronto without whose 'little bomb' in 1897 the first coming of NAYRU probably would not have occurred, and but for whom there might not be the Yacht Racing Union of the Great Lakes – the first umbrella yacht racing organization in North America – or the Canada's Cup and many other traditions of the sport.

HALIFAX REGATTA.

Wednesday, 17th August, 1836.

Sail Boats.

FISHERMEN'S BOATS,

The same Flags as are assigned to them in the following Classes.

FIRST CLASS.

Names.	Flag.	Keel.	Owners.	Names.	Flag.	Keel.	Owners.
La Hogue,		30ft	Edward Hayes,	Tral,		22ft.	Grieves & Shrioves,
Mary Ann,		32	W. A. Black,	Mermaid,		30	Charles Gay,
Victory,		20	John Martin,	Sir P. Halket		26	Eben Moseley,
Mary Jane,		28	John Flemming,	Mary,		29,6	Jas. Slachan[illegible],
Fair Maid,		25,6	John Flemming,	Lively,		33	Fred. Slachanwhaite
Spring Bird		26	Peter Martin,	Mary Ann,		22	Mr. Gray
Two Anns,		26	Fleming & Whaling	Water Witch,		29	83d Regiment,
Fire Fly,		24	Wm. Donaldson,	Wellington,		27	Mr. Tapp,
Coquette,		27,6	Mr. Miller,	Erin.		28	34th Regiment.
Kate,		32	Mr. Matthews,	Caroline,		34	Sir T. Ussher.

SECOND CLASS.

Names.	Flag.	Keel.	Owners.	Names.	Flag.	Keel.	Owners.
Winning Lass, 1		23	Andw. Henneberry,	Triumph,		20	Mr. Fullerton,
Melville,		19,4	M. Clancy,	Lady of the Lake		29	Mr. Maitland,
Linnet,		14	Mr. Howe,	Skipjack,		20	J. Jameson,
Ellen,		19,6	Mr. Ince,	Ondine,		29	Sullivan,
Magnet,		16	Mr. DeCourcy,	Lydia,		21	Cunningham,
Camperdown,		22	Jer. Holland,	Elizabeth,		[illegible]	Mr. Jeffery,
May Flower,		20	Peter Martin,	Tory,		20	Mr. E. Wallace,
Louisa,		18,6	Joseph Hawkins,	Brisk,		23	Mr. Glover,
Winning Lass, 2		20	John Pence,	Hornet,		19,4	Thomas Conrod,
				Molly,		22	Thomas Grey,

THIRD CLASS.

Names.	Flag.	Keel.	Owners.	Names.	Flag.	Keel.	Owners.
Splitt'g Knife		18	George Brown,	Friendly Intention,		17	David Smith,
Snake,		17	William Stone,	Fly,		18	Michael Lynch,
Fox,		18	Joseph Bisset,	Tom Cat.		13	A. Stevens.
Chance,		17,6	Thomas D. Young,	Gull,		18	James Cleary,

Captain DOUGLAS, R. N.
Captain JONES, R. N.
The Honble. T. N. JEFFERY,
Lieut. Col. SNODGRASS,
Dep. Com'ry. Gen'l. HEWETSON,
} UMPIRES.

CHAPTER I

BEGINNINGS

An example of a 'first' surfaces in the 1880 publication *Memorial History of New York*[1] which records that the yacht *Fancy* (a yacht being a vessel built for recreational rather than commercial purposes as the term is commonly used) is presumably the first American yacht.[2] We cite her as an illustration that yachting was an activity, albeit not on an organized level, a century or more before the advent in 1816 of George Crowninshield's *Cleopatra's Barge* – "invariably described as the first American yacht" even though his first yacht was the 22-ton sloop *Jefferson* built in 1801. The story of the *Fancy* can be found in an engraving composed of six large panels by William Burgis entitled *A South Prospect of ye Flourishing City of New York in Province of New York in America* and executed in London in 1718. A copy hangs in the New York Public Library and another is stored in the archives of the New York Historical Society. It depicts a celebration on the East River shore of Manhattan in honor of Governor Hunter on the eve of his departure for Albany in 1717 and shows numerous vessels, some of which are firing salutes. There are upwards of 30 captions describing vessels, buildings, etc. of which #25 states, "Collonel Morris's FANCY turning to windward with a sloop of Common Mould." Judging by the two gentleman standing waist high in the well deck, the yacht was designed for day sailing since there appears to be no space for cruising accommodations. An indication of the state of yachting in New York waters at the time is described in *The Memorial History* as:

> *Racing on the water was not much in fashion, though the gentry had their barges, and some their yachts or pleasure sail-boats. The most elaborate barge, with awning and damask curtains, of which there is mention, was that of Governor Montgomerie, and the most noted yacht was the Fancy belonging to Colonel Lewis (II) Morris (grandfather of renown Gouverneur Morris), whose Morrisania Manor on the peaceful waters of the Sound[3] gave a fine harbor and safe opportunity for sailing.*

Circa 1750 advertisements in New York and Philadelphia papers refer to the presence of "well-fitted" pleasure boats" and by the end of the century many small boats were moored outside of waterfront homes.

The Morris family also owned large plantations in New Jersey so that traveling to and fro under sail would have been much more expeditious and comfortable than by horse and carriage over King's Bridge (spanning the Harlem River) to Manhattan and down the Island to a ferry across the North River (known today as the Hudson River).

A legendary example of early yachting is mentioned in *Encyclopedia of Sailing* by the editors of *Yacht Racing/Cruising*, 1978, relating that at the time of the outbreak of the Revolutionary War, John Paul Jones was cruising on a hunting and fishing trip from the Chesapeake and first heard about the battle of Lexington on arriving in New York. Another item in the *Encyclopedia* reported that six months after Lexington a Boston physician, Dr. John Jeffries, had to obtain permission from British authorities to go down the harbor to shoot and fish, i.e. obtain a cruising permit.

Halifax Regatta, 1836
Royal Nova Scotia Yacht Squadron Records, Public Archives of Nova Scotia, Halifax, NS

Wherever there were populous towns on salt or fresh water, building and sailing of boats for pleasure became common and racing followed – sometimes impromptu and sometimes sponsored by a hotel or a waterfront business – until the advent of yacht clubs in the second quarter of the nineteenth century.

As early as 1802[4] John C. Stevens, founding member and first Commodore of the New York Yacht Club, was designing and building yachts for himself starting with the 20-foot LOA *Diver* in 1809; the two-masted 56-foot *Trouble* in 1816 – a pirogue dubbed by some as "probably the first American yacht;" and in 1820 a two-hull boat *Double-Trouble.*[5]

In 1835 a New York weekly called *Spirit of the Times – A Chronicle of the Turf, Field Sports, Literature, and Stage* carried a story about a race between two schooners for a wager of $500 witnessed by thousands of spectators. The race began and ended at Whitehall in lower Manhattan, and the one turning mark was a buoy off Sandy Hook, New Jersey. In the same year the weekly reported that there was a 'brush' between Robert Bennett Forbes's schooner, *Sylph*, and Stevens's *Wave* off Boston which was followed by two more in Vineyard Sound.

In 1836 a regatta, for which the notice of race is extant,[6] was held at Halifax, Nova Scotia a year prior to the formation of the oldest yacht club in North America – the Halifax (precursor to the Royal Nova Scotia Yacht Squadron).

John Cox Stevens, 1785-1857, first Commodore of the New York Yacht Club, 1844-1854
Photo courtesy of the New York Yacht Club, #1995.299

SHIFTING BALLAST

Stevens as an engineer pioneered using mechanical devices to replace manpower for shifting ballast, and while studying to be an engineer, N.G. Herreshoff may have had a hand in designing the shifting ballast box running athwartships that was fitted to his father's *Julia II* in 1864. Captain Nat also developed a technique for overcoming the delay and back-breaking work in heavy weather of shifting ballast after a tack, whether it be water, bags of sand, iron shot or a Herreshoff ballast box. As he observed in his correspondence with W.P. Stephens:[7]

> *... and wishing to get the box to windward, it was not pulled there, but a 'half-board' [half a tack] taken, and as the helm was put up, the "trigger" was released and the box would run to windward by momentum.*

As for shifting ballast, that was the practice in Great Britain, so that was the way it was done in North America. The more common method was not today's practice in offshore yachts of shifting water from side to side but by shifting bags of iron shot or sand – hence the term 'sandbaggers.' In 1871 the newly formed Seawanhaka Corinthian Yacht Club banned the practice adding the requirement that boats be crewed only by amateurs, and the Boston Yacht Club, also a Corinthian club, followed suit. Not only did shifting require an inordinate number of crew, but also, in heavy air it was counterproductive, since after a tack often the ballast could not be moved quickly enough. With those two clubs leading the way it was not long before the ban on shifting ballast became universal, e.g. the ban was adopted by the Yacht Racing Association of Long Island Sound in 1896. Paradoxically, deadweight was replaced by 'live' ballast, i.e. crew weight shifting to outboard racks, an example of which is the sandbagger sloop *David M. Lyle* built in Philadelphia before the Civil War (currently at Mystic Seaport Museum.)

Sandbagger, *E.Z. Sloat*, 1893
Charles Edwin Bolles, photographer,
The Rosenfeld Collection,
Mystic Seaport Museum, Mystic, CT

Apparently dumping sandbags on the leeward leg – similar to the current practice of the Bermudian Fitted Dinghies of some of the crew members jumping overboard – was not customary in North America, although it appears to have been so elsewhere. A comical episode is related about a match race off Melbourne, Australia between two early Six-Metres, *Eric* and *SJS*. After rounding the weather mark *Eric* dumped so many bags in shallow water that *SJS* ran aground on them.

NARRAGANSETT BAY TO HAWAII

Nathanael G. Herreshoff[8] recalls as a child his father's three earliest boats built for cruising and sailing on Narragansett Bay one of which was *Julia*, a Newport keel catboat 23-feet LOA built ca. 1833. In a letter to W. P. Stephens[9] he recalls in the 1830's a half-dozen boats in Bristol kept solely for pleasure sailing and that:

> *They would start in an imaginary line across the direction of the wind, with good water between, for then it was considered unsportsmanlike and an insult to get on the weather bow of an adversary or hold him back in any way to spoil her chances of success … This was quite a different aspect of yacht racing from the present.*

The above typifies how competitive sailing was conducted under a code, the genesis of which most likely was a congruity of the rules for rowing races and the Rules of the Road. A further sign of early racing activity in Narragansett Bay was the formation in 1837 of the Narragansett Bay Catboat Club.

Accounts in the press and periodicals serve as the source for early instances of brushes and matches. Research of these in other ports will show that similar tilts were commonplace contemporaneously with those in Boston and New York. By 1800, for example, Philadelphia as the largest city in North America and the second largest English-speaking city in the world, was a natural center for all forms of aquatic competitions; in Baltimore in 1819 the schooner-yacht *Hornet*, which records indicate was built along the lines of centerboarders designed by Captain Schlanck of the Royal Navy in Boston before the Revolution, wound up as a sloop in New York mid-century and re-appeared in Boston in the 70's.[10]

With respect to *Cleopatra's Barge* mentioned above, she was destined not only to usher in the era of yachting in New England but also in the Hawaiian Islands. Three years after Crowninshield's death in 1817 she was acquired by King Kamehameha II (Liholiho) for his personal use and renamed *Haaheo o Hawaii (Pride of Hawaii*). On a visit to the Island of Kauai, of which Kaumualii was King, he invited the King (who had brig of his own) aboard, whose loyalty he had suspected, and while entertaining him below gave orders to set sail for Honolulu making him a virtual prisoner. Unfortunately for the immediate future of yachting among the Islands, when King Kamehameha was away on a trip to England, the skipper and crew stranded the yacht on Monolau reef where she broke up.[11]

YACHT RACING: INFORMAL AND CLUB SPONSORED

Earliest of the yacht clubs, after the Halifax Yacht Club formed in 1837 (now Royal Nova Scotia Yacht Squadron), was the Detroit Boat Club founded in 1839 as a rowing club and holding its first regatta in 1842. Shortly thereafter came the New York Yacht Club in 1844; the Southern Yacht Club in 1849; the Neptune Yacht Club at Highlands, NJ in 1850; the Chesapeake Yacht Club at Baltimore in 1852; the Carolina Yacht Club at Wilmington, NC in 1853; and the Pacific Yacht Club (first by that name in 1856) in San Francisco Bay. While the Civil War slowed the formation of additional clubs, on its termination a proliferation of clubs developed to meet a pent-up demand.

Evidence of early yachting activity elsewhere, which often attracted many more spectators than watch yacht races today,[12] are: a report titled *1839 THE REGATTA – Fourth Annual Regatta of the Amateur Boat Club Association* (foremost a rowing club) *at Castle Garden* (New York Harbor) indicating that a club with sailing activity was formed as early as 1836; a description in *Sporting Magazine* describing a match in 1835 on the Delaware River from Philadelphia to Chester, PA and return between the schooners *Count Pilaski* and *Helen Mar* watched by thousands of people assembled on the wharves and small boats and steamers crowding the river. It is noteworthy that competitions in multiple aquatic sports – sometimes concurrently with equestrian competitions – were taking place in the 1830's and 1840's at different locations across North America and were a principal form of entertainment and a medium for betting by the public. An 1840 dispatch from St. John's (actually St. John, NB) by "Your old friend, The Turfman in Canada" describes three yachts competing including a cutter and a lateen-rigged boat. An 1841 edition of the *Toronto Herald* recounts a regatta with seven yachts.

The trip by *Cleopatra's Barge* to the Mediterranean her first year was not the only large yacht to have made a long ocean passage in the first quarter of the nineteenth century. An English lady, Mrs. Houston, in 1845 published her log[13] of a cruise on the 100-foot schooner, *Dolphin*, armed with six cannon that left England for the Caribbean, visited New Orleans and then was probably the first yacht to cross the bar at Galveston City (TX). Her detailed accounts of side-trips ashore and afloat, however, make no mention of any form of leisure sailing in the Gulf. Yet the fourth oldest yacht club in existence on the continent without suffering a lacuna was the Southern at New Orleans, founded as the Stingaree in 1849 indicating that there must have been recreational sailing activity there earlier in the decade.

From a clipping from a Boston newspaper datelined Newport, RI, August 12, 1844:

> *The harbor of this fashionable watering place has been enlivened for the last few days by the appearance of the Yacht Squadron of New York [yacht club] and the crack sailing craft of Boston. It had been announced ... that a Regatta for all yachts was to come off on a given day, but no arrangement of the kind had been made.*

The regatta that did not materialize had been bruited to take place as an open event on August 12. Actually a regatta was run – the first regatta in the history of the New York Yacht Club – on the 8th for New York and Boston yachts around Conanicut Island with four entries from New York including the *Gimcrack* on which the Club had been organized, and the *Belle*, a pilot schooner chartered by Robert Bennet Forbes of Boston – one of New England's most renown yachtsmen.

The Polynesian of Honolulu on April 25, 1846 reported a race from Honolulu to Lahaina, Maui, which became the great whaling ship rendezvous in the Pacific, between the Government schooner *Hooikaika* and the American schooner *Kamehameha III.*

In Puget Sound:

> *Informal matches may have taken place after establishment of Victoria in 1843,... Seattle in 1852 and Port Townsend in 1854 – U.S. Customs point of entry (situated en route from Victoria to Seattle)... whenever lumber, coal and fishing vessels gathered on holiday, crews most likely raced in ship's boats.*[14]

A newspaper article titled *The Boston Yachts, Gloucester, Mass. May 20th, 1846* refers to a sailing regatta to come off July or August "which will be duly announced in the Spirit." The January 1843 *Bermudian* reports a sailing race among pilot boats and a match race between yachts *Fanny* and *Harrington*; a yet earlier example of yachting in the Islands is a "Painting of a yacht in her native waters" by artist J. Lynn labeled "1834 A Bermuda Schooner."

The September 9, 1852 edition of the *Daily Alta California* recounts the formation of the Pioneer Yacht Club (lapsed after 1859) in San Francisco Bay at a meeting at which:

> *A number of gentlemen of this city have organized themselves into a Yacht Club, and have purchased the little pleasure yacht* Belle. *There are about thirty persons in this club. They meet today for the purpose of electing officers and naming the crews.*

THE CATBOAT ERA

A rare, both because they have never been published and because the writers' technical background make them eminently reliable chroniclers, overview of boats and yachting from Cape Cod to New Jersey are Letters #9 and #11 from *The Last Letters from the Master* consisting of 36 letters exchanged between Nathanael G. Herreshoff and William P. Stephens in the 1930's and annotated by John W. Streeter. The two letters describe the craft in use in the second half of the nineteenth century. From Letter #11 by N.G. Herreshoff:

> *The single-masted boats with gaff sail, as well as my information goes, were more prevalent in Narragansett Bay than at other parts of the coast, and what is known as 'cat-rig' was formally called 'Newport-rig'... Above the small gunter and spritsail size, the single-sail American boat, wherever found, was likely to settle into the catboat pattern.*
>
> *In my early days of cruising (ca. 1850's), if we turned eastward from Narragansett Bay we found nearly all boats about Buzzards Bay & Vineyard Sound, double-ended with two masts; the foremast carrying a gaff headed, lug footed sail and sometimes a jib on temporary bowsprit, the main-mast a gaff mainsail with boom. You are probably familiar with the old Block Island boats? "The Vineyard boats" were smaller – narrower in proportion, with more bilge and less flare, but well ballasted with stone, partly decked and good coamings. The masts not so tall and sails squarer cut. At Chatham we saw only small schooners such as fishermen use east of the Cape.*
>
> *"Cape Cod Cat-boats" were not known at that time. They were probably originated by the Crosbys at a later date. Going west, only pure Block Island boats were seen. Craft that were notoriously sea-worthy, and with surprising windward-going qualities in hard weather when properly handled; but now extinct. A very pleasing type were found about Stonington and Mystic; center-board boats with counter-sterns; of fine form with moderate displacement and generally jib and mainsail rig, with loose footed jib, but a few of the Newport rig. In the Connecticut River there was a distinctive type not seen anywhere else; the "Drag-net Boats." They appeared to be 20 to 22 feet long, of fine form, quite moderate beam, and light draft with centre-board. The rig, mainsail & jib on a short bowsprit, the mainsail with sprit and loose-footed with sheet block in*

William Pickard Stephens at his drawing board
Photo courtesy of WoodenBoat *Magazine*

traveler across stem. I well remember one of these boats that visited our waters in about 1858… When she left, two or three of our boats gave her a try in beating down the bay… Well! – our people had something to talk about that was unusual – by being beaten by the dragnet boat in their [our] own waters… Only 30 miles west an entirely distinctive type of boat was met with, – the New Haven Sharpie. These boats were evidently evolved by some bright Connecticut inventor for serviceable, cheaply constructed and rigged boats for oystering and fishing in those waters. New Haven Harbor appeared to be busy with them in the early '60s. Thus, in cruising 200 miles along our coast, no less than seven distinctive types of boats were met with.

From Letter #9 by W. P. Stephens:

What you say about early yachting on Narragansett Bay is all news to me… I do not know the origin of the catboat; of course Bob Fish was building them before 1850, but I have not been able to learn when and where the sandbag cat originated. Cary Smith went as an apprentice to Bob Fish in Pamrapo, NJ about 1853; he learned to build a boat, to sail a boat and drink whiskey. His father was a clergyman and Smith was a regular attendant at church in his latter years, but he could quote scripture and swear with equal facility.

Streeter notes: Not only was the catboat so ubiquitous that its origins were lost, but by 1852 the racing cat was extraordinarily refined.

He further comments:

The omnipresent New York Bay catboats in (W.P. Stephens') time were woefully ill-formed for hearty sailing and were little related, except by rig, to their present day counterparts which are descended from the Cape Cod boats in the Crosby and Hanley tradition.

Stephens echoes this:

> *It seems to me that the yachts east of Point Judith were far abler and better than those to the westward; the nearer one got to New York, the worse they were. The sandbag cats and sloops built by Pat McGiehan and Jake Schmidt... were a poor lot 'all deadrise and no bilge' (skimming dishes)... The ethics of sandbag racing were very low.*

In fact, it was the introduction of the Narragansett Bay and Cape Cod catboats that brought a new aspect of catboat racing to New York waters.

In Letter #13 N.G. Herreshoff refers to a "Newport Rig, or Point Boat as the Newporters called them," with rather high narrow sails, *Sachem*, having competed in a regatta in 1854 in the Providence River. Whether it was New Jersey, New York, Long Island Sound, Narragansett Bay, Massachusetts or Halifax in the east or San Francisco in the west or New Orleans in the south, before the Civil War racing under sail had taken hold and on a more egalitarian basis than it would be at the end of the century.

YACHT RACE SPONSORSHIP: FROM QUASI-PUBLIC TO PRIVATE YACHT CLUB

Early in the last half of the nineteenth century before the advent of yacht clubs at locations such as Southern Massachusetts on Buzzards Bay, Cape Cod and the Islands and along the Jersey Shore, which were resort areas with an influx of 'summer folk,' open regattas were sponsored by towns or hotels, or in some instances the commercial fishermen – often in conjunction with special holidays. This was a form of local promotion to provide non-sailors an alternative entertainment to swimming, walking the beach and sitting on the porch. As stated in the *History of the Monmouth Boat Club* (NJ):

> *Racing of sailboats seems to have originated as the invention of waterfront hotel-keepers who put up prizes, usually in the form of gold coin, to provide entertainment and sport for their guests.*

Often the races progressed from town to town each Saturday. As the financial status of the summer folk improved, a trend towards exclusiveness led to the formation of private clubs, and as a result of their proliferation, the quasi-public events began to decline.

An insight into the quality of life in Halifax, Nova Scotia is a painting of a regatta held there in 1857 in which, as described in the history of the Royal Nova Scotia Yacht Squadron:[15]

> *The 1857 fleet totaled thirteen boats, eight of which were Bermudian-rigged, a rig virtually unknown in racing in Europe and America until the next century... 'Bermudian' was the name used in the Halifax records because it was a model popular in Bermuda, which had many close ties to Nova Scotia.*

In 1866 the New York Yacht Club held a trans-Atlantic race in 1866 on which the press commented:

> *The feat of the three yachts, the* Henrietta, Fleetwing *and* Vesta, *in crossing the ocean in midwinter, at once proved that the yachts of the New York Yacht Club were not mere pleasure-boats, only fit to sail on summer seas or inland waters; but that they could, when the occasion demanded it, successfully brave the terrors of the Atlantic, and encounter its gales and seas unharmed. This act of daring at once placed the New York Club in the front rank of yacht clubs – a position maintained to this day.*

The occasion of the race was a late-night bet by the three owners, each of whom put up $30,000 for the prize. One of the yachts lost six crew members who were swept overboard by a huge wave during a storm. By today's 'safety-at-sea' standards the chase might be termed foolhardy, but for today's around-the-world races and single-handed challenges it might be accepted as not exceptional?

STARTING SYSTEMS

Aquatic Monthly and *Nautical Review – Devoted to the interests of the Yachting and Rowing Community* June, 1872 edition, as well as reporting that the Georgia Regatta Association had held a race near Savannah with six entries and that the Delaware Yacht Navy had raced up the Delaware River to Chester, PA, related:

> *Portland Yacht Club (Maine) – measures to be taken to get up a grand sweepstakes regatta in Portland Harbor in which the principal yachts of the New York and Boston yachting organizations will compete.*

Atlantic Yacht Club's (Brooklyn, NY) annual sailing regatta Sailing Instructions:

Schooners, first-class sloops (cabin sloops over 44 feet. LWL); second-class sloops (cabin sloops of 44 feet and under LWL); third-class sloops (open boats). All yachts will start from an anchorage off Bay Ridge, and shall be anchored in their respective classes in lines one hundred yards apart; first-class sloops in advance, second and third class sloops in the rear to northward, in the order of classification. All sloops shall be at anchor in line – with jibs down – promptly at 9 o'clock a.m.... Schooners will start flying.

The Atlantic Yacht Club was using two starting procedures – the 'standing start' for sloops and the 'flying start' for schooners, both patterned after British usage. The former was used by the Royal Yacht Club[16] at Cowes, IOW, England. Yachts drew lots for position at a series of mooring blocks in a straight line off the club property since one end was almost inevitably the windward end. The yachts would then pick up their assigned moorings and wait, all sails down, for the starting signal. Then they would hoist sail, slip moorings, and off they went.

In 1872, Albert, Prince of Wales, a fine sailor, offered a trophy for a schooner race, and he suggested a 'flying start.' Since he realized that could cause terror among the sailors, with a dozen yachts averaging 100 feet in length, all with long bowsprits, he further suggested that there be two starting signals five minutes apart, with each yacht to be timed as she crossed the line during the interval between signals. Although the portion of the Sailing Instructions of the Brooklyn Yacht Club quoted do not provide details, presumably schooners were to start according to this procedure.[17]

The standing start was standard in North America for many decades. The Oshkosh Yacht Club in Wisconsin (founded 1870), had a neat variation. Since windward boats had an advantage over the leeward boats, that was canceled by each boat to windward of another starting as far back from the starting line as it was to windward. Thus a yacht 100 feet to windward of the leewardmost yacht would take her position 100 feet back from the line. That was so sensible and fair one would expect it to have been emulated by other clubs, but there seems to be no record of this occurring – perhaps it was even more difficult position the yachts than jockeying nervous horses into the starting stalls?

CANOE RACING AND ORGANIZATIONS

By 1871 the New York Canoe Club was operational, and formally organized the next year with Roosevelt Schuyler as Commodore. Racing log canoes under sail became very popular; and clubs had been started at the Narragansett Bay Boat Club in 1837, at St. Michaels on the Chesapeake prior to 1840, at the Oakland Canoe Club in San Francisco Bay in the 1870's, Flushing Bay in 1872 and at the Buffalo Canoe Club in 1882. From the 1971 Yearbook of the Put-in-Bay Yacht Club (Lake Erie)[18] George Gardner, first Commodore and founder of the Inter-Lake Yachting Association, acquired Ballast Island in the Put-in-Bay island group and built a log cabin as a summer home. Three years later he formed the Ballast Island Club, induced the Longworth Canoe Club to make it its home and in 1885 formed the Western Canoe Association, a division of the American Canoe Association. A closing sentence captures the ambiance of this group of islands in Lake Erie north of Sandusky famous for the regattas which it hosts:

Probably few other places in this modern world can boast of such peace and quiet, free from automobiles, TV and telephones. Long may it last and God willing.

By 1880 there were enough clubs racing sailing canoes to form the American Canoe Association, a national sailing authority (albeit more akin to a class association) 17 years before the advent of NAYRU. Sailing canoes had become a mania in the U.S. during the '70's and '80's. After 1900, however, racing sailing canoes diminished partly by reason of the advent of the sliding seat[19] and advanced technology making the boats too athletic and expensive for the average sailor and partly by reason of the proliferation of one-design classes.

TOWARD THE END OF THE NINETEENTH CENTURY

In 1873 the Boston Yacht Club recorded 13 schooners, 25 sloops and two steamers; Eastern Yacht Club 32 schooners and 13 sloops; South Boston Yacht Club four schooners and 27 sloops; Dorchester Yacht Club six schooners and 51 sloops; Lynn Yacht Club one schooner, 23 sloops and eight cat-rigged boats; Beverly Yacht Club 37 sloops.[20]

Similar to how early racing on Puget Sound occurred before the formation of yacht or boating clubs, at Mattapoisett the first open catboat regatta was held in 1878, although the Mattapoisett Yacht Club was not founded until 1901; in the 1890's there were dory racing clubs in Massachusetts Bay and along the north shore; also, at Jamestown, RI. Sailors had been converting their catboats from commercial use to recreational use. This led to the formation of the Jamestown Yacht Club in 1891 (it changed its name to Conanicut Yacht Club the next year after the island on which it is located) by many of the same yachtsmen who had founded the Corinthian Yacht Club at Philadelphia – the city of their principal residence.[21] By 1903 there were 11 hotels in Jamestown with over 1,000 accommodations (only a fraction of this number are available today).

With the advent of clubs on bays such as Buzzards, Narragansett and other sections of the east coast, each club did not necessarily operate entirely by itself. Groups of three or more clubs could and did join to hold local regattas, particularly to the extent that they sailed common one-design classes and/or had enough cruising yachts sailing under handicaps. The main consideration was a willingness to share the costs and the effort. As to the yachts racing under handicaps, it is well to bear in mind that in other parts of the continent, similar to the northeast, there are hundreds of little yacht clubs, especially those for summer folk, that look just like they did a hundred years ago. In such clubs boats that cannot be raced by family members without the complications of handicapping and the discouragement of being beaten by a superior design quickly lost popularity and gave way to one-design classes as soon as there was a nucleus of members who could afford them.

The scale on which the sport of yacht racing had escalated a decade before the founding of NAYRU is the listing in the magazine *Outing* of regattas being held by clubs across the continent:

New England	26 clubs ranging from Portland Yacht Club, ME to Yale Corinthian Yacht Club, CT.
Greater New York	29 clubs from upstate NY and VT to Jersey City and Cold Spring Harbor, Long Island
Mid-Atlantic	Eight clubs from New Jersey to North Carolina
Great Lakes	21 clubs from Quebec to Minnesota including two associations
Gulf Coast	Southern Yacht Club
West Coast	Pacific Yacht Club, San Francisco

The listing should be read as representative but by no means complete. For example, there were at least ten active yacht clubs on the Gulf Coast by 1885. The decade preceding the first formation of the NAYRU was a period during which yacht clubs coalesced into regional associations thus providing the impetus for the formation of a national body to set standards for the sport.

C H A P T E R I I

ORIGINAL BIRTH OF NAYRU

At one time in the files of the United States Sailing Association there was a slim folder labeled "NAYRU, 1897." It contained two documents: the first was a report by J.O. Richardson from Toledo to the Inter-Lake Yachting Association, which he had recently represented at a meeting in New York; the second was a 14-page pamphlet entitled, "Articles of Association and Racing Rules of the North American Yacht Racing Union," with the legend, "Adopted 30 October 1897." Those were the sole remaining records left to tell the story of NAYRU, but fortunately newspaper articles and the reports of chronicler, William Pickard Stevens,[2] survive to tell much of the tale of the short-lived Union.

The meeting attended by Richardson was held in May for the purpose of exploring the possibility of establishing a national yacht-racing authority for the United States and Canada. As early as 1872 there had been at least one editorial voice calling for the establishment of a national organization. How early that was can be noted by the fact that in the northeast the Boston Yacht Club was only six years old, Eastern Yacht Club only two, Seawanhaka Corinthian Yacht Club was a yearling and the Larchmont Yacht Club not yet in existence. Elsewhere the San Francisco Yacht Club (#2, 1869) was struggling to survive, and the Southern Yacht Club at Lake Ponchartrain, MS was in the early stages of recovering from devastation of the Civil War. Nonetheless the magazine *Aquatic Monthly* was saying:

> *In another month or two, when the annual regattas and match races are over for the season, we will have abundant space to devote to yachting discussions respecting the vexed questions of time allowance, centerboard vs. keel, too much canvas and too little, heavy spars vs. light spars, and other questions that, today, notwithstanding the many folios written upon them in Great Britain and the United States, are probably as far from being settled as they were a score of years ago. What progress have we made when the New York Yacht Club, the largest yachting organization in the country… changes its time allowances almost annually?*
>
> *The only practical way… is to call a convention of yacht owners of the United States, to be held in the city of New York, when perhaps, the mooted points can be settled satisfactorily alike to the owners of large and small yachts; and standard rules adopted which will be readily acquiesced in by the yachting interests of the whole country. We are well aware that it is an exceedingly difficult matter to arrange, and that Great Britain has failed partially after attempting it at intervals for many years; yet we do not… despair of its accomplishment… At any rate, it is worthwhile to make the effort.*

To say that Great Britain had "failed partially" was an understatement. The coordination of yachting there was in far worse condition than in North America. Here, at least, the prestige of the New York Yacht Club was so great that new clubs, as they were rapidly being spawn-

"Full and By" – Commodore Æmilius Jarvis at the helm of the *Haswell*, his favorite of his many yachts. He sailed her to Jamaica and back.
Photo courtesy of Royal Canadian Yacht Club

ed, readily adopted its racing rules almost in their entirety. Later the prestigious quartet of New York, Seawanhaka, Eastern and Boston Yacht Clubs would serve as an informal national authority. They consulted with each other, and, as problems arose with the racing rules, they acted in consort. Eventually in 1903, along with several other clubs, they would produce the Universal Rule for measurement which quickly became the standard in North America for many years. Furthermore, Æmilius Jarvis of the Royal Canadian Yacht Club, who attended the 1897 meeting, led the movement to create the Yacht Racing Union of the Great Lakes the year before as a coordinating body on the Great Lakes for the very purposes for which the 1897 meeting was convened.

It took seven years, however, for the *The Aquatic Monthly*'s call to be heard. In 1879 a small club, the New Jersey Yacht Club, took action supported strongly by *Forest & Stream*[5] which had recently formed a yachting department. Only five small clubs in the vicinity of New York and the club at Salem, MA sent delegates to the meeting called by New Jersey – attendance by the person from Salem may have been happenstance rather than pre-planned. The outcome of the meeting was to form a committee of correspondence to attempt by letters to generate wider interest in the project. How they proceeded is not recorded, but nothing came of it. The clubs were too small and 'unimportant', and there was no response at all from the larger clubs which closely guarded their independence.

The next effort came in 1888 when 14 local and 'minor' clubs, ranging from Albany and down the Hudson River to the Staten Island Athletic Club, assembled in New York to form the New York Yacht Racing Association (NYYRA). Reflecting the thinking at the time was a resolution passed at the annual meeting of the Seawanhaka Corinthian Yacht Club:

> *Resolved, that the present Committee on Yachting Interests is hereby requested to consider the expediency of the formation of a general yacht-racing association, or of one to include the principal clubs of the Atlantic Coast, such formation to include, as far as possible, a uniform classification, a uniform system of measurement, and uniform racing rules; they are hereby authorized to do any and all things necessary to accomplish the object in view.*

By that time the major clubs had all adopted the Seawanhaka Rule for measurement. Most of the meeting, however, was devoted to creating a competing rule. Finally, the very simple 'mean length' rule (LOA + LWL divided by two) was adopted. It was almost identical to the successful rule that N.G. Herreshoff had created in 1866 for the Boston Yacht Club and later was in general use in Massachusetts Bay. It had little or no prospect, however, of unseating the Seawanhaka Rule which was in general use in greater New York waters. One objective of the NYYRA was to hold an annual regatta. Its first, on Labor Day 1889, drew 85 entries which may have been a record at the time. It also held a second and a third after which, as W.P. Stephens reported, the NYYRA "died quietly" – so quietly that he did not document exactly when (1897).

By 1896 there were six prominent area associations or unions with a strong interest in a national authority: the Yacht Racing Union of Long Island Sound (later Yacht Racing Association), the Yacht Racing Association of Massachusetts (later Yacht Racing Union), the Lake Yacht Racing Association (Lake Ontario), Inter-Lake Yachting Association (Lakes Erie, Huron, St. Clair and the Detroit River), Pacific Inter-Club Yachting Association (San Francisco Bay) and the Yacht Racing Union Great Lakes (an umbrella over the Great Lakes Associations). Among them were several yachtsmen who were protagonists of the concept: Frank Bowne Jones, founder of the Yacht Racing Union of Long Island Sound, another founder Oliver Cromwell of the Seawanhaka Corinthian Yacht Club, Louis Clark of Boston and President of the Yachting Association of Massachusett, Æmilius Jarvis (Royal Canadian Yacht Club), Joseph M. Macdonough of the Pacific Yacht Club and Pacific Inter-Club Yachting Association and Ernest Radder (Cleveland and Inter-Lake Yachting Association).

While they were working together to develop interest in a national Yacht Racing Association, three members of the New York Yacht Club petitioned its commodore, Edward Brown, to establish a committee of five with himself as chairman, to consider the possibility of New York taking the lead by:

> *Calling a convention of delegates from such yacht clubs in America as they may elect, for the purpose of considering the advisability of organizing a yacht racing league.*

Commodore Brown acted on the request but filled the committee with members of the 'old guard', including three former commodores. Its report to the club was predictable.

As minuted by the New York Yacht Club December 22, 1896, proposed was:

- *a Yacht Racing League to be composed of American Yacht Clubs in good standing having not less than 50 members and 15 yachts enrolled;*
- *its functions to be appoint an official measurer, frame and modify rules, assign dates for racing events and enforce penalties for violations of the racing rules;*
- *four Districts: Eastern, Gulf, Lake and Pacific, the Eastern District from Pennsylvania to Maine estimated to have 10,000 clubs.*

the objections to which were:

- *it would be unwieldy and composed of heterogeneous elements.*
- *favor (in lieu) a regional organization, e.g. Eastern District, in which the principal clubs are: NYYC, Eastern, Atlantic (Brooklyn), Seawanhaka and Corinthian of Philadelphia among which already a large degree of standardization exists;*
- *therefore no urgent need for the League;*
- *also, to give the Supreme Council power to rehear and to finally decide protests might aggrieve the Regatta Committee or members of a Club, even though this undoubtedly is the only means by which a uniform rule of decision can be obtained. This would be transferring the ultimate decision to a Council to hear the case upon evidence of others;*
- *unwilling to transfer authority to change racing rules and classification to a League dominated by small clubs interested only in small boat racing;*
- *the NYYC has never been a purely racing organization, i.e. it has a marked partiality for deep water cruising and therefore is unwilling to surrender its autonomy to the control of others and the fixing of dates.*

Therefore it would be inadvisable for NYYC to take the initiative but to condemn the project would hardly be just to those who have expended time and thought on the proposition...

The next day the *New York Herald*, owned by former Commodore James G. Bennett, editorialized – no doubt to his satisfaction:

> *This league business is totally unnecessary; it cannot add to the prestige of the Club and it may involve it in so many outside complications as to be both inconvenient and unpleasant. The NYYC has been able to care for itself in the past and is likely to do so in the future... It has a distinct antipathy to having its constitution tampered with...*

While the writer caught the essence of the Club's position, he failed to recognize the paradox of the Club agreeing that only through a single appeals body to decide protests could there be uniform interpretation of the rules while at the same time rejecting the procedure on the grounds that it would subordinate the Club to an outside authority. What he meant by "tampering" was that it would have required a members' vote to delete the line in its constitution prohibiting affiliation with any other organization – a prohibition that was not waived until the Club joined NAYRU in 1942. The rationale for the reaction to the proposal was: first, along with a few of the larger clubs that raced large yachts, vis-à-vis a plethora of clubs that raced in smaller classes, the Club considered itself self-sufficient to handle its own racing requirements; and second, it was leery of 'foreign entanglements' that might compromise its independence – the same type of 'isolationist' sentiment that was to retard the NAYRU for so many years after World War II from joining the International Yacht Racing Union.

MAY 1, 1897 MEETING

It was against the above background that a movement continued towards establishing a national body for the "Purpose of uniform measurement, classification and racing rules." Despite the uncertainty of the position of larger clubs such as New York, Atlantic and Larchmont, the issues were being addressed by the Yacht Racing Association of Massachusetts and Yacht Racing Union of Long Island, and on February 22 Boston and New York clubs conferred respecting a national association and called a conference of American Yachting Associations, initially for October but advanced to May 1, at the Fifth Avenue Hotel in New York. The four persons most responsible for the meeting were Æmilius Jarvis from the Lake Yacht Racing Association, Frank Bowne Jones from Yacht Racing Union of Long Island Sound, Oliver E. Cromwell of the New York Yacht Club and Louis M.

Clark president of Yacht Racing Association of Massachusetts.

All areas of North American yachting were represented except for the Gulf, the inland lakes of the Midwest and the Pacific Northwest. In attendance were:

Associations:

YRU of Mass.	*Louis Clark, 32 Clubs*
YRU of the Great Lakes	*Æmilius Jarvis*
YRU of Long Island Sound	*Stuyvesant Wainwright, E.B. Hart, Jr., O.H. Chellborg, Charles T. Pierce (NY), C.P. Tower, 22 clubs*
*Lake YRA**	*E.H. Ambrose (Royal Hamilton Yacht Club), five clubs*
*Inter-Lake YRA**	*J. O. Richardson of Toledo, Ernest Radder (Cleveland), 9 clubs*
*Lake Michigan YRA**	*E.C. Berriman of Chicago, 18 clubs*
Pacific Inter-Club YA	*Joseph M. Macdonough (Pacific Yacht Club), five clubs*
New York YRA	*Frank Bowne Jones, A.J. Prime (NY), E.A. Langerfield, George Parkhill, 17 clubs*

Clubs independently represented:

Atlantic, Brooklyn, Corinthian of Philadelphia representing Delaware River, Great South Bay, Hempstead Bay, Marine & Field Club, New York Athletic Club, Larchmont

** Members of Yacht Racing Union of the Great Lakes*

The 'climate' of the conference is summed up by the headlines in the May 2 edition of the *New York Herald*:

MANY YACHTSMEN MEET IN COUNCIL
Representatives of One Hundred and Eight Clubs
Favor a National Association
HASTE SHOULD BE AVOIDED
Committee of Seven Appointed to Report a Plan
of Organization in October Next.
VEXED POINTS PASSED BY

Oliver E. Cromwell was made chairman and W.P. Stephens secretary. Sanderson of the Larchmont Yacht Club echoed the quandary of most delegates – they had not been empowered by their club or association to vote for a national union nor on any of the issues. Hence, if it had not been for the positive position taken by Æmilius Jarvis, backed up by Jones, Tower and Pierce (the last three Yacht Racing Union of Long Island Sound) and implementation of same in a resolution by Clark of Boston, the conference might have wound up being only a forum without any action taken. To quote from the same article:

"MR. JARVIS' LITTLE BOMB"

Mr. Jarvis, of Toronto, had no power really to join an association, but believed that the clubs he represented would sanction what he did. Something should at once be done to broaden the sport of yachting and increase its volume... New rules must be made. Once length only was taxed. Then sail area came under the ban, and it was now universally recognized that lightness of construction could not be overlooked. Mr. Jarvis concluded with the offering of a resolution that it was expedient and advisable that a permanent body, national in its character and aims, should then and there be organized.

This little bomb called out many mild expressions of disapproval... The whole matter required deliberation of a serious nature, and that could only be given it by a committee having months at its disposal...

Others had similar views, but Messrs. Jarvis, Jones, Tower and Pierce believed in immediate action ...

Clark of Boston thought some action might be appropriately taken at present, and finally offered the following, which was passed:

Resolved, That it is the sense of this meeting that uniform racing rules should be adopted throughout the United States and Canada, and that for that purpose, that some kind of a national association should be formed.

Notably there was no mention in the resolution about a uniform measurement rule; the sensitivity of the subject and jealously of 'turf' that it engendered is sounded in Clark's position as summed up in the *Herald*:

In advocating the necessity of using the utmost precaution in the matter of measurement, Mr. Clark said Boston was particularly wary upon this point. If the New York rule was submitted Boston would up helm and soon be hull down. A compromise rule of some character must be decided upon, or there would be no union as desired.

Paradoxically this was the opposite approach taken at the formation of the Lake Yacht Racing Association, founded in 1884 making it the oldest YRA on the Continent, where its *History*[4] cites:

... the delegates immediately proceeded to tackle the most important subject which came up for discussion, viz. the measurement rule, for it was believed that if unanimity could be secured on this subject other less important details could easily be settled, and the association might be considered as formed.

This emphasizes how paramount the question of measurement and classification was to the sport and its organization and also the background that colored Jarvis' attitude. After discussing the Seawanhaka, New York and English Yacht Racing Associations rules it was decided to adopt the Seawanhaka Rule "as a happy mean between the two others."

Per resolution offered by John F. Lovejoy (Larchmont Yacht Club), a committee composed of Newbury D. Lawton (Atlantic Yacht Club), C.T. Pierce, Æmilius Jarvis, Louis M. Clark, J.M. Macdonough, A.J. Prime and F. Bowne Jones was empowered to:

Draft a plan of organization and submit such plan to the different clubs and associations of America for their consideration, to be reported back to the committee, which after due consideration shall be the plan of organization to be acted upon at a meeting in October...

The *Herald* sums up observing, "Further the meeting dared not to go."

Prescient of the issues that would be the subject of discussion among yachtsmen and clubs for the next hundred years and beyond, and also of the trend towards one-designs that would accelerate during the next decade, was a remark made by Æmilius Jarvis during a visit with Louis Clark at Marblehead when he was shown some of the local 21-foot keel boats which had been hauled out:

They are proper small boats, and one thing that I like about them is the restrictions placed upon the building of the hull. They are sufficiently light and will stand good for seasons. The Boston Herald will do yachting a great service if it argues for rules restricting the building of hulls. Argue for uniform, sensible construction, not basket-built boats... and put owners on an equal footing, both as to substantially built yachts, and a fair deal on construction. Go on and do this and you will help us out.

Jarvis's sentiments indicate a greater cohesiveness among the clubs on the Lakes than along the Eastern seaboard on the subjects of measurement and classification; the need for uniformity is reinforced in the above-mentioned letter from J.O. Richardson, Jr. to the Inter-Lake Yachting Association:

The meeting on the whole can be called a success as it clearly demonstrated that all Yachtsmen believed that uniform rules,[5] and united action would be beneficial. Some progress was made towards forming a national organization. Not as much was accomplished as desired by the Lake Representatives, but it was the best that could done all things considered ... It was the desire of the Representatives of the Lakes, and some of the New York Clubs, that an Association be formed at once, but a large number of the delegates from some of the principal Clubs had no authority to act, and were opposed to hasty action.

Resolved, that... uniform racing rules[6] should be adopted throughout the United States and Canada...

This was amended, and the Committee instructed to omit measurement, and classification rules.

The matter of rules [measurement], and classification, will be one that will have to be handled with much care, as some of the rules now in use are wholly satisfactory, the rules used by the Clubs on the Lakes are as good, if not better than any now in use, and similar rules are used by the Yacht Racing Union of Long Island Sound.

The Massachusetts Clubs use entirely different rules which work satisfactory to them, and they believe that they are at least as good as any that are used... They have a large representation both in members and yachts.

... and whatever rules are adopted will no doubt be picked from the best that now exist, and their adoption by Clubs gradual so as to protect Boats already built...

Richardson raised the twin specters of parochial resistance to change and change resulting in the obsolescence of existing boats that beleaguer every attempt to revise rules.

OCTOBER 1897 MEETING

On October 30 and 31 meetings were held, again at the Fifth Avenue Hotel, and presided over by Oliver Cromwell with W. P. Stephens as Secretary. Headlines in the *Boston Herald* announced:

YACHT RACING UNION FORMED

More than 130 Clubs Enrolled on Its Membership List
L.M. Clark of Boston Chosen
Chairman of the Council
No Agreement Yet on Measurement and Classification
A Long-Projected Yachting Scheme Realized

The new Union has as its object the encouragement of yacht racing and the promotion and adoption of uniform racing rules throughout the United States and Canada. Any yacht club in North America having a membership of 50 and an enrollment of 15 yachts and over is eligible for membership, and a club having 100 members is allowed one representative and an additional representative for each additional 200 members. The Union will be governed by a Council of 15 representatives.

The racing rules as published were adopted with slight amendments, but discussion over measurement and classification encountered a stumbling block. Discussion led to the concept that there might even be an international rule; to this end Jarvis and Macdonough, who were going to Europe, undertook to discuss the matter with the Yacht Racing Association of Great Britain.

After adjournment the Council elected as Officers: Chairman, Louis M. Clark; Secretary, F. Bowne Jones and Treasurer, Newbury D. Lawton (Atlantic Yacht Club).

Speculation about the chances of the Union surviving appeared in the Boston and New York papers. *The Sunday Herald – Boston*, November 7, 1897 predicted that without the strongest and best clubs in the country enrolled on the lists of the newly formed NAYRU, such as New York, Eastern and Corinthian (Philadelphia) the Union will be short lived. It refers to:

The two men who are to go to England with a view to talking over the club measurement rules with the British Clubs (Jarvis and Macdonough) [as both] English subjects... owning restricted boats built on rules wholly outside those which control the contests for the America's Cup, and on a rating rule which sets aside the waterline length. What good can come from such a visit abroad ?*

The article decries the British girth rule, observes that the (North American) rating rule for small boats has been a dismal failure in the case of the extreme boats designed for the Seawanhaka Cup. It reflects the division of opinion and the passions aroused in the yachting community stating:

So long as they assume the North American Association does not attack the interests of Massachusetts yachtsmen all will go well.

The next week the *New York Herald* editorialized:

Never before in the history of local yachting was such an unfair and unwise step taken as that of the YRA [LIS] in moving up class limits and at the same time cutting off the time allowance of older boats. It will doubtless make it impossible for them to be sold at anything like a fair figure... It will be a costly experiment, and it is hard to say just how far the result may go to breaking up the harmony of the Association.

Further evidence of the turmoil that NAYRU faced resolving, were it to achieve its purpose, appears in the report of the minutes of the annual meeting of the Yacht Racing Union of Long Island Sound, which changed its name to Yacht Racing Association of Long Island Sound, to avoid confusion with NAYRU:

Rule 2, regarding measurement, was debated at length. Objection was made to a portion of the rule on the ground that it did not conform with the rule upon the same subject in force at a 'large club' on the

* *Satirically speaking and certainly not the case with Macdonough.*

> *Sound, not a member of the Association. This brought several members to their feet, who insisted that if the Larchmont Yacht Club (which was using a length rule) does not belong to the Association, does not see fit to become a member, no further consideration should be given it.*

On December 12 the *Herald* reported, "International Rating Rule – Nothing Accomplished by the Union's Committee in London." In amplification the *San Francisco Chronicle* edition of February 26, 1888 reported:

> *Meager reports have reached the Coast from time to time concerning the reception that Joseph M. Macdonough and A. Jarvis, the representatives of the NAYRU, received when they went to London to try and formulate a plan by which it would be possible to bring the two countries together in unison in regard to a system of measurement for time allowances. All that was said would leave one to believe that they met with a very cold reception. This was caused by an unavoidable accident. When these gentlemen departed they were provided with letters to Dixon Kemp, the secretary of the English Association.*
>
> *That these letters miscarried was the cause of the trouble. They were forwarded to England, but Kemp was seriously ill at the time, the letters were not acknowledged, and, as it appears, were not laid before the Association. An invitation to attend a meeting was received. About this time Macdonough had to leave London on account of business. Jarvis alone appeared before the meeting, which, owing to the absence of the letters of introduction, was unaware of the reason for his visit... Later on Jarvis met several members of the Association in a social way and they began to realize that the object of his visit was misunderstood*
>
> *... From this time on things ran smoothly and the yachtsmen of the two countries will undoubtedly come to an understanding on this bugbear of time allowances.*

The Chronicle was much more optimistic than the *Herald* which opined:

> *... it transpired that neither the New York nor the Eastern Yacht Clubs had joined the Union and the chances of an international rule under these circumstances do not appear to be of immediate interest. In fact the attempt to launch such a rule would be about as abortive as that made two years ago by the YRA (British) and the Yacht Club de France.*

Domestically, moreover, there was the higher hurdle to surmount of assimilating the divergent views of New York and Boston. Because of the extremes of overhang and sail area that were occurring under the Seawanhaka Rule, Massachusetts clubs did not trust the rule of the New York clubs using a formula with the factors of LOA and LWL as the basis for determining a yacht's rating and hence the class in which she raced. They had had good experience in controlling excesses by classifying yachts according to fixed lengths of LWL instead of a length derived by formula.

At an April meeting of the Council the British girth rule was proposed, but in spite of two letters of recommendation it was tabled until the fall meeting of the Union. In the same month a continuing debate was going on in the *Boston Globe* about the Seawanhaka Rule and its effect on design. There had been a number of serious accidents in Massachusetts Bay resulting from collisions, and blame was leveled at the Rule. It produced unsafe yachts, it was alleged, that were most difficult to control in a fresh breeze. They were boats that had so little underbody that they were almost centerboarders (meaning like New York boats). While reporting the current views of physicist-yachtsman William E. Froude, namely that, if waterline and overhangs were controlled, sail area would take care of itself,[7] the *Globe* discussed the question of yachts under 30-feet. Slowly yacht designers were coming to realize that they could not make a successful small yacht merely by shrinking the lines of a large one. It was the intention of the YRA of Massachusetts Bay, like its counterpart on the Inland Lakes, to find a measurement rule that would assist in the development of such yachts, for which there was a steadily growing demand.

SECOND MEETING IN 1898

Despite the initial pitfalls of the Jarvis/Macdonough expedition to England, Æmilius Jarvis had persisted and did an exhaustive study of the YRA 1895 rule which included both a beam and girth factor – hence dubbed the 'girth' rule. At the second meeting of NAYRU on October 1, 1898 the Council reported the results of its consideration of all the rules currently in force, including the data brought back by Jarvis, and recommended that the 'girth' rule replace the length and sail area rule (Seawanhaka Rule) as the best means of equalizing boats. It recommended:

> *The adoption of this rule would promote international uniformity, the benefits of which to this Union would be incalculable.*

Pointedly the rule was adopted only for yachts with a minimum LWL of 30 feet; nothing was suggested for smaller yachts, nor was the subject discussed. NAYRU had missed an opportunity to offer leadership to one of its principal constituencies and to a multitude of clubs racing boats under 30 feet.

Several Associations were already working on filling the vacuum. The motivation was two-fold: first, inter-club racing was on the increase, and second, a uniform rule would create a wider market from Newburyport (MA) to Philadelphia for an owner wishing to sell his yacht. Typical of the discontent was the observation by *Field & Stream*:

> *At present, there is, within the YRA of Long Island Sound a decided difference of opinion as to the merits of the measurement rule recently adopted by NAYRU and its ability to produce a yacht of greater internal capacity than of late years resulting from the old rule.*

The negative comment was the only time during the year that *Field & Stream* quoted either Association as having mentioned NAYRU. During 1899 *Field & Stream* mentioned NAYRU only once, on the occasion of its third annual meeting. At the meeting NAYRU re-elected its original slate of officers, decided to retain the girth rule for another year and appointed a committee to consider possible revisions in the racing rules. At the annual meeting of the Yacht Racing Association of Massachusetts, on the other hand, the principal topic of discussion was revision of its racing rules, as if NAYRU did not exist at all.

Year	YACHT RACING ASSOCIATIONS	Area	1897 Meeting representative
1880	**American Canoe Association** (not an NAYRU YRA)	combination of clubs and classes	none
March 29, 1884	**Lake Yacht Racing Association** (Ontario) Toronto, Bay of Quinte Yacht Clubs	Lake Ontario including RCYC, Oswego, some Maritime	E.H. Ambrose
Jan. 17, 1885	**Inter-Lake Yachting Association of Lake Erie** Erie, St Clair, Huron, Detroit River Yacht Clubs	Lakes Erie, St. Claire, Huron and Detroit River	S.O. Richardson, Jr.
1889	**New York Yacht Racing Association** (lapsed ca. 1897)	New York waters and Long Island Sound	Oliver E. Cromwell
1890	**Newport Yacht Racing Association** (1921 Narragansett Bay Yachting Association)	Narragansett Bay	none
1891	**British Columbia Yacht Racing Association** (lapsed in economic slump)		none
Sept. 3, 1892	**Northwest International Yachting Association** (now PIYA) Victoria, Anacorte, Port Townsend, Seattle, Tacoma, New Whatcomb Yacht Clubs	Puget Sound	none
July 4, 1894	**Lake Michigan Yacht Racing Association**		none
May 15, 1895	**Yacht Racing Union of Long Island Sound** (1897 Yacht Racing Association) Corinthian Mosquito Fleet Douglaston Yacht Squadron, Harlem, Hempstead Harbor, Horseshoe Harbor, Hugenot, Huntington, Indian Harbor, Knickerbocker, Larchmont, New Rochelle, Pequot Casino, Riverside, Sea Cliff, Seawanhaka Corinthian, Waterside, Yale Corinthian Yacht Clubs	Western Long Island Sound	Frank Bowne Jones
March 19, 1896	**Yacht Racing Association of Massachusetts** (later Yacht Racing Union of Massachusetts Bay)	Massachusetts Bay	Louis M. Clark
May 12, 1896	**Pacific Inter-Club Yachting Association** California, Corinthian, Ecinal, San Francisco, Pacific Yacht Clubs	San Francisco	Joseph Macdonough
Nov. 7, 1896	**Yacht Racing Union of the Great Lakes**	Great Lakes Yacht Racing Associations	Æmilius Jarvis

The next month, when the Yacht Racing Association of Long Island Sound held its annual meeting, the President was obliged to report that two of the most important clubs on the Sound, Seawanhaka and Larchmont, which was not a member, refused to use the NAYRU measurement rule which had caused much confusion and embarrassment during the past summer. Since Larchmont had come to dominate inter-club racing at the Western end of the Sound, where the larger clubs were concentrated, the Association, perforce dancing to its tune, rescinded the girth rule and reinstated the old one in spite of its deficiencies. The young NAYRU was thereby dealt another crippling blow for in addition to losing the YRA it also lost one of its original and staunchest supporters – the Seawanhaka Corinthian Yacht Club. Most likely within the Club there also were older members who were reluctant to jettison the rule for fear that it would adversely affect the ratings of their yachts.

Although the girth rule had been adopted by NAYRU, only the Lake Yacht Racing Association put it into operation, and at the annual meeting of NAYRU on October 6, 1900 the rule was abandoned and the clubs were advised to shift for themselves. It appointed a committee to recommend a new measurement rule at the next meeting which never materialized.

Nonetheless, a committee led by Aemilius Jarvis convinced the Yacht Racing Union of Great Lakes to adopt the girth rule to which was added a table of restrictions including sail area, draft and hull dimensions for the establishment of restricted classes. What NAYRU had failed to accomplish nationally, the Yacht Racing Union of the Great Lakes succeeded in doing on a larger scale geographically than any other area in North America – no doubt as a result of the leadership of such strong clubs as Jarvis' home club, the Royal Canadian Yacht Club at Toronto and of Jarvis himself. As a member of YRU, the Lake Yacht Racing Association, for instance, embraced both Canadian and American clubs and extended to the Atlantic Seaboard. Jarvis was a remarkable person both for his contributions to the administration of the sport and his prowess as a yachtsman. Founder, as above noted, of the Yacht Racing Union of the Great Lakes, he also joined with Herrick Duggan (Toronto Yacht Club)[8] in founding the Lake Yacht Racing Association. Successfully competing into his eighties, in 1896 he represented the Royal Canadian Yacht Club and won a match race series against the Lincoln Park Yacht Club (Chicago) in the yacht *Canada* which the owners "deeded to the Yacht Racing Union of the Great Lakes for a challenge cup" named after the yacht. He also won the international match at Toledo where the Canadian yachts were painted black and dubbed 'the coffin fleet' by the Americans. As recounted in the *History of the Rochester Yacht Club*:

> *Skipper of the Canadian boats (competing for the Cup) in 1896, '99, 1901, '03 and '07 was Æmilius Jarvis, one-time Commodore of the RCYC and perhaps the most famous Canadian skipper of all time.*

He served as flag officer of the RCYC for 27 years and won over 300 regattas at home and internationally including the Canada's Cup in *Invader.* His range of yachting activity included cruising his yacht, *Haswell*, to Jamaica and return in 1897 – in one year attending meetings in New York in May and October, a trip to London on behalf of NAYRU and a winter cruise to Jamaica. During World War I when he was Commodore and head of the Navy League he recruited 2,500 men and bought 'mystery ships' on the Atlantic Coast. *The Annals*[9] record that:

> *In 1940 Jarvis, Canada's greatest sailor yachtsman for seventy years, dies in his eighty-first year. He had ridden the hounds on his last birthday, for he was Master of the North York Hunt.*

While the Union continued for a few years, either through lack of activity or loss of records, the nature and timing of its lapse is not known. The factors that caused the dissolution of the North American Yacht Racing Union are self-evident from the above account of its brief 'first chapter.' Even the British, who had failed in their attempt at harmonizing measurement in the United Kingdom and on the Continent, foresaw the effect of the lack of support from the prestigious clubs such as New York and Eastern. Another major factor was the failure of the rule that was adopted to address the needs of the smaller yachts in the under 30-feet range. It cannot even be said that NAYRU made any contribution towards achieving uniformity on the continent of the racing (right-of-way) rules. It announced that it had used the New York and Seawanhaka Yacht Clubs rules as models. The wording suggests that it followed Seawanhaka and just threw in New York for its prestige value. In point of fact, it made little difference whose rules had been used so alike were they in all important respects.

20
28
30
50
OFFICIALLY CERTIFIED
SWISS
CHRONOMETER
ROLEX—THE BLUE-WATER WATCHMATE

CHAPTER III

YACHT RACING ASSOCIATIONS

INTER-LAKE YACHT RACING ASSOCIATION[1]

The archives of the Inter-Lake Yachting Association are unusual among Associations owing to the persistence of two successive historians – the late A.A. (Al) Mastics and James A. Snodgrass – who have collected and microfilmed countless records. In this treasure trove, for example, are the Sailing Directions for a Regatta on Sandusky Bay, June 15, 1860 (four years before the Sandusky Yacht Club was formed) directing that yachts take pre-starting positions, for which they drew, and that certain stake boats, "must be rounded on the larboard hand."

In a letter Al Mastics recounts:

> *I-LYA has been an active organization since the day it was organized in 1885 by Commodore Gardner. He was Mayor of Cleveland at the time and Commodore of the Cleveland Yacht Club as well as (first) Commodore of I-LYA.*

Recalling, as a youngster, comments by delegates of the I-LYA to the 1897 meeting at which NAYRU was founded:

> *The reaction of the delegates to that meeting from the Mid-West was that the Atlantic Coast people were uncooperative and wanting credit for the national organization. They refused to vote claiming they were merely observers... The meeting accomplished what was needed and out of it came the Universal Rule (a few years after the lapse of NAYRU) which made interclub competition possible.*

> *Back in the '80's, yacht racing was the sport of large yachts – no one-designs – and every boat had a different measurement rating. They sailed long distances to get to their regattas and every club had its own racing and measurement rules. Wasn't that a beautiful mess?*

While at anchor in Put-In-Bay, a village on the southeastern of the three Bass Islands known for their wineries, on Lake Erie north of Sandusky and east of Toledo, a group of Cleveland yachtsmen listened to George W. Gardner remark that Put-In-Bay would be:

> *"... an ideal site for an annual regatta sponsored by an association of the yacht clubs on and near Lake Erie." From that chance remark has grown the world's largest freshwater yacht racing organization. January 17, 1885 at a joint meeting of the Cleveland Yachting Association and the Cleveland Canoe Club the Inter-Lake Yachting Association became a fact.*

Disrupted by the panic of 1893, the I-LYA reorganized in 1894. It's primary purpose was to standardize yacht racing rules to enable conducting the type of regattas proposed by Commodore Gardner. Today it is composed of over 140 yacht clubs representing some 40,000 sailors.

In 1908 the YRA held its annual regatta at Put-in-Bay. Aside from its charm, it was conveniently located for most of the member clubs, except Buffalo at the other end of the lake, and Columbus in the middle of Ohio. The YRA member clubs at the time were: The Buckeye Lake (Columbus), Buffalo, Cleveland, Detroit, Detroit Boat Club Yachtsmen,* Edgemere (Detroit), Erie, Lakewood (Cleveland), Monroe (MI), Maumee River (OH),

Put-in-Bay, Sandusky Yacht Club, the Country Club of Detroit, the Detroit Motor Boat Club and the Tawas Beach Yachting Association.

The program (the Notice of Race) for the regatta noted that all entries were to be made before 7 a.m. Monday, which no doubt reflected the wind conditions at Put-in-Bay; the breeze comes up in the morning and dies mid-afternoon after which competitors are free to retire to the wineries built by German wine barons modeled after those on the Rhine River. Sail racing took place on Thursday and Friday; power boat racing on Tuesday; and Wednesday was a lay day. There was a band concert before Thursday's racing, after which there were canoe races and swimming races. In the evening, the annual ball with two orchestras was held at the Hotel Victory – admission $1. After Friday's racing (there were four races in all), a baseball game took place between Toledo and Detroit yachtsmen, after which came a "smoker" at the hotel for the presentation of awards, ladies invited.

Cash prizes were in decline by the end of the 19th century and had been eliminated in many places, but they still existed on Lake Erie. The prizes were put up by the clubs, supplemented in most cases by the Association. The purse (sailors in those days were avid track fans) for Classes 'A' and 'B', for example, was $300 - $150 for first, $90 for second, and $60 for third. The winners also received a "Championship Flag."

Yachts in Classes 'A' and 'B' were ranked for handicap purposes under the Yacht Racing Union of the Great Lakes Rule which was, "fortified against the schemes of yacht designers by the addition of scantlings," e.g. whether tamarack could be substituted for oak. Class 'C' was ranked under the Seawanhaka Rule, with a variation that substituted LOA for LWL. The next three classes were ranked under the Association's rule for the 21-foot, 18-foot, and 16-foot classes, which were restricted one-design sloops. The last class, catboats, were ranked under the same, although how they fitted into it is difficult to figure. A unique provision in the YRU Rule was, "... Union will recognize no races sailed on Sunday..."

Participants at the 1908 regatta were given copies of a history of the YRA, about which, on the title page, the author complained of the great difficulty of accomplishing its mere 34 pages. He had found the Association's records in an unholy mess and grievously incomplete. As with many of club histories, it also fudged a year at the beginning. In this case, in 1884 there transpired only a conversation between three Cleveland lake sailors that amounted to a "Why don't we?"; implementation occurred the following year. Sometimes the date of adoption of by-laws or formal incorporation is used to record the date of origin of a yacht racing association or club.

Prior to the 1880's there had been only five yacht clubs on the American side of a lake that spanned 250 miles – one each at Detroit, Cleveland, and Buffalo and two at Toledo (which later merged). It was these that formed the I-LYA. During the next decade the Put-In-Bay, Erie, and Sandusky Yacht Clubs were formed and became members. The rule under which they raced was interesting: the sum of waterline length, maximum beam, and "the depth of hold from the underside of the deck to the top side of thc planking, at or as near the mast as possible." The third measurement was in common use on the Lakes before 1900 and appears to have been one more factor determinative of the relative size, i.e. speed potential, of a boat. The handicap was two seconds per mile for each foot of difference. Class divisions were determined solely on LWL, i.e. 35 feet and over for Class 'A' and less than 20 feet for Class 'E'. That was a common method of classification.

Note that on the Inland Lakes by the end of the century measuring of the hull had been abandoned, and the determination of whether a boat was 'in class' was whether or not it fitted in a rectangular box – an early form of template.

In 1895 the Association dropped its rule and adopted the Seawanhaka Rule, which was simply the sum of LWL and the square root of sail area, divided by two. At the same time it dropped the five-minute starting-interval rule under which a yacht's time was taken when she crossed the starting line during the first three minutes of the interval.

It worked. The very next year, it was adopted by clubs in North America, and it soon became the standard method for starting races everywhere. Probably no other rule change in yacht racing was ever adopted so quickly and so widely. Also, it introduced a new element to racing, the tactics of starting. As was often the case in yacht racing, as in life, change occurred not from the application of logic but from practical necessity. As the number of yachts on starting lines continued to increase, it became an onerous, often impossible, task to time them accurately when 15 or 20 of them were all crossing the line within four or five seconds. Race committees everywhere threw up their hands and said, "From now on, we'll time all of you from the starting gun." (See *Starting Systems* in *Chapter I.*)

In 1895 another remarkable thing happened. A new yacht appeared on Lake Erie with a Daimler gasoline engine and – wonder of wonders – a reverse gear. Naptha-powered launchers had been on the lake for a decade or so, but this was the first racing yacht with a real engine.

In the same year a Lake Erie boat sailed up the Detroit River and into Lake Huron and all the way around to the bottom of Lake Michigan to race against the Chicago fleet. The next year, several boats from Chicago reciprocated by visiting Lake Erie and taking part in the annual regatta at Put-in-Bay. There were also several Canadian boats from Lake Ontario on their way to race at Toledo for the Canada's Cup. The word "Inter-Lake" was beginning to take on a wider meaning.

In the history are several references to the Yacht Racing Union of the Great Lakes. The earliest 'umbrella' union of yacht racing associations, its sole purpose was to unify the racing rules and measurement rules of all the clubs on all the Great Lakes. In 1899 the I-LYA adopted a new measurement rule that taxed four factors; LWL, beam, girth (measurement only from waterline to waterline around the keel with measuring tape taut), and half the square root of sail area. Centerboards within keels were taxed and, if made of cast iron and/or lead, taxed as keels.

In 1901 the YRA saw the most dramatic example of what the Seawanhaka Rule had done to yacht design on the East Coast. A new yacht designed by B.B. Crowninshield of Boston appeared on the lake. It was 35 feet long on deck but only 21 feet on the waterline and drew only 3½ feet. With 730 square feet of sail she was very fast and was not beaten once during her first six years. Even the very sight of her made people shudder, and the Association made a number of changes in its rules. It also sent a circular to member clubs reiterating the YRU rule that it would not recognize races sailed on Sundays and urged them not to permit their members to enter such races.

The very next year, however, the I-LYA adopted the Yacht Racing Union rule, which also contained four factors but with limitations and penalties. For example, a yacht with a 25-foot waterline would be penalized for a draft of less than six feet or a sail area greater than 1,050 feet. Scantlings were also increased, so it is obvious that the purpose was safer and sturdier boats. It also made a lot more sense than the prior rule. Meanwhile, in New York a group of men representing the New York and Boston clubs were working on a rule proposed by N.G. Herreshoff (initially named for him but ultimately called the Universal Rule) adding limitations and penalties to it.

There were two developments in 1904. One was a rule banning, professional sailors as helmsmen. The debate over this resulted in a small concession. "Reformed" professionals were OK. The other was the adoption of the Massachusetts Bay 21-foot class. This was a cabin sloop about 30 feet in length with a rather tall rig. It did not displace, but supplemented, the "restricted" 21-foot class, and it seems to have been the first one-design on Lake Erie. Five were built the first year and it became a very popular boat.

It was in 1905 that the Verdi Band was first brought from Cleveland to Put-in-Bay to play from the deck of the schooner of the Yacht Racing Association's Commodore. There was also a fireworks display on Wednesday evening, sent up from a barge anchored in the harbor. The prospect of both brought many more people to the island than ever had attended the annual regatta before. It was also the first year that the catboat class raced.

The Association had been in the red for several years. It had gone from cash prizes to the presentation of medallions for first, second, and third places in the seven classes, which the Association paid for. As it turned out, the medallions were costing more than the contribution to the purses put up by the clubs under the previous system, so it went back to cash prizes in 1907. It also, through the Yacht Racing Union, adopted the Universal Rule, despite the objections of some that it was exceedingly complicated. That made the fourth completely new measurement rule in the Association's 24-year history.

It is not difficult to determine the size of sailboats on Lake Erie during this period. There are several references to schooners of more than 60 feet. The smallest recognized class of the I-LYA was the 16-foot restricted class, which meant about 23 feet in length. Catboats probably were a bit shorter, and those that remained at home because of the distance to Put-in-Bay were doubtless smaller. How many were racing is more difficult to determine. The only races described were those of the annual regatta, and the number of entries, class by class, was seldom given.

The year 1908 ended with a hope that some day a permanent clubhouse would be built at Put-in-Bay. That hope was realized in 1923. A Put-in-Bay Yachting Association was formed in 1886 but soon went bankrupt. It was re-formed in 1894 by local businessmen whose businesses did very well every August when all the people came for the annual regatta. In short, it was a public relations gesture. Eventually, it became a yacht club in the usual sense, although it didn't have a home until a piece of waterfront land became available in 1922. The club promptly built a clubhouse on it the next year.

Put-in-Bay continues to host the annual regatta of the Association amidst a bucolic Victorian setting free of automobile traffic.

LAKE YACHT RACING ASSOCIATION[2]

The Lake Yacht Racing Association is the oldest district sailing association in North America, having preceded the next oldest – the Inter-Lake Yachting Association – by a year. The Lake in the title is Ontario, and it was a joint Canadian/American venture combining yacht clubs on the shores of the Province of Ontario with those on the shores of the State of New York. The impetus for the venture came from the Toronto Yacht Club[3] which found, after a brief survey of opinion around the Lake, that there was considerable interest in establishing an association.

A meeting was called in January, 1884, but only three clubs were directly represented: Toronto, Royal Canadian and Oswego. The Bay of Quinte and the Kingston (#1) Yacht Clubs wrote their regrets and offered their proxies to Toronto. The Chairman, G. Herrick Duggan of the Royal Canadian and Toronto Yacht Clubs initially sought to create a national Canadian Yachting Association, but as events turned out, this was deflected to become a yacht racing association. The Chairman began with an effort to obtain agreement on a common measurement rule. He reasoned that, if this could be done, the rest would be easy. The Seawanhaka Rule (LWL plus the square root of sail area divided by two) had been in use for eight years, long enough to have proved its worth, and Toronto and Kingston had already adopted it. Agreement on the Seawanhaka Rule took only a few minutes, and the delegates turned to drafting a constitution.

The constitution in Article I states:

> *The object of this Association shall be to encourage yacht building and yacht racing, and to establish and enforce uniform rules for the government of all races in which the yachts of two or more clubs compete.*

It was hoped that adoption of the Seawanhaka Rule would encourage yacht building. To encourage yacht racing the Association sponsored a port-to-port regatta each year. The regatta began in one port, and the yachts would race to another, where they would spend a day or two racing around-the-buoys and so on until the fleet had almost circumnavigated the lake. One owner in 1892 reported that his taffrail log had recorded 607 miles for the entire regatta. The next year's regatta was the last port-to-port event; apparently, it was too strenuous and time-consuming. Thereafter every regatta was held in a single location.

By 1894 the LYRA had at least four new members: Rochester Yacht Club, the Royal Hamilton, Victoria Yacht Club (also in Hamilton) and the Queen City (Toronto). Buffalo (technically a Lake Erie Club) and Kingston (#2 as the original one had lapsed) Yacht Clubs joined three years later. In 1896 a new group called the Yacht Racing Union of the Great Lakes was formed as an umbrella organization for the three associations functioning on the Great Lakes – Lake Michigan Yachting Association, Inter-Lake Yachting Association (Erie) and the LYRA. Its function was to be purely advisory and to help coordinate events and rating rules involving clubs from two, or all three, associations, but note that it assumed a leading role and made some binding decisions from time to time, albeit with the acquiescence of the three associations in most cases. It remains the first organization in North America to serve as an umbrella for a combination of Yacht Racing Associations.

LYRA adopted the girth rule in 1898 since the usefulness of the waterline and sail area rule had come to an end with the building of yachts with extreme overhangs and very limited displacement. A committee led by Æmilius Jarvis of the RCYC resulted in the adoption in 1902 by the Yacht Racing Union of the Great Lakes of a table of restrictions including sail area, draft and hull dimensions for the establishment of restricted classes. Note that under the aegis of the YRU the rule would have much wider coverage than merely under the YRA.

In 1906 the three associations adopted said rule and its scantling minimums. The Rule was the Universal Rule that had been developed by N.G. Herreshoff at the behest of the New York Yacht Club to which the YRU had added the scantlings. The Rule, created to curb the havoc wrought by designers under the Seawanhaka Rule, added to the elements of LWL and sail area a displacement factor resulting in LWL times the square foot of sail area divided by 5.5 times the cube root of displacement.

In 1909 the LYRA voted to allot 25 percent of the prize money for the annual regatta to the "veteran cruising classes." Did this mean older boats that were no longer competitive, either because they had been out-designed by newer ones, or because of scantlings that were not stout enough and caused rapid deterioration? No exact definition of a "veteran" appears in the History, though one owner defined it as, "any yacht in which the bilge pump was a more important piece of equipment than the mast." The prizes, incidentally, ranged from $35 for the first place in the largest class to $8 for third place in the smallest. The money came from subscriptions from member clubs, some of which did not always come through. The amounts ranged from $50 for the smallest clubs up to $400 for the largest – the Royal Canadian

Yacht Club. Surprisingly, the LYRA often wangled contributions from the town or city in which an event was to be held. Sometimes as much as $1,000 came from the public coffers.

Racing was curtailed greatly during World War I, and no LYRA events were held. In 1919 the questions of port-to-port racing arose, and it was decided to try it again, this time on a much modified basis of three day-long distance races, two days of round-the buoys racing at a third port, and then two more distance races. The following year was the one in which the great switch from gaff to Marconi/Bermuda rigs began, but the LYRA banned them for use in handicap racing for two years. It then accepted them but penalized the masthead rig by ten seconds per mile! One more year and the flood was too great; the LYRA capitulated.

In 1921 the port-to-port question became academic with the presentation to the Association of the trophy to be called the Freeman Trophy. It quickly became the principal distance event on the lake. The first sailing for it that year was the longest straight-line course that Lake Ontario can provide: 190 miles from one end of the lake to the other – Hamilton to Kingston. The winner was a schooner owned by Æmilius Jarvis, former Commodore of the Royal Canadian Yacht Club and a man judged by many to have been Canada's greatest sailor.

In the same year the LYRA took a census of all the handicapped yachts belonging to member clubs and issued blocks of numbers to be assigned permanently. The size of the blocks was to provide each club with the potential number that it might need. Nine of the clubs received ten numbers and the Royal Canadian 20. Thus, in 1921 there was a potential of 110 such racing yachts on the lake. In actuality there probably were no more than 75.

In 1923 a new class of yachts, called 'C' boats, appeared fostered by the Royal Canadian Yacht Club. They were 25 feet LOA with cabin accommodations for three. They were stout little vessels and became very popular. Some were still racing more than 30 years later. Apparently they were one-designs, but whether they sailed with the offshore fleet or amongst themselves is not mentioned in the history. As one-designs they joined the Stars and the local intra-club knockabouts as the only such classes on the Lake.

By 1925 so many amendments had been made to the racing rules that a committee was appointed to tidy them up. A new condition for membership was set at a minimum of 50 members and at least five regularly sailed yachts with LWLs of 15 feet or more. At the same time a new rule was instituted banning the use of spinnakers and other light headsails between 7 p.m. and 5 a.m. The purpose of the rule was to prevent obscuring running lights which, carried on sideboards high above the deck, were easily masked by such sails. The most important event of the year, however, was an invitation from Clifford D. Mallory, President of the Yacht Racing Association of Long Island Sound, to send a delegate to New York to attend a meeting at which an effort toward the re-formation of the North American Yacht Racing Union, which had been defunct for 24 years, would be undertaken. Before the meeting was successfully completed, George Gooderham of the Royal Canadian Yacht Club was appointed Vice President, and W. P. Barrows, retiring President of the LYRA and a member of the Rochester Yacht Club, was appointed a member of the Racing Rules Committee.

In 1927 there were 40 entries for the Freeman Trophy race, a record number for the event that erased the 1926 record of 38. The same year the Prince of Wales (later the Duke of Windsor) visited the annual regatta at Kingston aboard a steam yacht. That he showed up exhibited a dutiful attitude, since it was well known that he had no interest whatsoever in yacht racing. Indeed, he had once been seen aboard the royal yacht *Britannia*, while she scudded before the breeze under spinnaker, hitting golf balls off her stern. The lack of interest was one reason King George V ordered that she be taken out to sea and scuttled when he died.

At the 1929 annual meeting LYRA adopted the measurement rules and racing rules of NAYU – "subject to such amendments and additions as might be decided to suit local conditions." Later in the year it was reported:

> *The NAYRU racing rules, measurement rule and time allowances were so 'jumbled up' that a joint committee of NAYRU and the New York Yacht Club had been set up to re-arrange and simplify them.*

The report was misleading. The International Yacht Racing Union was intent on having uniform racing rules on both sides of the Atlantic. To that end, it invited the New York Yacht Club and NAYRU (in that order, incidentally) to send two delegates each to the annual meeting in London to discuss the matter. The result was that the right-of-way section of the rules became conformed, with both sides accepting compromises amicably where the two differed.

One of the primary purposes in re-creating NAYRU had been to secure uniform racing rules throughout North America. Yet, NAYRU was most careful not to display a dominating attitude and relied on time and persuasion; in Clifford Mallory it had a perceptive and diplomatic leader. As late as 1931 the racing rules of the LYRA governed on Lake Ontario, and they still had not been fully conformed to those of NAYRU. It was not the only association or individual club that differed; many did in minor ways.

SAN FRANCISCO BAY AND NORTHERN CALIFORNIA[4]

ON SAN FRANCISCO BAY

[Lloyd Ryland] I have located the dates of the first yacht regattas and yacht clubs in the San Francisco Bay area – the first on the Pacific Coast. The existence of them was ignored by Eastern and Mid-Western yacht clubs and publications. I think this was, in part, because of the false conception that the Industrial Revolution had not yet reached the west coast in the early days and, in part, because there was a lack of communication between this and the Eastern areas. Early major Eastern magazines rarely published on Pacific Coast yachting, unless correspondents forwarded articles.

During the 1840's and for some time thereafter, there was no continental telegraph, no 'pony express' nor railroad communication. Information was transmitted both ways by ships that had to go 'around the Horn.' Starting in the 1850's, communications from the East were sent to the Caribbean side of the Isthmus of Panama, transported across Panama to the Pacific side, and thence by 'shuttle ship' to San Francisco – and in reverse.

By then the Gold Rush years had transformed the Spanish mission village of San Francisco to a port with more ships than any other on the globe and a frenzy of activity.

Our earliest yacht club was called the Pioneer, formed in 1852 [during a cruise of yachtsmen to Angel Island]. [That] was only eight years after the New York Yacht Club was formed and only one year after the first America's Cup race at Cowes [Isle of Wight], which was duly reported here. It never had a clubhouse, but it did buy a small schooner, and it participated in some regattas of the later clubs. [There are reports of yacht racing from 1852-54 including a race between Michief *and* Eclipse *for stakes of $50]. It had a desultory existence and was last heard from in 1895.*

Other short-lived yacht clubs were formed whose names were later adopted by present durable clubs, thus leading to confusing duplicate names. There was the first San Francisco Yacht Club ca. 1855, a first Pacific Yacht Club ca. 1856 and a first Oakland Yacht Club ca. 1860. Later duplicate name yacht clubs were the California Yacht Club 1894-1920; the first Golden Gate Yacht Club 1906-1910; and the first Sausalito Yacht Club 1910-1918. The second local Pacific Yacht Club existed from 1878-1899. Some of the abandoned names were taken by Southern California Yacht Clubs, i.e. California 1922 and Pacific Yacht Club 1907 which used different burgees.

The first 'sweepstake' race was held by... the first San Francisco Yacht Club on the 4th of July, 1855... Three prizes were put up: first, $500 and a silver pitcher; second $50 and a silver cup; third, a silver cup. The contestants were a mix of sailboats carried on the decks of square-riggers [many from the East coast] and local work boats... This early club continued its annual regattas until at least 1859. How long it existed after that is unknown. The present San Francisco Yacht Club was formed in 1869 and was the first permanent club on the Pacific Coast.

In 1869 the Master Mariners Benevolent Association (MMBA) took over the Boatmen's Protective Association and held races for dissimilar cargo vessels from 1869-79, 1884-85 and in 1891. In 1965 the MMBA was revived under the direction of William Vaughan of the Encinal Yacht Club (Alameda) for sponsored yachts, "designed or built using materials in common use before World War II."

Of the East Bay clubs a few short-lived ones are reported to have held regattas such as the Oakland Yacht Club in 1860, the Sea Bird Club (San Leandro Bay) from about 1875 to the early 1880's. From 1890 to the early 1920's the Alameda Boating Club, primarily a rowing club, ran races for sailboats.

Regarding the first one-design sailboats in San Francisco Bay, the first was probably the common, multi-purpose Whitehall. The first of these came on the decks of square-riggers and later were built in small local shipyards. Informal, unrecorded stake races, for money or merchandise, undoubtedly occurred with those fitted with sail, when there was leisure time. [More on the Whitehall in Chapter VII – Classes and One-Designs.*]*

The Corinthian movement on the Bay began in the mid 1880's with the establishment of the Corinthian Yacht Club at Tiburon, which limited its races to boats up to 45 feet LOA. The Encinal Yacht Club (Alameda) was, likewise, founded as a Corinthian club in 1890. The trend in this direction in the latter quarter of the past century encompassed the East Coast, the Inland Lakes and the West Coast.

[Rudder][5] *The San Francisco Perpetual Challenge Cup: a little over a year ago (1895) some cranky individuals [members of the Corinthian Yacht Club]... conceived the idea of getting up a cup which should have as its object primarily the encouragement of the smaller classes of yachts, and which should not be liable to degenerate into a "class distinction", or become a possibility for millionaires only. A second aim was the encouragement of all classes in a club, the tendency of all or most [match racing] challenge cups being to favor one particular class at the expense of all others... the guiding principle was, "bar no class, and take a fellow of your own size." ... It had been intended to give it to the San Francisco Yacht Club, because it was the parent club... But the usual childish jealousy, which has never failed to come to the surface when anyone ever attempted to do anything for yachting here, made itself largely in evidence, and the first custodian [Encinal Yacht Club] was chosen by lot.*

The cup fell, as it happened, into apparently the worst possible hands – a club devoted to sociability and the cultivation of "family virtues", with a little yachting thrown in as an incidental... The SFYC... promptly challenged (and lost to a slower boat which the defenders managed to re-rig, re-ballast and tune up by taking advantage of an exception to the prohibition forbading the building of a new boat after the date of the challenge but not forbidding unlimited tuning up).

[Lloyd Ryland] During 1897 the Pacific and the present Corinthian Yacht Club's first held regattas using 15-foot and 17-foot one-designs. The former could have been the North Haven one-design. [The] boats were either imported and/or built locally. No design or description of either boat has been found... After that, a great many small one-designs came gradually into use. [Per] the first Pacific Inter-Club Yacht Association [PICYA] yearbook,by 1922 there was a short-lived and unseaworthy one-design called Coyote Point class, fostered by the first Coyote Point Yacht Club. Both existed only until 1923. At this time, the Cub and Dory classes were popular for junior training. Later the Moons, Stars, Snipes, Mercuries and many others became popular. Larger one-designs started with the 'Q', 'R' and 'S' boats [Universal Rule class designations are in descending order of their size, i.e. the 'S' class at about 26-30 feet LOA was the smallest of the three; the largest class to sail in North America was the 130-foot LOA 'J' sloop during the 1930's America's Cup matches].

The San Francisco Challenge Cup and the Seawanhaka International Challenge Cup For Small Yachts (known as The Seawanhaka Cup) were created in 1895 four days apart and first raced for 28 days apart. The latter, however, is not scheduled annually, but both served as prototypes for other match race competitions.

Lloyd Ryland furnished a clipping from the Aug. 2, 1897 *San Francisco Chronicle* that is typical of yachting reportage in the Victorian era, "Dr. Thomas L. Hill Wins – Fine Display of Seamanship Witnessed":

> *It was a merry old wind that welcomed the new era in yachting on San Francisco Bay yesterday, when the first race of the [15 foot LOA] one-design class was sailed under the auspices of the Pacific Yacht Club ... The boats were beached in the middle part of last week and painted, making them in fine condition for the close contest. Early Sunday morning all was activity about the boathouse of the club, for five of the boats had to ship their masts and set up the rigging.*
>
> *As early as ten o'clock the members began to arrive on the grounds coming over in time for lunch. As the hour drew near for the starting time the gigs of many yachts anchored off Sausalito put off for the clubhouse, loaded down to the plimsoll mark with pretty girls dressed in yachting costumes, who, when they took possession of the clubhouse and grounds made one think the whole world loves a sailor. The 'landlubbers' with tall hats and long-tail coats looked as though in despair they would have to take up the sport to be within the magic circle of the smiles of the daughters of Neptune.*
>
> *Promptly at 1:50 p.m. the preparatory gun was fired from the flagship* Sappho. *[Only] two of the yachts were underway... Both started before the race for a trial spin with full sail. It was warm work, and Dr. Hill thought, as the wind was increasing, it would be best to turn in a reef. To this he attributed his victory. The yachts were sent up and down Hurricane Gulch. As the squalls, with the strength of a 50-mile breeze, would strike them they would be sent over on their beam ends, exposing the rudder and most of the centerboard. It was exciting and looked to be bordering on recklessness, which undoubtedly made the timid and faint-hearted desist from entering in the prevailing winds... The ladies would scream and plead with the yachtsmen present to send a boat out to the racers and save them.*

The start was delayed five minutes so as to allow Dr. Hill to finish putting in his reef... The Doctor got the best of the start... He was closely followed [by the other yacht]. Just as the latter reached the line a terrific squall struck the boat, which luffed it up into the yacht Lurline, *which was laying at anchor. No damage was done, and she was soon on her way again.*

On the run to the Belvedere stakeboat Dr. Hill led by four minutes at the turn and was going easy, while the other boat was laboring badly. The Doctor after making the turn stood off into the Raccoon Straits channel breeze, holding on for an unnecessary time. He slipped into light winds and a heavy flood tide which carried him out of position

[The other boat] saw this and after following the Doctor for a short while went about and stood in shore. When the yachts crossed tacks a short while after it was seen that the Doctor had lost his advantage and some minutes besides.

In the meantime, the Doctor went well into the ferry slips before he went about for the finish. This proved to be one of the winning points of the race.

Commodore Law entertained the judges... at lunch aboard the Sappho *before the race. After the start [she] began to drag her anchor, which was caused by the great number of flags with which she was decorated.*

PACIFIC INTER-CLUB YACHT ASSOCIATION - 1896

The PICYA was the first continuous yachting association on the Pacific Coast and the sixth in North America; although the Northwest International Yachting Association was founded four years earlier, it was reorganized and succeeded in 1920 by the Pacific International Yachting Association. The statement of purpose of the PICYA reflects the factors that militated the formation of most regional organizations as well as the founding of NAYRU the next year. The first President was Charles G. Yale, a charter member of the San Francisco Yacht Club and its Secretary for 16 years. The founding clubs were: San Francisco Yacht Club 1869, the first permanent yacht club on the Pacific coast; Corinthian Yacht Club 1886; Encinal Boat Club a.k.a. Yacht Club or Encinals 1890; California Yacht Club 1892 at Alameda and later disbanded; Pacific Yacht Club 1878, lapsed in 1899. The South Bay Yacht Club initially declined and later joined in 1897.

At the 1897 meeting, out of which arose NAYRU, the PICYA was one of the six associations most active in accomplishing its formation and was represented by Joseph M. Macdonough, a member of the Pacific and New York Yacht Clubs. He spent much of his life in New York, was donor of money for trophies for which yachts of the PICYA competed for 22 years and was delegated by NAYRU, along with Æmilius Jarvis of Toronto, to discuss measurement rules with the British Clubs.

The Bay was one of the last centers of yacht racing to adopt the Universal Rule. We noted in *Room at the Mark*[6] that New York and Boston Clubs and others in the east could hardly wait, while the rule was reviewed, strengthened and approved by the Atlantic Coast Conference in 1904, to substitute it for the Seawanhaka Rule. The switch-over was instantaneous, so despised had the Seawanhaka Rule become for the ridiculous 'skimming dishes' it ultimately produced. The Universal Rule had been adopted by the Yacht Racing Union of the Great Lakes in 1906 along with scantling requirements, and since, as Ryland reports, the same dissatisfaction with the Seawanhaka Rule existed on the West Coast, one would have expected its quick adoption on San Francisco Bay. After discussion by the Pacific Inter-Club Yacht Association in 1908 about replacing the Seawanhaka Rule, it was decided to delay so doing until the next year, but no action was taken until 1910, nor did it appear in the revised PICYA by-laws until 1912. Apparently reluctance to change and apprehension over outmoding existing yachts caused the delay.

As Ryland relates in a letter:

When PICYA was formed during May 12, 1896, "to encourage yacht building and yacht racing and to enforce uniform rules for the governance of all races in which two or more clubs, members of the Association, may compete. Any recognized yacht club on the Pacific Coast in good standing is eligible for membership," virtually all sailboats were non-identical and were handicapped by the Seawanhaka Rule. Separate allowances were made for yawls and schooners. A so-called 'San Francisco Bay Yawl' was designed to take advantage of this rule. This led eventually to freak designs of 'racing machines' and general dissatisfaction. As early as 1907 the San Francisco Yacht Club was recommending using the Universal Rule.

The 'freak' yawl was 56 feet LOA, only 24 feet LWL, 14-feet, 6-inch beam and drew only eight feet with her centerboard down. To keep her overhangs from falling off she had to be fitted with internal steel trusses.

In 1900 the PICYA had its second new member since its founding, the Vallejo Yachting and Rowing Club. Vallejo had become a favorite cruising destination, which led to its eventually being a venue for one of the Association's inter-club regattas. By the next year the Association was in trouble with its member clubs over regatta costs and insufficient trophies. The solution was to charge clubs according to the number of entries each had and charging people who went out on private spectator boats a fee of $1.

In 1911 the Panama Yacht Club was established (on the Alameda side of the Oakland Estuary), apparently named in anticipation of the completion of the Panama Canal in honor of which the Panama-Pacific International Exposition was schedule to take place in San Francisco in 1915 – "the first truly international cultural exposition to be held in the U.S." Unfortunately the Club was short-lived.

During Sir Thomas Lipton's visit to San Francisco in 1912 he was entertained by Exposition officials, the PICYA and member yacht clubs. He issued the following challenge:

> *I will bring a 23 Metre cutter to race here at your great Exposition regatta in 1915, and I will hoist my fighting flag and challenge the world to a race for the championship of the seas.*

Sir Thomas presented his 'customary' trophy – dubbed the 'Big Lipton' [to distinguish it from a later donation of his] for which the deed of gift provided that it was to be raced for annually by sailboats of PICYA clubs under a rating according to the Universal Rule. The first race, held in 1914, was participated in by seven yachts in the 'N' Class – a class recorded only in California and the Great Lakes – and won by the gaff-rigged sloop *Yankee* now rigged as a schooner. At the Exposition regattas the next year the PICYA conducted 26 races, an extraordinary number for the period and probably not matched elsewhere in North America for years to come. It was, also, the first large-scale racing in 'R' boats on the West Coast. Like the 'R's at Marblehead, where the class began, they sailed as a class without handicap, as though they were one-design. Similar to Marblehead, the class was an instant success and was destined for more than 35 years of racing on the Bay. This, also, was the first year for Six-Metres, although there were only two of them, the gaff-rigged *Lady Betty* (US 6/1) from the San Francisco Yacht Club and *Nordug IV* from Denmark sporting a Marconi/Bermuda rig and roller reefing. This represented the first Six-Metre racing in North America and, but for the outbreak of war in Europe, would have been attended by Sixes from other countries.

After the first race for the 'R's a bizarre set of circumstances occurred. It was won by *Fleur de Lys* from the San Francisco Yacht Club but was protested by *Sir Tom* from the Seattle Yacht Club on a measurement allegation. The latter was the first 'R' in the Northwest, having been designed, built and owned by Ted Geary, a talented and prolific naval architect and sailor. The Regatta Committee heard the protest and dismissed it as without merit. Geary appealed to the Board of Directors of the Exposition which overturned the decision of the Regatta Committee, disqualified *Fleur de Lys* and awarded the trophy to *Sir Tom.* That was tantamount to the Port Authority overturning a decision of the Jury at the America's Cup in San Diego. The matter ended up in court and two years later the second decision was overturned and the trophy returned to the original winner. Meanwhile:

Lloyd Ryland, historian of the Pacific Inter-Club Yachting Association
Photo courtesy of Lloyd Ryland

C. Stanley Ogilvy, author of *A Centennial History YRA of Long Island Sound; A History of the Star Class;* and *Diamond Jubilee, A History of the Larchmont Yacht Club*
Photo courtesy of the author

> *her disgusted owner retired [her] from racing, had a motor installed and devoted his time thereafter to fishing.*

Retired in 1919, the Trophy was raced for 40 years later under a revised deed designating it for team racing. In 1965 the deed was altered by substituting the Cruising Club of American Rule for the Universal Rule; the Trophy was destroyed in the 1976 fire at the St. Francis Yacht Club. It was replaced in 1980 by a model of one of Sir Thomas's *Shamrocks* and is known as The Sir Thomas Lipton Challenge Trophy (1913/1980).

A second trophy, 'The Little Lipton,' was presented by Sir Thomas in 1934 to foster a race back to the mainland after each Transpac race. This proved impractical, and it was turned over to PICYA for Six-Metre racing in 1934 and won by *Maybe* of the Corinthian Yacht Club.

Mission statements often provide an insight into how sports organizations became more complex and government regulations more intrusive with the passage of time. The original statement of the PICYA sufficed from 1898 - 1952:

> *Encourage yacht building and yacht racing.*
>
> *Establish and enforce uniform rules for governing races in which two or more clubs shall compete.*

By 1995 the statement had been revised and expanded to include:

> *(2) Constitute an association of yacht clubs and organizations, to promote inter-club communications, yachting activities and social interaction relating thereto, and to organize and conduct programs which enhance the general welfare of the member organizations.*

Likewise, the membership requirements underwent change from:

> *Open to any yacht club (in good standing) located on the Pacific Coast*

(to)

> *Open to non-profit yacht clubs or recreational boating organizations located in Northern California which meet the following qualifications: (1) shall be committed to the promotion of recreational boating, (2) shall have been in active existence for a minimum of two years, (3) shall have a regular dues-paying membership whose members own a minimum of twenty recreational watercraft, and (4) shall have interests compatible with Member Clubs.*

While the territorial scope of the Association contracted, conversely the spread of the recreational boating became more comprehensive.

THE PACIFIC COAST YACHTING ASSOCIATION

Before 1921 contact among PICYA clubs and those to the south around Los Angeles had been mostly on a club-to-club basis involving special events. In 1921, however, the Southern California Yachting Association (SCYA) was formed. The same year two representatives of the Pacific International Yachting Association came to San Francisco to talk with PICYA and SCYA to see what might be done to encourage and promote racing on the entire West Coast. The result of that initiative was the formation in 1923 of an umbrella organization to cover all three groups called the Pacific Coast Yachting Association. Its role was mainly to assist in communications and scheduling regattas on the west coast to obviate conflicts. Dr. Albert Soiland, Commodore of the South Coast Yacht Club (Los Angeles) which staged the first Transpac Race, was made Admiral. - now Commodore

At the time the SCYA had six members: San Diego, Newport Harbor, Los Angeles, California and Santa Barbara Yacht Clubs and the Los Angeles Athletic Club. The PICYA had six members: San Francisco, Corinthian, Aeolian, Oakland and South Bay Yacht Club's and the Vallejo Yachting and Boating Club. The PIYA had seven: Seattle, Queen City (Seattle), Royal Victoria, Royal Vancouver, Cowichan Bay, Tacoma and the Portland Yacht Clubs.

With only 19 member clubs under three umbrella groups spanning a coastline of 1,300 miles there hardly seemed need for an overall coordinating organization, especially if the more densely populated East Coast with many more clubs spanning a roughly equivalent distance had not been impelled to form one. The need stemmed from a type of inter-regional competition for special trophies that drew yachts from as far away as San Diego and Vancouver to compete with each other. For example, it did not phase Clarence MacFarlane, after sailing his schooner *La Paloma* from Honolulu to San Francisco in 1906 to start the first Transpac Race and finding the City devastated by the great earthquake, to sail to Los Angeles and start the race to Honolulu from San Pedro. Ever since its formation the PCYA annual regatta have been a great draw, and the site of the competition moved up and down the coast.

YACHT RACING ASSOCIATION OF SAN FRANCISCO BAY

In 1928 two clubs, the St. Francis Yacht Club, established the year before by members of the San Francisco Yacht Club who wanted to locate on the City side of the Bay, and the much older Corinthian Yacht Club formed the Yacht Racing Association of San Francisco Bay to provide more direct services to the racing sailors than were available from PICYA; in fact the Corinthian Yacht Club had recently resigned from PICYA. Its first Chairman was Charles A. Langlais who served for many years as a Director of NAYRU. The Association conformed race management techniques, established standard starting signals, a standard scoring system, a percentage handicap system based on prior performance and set a schedule of championships around the Bay. Two classes that especially benefited from this were the 'R' and the Six-Metre most of which were owned by members of the two clubs.

The St. Francis Yacht Club, whose founding members consisted of the most experienced and financially eminent members of the San Francisco Yacht Club with many of the largest yachts, immediately became a strong player in the YRA, and today it conducts a significant portion of the regattas on the Bay. This, coupled with its associations with the New York Yacht Club and the Royal Thames Yacht Club (London), soon made it one of the most influential clubs in North America.

SMALL BOAT RACING ASSOCIATION

Unlike the majority of Yacht or District Associations, which normally conducted only championship regattas or race weeks, the YRA operated more akin to the YRA of Long Island Sound; both scheduled races for season series on a rotational basis among their member clubs. The smaller classes, traveling a long distance to regatta sites that were not suitable for their type of boats, found this incompatible with their needs; hence, these classes and the clubs at which they were located formed in 1937 the Small Boat Racing Association. The new Association was especially convenient for clubs located on the Eastern side of the Bay and their smaller one-design classes.

YACHT RACING ASSOCIATION OF LONG ISLAND SOUND[7]

Strange as it may seem, there was no inter-club racing on Long Island Sound until 1880, save for a few youngsters who sailed small catboats and presumably raced informally from time to time. In the Lower Bay of New York Harbor there were at least ten yacht clubs, but the western end of Long Island Sound there were only three – North Shore (later Port Washington) and Knickerbocker Yacht Clubs in Manhasset Bay and Stuyvesant Yacht Club at City Island. They were augmented by the formation of the Larchmont Yacht Club in 1880. Within three years it had almost 300 members. By 1891 the Seawanhaka Corinthian Yacht Club had located on Centre Island, Oyster Bay, and the American Yacht Club was formed at Rye NY. By 1895 there were at least 19 clubs in the western end of the Sound. All initially conducted regattas only for their own members so that there was no inter-club competition.

As soon as clubs began to invite members of other clubs to participate in their races, problems arose. They were not caused by the racing rules, for the clubs all copied the rules of the New York Yacht Club, which in turn developed rules in conjunction with the Eastern Yacht Club of Marblehead MA and the Seawanhaka Corinthian Yacht Club. The problems lay with measurement rules and time allowance tables which not only were at variance with one another, but also had problems respecting interpretation and race procedures. Conflicts of race dates were also becoming most annoying to many competitors.

In January, 1895 the Race Chairman of the Indian Harbor Yacht Club arranged a meeting of the race chairmen of 19 clubs on the Sound. These men attempted only to establish a satisfactory regatta schedule for the coming season and did so. Other more formal steps could await the reception of the clubs to that accomplishment. Absent from that meeting, unfortunately, was the Larchmont Yacht Club, the largest and the most active club holding regattas. It wished to have nothing to do with any group that threatened its sovereignty or its programs. By contrast, Seawanhaka Corinthian was willing to do anything to help. Ironically, many of the most prominent yachtsmen in the area held membership in both clubs.

The next month the Chairman of the Race Committee of the Huguenot Yacht Club (Westchester, NY) also the editor of *Rudder* magazine, gave Larchmont an editorial tongue lashing. Apparently it stung, since Larchmont sent a representative to the group's next meeting. Apparently, also, the reaction to the scheduling work had been swift and favorable, for the meeting was held on April 15. It was the formal beginning of the Association. One of the regulations adopted was that the Association be open to membership to any club of 50 members or more, and each member club was to have representatives in proportion to its membership – one for each 100 members or fraction thereof, to a maximum of five.

The seven officers and executive committee members elected that day set to work on the problems that had caused the creation of the Yacht Racing Association of Long Island Sound. They proposed that all clubs use the Seawanhaka Rule, which most already did; they laid out a standard time allowance table; and they proposed a standardized manual of procedures for race committees, including a single-gun start in place of the three-minute interval [used for large yachts] during which race committees had to time each yacht as she crossed the line. The larger yachts could start the same way everyone else had been starting for almost 20 years – on one starting gun. Another proposal, incidentally, was to permit racing on Wednesdays as well as Saturdays and holidays. No racing was permitted on Sundays in those times.[8] All of the voluminous proposals met with almost unanimous approval at the annual meeting of 1896.

Up to that point no application for membership had come in from Larchmont. By 1902 12 more clubs had been added to the membership, but still no Larchmont, and four of the original 16 had dropped out – probably because they had been dissolved. Finally, after 16 years the Executive Committee decided in 1911 that Larchmont, which:

> *had been in the awkward position of participating in some YRA affairs without belonging, should be invited to join. The club accepted with alacrity.*

In 1913 the Executive Committee, having received complaints about the management of races, sent a letter to the Race Committees of all the YRA members. Among other things, it recommended that:

> *Whenever possible, the first leg of the course should be to windward, and the line should always be laid to accord with the course [square to the wind].*

However well or badly the clubs may have responded to the second part of the request, the first part fell on deaf ears. The standard procedure, not just on Long Island Sound, was to use government marks, and if there were not enough of them handy, to set out some club marks before the season began and pull them when it ended. If on a racing day one of them happened to be to windward, fine. If none, the race committee had no alternative but to use the one closest thereto, thus compromising the integrity of the course.

It was not until the 1930's, partly because of the influence of frostbiters at Manhassett Bay and Larchmont Yacht Clubs, who insisted on all races being run with the first mark dead to windward, that the twenty-year-old request was generally being honored. The availability of better materials for mark boys and of launches that could do the mark-setting job in matters of minutes also helped.

The part of the letter, however, that appears to have startled the author of the YRALIS history was:

> *If the committee sees infractions of the rules, they should take immediate action, call for witnesses, etc., if they deem it advisable, and disqualify offenders in accordance with Rule XIX, Section 4.*

The entire protest procedure was loaded. Guilt was assumed unless innocence could be proved, and an innocent victim had little chance of redress. Rule XIX, Section 4 stated:

> *The Regatta Committee shall, without a protest, disqualify any yacht, should they know prior to the conclusion of the race, that she has committed a breach of these rules [What were the rules of evidence?]*
>
> *They may disqualify any yacht for a breach of these rules, should such breach be brought to their attention prior to 6 p.m. of the weekday following the race.*

By this was meant a protest, but again guilt was assumed.

If a yacht wished to appeal an RC decision, there was a substantial hurdle: a filing fee of $25, which amounted in today's dollars to about $250. It was a strong hint to forget the whole thing, especially since the odds against any decision being overturned were very high. Long Island Sound was not unique in its rules and procedures; absolute authority and the dictatorial use of it by race committees was most common in other areas at the time.

Unfortunately, most race committees were not very good at what they did. While resplendent in their braid and badges and handling the ceremonial aspects of their functions with pomp and dignity, few of them could run races or dispense justice competently. Fully a decade later, when committees had more and more experience with larger and larger fleets, William U. Swan[9] wrote at length in *Yachting* about them. After a full summer of observing committee work on Long Island Sound, he found their sloppy, arbitrary procedures and decision-making to be appallingly inept.

When the New York Yacht Club finally gave up its Staten Island site because of the incessant commercial traffic in the Lower Bay, its members had to join other clubs in order to have a place to moor their yachts and to have access to them. The majority chose a club, or clubs, on Long Island Sound convenient for residents of Manhattan and the departure point for the Club's cruises eastward. By the 1930's the cycle had reversed so that it was members of clubs on the Sound that were joining New York. Regardless, it came to pass for a period that all seven persons on the Yacht Racing Association of Long Island Sound Executive Committee were New York members and held their meetings at 37 West 44th Street (site of the NYYC clubhouse after 1900) – paradoxically, a club that still disdained membership in the YRA. Eventually the clubhouse became, and continues to be, a Mecca for meetings of yachting organizations and their committees. In fact, the office of the YRA is currently located there.

By 1922, with 28 member clubs on board, the amount of detail work became too onerous for one voluntary Secretary, so the YRA hired a person to perform most of those duties, and the clubs were assessed for the cost. In the same year it tried to do something about one-designs. There still was only the Star as an inter-club yacht, and most of the clubs had their own intra-club one-designs. The YRA reasoned that there would be much more competition if all the clubs would agree on a single one-design as a common class. Predictably, agreement could not be reached, and the idea had to be abandoned.

An Atlantic Coast Conference, another loose union of yacht clubs, had faded away. For a brief period it had achieved a degree of unanimity among the leading yacht clubs on the eastern seaboard, but its proposals do not appear to have become codified and put into general practice. An indication of the direction that yachting was taking is the publication of the Conference labeled, "Proposed Amendments to Racing Rules, Submitted to the Atlantic Coast Conference, October, 1912." Much of the publication, which was in the exact format of the rules of the New York and Eastern Yacht Clubs, was in italics – presumably representing revisions, or additions, to existing rules. Some of them, for example, the 'string principle' for sailing the course, would ultimately become part of the present racing rules, but that would be 35 years into the future.

Several unsuccessful efforts had been made to resuscitate the defunct Atlantic Coast Conference. Hence, Clifford D. Mallory, President of the YRA of LIS, who had long been desirous of reviving the NAYRU, proposed to the annual meeting of 1924 that it support his intention to call a meeting to consider such revival. The prestige of the YRA was such that it would give him a solid launching pad. (The story appears in *Chapter IV - Revival of NAYRU in 1925*).

Following the revival of NAYRU not all the clubs and YRA's used the Union's rules. Five years later at the annual meeting of 1930 a delegate rose to lament the fact saying that the rules are still different. He exaggerated badly, of course, but he made his point. At the beginning the Executive Committee had appointed an impressive Appeals Committee and announced that it would accept appeals from decisions of YRAs and many member clubs unaffiliated with a YRA. Yet, when its chairman, C. Sherman Hoyt, rose to make the Committee's report, he had to say that it still had to receive its first appeal. During those five years the Yacht Racing Association of Long Island Sound, which had risen to preeminence among the YRAs nation-wide, was as much a national authority with respect to the rules as the Union, perhaps more so.

Had Clifford Mallory been able to read the centennial histories of the clubs that were in existence in 1897, he would not have been the least surprised at the reaction to the union's re-birth in 1925. There was no leaping in the air, no dancing on the docks and no throwing of hats aloft. Clubs and YRA's were reluctant to give up long-standing practices and to relinquish authority, but Mallory was a patient man. It was not his intention to have NAYRU run the show; he was determined simply to have it survive and to innovate based on consensus. Increased authority would come when it was earned. The dues or membership had been set at a very nominal amount, and it soon became apparent that they were not covering costs. Rather than ask for an increase, however, Mallory simply paid the shortfall out of his own pocket for the ten years that he remained at the helm.

Until 1932, by which time the Yacht Racing Association of Long Island Sound had acquired a sizable number of trophies to award, the annual meetings of the Association were limited to officers and club delegates. It meant that anyone not in that category who won a YRA championship could not attend the dinner at the annual meetings to receive an award. While that defied common sense, the reason for making the dinner open to all was really economic. The year, as we have noted with respect to the state of yachting virtually everywhere, was the nadir of the Great Depression, and everything possible had to be done to maintain interest in the sport.

Among other things, entry fees were cut in half, and to make it easier for sailors to reach starting lines the Seawanhaka and Larchmont Yacht Club's moved theirs westward; and others, clustered at the end of the Sound west of Execution Rocks, moved theirs eastward.

One of the first acts of the Union had been to establish a Racing Rules Committee. Yet, nine years later the YRA still had its own, and the composition of both was identical, and they were all members of the New York Yacht Club, which belonged to neither organization; nor did the home clubs of the Committee members. If this seems a tad parochial, by contrast, US SAILING's present Racing Rules Committee consists of persons who hail from the States of Washington, Wisconsin, Illinois, Virginia, Maryland, New York, Connecticut and Massachusetts; also, the criterion for membership is willingness to do the tedious leg work, not prestigious connections.

The American Yacht Club of Rye, NY had an idea at the time. It was to put a chart in the sailing instructions that identified by letters all the racing marks, both government and club, that might be used for establishing a course. This would provide some variety in courses which was lacking at many clubs. More important, rather than setting a course in the wardroom, the race committee could wait until it got out on the water, sniff the breeze[10] and form an informed guess as to what it might do later. After deciding on a course, the RC had only to display the marks chosen by letter boards. The wonder is that someone had not thought of that many years before. Quickly adopted by other clubs, it was not long before the American Yacht Club race committee boat added to its flexibility by carrying a spare mark on board so that they could set a beat to windward if one of the fixed marks did not align with the direction of the wind.

During World War II clubs on the Atlantic Coast were out of business. The Coast Guard, however, permitted sailing in Long Island Sound provided that courses did not cross the main channel. The Sound was heavily trafficked by ships which, in order to avoid German submarines, took the inside route from New York to Boston and beyond. These clubs fared much better than those in a major naval port such as San Diego where yachting came close to a standstill during the war years. The classes were much reduced in size, of course, but there was one delightful aspect to it: there were no power boats out there – no gas for guzzling.

Recovery of racing at the end of the War was rapid, and the growth in numbers was almost exponential. The 1955 Yearbook recorded that there had been 3,745 starters (in various classes) on the Sound itself, 13,431 (in classes of smaller boats) in the peripheral harbors and bays, 609 distance races and 1597 Junior YRA starters. The peak was reached in 1960 after which the numbers began to decline. By 1969 the average number of starters in YRA races on the Sound (presumably including Larchmont Race Week) was down somewhat to 128, but by 1973 it had dropped to 80. Today it is seldom over 50. Long Island Sound is not alone; one-design racing is down everywhere. The number of clubs, however, has continued to grow, and the Yacht Racing Association of Long Island Sound today has, in addition to a dozen or so related groups, over 55 yacht clubs on its roster.

These numbers were partially offset by a considerable growth in distance racing augmented by annual fixtures sponsored by clubs such as the Larchmont, Stamford and Storm Trysail Clubs. Another offset recently has been the growth of the PHRF fleet, which today has more than 700 members among the clubs on Western Long Island Sound (the jurisdiction of the YRA extends eastward to Port Jefferson on Long Island and Bridgeport in Connecticut.)

As a final note, the New York Yacht Club finally joined the Yacht Racing Association of Long Island Sound and the NAYRU in 1942 largely through the persuasion of Clinton H. Crane. Since both had been using space in the club for offices since 1937, it seemed only fitting. Chronicler John Parkinson, Jr. observed that the members of both, "... had seen the handwriting on the wall."

YACHT RACING ASSOCIATIONS after 1897 through 1929

1898	**Inland Lake YRA**, Wisconsin and Illinois
1901	**Southern Gulf YA** (1920 Gulf YA), Gulf Coast/Pensacola
1906	**Great South Bay YRA**, South Shore Long Island, NY
1909	**Chesapeake Bay YRA**, Maryland and Virginia
1914	**Barnegat Bay YRA**, New Jersey
1920	**Pacific International YA**, Puget Sound
1921	**Southern California YRA**, Santa Barbara to San Diego
1923	**Pacific Coast YA**, West Coast YRAs
1924	**Junior YRA of Long Island Sound**, Western CT, Long Island

CHAPTER IV

REVIVAL OF NAYRU IN 1925

Rudder magazine in its April, 1920 issue reported that following the lapse of NAYRU after the turn of the century there were attempts on a regional basis to coordinate activities and develop uniform rules. As an example, the New York Yacht Club in 1902 had taken the leadership in finding a measurement rule to replace the outdesigned Seawanhaka Rule and had enlisted the assistance of a dozen other clubs in creating what came to be called the Universal Rule. That group called itself the Atlantic Coast Conference and held meetings from 1908 to *1912* after which it dissolved rather than seize the opportunity to promulgate the measurement, classification and racing rules that its committee had formulated. The Conference included Associations and Clubs ranging from Philadelphia to Halifax and the Yacht Racing Union of the Great Lakes. Even though it had acted in only an advisory capacity, its suggestion to the clubs that they should adopt the new rule in the interest of the good of the sport certainly had an effect on the spread of the Universal Rule. The degree of authority that associations exercised varied from being purely advisory to administering rules ratified by constituent clubs and acting as court of last resort to which appeals from decisions of race committees could be taken. *Rudder* mentions at the other extreme clubs that either because of size, or being located where no association existed, "paddled their own canoes" such as New York, Eastern, Corinthian of Marblehead, Southern at New Orleans and Beverly on Buzzards Bay.

> *The New York Yacht Club has always held aloof from joining an association, because it does not hold any open regattas and the smallest yacht that can be enrolled in that club and for which races are held is Class 'P', sloops which rate from 25 to 31 feet. The New York Yacht Club, however, favors uniformity in measurement and racing rules, and it was largely through its action that the present rules became adopted generally. The Eastern Yacht Club and the Corinthian Yacht Club give open races. They also hold races for all classes of yachts and work in harmony with the Massachusetts Union in arranging schedules and in all matters for the betterment of the sport.*

An instance of how various associations were tracking changes in the rules is a letter of February 18, 1913 from the Secretary of the Yacht Racing Union Great Lakes, J. S. McMurray, to the Secretary of the Atlantic Coast Conference, Charles Lane Poor, indicating that he had heard that there had been amendments to the racing rules which had been published by the Conference the previous October and asking for details. By 1924 there were 17 YRAs in operation and two regional, or umbrella, organizations – Yacht Racing Union Great Lakes and Pacific Coast Yachting Association – most of which served in an advisory capacity respecting rules, schedules, and similar. The impetus for their formation was similar to that for the original formation of NAYRU, and typically, as expressed by Secretary Daniel Pratt at the 1921 meeting at which the Northwest International Yacht Racing Association (1892) consolidated with the Pacific International

Commodore Clifford D. Mallory
at the helm of his *Bonnie Dundee III*
Photo courtesy of
Mystic Seaport Museum, Inc.

Power Boat Association to form the Pacific International Yachting Association:

> *... to get the clubs of this district thoroughly organized so they would act as a unit in promoting the sport of yachting in these waters, and also to provide the machinery through which big inter-club and international regattas could be promoted and conducted.*

Such a high degree of coordination on an Association and regional basis, combined with dissatisfaction with the measurement rule on the Lakes and both coasts inevitably resulted in mounting pressure for coordinating on a continental basis. It was the invitation from the Executive Committee of the Yacht Racing Association of Long Island Sound, of which Clifford D. Mallory was President, to all YRAs and Unions that brought their representatives together at the Racquet and Tennis Club in New York City on November 12 -13, 1925 for the purpose of:

- *uniform racing and measurement rules*
- *appoint a committee to consider periodic changes to the rules*
- *appoint an Appeals Committee*
- *establish a medium for constant and widespread exchange of ideas for the development of the sport.*

As reported in *Bulletin No. 1* of NAYRU:

> *... it was the unanimous opinion of all present that an organization should be formed representative of all sections of the United States and Canada, for the purpose of obtaining uniformity of Measurement and Racing Rules. Within thirty hours a constitution and by-laws had been adopted.*

The *Bulletin* also notes:

> *The Executive Committee has been requested by two of the Associations, members of the Union, that they make a careful study of the Universal Rule of Measurement, for the purpose of strengthening that rule in order to develop what is expected to be a more wholesome type of boat.*

This time the subject of measurement was placed first on the agenda of the reconstituted NAYRU instead of "Vexed Points Passed By" as occurred in 1897. NAYRU was formed as a body "largely advisory in scope" comprised of local YRAs and individual members of 'recognized' yacht clubs. Appointed as officers were President Clifford D. Mallory of New York, Vice President Norman Gooderham of the Royal Canadian Yacht Club, Secretary Donald H. Cowl of the Yacht Racing Association of Long Island Sound, Treasurer F. D. Porter of Lake Michigan Yacht Racing Association and on the Executive Committee Joseph V. Santry of the Corinthian Yacht Club (Marblehead), Ernest Lee Jahncke of the Southern Yacht Club and Ben Weston of the California Yacht Club (Los Angeles).

W.A.W. STEWART RECALLS

W.A.W Stewart,[1] who served the sport in many capacities, e.g. Commodore of the Seawanhaka Corinthian and New York Yacht Clubs, Chairman of the NAYRU Measurement and Appeals Committees, principal draftsman of the NAYRU Constitution, was asked in 1950 by Henry S. (Harry) Morgan, President of NAYRU 1950-56, to give an overview, on the occasion of the 25th annual meeting of NAYRU, in regard to its organization and activities since 1925. Clinton Crane in *Yachting Memories*[2] observes:

> *No one of my lawyer friends has more ability to express himself tersely and clearly in the English language... Will's eagle eye picks out errors in words, just as a chartered accountant picks out an error in figures. Besides this, he has always been very understanding of human beings, being very human himself.*

Stewart's address provides further insight on how the Union came into being:

> *... As you all know, the formation of the Union was Clifford Mallory's idea; he was the mainspring of the activities which brought about its formation and it was his wide acquaintance with yachtsmen throughout this country and Canada and their high regard for him as a man and yachtsman which brought together on November 12, 1925, probably the most representative body of American and Canadian yachtsmen which had, up to that time, ever assembled in this country.*

Mr. Mallory opened the proceeding with a speech in which he emphasized the fact that yachting was the only major sport in our country which had never been nationally organized and dwelt upon the benefits which had accrued to other sports through organization. He also mentioned the fact as important and I quote, "We have no central body that is competent or empowered to confer with European representatives for the country at large. It is known, I believe, by all of you that there has been an effort made on the part of our European yachting friends to bring about a closer relationship between this country and Europe." I mention this because it was one of the several important considerations which were in the minds of Mr. Mallory and his associates in believing that the formation of a national association would be for the best interests of yachting not only here but everywhere.

Mr. Mallory was followed by George Nichols, then Commodore of the New York Yacht Club. You will all recall that it was many years (1897-1942) before the New York Yacht Club joined the Union,[3] and it really required some courage for George to attend the meeting. This is well indicated by his opening remarks which I quote, "I speak with some diffidence because I was told last night by a yachtsman in whose opinion I have the greatest confidence that the New York Yacht Club had no business at this meeting; that the Club represented only the larger yachts; that its membership was very wide; that, as I understand it, a large majority of the larger yachts were in one way or another represented in the New York Yacht Club, and secondly, so far as I could gather, in the larger yachts the Club was practically national in its scope." He then proceeded in general terms to give the proposed national association his personal blessing.

Mr. Nichols was followed by Mr. Benson, speaking for Canada in general and Lake Ontario in particular. He stressed the desirability of a governing body that would make the rules throughout North America the same and not only establish such rules but provide a body to interpret them so that the interpretation thereof should be the same everywhere, and its decisions should be final and binding everyone.

Frank Paine (a naval architect) was asked by Mr. Mallory how Boston felt about the proposed association. I think his answer is sufficiently interesting to quote it, "I am sorry to tell you that I do not know how Boston feels as they have not in any way made up their minds. As a matter of fact they are waiting to hear the result of this meeting and what this meeting does and what it is organized to do before they put their foot in it. Personally I think that Boston will favor any national organization that is got up on a basis which will represent the various sections of the country equitably."

Mr. George W. Elder[4] spoke briefly expressing the approval of the Southern California Yacht Racing Association and was followed by C. Sherman Hoyt who spoke enthusiastically in favor… He was followed by Mr. Davis, speaking for the Narragansett Bay yachtsmen and Mr. Crabbe speaking for the Barnegat Bay yachtsmen. Both in favor…

(After a resolution to form a national body) Mr. Mallory asked me to read a tentative plan which I had prepared at his request for submission to the meeting. This tentative plan provided, among other things, that membership in the association should consist of (1) the various yachting associations then in existence which desired to affiliate themselves with the proposed organization, (2) member Yacht Clubs, and (3) individual memberships, but that the voting power be given only to the member associations. I then stated that Mr. Johnston deForest (Long Island Sound) had produced another plan which differed substantially from mine only (mainly?) in that under his plan the membership should consist of the individual yachtsmen who joined the association and the voting privilege be confined to them… Mr. Nichols spoke in favor of Mr. DeForest's plan. Mr. Dauchy of Chicago spoke in favor of my plan. The whole matter of the organization of the proposed association and its functions and the question of voting was then referred to a Special Committee consisting of Dauchy, Benson, deForest and myself. Mr. Nichols and Mr. Paine did not wish to act on this Committee in view of the uncertain attitude of the New York Yacht Club and the Eastern Yacht Club, but at Mr. Mallory's request they agreed to sit with the Committee and take part in its consultations.

(Stewart relates the proceedings of the Committee and notes): This Constitution provided for the voting by associations and is, I believe, apart from the provisions constituting an Appeal Committee adopted many years later,[5] practically the same as the Union is operating under today.

At the meeting on November 13th (the following day) the formal organization of the Union took place. It was attended by representatives of 14 yacht racing associations.

You will notice that the men elected to the leadership of the Union in its infancy represented all sections of our country and included as Vice-President one of the leading yachtsmen of Canada.

W. A.W. Stewart's address is presented in detail since it reveals the interplay of persons and issues affecting the outcome of the meeting, to wit:

(1) How might the Union have evolved if the plan of deForest Johnston to place the voting power in the hands of the yachtsmen rather than the associations had been adopted? Of all the major National Authorities for yachting in the world US SAILING ranks lowest in terms of the percentage of individuals who race being members. The Johnston proposal was similar to the system under which the British Yacht Racing Association operated until after World War II; its membership was open only to individuals (in the beginning by invitation only) and there were no sub-associations. The founding district Yacht Racing Associations of NAYRU were:

Barnegat Bay (NJ)
Chesapeake Bay (MD and VA)
Gravesend Bay (NY)
Great South Bay (Southern Shore Long Island, NY)
Gulf Yachting (LA to FL)
Inland Lake (WI and IL)
Inter-Lake (Lake Erie, Lake Michigan, Detroit River, Lake Huron)
Lake (Ontario and St. Lawrence River)
Long Island Sound (Western CT and Long Island)
Massachusetts Bay
Narragansett Bay (RI)
Pacific Inter-Club (San Francisco Bay)
Southern California

(2) George Nichols, a conservative person by nature and son-in-law of J. P. Morgan, exercised unusual prescience respecting the direction in which the sport was heading in taking the position that he did. His sailing experience ran the gamut from a Herreshoff Suicide Class boat to the Herreshoff-built Class J *Weetamoe*.

(3) Frank Paine was in an ambivalent position inasmuch as a member of the Eastern Yacht Club he was echoing its view rather than that of the YRA of Massachusetts Bay which was one of the associations that militated for convening the meeting.

(4) Persuading Messrs. Nichols and Paine to take part in the Committee that not only was responsible for recommending a proposed Constitution but also served as the nominating committee revealed the leadership qualities and diplomacy of Mallory that were key to steering the Union to fruition.

ABOUT CLIFFORD D. MALLORY

Clifford Day Mallory was the 'Æmilius Jarvis' of the rebirth of the Union and a yachtsman of many parts. Born in 1881, he was 44 when NAYRU was founded and already had become President of the YRA of Long Island Sound in 1923. His early racing was in half-raters and knockabouts, and he established his reputation in the New York Thirty, *Bonzai*; then in a Crowninshield American Yacht Club One-Design; a Goeller designed 'R'; and a Herreshoff 'P'. He became renown competing from 1923-32 in the Six-Metre *Clytie* winning first in class and was captain of the American team racing Sixes at Cowes in 1923. He was founder of the Ten-Metre and Twelve-Metre Classes in North America and owned US Twelve No. 3 *Tycoon* – one of the Burgess & Morgan designs built in Germany. He served as Commodore of the Indian Harbor Yacht Club and was Chairman for Yachting for the 1932 Olympic Games at Los Angeles.

His power of persuasion and ability to persuade and engage people in enterprises which he felt had merit were supplemented by being well liked by everyone and having a wide range of friends.[6] He was successful in rallying key members of the New York Yacht Club, including Sherman Hoyt, Henry Plant, Clinton Crane and George Roosevelt to support his move to consult with the Scandinavians and British when forming NAYRU – a move being opposed by other New York members, including the Vanderbilts, Winthrop Aldrich and Vincent Astor.

His enthusiasm for new classes included ordering for his son a cat-rigged International Fourteen in which class he had sailed during the 1930 Canada Cup Races at Port Charlotte, Lake Ontario. He took the Fourteen to New-

Distinguished yachtsmen visiting the Royal Canadian Yacht Club, Toronto, on December 10, 1927 – George Gooderman, Commodore RCYC, Toronto; Clifford D. Mallory, President NAYRU, New York; C. S. Hoyt, Chairman of the Racing Rules Committee, New York; H. H. Macrae, Vice Commodore, RCYC, Toronto. Following adoption by NAYRU of the International Rule the RCYC did likewise at the end of the 1927 season. Mallory and Hoyt gave an address at the King Edward Hotel on the rule to, as Mallory declared, "The finest gathering of yachtsmen he had ever attended."
Photo courtesy of the New York Yacht Club #1995.299

port during the America's Cup Trials where it provoked a heated debate over the relative merits of the Canadian cat-rigged versus British sloop-rigged Fourteen leading to the international team race in 1933 at the Seawanhaka Corinthian Yacht Club. He was active in training youth to handle boats; he supported the Sea Scouts at Mystic, and he put up the trophies for the national championship of both the Inter-Scholastic national fleet racing championship and the U.S. Men's National Championship which are named in his honor.

His pioneering spirit was manifested in his development of the wishbone boom,[7] testing equipment like a fathometer on his own boat before putting it to use on vessels of the family shipping firm and in developing the concept of a motor-sailer with good sailing capabilities which started with his series of Bonnie Dundee's.[8] What is even more remarkable is that he was able to carry on all these pursuits while suffering from a painful illness that had the characteristics of ulcers for which there was no cure during his lifetime.

Bulletin No. 1 of NAYRU, a low-key document, set the mission and initial functions of the Union and was signed by President Mallory and Ernest Stavey, Corresponding Secretary.

> *We trust that the members of the Union... will make suggestions at any time or call to our attention any matters that they may feel to be of universal interest. We are trying to render a service to the racing men and continent, and it will be our pleasure to co-operate to further the sport in every way possible, but suggestions must come from those who have the active interest of the sport at heart.*

> *On May 6, 1926 the Executive Committee met with the Committee on Racing Rules... Both Commodore W.A.W. Stewart, Chairman of the Measurement Committee, and Mr. C. Sherman Hoyt, Chairman of the Rules Committee, are to be congratulated on the work which they have accomplished.*

As early as 1920 the yachtsman who would have the greatest influence of any person in the history of the sport on the racing rules, Harold (Mike) Stirling Vanderbilt, was already working on their simplification and, as Clinton Crane stated in his autobiography, on "unmistakable right of way determinations."[9] (*Appendix H*)

The role of the new Union in dealing with both measurement and racing rules is related elsewhere in this History, but as an indication of the direction in which the sport was moving, in November the Executive Committee of NAYRU and the Yacht Racing Association of Long Island Sound went on record, "except for the Marblehead crowd," adopting the International Rule for boats up to Class 'P' thereby sowing the seeds for further erosion of the Universal Rule. Chairman Stewart's report in December provides further evidence of discontent over the Rule and the direction that the Union would eventually take:

> *... that not only was it desirous to bring about an improvement in the measurement rule but also to bring about, or tend to bring about, a uniform racing rule throughout the world.*

ROBERT N. BAVIER, JR. RECALLS

Over the decades NAYRU, of course, provided a multitude of services never contemplated at the outset some of which were national championships for men, women, juniors, open youth, match and team racing, uniform measurement rules, certification of judges, measurers and instructors, liaison with the International Yacht Racing Union (now International Sailing Federation) to name a few. Its growth and expansion are covered elsewhere in this history, but for a thumbnail sketch we turn to the report of Robert N. Bavier, Jr. delivered at the annual meeting in 1971 at the end of his five-year stint as President.

> *... It is important to note that the Constitution authorizes NAYRU to exercise advisory jurisdiction over its many members and member associations, its only authority stemming from consent of those it governs. Should we drop the ball, we have no authority over any association or area which disagrees with us. The fact that NAYRU's authority has seldom been challenged indicates that the ball has seldom been dropped. This is not to say that we have not made mistakes but rather that yachtsmen in North America recognize the need for an overall coordinating body for their activities and, despite our shortcomings, have entrusted NAYRU with more and more responsibilities. We are now truly the National Authority in the United States and the Coordinator of yachting on the North American Continent.*

> *In its early years NAYRU was largely an eastern organization and it still to this day is criticized for being (so)... There is some truth to this as witness the fact that... Presidents – Clifford Mallory, Philip J. Roosevelt, Clinton Crane, Henry S. Morgan, George Hinman and myself to present have come from the general New York area. Our sole departure from this norm was the presidency of J. Amory Jeffries from the Marblehead-Boston area.[10] Appearances are somewhat deceiving, however, since the Vice Presidents and other officers, the members of the Executive Committee, and various committee chairmen represent all areas of the United States and Canada.*

... At that time (1950 when Bavier became Corresponding Secretary) we had no Adams Cup Committee, no North American (Men's) Sailing Championship, no U.S. Olympic Yachting Committee and no Offshore Racing Committee. We were not members of IYRU and sent no one abroad to their meetings, in marked contrast to the ten or more of us who now go abroad for meetings each year.

... The day to day operation was done by Catharine Evans (part-time secretary) and by myself. I used to spend two or three lunch hours a week eating a sandwich in our then tiny office (hardly room for a desk and two chairs), dictating letters, and going over the work Catharine had been doing.

By contrast... We have two offices... Harry Anderson operating full time as Executive Director (dividing his time, however, as Exec. Dir. of the YRA of Long Island Sound, Junior YRA and U.S. International Sailing Association)[11] *of the main office (in a room and half at the NYYC with a connecting bathroom for storage of files), and Bob Hall in the same role for our Offshore Office...*

NAYRU has been criticized by a number of yachtsmen for foisting off on them, during my term of office, the new IOR Rating Rule.[12] *It's important to remember that we did not initiate the IOR Rule.*[13] *The CCA was instrumental in phasing out its own rule and in getting together with the RORC to develop a new worldwide rule, and when it came into being they asked us to administer it... The progress made in yacht design is more at fault for outdating older boats than is the new IOR Rule... we remain convinced that after this period of growing pains and evolvement, it (IOR Rule) will be best for the country's yachtsmen... Last fall I formed a Rating Rule Committee of NAYRU, composed of the continent's leading yacht designers and builders plus representatives of yachtsmen, notably Dan Strohmeier, Chairman, and Tom Young, who heads the Storm Trysail Rating Rule Committee. This group will insure that the rule does reflect broad thinking.*

The other thing I am proud of accomplishing during my administration is bringing more young new blood into the organization. It's not true that no one ever resigns from a NAYRU committee – it just seems that way. As vacancies have occurred, I've filled them with young, extremely active, and extremely competent sailors. Some of our new officers are in their thirties, and I feel this trend should be accelerated. Our new Class Advisory Committee is composed solely of young and very active top sailors...

In line with Bavier's remarks about geographical representation, his successor as President, James Michael, was from San Francisco and had succeeded Charles Langlais as a west coast Director of NAYRU.

"Nothing gives you a greater appreciation for timing and equipment than a lifetime of competitive sailing."
COURTENAY DEY
Olympic medalist, two-time
Rolex Yachtswoman of the Year,
America's Cup competitor.
ROLEX
Rolex Oyster Perpetual Lady Yacht-Master in stainless steel and 18kt gold with matching Oysterlock bracelet.
For the name and location of an Official Rolex Jeweler near you, please call 1-800-36ROLEX.
Rolex, ♛, Oyster Perpetual, Lady Yacht-Master and Oysterlock are trademarks.

CHAPTER V

INTER-COLLEGIATE YACHT RACING[1]

EAST COAST

The earliest sailing at colleges appears to have occurred as a recreational exercise usually by way of cruising in company in yachts owned by undergraduates or on loan from their parents. 'Yearbooks' at Yale, for example, log an episode on July 15, 1870 during a cruise from New Haven to New London, and soon squadron runs to New London became a prime activity among Yale sailors after the end of the academic year. In 1872 and '73 two races in October were conducted from Long Wharf, New Haven to Adam's Fall buoy and return in which six yachts competed. By 1873 the activity was listed as a 'Yacht Club' and a few years later adopted the motto "Hard-A-Lee" to which wags covertly added "ever."

There were catboats for hire in New Haven Harbor which students would rent and sail to the Thimble Islands on the half-holidays of Wednesday and Saturday afternoons.[2] In 1881 the proprietor of one of the boat liveries built nine boats for the members of the Yale Corinthian Yacht Club in which informal races were held, but as was the case with many colleges over the years, graduating seniors took the boats with them. The Club reorganized in 1893 with over a 100 members, many of whom brought their families' yachts from home.

By 1894 sailing was an activity at Harvard as evidenced by what is claimed to have been the first inter-collegiate regatta when Harvard and Yale competed, immediately following the Yale-Harvard crew race (rowing), on the Thames River, New London in boats as large as 40 feet divided into five classes (both yacht clubs were listed in Lloyd's Register of American Yachts).[3] Frederick Coonley[4] describes the status of college sailing at the end of the century as:

> *College yacht clubs in the United States first blossomed in the Gay Nineties with the founding of undergraduate organizations at Brown, Harvard, MIT, Tufts and Yale. In the main, these were social organizations devoted to sponsoring an occasional open regatta or annual cruise.*[5]

A indication that college sailing was destined to be conducted on a more serious and competitive level is his observation that at Yale after the 1896 season:

> *... several members felt that the club was not fulfilling its mission. They desired to furnish an opportunity for a larger number to enjoy the sport and make yachting more popular in the university. At the suggestion of W.N. Low, Jr., E.C. Perkins and C.A Goodwin, W.H. Hand designed a 15-foot boat...*

> *Actually the boats were 21-feet 9-inches LOA, 15-feet LWL, six-feet three-inches beam and six inches draft with board up – 'skimming dishes' – carrying 350 square feet of sail and crew of three. The importance of these boats, which were called the 'special Yale 15-foot class' was twofold: First, small boats (which they were for their time) greatly expanded participation because of their lower cost. Second, the fleet of 16 boats built at New Bedford (Gloucester according to Downey), Massachusetts, was among the earliest of one-design racing fleets...*

According to Coonley, "A series of races was held twice a week during the season, and soon became the leading feature of the club's races".

Prior to World War I Yale successively purchased fleets of Swampscott, MA dories and Hartford, CT dories. The War, unfortunately, brought an end to such development, but not before sailing at Harvard, for instance, included such notables as Franklin D. Roosevelt, Charles W. Eliot (later President of the University), Harold S. Vanderbilt and Samuel Eliot Morison. Cmdr. C. Sherman Hoyt in his autobiography[6] recalls sailing activity at Brown University when a team from the sailing club in 1900 rolled a beer barrel down Thames Street in Newport, RI.

It was not until 1928 that organized inter-college competition developed in its 'modern' mode. Briggs S. Cunningham, then a freshman at Yale, conferred with Frederick T. Bedford, a long-time sailing enthusiast from Southport, CT who later became his father-in-law. They concluded that it might be fun to hold a series of yacht races with Harvard, Yale and Princeton after the colleges recessed in June. At that time the Yale Corinthian Yacht Club was a going concern; Harvard had a similar organization, but Princeton lacked one, since its location was distant from suitable sailing waters. Nonetheless, Princeton had Arthur Knapp, Jr. who was instrumental in turning the informal series into a major annual inter-collegiate competition. Subsequently George O. May, a neighbor of Bedford, whose son Oliver sailed with Briggs Cunningham at Yale, offered to donate a trophy. Invitations were sent out to Harvard and Princeton and thus was born the nucleus of what was later to become the larger organization known as the Intercollegiate Yacht Racing Association (as distinct from later ICYRA/NA).

There were many first-rate sailors at all three colleges; to name a few: Princeton had Arthur Knapp, Jr. '28, Charlie Hewitt, '28, Bill McMillan, '28, Rufus Smith, '29, Bob Garland, '29, Osborne Willauer, '30 (later a Director of NAYRU), Bob Bryant, '30. Harvard's formidable contingent was headed by John L. King and a high-powered group from Marblehead; at Yale Cunningham and May already referred to; and Brown had Zenas Bliss – navigator in 1934 on the America's Cup defender *Rainbow*.

Harvard and Princeton accepted Yale's challenge and plans were announced for a triangular series of three races to be held off Southport using Eight-Metres loaned by three generous members of the Pequot Yacht Club.

On February 20, 1928, the first meeting of a newly formed Princeton Yacht Club was held followed by meetings during the spring term at which a crew was chosen with Arthur Knapp, Jr. as skipper. Princeton won the first two races and thereby accumulated enough points to gain a leg on the Oliver May trophy. The races were such a success that by 1929 Cornell announced that it would like to compete, but the problem of finding owners of such expensive yachts to loan them to a group of young college students seemed an almost impossible task. At this point the extraordinary talents of C. Sherman Hoyt, a graduate of Brown University living in Oyster Bay were sought. He took a great interest in the efforts of the fledgling college students and was able to assemble a fleet of Herreshoff 'S' boats which were a popular class at the Seawanhaka Corinthian Yacht Club.

Each college provided two teams consisting of a skipper and two crew for each of two boats. This changed the original format from a one-on-one challenge to fleet racing in two divisions – the position of each college being the multiple of points earned by its entry in each division – thereby enabling more students to take part. With the addition of Cornell, whose formidable skippers were Carl Weagant, '29 and Roderick Stephens, '32, the competition looked keen. Unfortunately Harvard failed to show up as a result of a car breakdown leaving only Yale, Princeton and Cornell to compete. Yale won thus tieing Princeton for a leg on the Oliver May trophy.

By 1930 applications to compete began to multiply. Dartmouth and Williams wanted to join the four. Again Sherman Hoyt came to the rescue, having corralled 12 Atlantic Class boats from the fleets at Pequot and Black Rock Yacht Clubs. The entries of Dartmouth and Williams were accepted, but other colleges who wanted in were rejected as being too late. The site was Southport with Pequot as host club. The deed of gift for the Oliver May Trophy, however, stipulated not only that it became the permanent possession of the first winner of three events, but also that only Harvard, Yale and Princeton could compete for it. Fortunately William McMillan, Princeton '28, offered a trophy named after him open to all competitors.

A series of six races was held off Southport. Princeton skippers, William L. Crow '33 and Peter H. Cummings '33 were victorious thereby gaining a second leg on the May trophy and winning the first series for the McMillan trophy. Everett B. Morris's account in the August issue of *Yachting* cites as outstanding skippers Billy Crow and P.H. Cumming (Princeton), W.D. Taylor of Harvard as "the outstanding skipper of the day," John Muhlfeld (Yale) and James Moore and Victor King (Dartmouth). In the evening after the first day of racing a meeting of all 12 crews was held at the Pequot Yacht Club, and it was decided that such races were so much fun, and that so many other colleges had expressed an interest in participating in them, a new overall governing body would have to be formed. Thus was the Intercollegiate Yacht

Racing Association (IYRA) born. James O. Pease, '31, Commodore of the Princeton Yacht Club[7] was elected Chairman of the Association, being its only officer.

> *During the school year of 1930-31 the Chairman corresponded in great volume with the Commodores of Harvard, Yale, Dartmouth, Cornell and Williams and met with all of them at the Princeton Club in New York during the Christmas holidays. A set of By-Laws was gradually hammered out and submitted to the member college yacht clubs for ratification.*

Applications poured in from scores of colleges, but being unable to obtain the loan of a enough boats of one class compelled turning all of them down. At that time none of the clubs were affiliated with their athletic associations. In those depression years large fleets of small boats were simply not available. The 1931 races were held back at the Seawanhaka Corinthian Yacht Club on Oyster Bay, and again "our beloved mentor," Sherman Hoyt (referred to by Everett Morris in *Yachting* as "unofficial godfather of the college sailormen"), performed his miracles by obtaining ten Atlantic Class boats." Cornell failed to show, and after five races Princeton skippers Bill Crow and Peter Cumming prevailed thereby retiring the Oliver May trophy.[8] Hoyt's interest in college and junior sailing remained unflagging until long after WW II, and during the early years of intercollegiate competition prior to the formation of the ICYRA/NA he coordinated the scheduling of regattas among New England schools paving the way for Leonard Fowle as Graduate Secretary to formalize the process.

Six colleges raced for the McMillan Cup in 1932 in Atlantics at the American Yacht Club. Bill Crow of Princeton succeeded Pease as President of the Intercollegiate Yacht Racing Association; Harvard won; and from Princeton skipper, Pete Cumming's recollections:

> *Bill Cox (William S.) came aboard the first day with a tool kit and two sheets, one green and one red. When I asked him why the lines and why the colors, he replied that they would be used on the spinnaker for guy and sheet. Not knowing Bill, my reaction was that a man who needed colors to keep from getting mixed up was not my idea of an ideal crew. Result: I would not allow the use of those sheets and for the first time Princeton did not win the Cup.*

Following the (first) Frostbite Regatta of January 1, 1932, frostbiting became popular, and an intercollegiate regatta was held among seven colleges at the Knickerbocker Yacht Club in Manhasset Bay in Dyer dinghies in 1932. This was a very brief series (one race) as a nor'wester and cold took their toll; Oglethorpe University (GA) won with a crew of Ed Miller and Jean Belden (a Barnard student). Others over Christmas vacation were held at the Indian Harbor Yacht Club, Greenwich CT in 1935 and 1936.

From the history of the Cruising Club of America[9] by John S. Parkinson, Jr.:

> *Like so many events that were to have a widespread impact on the sport of yachting, the 1932 New Year's Day first frostbite dinghy race on record was the result of a bet – a bet at the bar of the Larchmont Yacht Club during Race Week when Sam Wetherill bet another sailor that he would beat him sailing a dinghy on New Year's Day. William H. Taylor from Manhasset Bay (Long Island) who was a sports writer for the* Herald Tribune *induced others to enter the contest which was held at the Knickerbocker Yacht Club (on the Bay). It quickly spread to clubs as far afield as the Essex Yacht Club on the Connecticut River, but the annual Frostbite Regatta was held thereafter at the Manhasset Bay Yacht Club.*

As told by Arthur Knapp, Jr.:[10]

> *First frostbite regatta was held January 2, 1932 in Manhasset Bay at the Kinckerbocker Yacht Club in a mix of dinghies, e.g. 11½-foot Ratsey Prams, 11½-foot Dyer Dhows. Knickerbocker was founded by a group of members of the Manhasset Bay Yacht Club who rebelled against the $1,000 assessment levied to pay for an extravagant (for the Depression era) new clubhouse. The next year the newly formed Frostbite Club, which had no dues, met at the Manhasset Yacht Club. A number of those who pioneered winter sailing journeyed as far afield as the Essex Yacht Club on the Connecticut River which quickly caught the bug. (He winds up remarking) "I was a founding idiot".*

By the mid 1930's[11] sailing facilities existed, or were in planning, at numerous colleges, e.g. Cornell on Lake Cayuga in Class 'X' one-design frostbite dinghies, Dartmouth on Lake Mascoma in Wee Scots (later replaced with Tech dinghies). According to one report the first college fleet of dinghies was the Tiger Class 10½-foot dinghy established at Princeton in 1934, and the first intercollegiate 'dinghy' series occurred in the Tigers on Lake Carnegie between Princeton and Dartmouth. Actually the Naval Academy started a fleet of four Stars in the 1920's, but they were not permitted to compete outside of the Academy. It was the innovation of frostbiting that created the popularity in dinghy racing that caught on in the colleges. The sport really owes its initial and continuing growth to the establishment of this type of racing at MIT in 1936 when the Sailing Pavilion and 40 Herreshoff-built 'Tech' dinghies designed by Professor George Owen (head of the Department of Naval Architecture and Marine Engineering) were launched with the aid of alumni support. The boats were lapstrake one-designs 12½-foot LOA, 5-foot beam and constructed at the Herreshoff plant in Bristol. Dean Erwin H. Schell originated the idea, over 300 students were enrolled for lectures on the art of sailing and seamanship and Walter C. Wood was appointed sailing master of the MIT Nautical Association.

Some years later Leonard Munn Fowle as graduate secretary of ICYRA wrote:

> *It is not extravagant to say that without the contributions of MIT no such expansion of college sailing as has taken place would have been possible. Walter C. 'Jack' Wood, Director of Sailing at Tech, has always been willing to lend the Institute's facilities to the ICYRA or any of its individual members; but Tech's generosity has reached further and many non-members, as well as women's colleges, preparatory schools, Sea Scouts and numerous yachting organizations and yachtsmen have been recipients of Tech's bounty.*

Concurrently[12] with the MIT project, Brown established a fleet of Dyer Dinghies on the Seekonk River. MIT was, of course, welcomed as a new member of ICYRA, as was Brown. There were now eight members, and with MIT's large fleet more applications could be accepted, especially as facilities at the Naval and Coast Guard academies expanded. With the founding of the Boston Dinghy Club Challenge Cup held at MIT, 19 colleges competed in 1937 including McGill University of Montreal making it the first international competition in college sailing in North America. The next year the Midwest was represented by the University of Michigan and Canada by McGill and the University of Toronto. In the meanwhile women's colleges, besides competing among themselves, were engaging in matches, e.g. Princeton competing with Vassar and Sarah Lawrence.

Racing for the McMillan Cup continued in 1934 in Herreshoff 15-footers at the Beverly Yacht Club in Buzzards Bay – the year in which Leonard M. Fowle* was appointed Graduate Secretary-Treasurer of ICYRA; in 1935 on Long Island Sound in two divisions – Atlantics and Interclubs; and in 1938 at the Wianno Yacht Club in gaff-rigged Wianno Seniors. Ten schools competed including Trinity and Penn. The two Harvard skippers were Joe and Jack Kennedy, and since they both owned Wiannos, it was not surprising that Harvard won, although it was not an easy victory; Dartmouth and Williams were very close behind after eight races. In the dinghies the first Morss Bowl in 1936 was won for the first of three in a row by MIT.

*Fowle (Harvard '30 and a reporter for the *Boston Globe*) apparently had made a casual remark:

> *What the ICYRA needs is some graduate to hold it together and promote it just as Everett B. Morris (reporter for the* N.Y. Herald Tribune*) is doing for the Intercollegiate Power Boat Assn. [To what extent there was competition among colleges in power boats is not evident].*

Thanks to fine reporting in the *Herald Tribune*, *Boston Globe*, *New York Times* and *Yachting* magazine by respectively Bill Taylor, Leonard Fowle, Everett Morris, James Robbins and Alf Loomis there was good publicity further enhanced in 1950 by the publication of the newsletter of The Afterguard edited by 'Doc' A. R. Lukens (MIT) who coached its team during the War years. His method of coaching on Sundays was to observe the racing with field glasses from his apartment on the South bank of the Charles River while listening to the Philharmonic orchestra and at the end of the day driving across to the MIT Pavilion to conduct a briefing. Founded as the graduate arm of college sailing, The Afterguard held an annual regatta and for a few years published a yearbook; after a long lapse it has been revived under the leadership of Lawrence A. White whose many services to college sailing included being administrative coach at the U.S. Coast Guard Academy. The participation of the Naval Academy and the Coast Guard Academy assured the continued expansion of college racing along the east coast. Simultaneously under the spontaneous leadership of Bob Allan, Stanford '39, the sport grew in southern California as well as in the northwest and Hawaii.

In 1939 the McMillan Cup was held at the Cold Spring Harbor Beach Club (on Long Island Sound) in three-man boats. Harvard, absent the Kennedy brothers, came in a distant third to the winner, Williams, captained by Bob Bavier, and MIT finished second. In 1940 the ICYRA found a partial solution for borrowed boats by reducing the number needed through holding eliminations in keel boats on Long Island Sound and at the Naval Academy from which five schools qualified for the finals held in Class 'E' and 'G' Scows provided by the Mantoloking Yacht Club on Barnegat Bay. After winning it again for Williams, Bob Bavier commented that his team had been lucky that MIT's star sailor, Runyon Colie, who was a member of Mantoloking and a whiz in scows and dinghies, was unfamiliar with keel boats and had not survived the eliminations. Runners up were Yale, Harvard, Coast Guard and Navy – the first attempt at the big time for the latter two.

Until the venue for the McMillan Cup finally became the US Naval Academy, it led a peripatetic life depending on where fleets of one-designs could be borrowed. For example, in 1941 after three elimination series finalists, including Boston U. (Thomas Coleman and Russ Mattern), Yale (John Ware and Richard Besse), Navy (William Hurst and Robert Kunhardt), Coast Guard (Roy Hutchins and Austin 'Red' Wagner), Harvard (Roger Wilcox and George Nichols, Jr. – a recent winner of the Scandinavian Gold Cup in Six-Metres) and Dartmouth (Emil Mosbacher and Warner Willcox) competed at Marblehead in 110's and Massachusetts Bay One-Designs (MB's). Dartmouth won with Harvard second and Yale third – one point only separating first and third. Len Fowle in his account stated, "As grand a series as this observer has ever seen."

In the spring of 1939 the first women's regatta was held at MIT. In order of their finishing scores the schools competing were: MIT 67 points; Connecticut College for Women (now Connecticut College, New London), 65 points; Katherine Gibbs (a Boston secretarial school); Jackson (then the female division at Tufts); Sarah Lawrence; Pembroke (then the women's division of Brown); Sargent (part of Boston University); Vassar; and Wheaton. The first winning women's skippers of ICYRA were Edith Cameron and Domina Spencer. Unlike among midwest colleges, co-ed sailing in New England encountered inhibiting athletic regulations and policies among the universities and the NCAA. At the instigation of the University of Rhode Island, in 1961 the New England Women's Intercollegiate Sailing Association (NEWISA) was formed. This resulted in NEWISA and the Middle Atlantic Association of Women Sailors (MAAWS) organizing the first women's nationals in 1967. Under the leadership of Georgetown University coach, Gerald C. Miller, the first event was launched with only three teams attending, but by 1976 the concept had taken hold to the extent that the ICYRA assumed control. The east, however, could not catch up with the northwest where Louise Anstey from the University of Victoria, BC became the first woman to earn All-American status after skippering 'A' Division at the Nationals.[13]

Nonetheless, as colleges in New England went co-educational, the separation of men and women created social and logistical problems in conducting competition both at home and in outside. At the 1973 annual meeting of the New England ISA remedial action was taken with the passage of the so-called 'Yale Amendment':

> *Supported by fellow humanists at Yale and sailors from Brown and Dartmouth [the Yale Amendment] was adopted; this amendment [to the by-laws] allowed women to compete on the previously all-male varsity and on freshman teams. Since then names of five woman sailors on New England teams, including three from Yale... have been inscribed on either the first or second place North American Dinghy Championship trophies.*[14]

By WW II the ICYRA after 14 years had grown from three to 28 schools and become the prototype for similar organizations on the west coast and in the midwest. Perforce, the elimination series became standard procedure when college sailing resumed after WW II in an organization that consisted of four YRAs within a re-organized ICYRA

Walter C. (Jack) Wood after moving to San Diego
Photo courtesy of MIT Sailing

Leonard M. Fowle founder of ICYRA
Photo courtesy of Jack Wood

WEST COAST

College sailing on the west coast began in the early 1930's, even before MIT and Brown launched their fleets, when Donald Douglas, Jr. gathered a group of sailors attending Stanford and the University of California, Berkeley, for a few challenge races in San Francisco Bay. Subsequently there is a record of Douglas Giddings of San Diego competing for the University of Arizona in the Pacific Coast Intercollegiate Yacht Regatta which was reported in the *Union* on June 14 and 15, 1936:

> *Intercollegiate racing will be inaugurated on San Diego Bay when representatives of Stanford, UC at LA, Cal Tech and Univ. of Arizona meet... in a round-robin series, using Pacific Coast class one-design boats of the San Diego Yacht Club... Cal Tech will be represented by Frank Jewett, winner of the Olympic trials in the monotype class.*[15]

The first college club on the West Coast was organized at Berkeley as the Windjammers. Without a formal organization, however, racing died out until 1939 when Stanford again challenged Berkeley. Ten Snowbirds (the singlehander in the 1932 Olympic Games) were used by each team. The following year the Pacific Coast Inter-Collegiate Yacht Racing Association (PCIYRA) was formed to expand college sailing when Stanford and Berkeley were joined by San Jose College and Menlo Junior College. Another boost for college sailing was the recognition of sailing by Berkeley as an official sport.

Robert M. Allan, Jr., co-founder of ICYRA and co-founder with his wife Harriet Spicer Allan of PCIYRA
Photo courtesy of Robert M. Allan, Jr.

Those two steps paid off, and the call for more participants was heeded when six colleges appeared at the Newport Harbor Yacht Club for the first West coast championship in 1941 held in Dyer Class dinghies and organized largely through the efforts of Robert M. Allan, Jr. (Stanford '41), Commodore of PCIYRA, and the Newport Harbor Yacht Club. Cal Tech won, followed by Oregon State and Stanford. UC Berkeley was there, of course, as was UC Los Angeles. The sixth school was not identified. The two-division system used in the east was inaugurated. The Stanford team captain was Allan who had sparked the 1939 challenge resumption and was the principal mover, along with Harriet Spicer (Allan) (Stanford '43) in establishing the PCIYRA. After graduation, following a hiatus during WW II, he remained involved for 16 years as graduate secretary. He is deservedly credited with making it all happen. Bob Allan started militating for a national inter-collegiate association as early as 1939 when as he recalls:

> *This (1989) is also the 50th year from when I wrote Len Fowle at MIT and worked out with him and Jack Wood the framework for the "true national college sailing association... we wanted larger boats that would improve crew training; seamanship at sea; women or partly handicapped people who could not race in dinghies (and shift the emphasis away from lightweight crews). Thus, early on we tried to get the McMillan Cup reorganized for a National Event, but properly it was held by tradition for the "east only"... so we then worked out the event (the John F. Kennedy Cup) at the US Naval Academy, and our first thanks is to the USNA for their cooperation... we soon had a true National set of big boat races (on a National scale)... As a sidelight, the first three JFK championships were won by the three colleges that JFK attended... lst year Harvard... 2d year the Navy Training School at USNA... 3d year Stanford (JFK attended graduate school there)... Stanford in its way was as strong on the West Coast for many years as was MIT in the dinks in the East.*

Bob Allan's emphasis on offshore boat experience resulted in informal collegiate participation within the Transpac Race – informal since Transpac would not recognize a race within a race. Navy had the loan of *Duello* and raced with UC Santa Barbara on *Fickle Duck* and Cal Western on *Chinook*.

Rev. Theodore 'Ted' Livingston (San Diego State Univ. '48), who served as Varsity Sailing Coach at the Univ. of Hawaii 1968-89, cites the inscription on a memorial plaque summarizing the contribution made to intercollegiate sailing by Bob Allan's counterpart at the Univ. of California, Richard H. Lough (1907-1956):

> *Dick Lough overcame incredible physical handicaps to become one of the most formidable and likable racing skippers on the West Coast. His enthusiasm for the sport of sailing found expression in his unflagging support of junior sailing, and his willingness to share his secrets of success and the ideals of sportsmanship with all who wished to learn. While a graduate student at the University of California, he and Bob Allan, then a student at Stanford, sowed the seeds of friendly rivalry which would grow to become the PCIYRA.*

In 1948 the PCIYRA expanded its scope by encouraging junior colleges to join. Orange State (in Orange County) was one of those to apply, and it soon became a powerhouse in the organization. In the same year the UC Berkeley Sailing Team managed to obtain a loan from the university (recognition of a sport goes only so far where there are no gate receipts) to build a fleet of International 14's (built to the same dimensions, i.e. without the latitude provided under the restricted formula used by the Class). One of the disadvantages of development classes is that one-offs are more expensive than boats from a production run which enables builders to recover their start-up costs and reduce the man-hours of labor. The fleet became the nucleus of college sailing in the San Francisco Bay area for the next decade.

When the initial Intercollegiate Yacht Racing Association, which had sponsored college sailing in the northeast for 20 years, joined in 1949 with the more recently formed Midwest Yacht Racing Association and the PCIYRA to form the ICYRA of North America, intersectional racing became possible. It began with teams from schools that were participating in the Rose Bowl, i.e. the Big Ten and the Pacific Coast Conference. Meanwhile, the original IYRA was splitting into New England and Mid-Atlantic states resulting in there being four regional YRAs. The venue for the Henry Morss Bowl held in dinghies – the equivalent of the national championship for college sailing – was rotated among them. Two schools from each YRA competed in the nationals, each with an 'A' and a 'B' division, for a total of 16 crews; a school's score was the combination of points earned by its 'A' and 'B' division crews.

The Pacific Coast's first hosting assignment was in 1950 at the Newport Harbor Yacht Club. The regatta came down to a three-way tie between Stanford, Berkeley and Yale. In the sail-off Bobby Monetti beat Bill Ficker by inches to win the championship for Yale. In 1954 MIT and Harvard, which had been dominating New England, also dominated the Nationals. At its third hosting, again at Newport Harbor, the Lipton Trophy for team racing (later changed to the Wood Trophy) and the Morss Bowl were held respectively in eight International 14s and eight Metcalf dinghies enabling both divisions to race at the same time. Occidental and Stanford represented PCIYRA.

June, 1961 the Northwest Intercollegiate Yacht Racing Association was formed including the Universities of Washington, British Columbia, Puget Sound, Seattle University. and Western Washington College all of which had been members of PCIYRA. The University of Hawaii, where Charlie Dole (Stanford '36) coached for ten or more years starting at age 65, remained in PCIYRA.

MIDWEST[10]

What started as a talk between a bunch of naval architecture majors at Michigan and another group from Wisconsin in 1938 has developed into the Midwest Collegiate Sailing Association (MWCSA). The Univ. of Michigan spearheaded interest in college sailing and founded a club in 1934. Weekly ladder races were started and in 1939 Michigan was elected a member of ICYRA. The first recorded midwest collegiate regatta was in 1941 at Sandusky Sailing Club in Snipes with Michigan, Wisconsin, Kenyon and Illinois participating. Michigan's club originated in the Quarterdeck Society of the College of Naval Architecture one of whose most promising members designed the Double Trouble Dink for the club.

In the spring of 1947 the University of Michigan Sailing Club with six dinghies began exploiting the sailing interests in other Midwest colleges by holding several invitational regattas on Whitemore Lake. This was prompted by Paul Moote and Robert Schroder, both of Michigan, James Parker of Denison and Timme Angsten of Northwestern getting together in the winter of 1946 to organize an event for the next year. The meeting is noted as the founding of MCSA, the original members of which were Michigan Sailing Club (University of Michigan), Michigan State College Sailing Club, Northwestern Sailing Club and Denison Sailing Club; Youngstown College Sailing Club joined but later dropped out. It was Timme Angsten and his club that approached the Chicago Yacht Club for assistance in loaning its boats and permitting holding the regatta that bears his name.

In 1947 Midwest joined New England, Middle Atlantic and Pacific Coast to form a temporary Union of Intercollegiate Yacht Racing Associations at a meeting held at the New York Yacht Club for the purpose of organizing an annual representative National Inter-collegiate Dinghy Championship. Leonard M. Fowle of Marblehead was named Executive Secretary, and the first meet was held in 1948 at the U.S. Naval Academy in a new fleet of 30 Tempests with colleges from all over the country and the second the next year at the University of Michigan. Initiating the championship led to New England, MCSA and PCIYRA forming in 1949 the ICYRA of North America. Almost concurrently the Afterguard was formed for the purpose, as Bob Allan stated:

> *... in 1948 when we formed the truly national ICYRA we also formed an Afterguard... to carry on after graduation... From experience gained during the past two decades of active college sailing in the United States, particularly in the former IYRA, it has been proved that the sustaining graduate interest can be a most important asset for the future of college yachting... the Executive Committee at Ann Arbor, Michigan on June 20, 1949 formed and incorporated in its By-Laws a graduate organization... One of the principal functions of the Afterguard is to furnish a reservoir of experienced sailors to act as officials (a precursor to the concept of the US SAILING judges program).*

Growth, however, of sailing clubs in the Midwest was hampered by lack of interest by the colleges in recognizing sailing as a sport worthy of financial assistance thereby making it difficult to find funding for fleets. By 1950, nonetheless, the Midwest had 21 schools, Middle Atlantic 25, New England 21 and Pacific Coast 19. Although ICYRA, unlike the customary member Yacht Racing Association, was not an association representing, and responsible for, a group of yacht clubs and classes in a contiguous area, Leonard M. Fowle working with C. Eric Olsen, Harry Anderson and others persuaded Commodore Henry S. Morgan, President of NAYRU (1950-56), to provide an avenue of appeal from protest decisions via the ICYRA Appeals Committee to the NAYRU Appeals Committee. The first intercollegiate appeal to reach NAYRU arose from a Timme Angsten regatta – No. 46, the case of the 'wayless' yacht – in which the decisions of the protest committee and ICYRA appeals committee were reversed, but later, when the NAYRU Appeals were revised, they were reinstated.

The MSCA has been a leader in many ways. Its newsletter, *The Tell Tale*, is unique in college sailing and was first published in the fall of 1947. In the same year the method of figuring skipper standings was introduced, women were encouraged to participate and a boat loan fund was established.

Sailing collegiately in the Midwest takes commitment – especially the stint of long distance travel that is part of the package. The MSCA at one time or another has claimed over 70 different member schools in ten states and a Canadian province in an area about 800 by 600 miles.

In recognition of George Griswold's (Wooster '61 and Hall of Fame) outstanding service to the MCSA – Graduate Secretary of MCSA since 1962 and for a period Graduate Secretary of ICYRA – the Executive Board established the George H. Griswold MCSA Team Race Trophy in 1966.

Not only was 1996 the 50th anniversary for MSCA; it also is the 50th for one of the oldest intercollegiate intersectional events – the Mark Timme Angsten Memorial Regatta held at the Belmont Street Station of the Chicago Yacht Club over Thanksgiving weekend in dinghies – currently in the 420.

THE SOUTH[17]

Shelby and Buddy Friedrichs join the Bob Allan, Bill Cox, David Minton,[18] Corny Shields and Butch Ulmer families in the distinction of having two generations from the same family in the Inter-Collegiate Hall of Fame.[19]

G. Shelby Friedrichs (Tulane '33) is recognized by many as the father of southern intercollegiate sailing. His contacts in 1954 with Leonard M. Fowle, Graduate Secretary of the ICYRA, set the wheels in motion to form the fledgling Southern Intercollegiate Sailing Association (SISA) in 1957 during the first intercollegiate regatta held in the south. Shelby was commodore of the Southern Yacht Club and worked together with John H. Stibbs, then new Dean of Students at Tulane, to lay the groundwork for the entry of the SISA into the national picture.

In the absence of dinghies in the south, G. Shelby (Buddy) Friedrichs, Jr. (Tulane '62) concentrated his efforts primarily in keel boats and won an Olympic Gold Medal with fellow Tulanian Barton W. B. Jahncke and Click Shreck in 1968 in the Dragon Class. For over 20 years thereafter Buddy and his father were supportive friends of sailing at Tulane.

Commodore Friedrichs joined with Southern Yacht Club Commodore, Garner Tullis and Dean Stibbs to acquire the first southern collegiate dinghy fleet – ten O'Day Gannets (modified version of a Fourteen in GRP) – for Tulane in the spring of 1961 in which the first Southern college regatta, the Garner Tullis, was held. As sailing grew at Tulane and spread throughout the southern colleges, SISA applied in 1961 for entry into ICYRA at the same time that the SEISA (comprising colleges in the southeast) applied. It was decided to merge the two organizations into one district – SEISA – covering an area from Texas to Florida to Virginia. The first SEISA graduate secretary was John Taylor (Hall of Fame, UCLA '56).

Over the years many SEISA sailors have done well at the national level: notably John Dane, III (Tulane '71), a three-time All American who won the 'A' division at the 1969 Dinghy Nationals and both the Douglas and Kennedy Cup regattas twice successively; also Augie Diaz (Tulane '74) who was named College Sailor of the Year and won both the Dinghy and Singlehanded championships.

Southern college sailing actually began on November 15, 1941 when Herbert O'Donnell won the first Tulane Sailing Club regatta held in the Gulf Fish Class at Southern Yacht Club. The 1991 Nationals marked the 50th anniversary of the long relationship between college sailing, Tulane and the Southern Yacht Club.

In 1963 the areas of Florida, Georgia, Louisiana and Tennessee were embraced under the South East Intercollegiate Sailing Association (SEISA) including Univ. of Florida, Georgia Tech, Rollins College, Tulane University, Springhill College, Auburn College, Amory, University of Georgia, Louisiana State, Stetson University College of Law at Vanderbilt University, Florida Presbyterians, and St. Johns River. The vast geographical spread of the colleges militated in 1983 subdividing the Association into the original SEISA west of Pensacola and SAISA east and north of Pensacola.

INTERCOLLEGIATE SAILING IN PERSPECTIVE

Tripp Alyn comments on the diversity of college sailing which includes sailboarding, dinghy racing, singlehanded, one-design keelboats and offshore boats; also it pitches young and old, light weight and heavy against one another. Further, intercollegiate sailing with its graduate and undergraduate components have introduced numerous innovations to the sport of yacht racing. Special procedural rules have been created to meet matters peculiar to college sailing such as eligibility, the two-division system of competition, three-minute starting sequence using a whistle and no flags, accelerated protest procedure, conforming ICIYRA eligibility rules to NCAA regulations, the US Olympic Committee's Tuition Assistance Program and others. ICYRA was the first national organization to test and adopt the new racing rules prepared and advocated by Harold S. Vanderbilt. Also, *Appendix D – Team Racing Rules of the RRRS* (1997) had its genesis in collegiate sailing, and college sailing has been a proving ground for the development and administration of *RRR* 42 – Propulsion. Coincidentally Mike Horn, Executive Vice President of ICYRA, reporting in the *American Sailor* in 1989 was advocating that the most effective way to strengthen future Olympic efforts would be:

> *to broaden the base from which junior sailors (the future college and Olympic sailors) are drawn. And I would do that by contributing to the establishment, development and growth of community sailing programs... initiate a program to help struggling 'small' college programs to acquire boats and/or facilities.*

... very much along the lines of the Olympic Path program adopted at the 1996 annual meeting of US SAILING.

The climate in 1966 was more parochial. Women, for example, could not compete at varsity level in NEISA, but even where they could in other Associations of ICRYA, as Lester Rhoads describes it:

> *At schools where this condition prevails athletic associations are reluctant to grant recognition, as the present eligibility standards of all United States college athletic conferences are defined for male students. In New England and the Middle Atlantic the NEISA and MALSA have set up separate Women's ISA's. In the Midwest and West, however, sentiment favors coed competition.*

By the mid '70's the practice had ended in NEISA, although women still have the option to compete in women's only competition under NEWISA and in certain National Championship events.

While intercollegiate sailing had been 'international' at a 'continental' level, i.e. Canadian teams from Districts of the CISA* and U.S. teams competing together, it finally became fully international in 1954 when a team from the Oxford University Yacht Club (founded 1884) visited for eight weeks and competed for the newly created Sir Thomas Lipton Memorial Trophy. The next year an additional award – the British Universities Trophy – was created and both are competed for biennially on alternate sides of the Atlantic in team racing format.

SAILING AT THE U.S. NAVAL ACADEMY[20]

In one respect the U.S. Naval Academy is the first institution in North America to have had, perforce, a formal curriculum on the subject of sailing and seamanship and, although not at an inter-collegiate level, is the first 'college' to have competed in an international regatta.

On the first score, in 1851 the Secretary of the Navy prescribed that midshipmen embark on a "vessel of war, equipped and kept in order for sea service and gunnery practice." On the second, the yacht *America* was stationed in 1863 at Newport, RI as a practice ship for the Naval Academy. In 1870 she was assigned to represent the Navy and Naval Academy under the command of Vice Adm. David Dixon Porter, U.S. Navy, recently superintendent of the Academy, to participate in the defense of the America's Cup.

Sailing as an intra-mural sport at the Academy, however, did not begin until the turn-of-the-century when racing took place for the Thompson Trophy in half-raters (gaff-rigged centerboard sloops)[21] and catboats. In the late 1920's "four Star-class racing" boats were purchased but "were not permitted to enter local races."

The history refers to the 'first' organized intercollegiate racing as occurring in 1928 between Harvard, Princeton and Yale and competition in 1929 for the Oliver May Trophy. In addition it notes that as early as 1920 there was informal competition among the three colleges and that the first recorded competition on the west coast was when "the Stanford team captained by Donald Douglas, Jr. (after whom was named the Douglas Cup annual invitational) beat the University of California-Berkeley (in the 1930's)."

It was not until 1932 when yachting writer, Alfred F. Loomis (renown for his column in *Yachting – Under the Lee of the Longboat*) fired the broadside, "Are there any sailors in the Navy?," that it was recognized that:

> *Small-boat experience developed better ship handlers, provided great recreation for sailors and officers, and encouraged cooperation with civilian sailors who would become naval reserve officers in time of war.*

Four years later midshipmen at the Academy "organized a boat club (the Midshipmen Boat Club[22]) with a membership larger than any other extracurricular activity". Racing was conducted in a fleet consisting of 30-foot centerboard, ketch-rigged, sailing whaleboats which also were carried aboard the large naval vessels.

The Academy's entree to offshore racing came with a gift in 1936 by Vadim S. Makaroff, of his 72-foot main trysail ketch *Vamarie*. This did not immediately transpire, since a request by midshipmen to enter her in the 1937 New London, CT to Gibson Island, MD race was turned down by the commandant of midshipmen with the comment that he could not even recommend this action to the Superintendent because:

> *the only requirement for amateurs in all these races is that the owner and navigator must be amateurs, and it will be found that those engaged in racing, even including the afterguard, are pretty tough characters. Apparently ocean racing bears no more relationship to (events where) small boats of one class are raced than does intramural boxing compare with the heavyweight championships.*

The history cites some intercollegiate watersheds such as Princeton establishing a fleet of Tempest-class dinghies in 1934,[23] and MIT building its Sailing Pavilion in

*By 1981 the CISA had ceased to participate as an Association of ICYRA.

1936 and equipping it with 36 Herreshoff-built dinghies designed by Prof. George Owen.

In the fall of 1936 Navy sent a team to MIT to race and a return engagement occurred the next year with MIT twice victorious. In an effort to provide outside competition in some high-performance boats, two Star boats arrived in April, 1937, and a practice of enlisting help from expert yachtsmen in training midshipmen in tuning and tactics began. The Naval Academy can probably claim to be the first college to have competed internationally (excluding the 1870 foray in the *America*) by dint that year of taking the Stars on the decks of three battleships and racing against the German Naval Yacht Club at Kiel, Germany and then racing in dinghies against the Britannia Royal Naval College in Tor Bay, England – a precursor to today's British Universities versus ICYRA exchanges in dinghies.

While the Academy's participation in inshore intercollegiate racing was proceeding apace, the struggle to obtain permission to race offshore by entering *Vamarie* in the 1938 Newport to Bermuda Race met with repeated rebuffs. As was the case with numerous 'firsts' in the development of sailing at the Academy, many insights related in the History are firsthand since author Admiral McNitt, both as a midshipman and later as a mentor for the sailing program, was a key player. Vice Commodore of the Boat Club, he was among a group of senior classmen who not only went to the media for support by inducing editor of *Yachting* Herbert L. Stone to state in an article "*Vamarie* – Will She - Won't She?", but also bypassed the chain of command by going directly to the Secretary of the Navy seeking permission. Permission was granted, and so a tradition of midshipmen competing in offshore yachts and events was established, albeit in this instance the midshipmen were newly commissioned ensigns including the author. Fifty-four years of unbroken participation in the race elapsed before the Academy would win the Bermuda Race.

The reflections of one of the ensigns on *Vamarie* presaged the significant role that competitive sailing would play half a century later as a major component in professional development training at the Academy and the type of influence that collegiate sailing has had throughout the ICYRA:

> *We did race, had a great time, did become better ship-handlers, better navigators, and better shipmates, but perhaps most of all we learned some things we didn't appreciate until later... Between bouts of seasickness, I expect there may have been some appreciation that keen alertness to changing conditions, getting the most out of crew and equipment, decisiveness in acting to take advantage of sudden opportunities, and a fierce determination to win were characteristics we would need later in the combat all of us saw within four years.*

When in the spring of 1939 dinghy racing was officially recognized as an intercollegiate sport at the Naval Academy, a dinghy team coach was assigned and a fleet of ten International 14's was ordered. The same year the first three of a fleet of twelve 44-foot Luders yawls were delivered. Thenceforth the offshore fleet has been regularly augmented by gifts of highly competitive offshore yachts which comprise the Yacht Squadron composed of members of the Midshipmen Boat Club.

Support of the sailing programs by yachtsmen has not been solely material; from the late 1930's counsel and advice has come from such as Alf Loomis, Herbert Stone, Rod Stephens, Lt. Comdr. C. Sherman Hoyt, Bob Bavier and after World War II Carlton Mitchell, Barklie Henry, John Nicholas Brown and DeCoursey Fales among others. The Academy became more deeply involved in offshore racing in 1947 as a co-sponsor with the New York Yacht Club and Annapolis Yacht Club (joined later by the Ida Lewis Yacht Club of Newport, RI) of the Newport to Annapolis Race (eventually reversed to start at Annapolis and finish in Newport). Concurrently Carleton Mitchell, other local yachtsmen and especially John Nicholas Brown (Assistant Secretary of the Navy for Air) were responsible for the appointment of Commodore DeCoursey Fales (New York Yacht Club) and Mitchell as a Sailing Council for the Academy sailing program. This led ultimately to the formation of the Sailing Advisory Council in 1966, quickly named the Fales Committee in honor of the Commodore. Its initial members were Robert

M. Allan, Jr., Henry H. Anderson, Jr., Clayton Ewing, Capt. Everett B. Morris, Cornelius Shields, Albert Bel Fay, Richard Latham and H. Irving Pratt. Its basic mission was:

> *to provide the basis for actions in the Navy Department that could make it possible to turn ideas into reality. That called for members whose experience, reputation, judgment and willingness to work outside the academy, both with the Navy Department and the yachting community, were established and demonstrated.*

With the creation in 1949 of the Naval Academy Sailing Squadron (NASS) nominally:

> *The commanding officer of the Naval Station became the commodore of NASS, and was charged with representing the Academy in all sailing activities, and with fostering cordial relations with civilian yachting organizations. In reality, the commodore of NASS managed only the ocean racing and local recreational sailing, since the intercollegiate varsity dinghy competition remained under control of the Athletic Association. There were periods, however, when the crews selected for the 'big boat' events, such as the ICYRA McMillan and Kennedy Cups, were composed of the best talent from both offshore and dinghy programs.*

These changes came under the watch of Superintendent Rear Admiral James L. Holloway, Jr. who:

> *Was the first Superintendent since Admiral Sellars to demand a strong sailing program, knowing that anything less was not an option for the school charged with setting the professional seagoing standard for the entire naval service.*

In 1950, the final year of his tour of duty, the Naval Academy at the invitation of the ICYRA hosted the McMillan Cup in the 44-foot Luders yawls.

> *Heretofore McMillan Cup races were held each year wherever a host yacht club could be found with enough boats of one class to schedule the regatta. This soon became increasingly difficult as many more colleges wanted to participate than could be accommodated by the boats available. In 1949 the Naval Academy's Sailing Council saw an opportunity to ease this problem and assure the midshipmen of a chance to compete every year. They suggested that the Superintendent offer to host this regatta at Annapolis… The winner of the first McMillan Cup Regatta to be held at the Naval Academy was Glen S. Foster II of Brown University.*

In 1965 this type of racing, which for the McMillan Cup initially was open only to New England colleges and later to some from the midwest, became nation-wide with the founding of the John F. Kennedy Memorial Regatta (in memory of his early interest in intercollegiate sailing; JFK was on the Harvard team that won the 1938 McMillan Cup) for which the Naval Academy has traditionally been the host.

> *The event was proposed by Robert Allan, Jr. who worked out the details with Leonard Fowle at ICYRA and Walter C. (Jack) Wood at MIT.*

In the interim years Academy teams were making their mark in such offshore events as the Bermuda Race, Buenos Aires to Rio de Janeiro and eventually Mackinac and Transpac in yachts donated to the Academy via the Naval Academy Sailing Foundation established by members of the Fales Committee.

In 1963 the gap between offshore sailing and dinghy racing was bridged with a gift volunteered by Cornelius Shields of the Larchmont Yacht Club from the Paul V. Shields Foundation to purchase a fleet of Shields Class Sloops. He was instrumental in developing fleets of Shields at the U. S. Coast Guard Academy and along with Robert M. Allan, Jr. at the University of Southern California at Irvine. For a number of years the ICYRA sloop championships were held in these fleets.

Allan as a member of the Fales Committee in 1967 recommended establishing a Collegiate Hall of Fame – a proposal gratefully accepted by the ICYRA and implemented at the Naval Academy's Robert Crown Center on its completion in the early 1970's. During the decade 1965-75 various factors and individuals combined to raise the level of performance in the sailing program and set up operating systems to optimize seamanship and teams capable of winning inshore and offshore. For example, when Rear Adm. Draper L. Kaufman became Superintendent he addressed concerns about the programs expressed by Charles L. Ill and Morton Gibbons-Neff, Jr. – Chesapeake Bay sailors – and both he and Commandant of Midshipmen, Capt. Sheldon Kinney, developed a strong working rapport with the Fales Committee. During this period 420's replaced the dinghy fleet, midshipmen competed in trans-Atlantic and trans-Pacific races, and the 44-foot wooden yawls were replaced in GRP.[24] In 1975 Capt. Alexander G. B. Grosvenor became the commanding officer of the Naval Station and was destined to make major innovations and further improve the competitiveness of Navy teams.

How he came by his assignment is an example of the sometimes bizarre ways in which the Fales Committee has been of assistance. When Charles Ill called on Vice

Admiral David Bagley, the Chief of Naval Personnel, to proselytize on behalf of Capt. Grosvenor, Admiral Bagley:

> *Made it pretty clear that... he didn't want any names... he asked me to write up specifications (for the post)... I called my aide... and he produced Capt. Grosvenor's personnel file. We worked up a specification from the file and sent it to Dave (Bagley). Lo and behold the computers digested the specifications and in a short time later I got a note asking what I thought of BuPers recommendation of Capt. Alexander Grosvenor for the job.*

Under Superintendent Vice Admiral Kinnard R. McKee and Capt. Grosvenor who, "believed that racing inshore as well as offshore is the ultimate expression and test of seamanship and competence in sailing," the Division of Professional Development was established to develop skills of seamanship, navigation, piloting, small-craft maintenance and leadership. As Admiral McNitt describes it:

> *This was the beginning of structured sail training while cruising, which would lead to the cruise-credit concept (heretofore only earned on 'gray' ships) in just a few years.*

It also reflects that inter-collegiate sailing as a sport has a reach far beyond merely recreational sailing. A measure of its significance at the Naval Academy was the awarding to Capt. Grosvenor, after his untimely passing, of the Legion of Merit.

> *This extraordinary man left a standard of excellence that would be his legacy to the Naval Academy for many, many years.*

In 1979 under Capt. Edwin A. Shuman, III the Naval Academy began holding Safety-at-Sea seminars involving, for example, Richard C. McCurdy Chairman of the joint Cruising Club of America and U.S. Yacht Racing Union Safety-at-Sea Committee. This led to year-long tests in 1983 that culminated in the 'quick stop' technique for recovering a man overboard.

When Capt. John B. Bonds (later Executive Director of US SAILING) took over as commanding officer of the Naval Station in 1984, he continued the safety-at-sea research and the composing of manuals on the subject. Also, it was during his tenure that, thanks to the gift of Cornelius Vanderstar, over 70 windsurfers were purchased and that under the guidance of Fales Committee member, Charles Ill, plans were implemented for replacement of the yawls with twenty McCurdy & Rhodes designed 44-foot sloops.

In 1987 the importance of sailing as part of professional development of midshipmen was highlighted by separating the posts of commanding officer of the Naval Station and Commodore of the Naval Academy Sailing Squadron, making the latter Director of Naval Academy Sailing and requiring all 1,300 plebes in the new class to learn to sail as part of their introduction to the Navy.

The success of the Naval Academy's sailing program was attested by the Varsity Intercollegiate Sailing Team winning in 1991 all three (Dinghy, Women's Dinghy and Team Racing) of the ICYRA championship events – the first college ever to do so. Subsequently Navy went on to become First Overall in the 1992 Bermuda Race in the Swan 48, *Constellation*, thereby winning the St. David's Head Lighthouse Trophy.

Historically the role of the Naval Academy in intercollegiate sailing has been a unique one both as a pilot program for the other service academies and in providing fleets of dinghy and offshore boats for major intercollegiate and interscholastic regattas. Further, as in the case of the other service academies, Navy has demonstrated that sailing has been much more than a sport; it has served as an integral factor in professional training and character building.

YALE CORINTHIAN YACHT CLUB[25]

Although it existed in some organized manner only since 1881, sailing as an activity at Yale can be traced back more than 200 years. An order in the Yale Rule Book of 1759 reads as follows:

> *If any scholar shall go a-fishing, sailing, or move more than two miles from college upon any occasion, without leave of the President, a professor, or a tutor ... he may be fined not exceeding 34 cents.*

Apparently the Puritan leaders of the college were not in favor of the sport. That attitude lasted a long time; as late as 1914, compulsory chapel meant that no one could leave the campus for the weekend. If that rule were still in effect, the sailing team could never attend an outside regatta.

After the Civil War, and before the upper part of New Haven Harbor had been taken over by industry, there were catboats for hire there. On the half-holidays of Wednesday and Saturday afternoons, students could rent them and sail off the Branford or the Thimble Islands for a bit of recreation. Indeed, it was the proprietor of one of those boat liveries who taught two students who would become the first and second commodores of the Yale Yacht Club how to sail. It was the first one, John Phelps, who organized the club in 1881. The man who had been his instructor was commissioned to build nine boats for the members. The races they held were most informal, but they were races.

The problem was that, as these nine graduated, they took their boats with them. The third commodore, Henry B. Anderson[26] was forced to watch them go, and none of the younger members had any interest in having boats built. The club sank into total inactivity for eight years.

When it was re-organized in 1893, the atmosphere was different. Across the country, new yacht clubs had been forming at the rate of nine or ten a year, and sailing was in the air. The name was changed to Yale Corinthian, a burgee was designed, a trophy was acquired as a carrot for competition and the membership almost overnight reached 100. Also, many of the members brought to school their larger yachts from home (akin in the 1920's and '30's, to the most affluent students bringing their automobiles to school), and some of them were well known along Long Island Sound and the East Coast as having excellent racing records which added even more interest.

The club then rented a house at Morris Cove, put in a float, paid a steam launch to make two round trips a day from downtown to the Cove, and hired a "first-class" cook for the dining room. Racing activity was three or four times as large as in the decade before, both formal and informal (the rental catboats were still available), and the first annual regatta was held in June, open to all and with three classes. Another such regatta was held the second year, followed by the "first annual cruise." In 1895, the club joined the Yacht Racing Association of Long Island Sound, which conferred some real status. By this time the membership had climbed to 200.

The club had another incentive: beat Harvard. The Harvard Yacht Club had been formed in 1894, and both clubs donated $100 for a challenge trophy. Arrangements were made for the first inter collegiate sailing regatta, which was to be held at New London on the last day of Yale's annual cruise of 1894, and the day before the traditional Yale-Harvard crew race. There were to be five classes: three of sloops, 30+ to 40 feet, 26+ to 30, and up to 26 feet; and two of catboats, 20+ to 26 and up to 20 feet. Scoring points: 5 for first, 2 for seconds, 1 for thirds. The larger yachts were to sail a 20-mile race and the smaller ones, 15 miles.

Yale won 21-16, in part because Yale had five more entries. The three larger Harvard sloops were fog-bound in Newport and never made it to New London. Even had they reached the venue, Yale had two more entries than Harvard. Also, it was found that one of the Harvard boats had been chartered. The event was sailed under the rules of the New York Yacht Club which specified that no chartered yachts may enter. Before the event the *Yale Daily News* reported having heard from several alumni who were opposed to the regatta on the ground that it would eventually deteriorate into a match race for which the representative of one school, or the other, would attempt to win simply by building a more expensive yacht. The paper rightly pooh-poohed the idea.

Harvard did not show up the next year, and the year after that a brief rupture of athletic relations between the two schools meant that there could be no Yale-Harvard racing at all. Meanwhile, in an attempt to provide a wider range of sailing for members, the Yale 15-foot Class was designed, and 16 were ordered. They were bought by members, or syndicates of members, and would be distributed by lot upon delivery from Higgins & Gifford of Gloucester.

The class was an example of the influence of the Seawanhaka Rule on yacht design: they were "skimming dishes" – 21 feet LOA, 15 feet LWL, 6 feet 3 inches in beam, and a draft of six inches with the centerboard up. They carried 350 square feet of sail and a crew of three. They were powerful, fast, and they could beat to windward in a smooth sea like a greyhound. But in a chop they could shake one's teeth loose. A student who sailed in one said later that he was always chosen to go on the foredeck to tend to jib because he was the only one light enough to do it without burying the bow, which carried the risk of submarining the entire boat.

As had happened before, when the students left New Haven, their boats left with them. By 1900, interest had waned to the point that the club didn't hold its annual regatta. Once again, however, the club bounced back, this time with a fleet of twenty 21-foot Swampscott dories, purchased and distributed in the same way as the earlier 15's. Their dimensions were much the same, too, except that they were dories and carried leg-of-mutton mainsails, named after the billowing sleeves of the blouses that women were then wearing – deep draft and high roach. The cost was $70 a copy. Three years later a fleet of 15 Hartford dories were acquired, a number of trophies were donated for internal competition, and membership grew to 255. Yet, the interest, while intense, was shallow. Within a few years, there seldom were more than 12 of the 35-boat fleet in any race. Interest and membership declined and were at a low level, with little or no racing, for many years.

In the 1907 season the club membership peaked at 450 and had the same two classes of boats. Yet racing did not become popular, and the main interest among the members appeared to be social and cruising jointly with Harvard. The period 1908 - 1927 could be characterized as one of doldrums.

The modern era of college sailing began in 1928, when Yale, Harvard, and Princeton banded together, under the patronage and leadership of C. Sherman Hoyt (Brown '01), who had obtained a degree in naval architecture at the University of Glasgow, to form the Inter-Collegiate Yacht Racing Association, the only function of which, originally, was to conduct a summer regatta somewhere along the East Coast. One of Hoyt's major contributions was the scheduling of regattas among the colleges. The first was held at Southport, Connecticut, sailed in Atlantic Class sloops. In 1930, Cornell, Dartmouth, and Williams were admitted to membership, but further applicants were denied for several years. In 1930, also, the ICYRA acquired the McMillan Cup for an open championship – by William McMillan of Princeton University. The cup, no longer representing the national championship, is still being raced for at Annapolis in the Naval Academy's 44-foot sloops.

By 1934, interest was turning to dinghy racing, but it was two outsiders, MIT and Brown, that had led the movement. At the annual meeting in June, those two schools were admitted to the Association, and Leonard M. Fowle, a Harvard graduate and yachting editor of the *Boston Globe*, was elected Graduate Secretary - effectively its CEO. Fowle, almost messianic in his fervor, had two urgent goals – to make dinghy racing the primary function of the ICYRA and to make it a national institution. He succeeded brilliantly in both.

CHRONOLOGY OF THE EARLY YEARS OF YACHTING AT YALE

1870 July 15th: cruise of the *Good Ship Washington*. The records contain the comment, "Owing to the illness of the Chaplain morning prayers were omitted." Cruising – later squadron runs to New London (from New Haven) after the end of the academic year were to become a prime activity among Yale Yachtsmen. The history of the Oxford University Sailing Club (with which from time to time Yale sailors have had a close relation) parallels that of Yale's, i.e. in the nineteenth century the two clubs were comprised of cruising or offshore racing members. World War I saw a cessation of activity, and in the 1920's the clubs revived – first as cruising racing organizations and later blossoming into small boat, one-design racing which today is the backbone of inter-collegiate competition.

1881 The Yale Yacht Club registered seven yachts ranging from 21-to-41 feet LOA; John J. Phelps as Commodore; 21 members; and its burgee a white 'Y' on a blue field.

1884 Eight yachts registered; officers – Henry B. Anderson, Commodore and Sheffield Phelps, Secretary-Treasurer.

1885 The Yale Yacht Club registers in Lloyds. Judges at the Spring Regatta were Henry B. Anderson and Carl W. Cutler.[28]

1893 Reorganized, the club adopted the term 'Corinthian' in its name and reversed its burgee to a blue 'Y' on a white field.

1894 The yacht club again appears in Lloyds and lists 21 yachts; Secretary-Treasurer is Harold W. Buck. This also was the year in which the Harvard Yacht Club was founded.

Hood sails. Rolex watches. Ultimates each.

For over twenty years, Frederick E. "Ted" Hood has designed and manufactured the most desirable, durable and efficient sails ever to drive the competitive yachts of the oceans of the world.

He's raced and won with the best. His list of prestigious victories include the Mallory Trophy in '56, the Bermuda Race in '68, and the SORC and the America's Cup in '74.

He knows his sails and he knows his sailing. His philosophy contains no room for anything less than maximum application of ability.

Durability. Excellence. Exactness. The words fit the man... the way he works. With ultimate care. With attention to detail. With the pride that comes from making the best that can be made.

The result is that every skipper worth his salt wants a suit of Hoods on his mast. And, chances are, he wants a Rolex on his wrist. Because uncompromising performance counts.

Rolex. The totally uncompromised machine. Handcrafted in 192 individual steps from a solid block of gold or stainless steel. Mechanically unequaled. Esthetically unparalleled. The world's idea of what a watch should be.

Indeed, Mr. Hood and Rolex have precisely the same opinion toward accomplishment. The only true measure of achievement is result.

ROLEX

Pictured: The Rolex Submariner Date Chronometer in stainless steel with matching Fliplock bracelet. Pressure-proof to 660 feet. Also available in 18 kt. yellow gold.

Write for brochure. Rolex Watch, U.S.A., Inc., Dept. 111, Rolex Building, 665 Fifth Avenue, New York, New York 10022. World headquarters in Geneva. Other offices in Toronto and major cities around the world.

CHAPTER VI

INTERSCHOLASTIC SAILING ASSOCIATION[1]

The year 1930, the first of the Great Depression, was not a good year economically, but it was the year in which the Interscholastic Yacht Racing Association was formed.[2] The prime movers were George H. Tilghman, headmaster of the Morristown (NJ) School, W. Huston Lillard, headmaster of Tabor Academy (Marion, MA), H. Nelson Emmons of the Beverly Yacht Club (Marion, MA), and Clifford D. Mallory, President of NAYRU and Commodore of the Indian Harbor Yacht Club (Greenwich, CT). The purpose was to "give schoolboys a chance to develop their yachting interests just as college men had been doing for some time." The four men enlisted the support of the headmasters of 12 other schools and launched the first regatta, at Mallory's invitation, at Indian Harbor Yacht Club, sailing in the club's Atlantics. All 14 of the original schools competed.

It was an unusual organization, stretching geographically from Concord, NH (St. Paul's) to Morristown, NJ. Thus, membership was far beyond the traveling range of the schools' normal competition in the standard sports, such as football and baseball. Most of the students' experiences in sailing occurred during their summer vacations at home, local clubs and summer camps. Since all of the members were, and would continue to be for many years, private preparatory schools, it was elitist. Yet, it had to be, if it were to exist at all, for a sailing team was unheard of at any public high school. None of the schools had any sailing equipment, i.e. boats. Even if they had, they could not take them aboard a transporting bus, as the baseball teams could. They were entirely dependent for regattas on the hospitality of yacht clubs which could readily be hosts, but which had to rely on members to lend boats that were still being fitted out the beginning of the season.

The wonder is that the Interscholastic Yacht Racing Association was created at all. It was sure to fail. That it did not was a tribute to the determination and the nurturing of a great many people whose love of sailing was stronger than the adversities they faced. The second regatta was held again at Indian Harbor, this time for a handsome trophy donated by Clifford Mallory – known ever since as the Mallory Trophy. As was the first, and as all regattas were to be for many years, it was a three-day event – two days of eliminations and a third day of finals, round-robins if wind and time permitted. The format was dictated by the availability of boats, since the association learned not to count on more than five or six so early in the season.

In 1932 the Beverly Yacht Club offered to host the annual Interscholastic regatta with its Herreshoff Twelve-and-a-Half's, and the BYC continued as hosts for all the years up to 1940 but one, which was hosted by the Manhasset Bay Yacht Club of Port Washington, Long Island. In 1940, by which time entries were exceeding 20, the venue became the Naval Academy at Annapolis in its 26-foot knockabouts, that year and in 1941. With dues originally $25 per school and then $50 the annual income was only $1,100. It is apparent that a number of people were digging into their pockets to make anonymous donations while many others donated time and services.

World War II halted sailing until 1948, when the Naval Academy resumed hosting duties for another five years. The number of schools entering in those years was lower than it had been during the several years before the war. Despite its excellent facilities, the Naval Academy was well south of all the member schools, so the ISYRA found another willing host at the Coast Guard Academy in New London, which served as the venue for the Mallory Trophy for five years beginning in 1954. The Academy provided its 24-foot Raven sloops or 26-foot knockabouts for these events.

In 1957 a record number of 24 schools entered, and the Association had to begin thinking of limiting membership. While it was loathe to do so, it was fearful of overloading its hosts, so at the December meeting it established a limit of 30. In 1959 three significant things happened. For the first time a member school, St. George's at Newport, was host for the Mallory, sailing its Fireflies and Sprites out of Ida Lewis Yacht Club; schools were invited to send two teams to compete; and a school from outside the east– the Park School of Indianapolis – became a competing member.[5]

Between then and 1971 the Association's annual regatta moved around from Manhasset Bay to the Naval Academy to the U.S. Merchant Marine Academy at King's Point, NY to the Corinthian Yacht Club at Marblehead. In 1971, however, a venue could not be found, and the regatta had to be canceled. This led to some serious thinking about the Association's future. From the beginning, regattas had been raced in Atlantics, Shields, Ravens, 210's, Ensigns – whatever host clubs could offer. Should not these youngsters be sailing high-performance dinghies, as the college sailor were? Also, a number of schools had become co-educational, and girls were on their teams. Finally, an inquiry had come from Wellesley High School (MA) about membership, and it would become the first public school member.

The solution was to hold the 1973 regatta at the Yale Corinthian Yacht Club, an Intercollegiate Yacht Racing Association member, and the owner of a fleet of 420 dinghies. The Interscholastic Yacht Racing Association was invited to send its winners to the first U. S. Youth Championship regatta on Lake Michigan. Thus, the 'A' division team of Phillips Academy (Andover) was sent to sail in the 470 division, and the low-point skipper (from Greenwich High School, the second public school member) was sent to sail in the single-handed Laser Division. The Association now seemed to be on the right track.

The next development would be regional associations. That was how the Intercollegiate Yacht Racing Association was organized, and New England, with by far the largest number of schools in the national organization, already had its NESSA, with a dozen schools in 1959 and increasing to 60 by 1997. Five schools in the Charleston area had formed South Atlantic SSA, and other areas were becoming ripe for regional associations. The first and second annual Cotton Bowl Regattas at the Fort Worth Boat Club attracted schools from Texas, California, South Carolina, Louisiana, and Massachusetts, and the second was won by the Woodrow Wilson High School of Long Beach (CA). Thus, the Board of Directors authorized the establishment of regional associations in any area where there were three or more schools, public or private, that wished to create one.

The Mallory remained at Yale for several years. The growth of regional YRAs meant that local eliminations could be held, and the regional groups were given entries according to the ratio of the membership of each to the total member schools. (New England seemed always to have six or seven, while the smallest of them had only one.) Of the seven districts, Pacific and Mid-West rivaled New England in strength with the South and Middle Atlantic close behind.

Meanwhile, a new problem, albeit an easy one, arose: what to do with the Mallory Trophy itself. Clearly, it was too valuable and the insurance too costly to risk it traveling around the country. The first institution to step forward with a housing offer was the Peabody Maritime Museum in Salem, which was happy to display it in a glass case in a prominent location. There it sat until 1990, when it was moved to the Mystic Seaport Museum, a more appropriate location, since Mallory had been one of the original organizers of the championship and was one of the three founders of Mystic Seaport.

In 1976 the Mallory was won for the first time by a high school, Amity Regional of Woodbridge, CT. The next year, the venue was moved to the Harvard Yacht Club on the Charles River, which was able to provide 18 Interclub dinghies. That began a string of ten years in which, except for one, the winner was either Tabor or St. George's. It illustrated the advantage of a school of having its own boats to sail every afternoon, having a coach and being able to hold weekend regattas with other New England schools.

For three years the venue moved to the Coast Guard Academy and then it stayed at the Naval Academy until 1990. The championships now are rotated through the

MALLORY TROPHY

1930	Middlesex School
1931	Lawrenceville School
1932	St. Mark's School
1933	St. Mark's School
1934	Belmont Hill School
1935	St. Paul's School
1936	Loomis School
1937	Belmont Hill School
1938	The Hill School
1939	St. Paul's School
1940	Loomis School
1941	Hotchkiss School
1948	St. George's School
1949	Belmont Hill School
1950	Choate
1951	Noble & Greenough School
1952	Noble & Greenough School
1953	Phillips Academy
1954	Roxbury Latin School
1955	St. Paul's School
1956	Phillips Academy
1957	Pomfret School
1958	Pomfret School
1959	St. George's School
1960	Phillips Academy
1961	Loomis School
1962	Cheshire Academy
1963	Williston Academy
1965	Phillips Academy
1966	Wilbraham Academy
1968	St. George's School
1969	St. Andrew's School
1970	Williston Academy
1972	Phillips Academy
1973	Phillips Academy
1974	Hotchkiss School
1975	Hotchkiss School
1976	Amity Regional School
1977	Tabor Academy
1978	Tabor Academy
1979	St. George's School
1980	St. George's School
1981	Tabor Academy
1982	Tabor Academy
1983	Tabor Academy
1984	Isadore Newman School
1985	St. George's School
1986	Tabor Academy
1987	Corona Del Mar High School
1988	St. Petersburg High School
1989	St.Petersburg High School
1990	St. Petersburg High School
1991	St. Petersburg High School
1992	Hotchkiss School
1993	Point Loma High School
1994	Palmetto High School
1995	Newport Harbor High School
1996	University of San Diego High School
1997	Newport Harbor High School

BAKER TROPHY

1989	Tabor Academy
1990	Tabor Academy
1991	Tabor Academy
1992	Corona del Mar High School
1993	Newport Harbor High School
1994	Palmetto Senior High School
	Tabor Academy
1995	Tabor Academy
1996	Newport Harbor High School
1997	Tabor Academy

CRESSY TROPHY

1979	Newport Harbor High School
1980	Wilson High School
1981	Tabor Academy
1982	Annapolis High School
1983	Woodrow Wilson High School
1984	St. George's School
1985	St. George's School
1986	Miami-Killian Senior High School
1987	Sarasota High School
1988	Isadore Newman School
1989	Palmetto Senior High School
1990	Largo Senior High School
1991	Largo Senior High School
1992	Largo Senior High School
1993	Avon Old Farms
1994	Hotchkiss School
1995	The Bishop's School
1996	St. Petersburg High School
1997	Clearwater Central Catholic High School

districts. The Naval Academy with its enormous facilities can provide 20 420's, 20 FJ's, and 40 Lasers, which means that 120 sailors can be sailing in four races simultaneously. Similar venues are now available elsewhere. Your editor had the great pleasure of serving on the Jury for this event with long-term board member and close friend Frederick D. King, who devoted may years to the Association and passed away in 1996.

In 1990, while celebrating the 60th anniversary of its founding, the Association, now called the InterScholastic Sailing Association (ISSA), was given two trophies: the Cressy Trophy for single-handed championships and the Toby Baker Trophy for team-racing championships. The above are the winners of the trophies for the national championships:

JUNIOR AND YOUTH PROGRAMS

YACHT CLUBS

The Pleon Yacht Club founded at Marblehead, MA in 1887 was the earliest junior program to operate independently of a senior yacht club and the only one to survive in this status. All the officers are under age twenty-one, and except for the Commodore and Treasurer having adult advisers looking over their shoulders, the young members conduct their own operation. Originally it was created for the children of members of the three clubs in the harbor – Boston, Corinthian and Eastern – but soon was open to children of non-members.

The fees were modest, and as the years went on, its alumni were most loyal in making contributions to cover operating costs. To be an 'alum' of Pleon was a badge to be carried through life.

Runners-up to Pleon, although none remained independent, were the Junior Squadron of the Royal St. Lawrence Yacht Club formed in 1888, the Queen City Yacht Club of Seattle (#1 of that name) in 1897 and the Junior Yacht Club at San Diego in 1908. Respecting Queen City:

> *Another event of note in 1987: many avid teenage boaters (including Ted Geary) moored their vessels near Brighton Boathouse... Neither Seattle nor Elliott Bay allowed membership for those under 21.*[4]

They created the first Queen City Yacht Club which expired a few years later when the Elliott Bay Yacht Club arranged for junior memberships. The vessels included, among others, the vee-bottom Skipjacks similar to a Snipe, but on a larger scale with inboard rudders, and some of the 16-foot, shovel-nosed scow catboats the plans for which appeared in *Rudder*.

The Junior Yacht Club at San Diego was founded by Dr. E. W. Gahan, a member of the San Diego Yacht Club, with separate quarters from SDYC for the sole purpose of training juniors for racing. Within the decade he persuaded SDYC to adopt the club only to let it lapse for a period of years. It took another dynamic member, Joe Jessop, to revitalize it in 1928 at the behest of several youngsters. Starting with the 16-foot, gaff-rigged Flapper class, the program acquired a small edition of a Star, the Starlet 16 feet 14 inches LOA and capable of being home-built from a kit. Today the San Diego Yacht Club employs ten instructors augmented by 50-to-60 volunteers to conduct junior training and racing.

Elsewhere in North America junior programs, whether or not organized along club lines, were small in number even in the 1920's. The movement picked up velocity in the 1930's, often as a feeder for potential members to its affiliated senior club during the depression years. After World War II the majority of yacht clubs had a full-scale junior program usually employing college sailors as instructors.

The programs that began in the 1920's had a variety of origins. The one at the Neenah-Nodaway Yacht Club in Neenah, WI on Lake Winnebago is novel.[5] In 1926 two members bought three dinghies and donated them to the club. Instead of using them to teach the children of members, however, they drew recruits from two of the town's boys clubs. In short, these were boys whose parents could not afford to join a yacht club – or any club. Applicants had to be between 13 and 18, be able to swim 50 yards and have parental consent. The boys were not only taught sailing but the care and maintenance of boats. After a race crews were required to stand by until their boats were inspected. Instruction and racing were conducted each Saturday during July and August.

As boys gained skills they were frequently invited to sail with seniors as crew. Since most of the yachts on the lake were relatively small, teen-agers on the sheets and halyards were ideal. After a while sons of members began to apply for the program. By 1932 there were as many juniors as seniors sailing , and the youngsters had racing on both Wednesdays and Saturdays. Two years later the Inland Lake Yacht Racing Association adopted a boat called the Cub, a small sloop designed especially for juniors. In turn most of the clubs in the Association bought a fleet, and soon there was a Cub championship in the area. One held a few years later on Lake Geneva drew 45 entries. Thus did junior programs begin in Wisconsin.

The Junior Squadron of the Royal St. Lawrence Yacht Club was short-lived, but in 1919 the club sponsored possibly the first Sea Scout Troop in North America. The Scouts trained in boats ranging from a 46-foot cutter to a navy gig.

The Seattle Yacht Club revitalized its junior program by purchasing in 1913 ten small one-designs. The aim was to encourage young men to learn to sail in the expectation that they would become interested enough in the sport to buy their own boat.

The concept of a separate facility under the administration of the senior club also gained favor at the Royal Canadian Yacht Club:

> *In one sense the most important development of the year was the bringing into being of the Junior Club, composed of sons of members and lads proposed by members in the senior club. The age limit was fixed at 10 to 15 years. A special clubhouse was built on the south side of the lagoon, and an initial fleet of six safe and sound flat-bottomed sailboats was built in the club workships... as gifts of Officers and others... By 1927 the RCYC had a full-fledged Junior Club with maximum membership of 60.*[6]

The Seawanhaka Corinthian Junior Yacht Club, in order both to honor a past Vice Commodore, Sheila Curtin Gross, who came to an untimely death in 1953 and to help the current members understand that they are an integral part of an organization that has a continuing tradition of Corinthianism, presented a plaque in her memory to be awarded to the member who has best exemplified the Corinthian spirit. The signature on the bronze plaque at the end of the text is that of Henry H. Anderson, Jr., the Junior Club's first Commodore; inscribed is:

> *A 'Corinthian' is a person who plays a sport as an amateur, that is, for the love of it without thought of personal gain, and who brings to the sport the finest qualities associated with the terms 'sportsmanship' and 'gentleman'. Historically the term 'Corinthian' stems from the town of Corinth, a port located on the isthmus joining the two parts of Greece. The Corinthians were seafaring men of renown and were gentlemen sportsmen who handled their own ships and hunted with their own horses instead of paying others to do so. Undoubtedly, the yachting fraternity adopted the term 'Corinthian' and incorporated it into the names of their clubs because of the world-wide reputation that the men of Corinth acquired for maintaining such high standards of conduct as amateurs in the pursuit of sports.*[7]

NATIONAL SEA EXPLORER CHAMPIONSHIP

As above noted, Sea Scout programs, normally unaffiliated with yacht clubs, served in parallel with club programs and came closest to being today's version of 'community sailing' services, although without an adult constituency. D. Verner Smythe, Chairman for many years of the NAYRU Junior Yacht Racing Committee, was also a national Director of the Boy Scouts of America National Sea Explorers (in 1949 Sea Scouts were so renamed) so that it was an easy step for the Committee to undertake to become involved in assisting the Explorers in developing a national sailing championship conducted along the lines of the Sears Cup. In 1964 a member of NAYRU, on behalf of the Union, offered to put up a trophy for the event on the premise that "Although NAYRU would not be the sponsor, members of the Junior Committee volunteered to assist." It was not until 1970 that the first national championship was held under the aegis of the Sears Committee, and the Chicago Yacht Club held a regional championship for crews from 12 Scout Regions. Actually the Chicago Yacht Club in 1925 had assumed support of Boy Scout Troop No. 870 which was re-organized under a Sea Scout charter. The winners of the Union's trophy were the team of Thomas E. Bissett and James C. Rogers of the Crescent Boy Scout Council, Madison, California.

JUNIOR BOATS

Classes for junior sailing, unlike those for collegiate racing, tended to develop locally resulting in a tremendous proliferation of types. In spite of the fact that today the classes for juniors more and more represent smaller scale versions of classes used in the Olympic Yachting Games, those used for junior training in North America lack the sophistication of the ones found, for example, in Australia. There the popular Flying Ant with its open transom, trapeze, spinnaker, etc. incorporates all the elements of a Flying Dutchman and is handled with amazing expertise by youngsters in 20 knots of breeze.

The chapter on yacht club histories describes how numerous classes originated, and as an example of the variety we note three in chronological order. First, when in 1936 the Seawanhaka Corinthian Yacht Club converted its junior program into a Junior Club format with its own clubhouse, lockers and pier, it commissioned Sparkman & Stephens to design a 24-foot keel sloop. Built by the Penn Yann Canoe Co. near Lake Cayuga, NY, the first boat was tested in a blizzard shortly before New Year's Day by a delegation including Roderick 'Rod' Stephens, Jr., who, as ice started to form on the deck, took the opportunity to try out the new Topsider deck shoe. At $750 complete with sails the Seabird served the junior program for several decades and after conversion to GRP the women's sailing for almost as long.

Second, the scenario for choosing the El Toro as junior boat at the Richmond Yacht Club (San Francisco Bay) four years later, and the result, were quite different[8]

> *A literal stampede of boat builders came in the fall of 1940 when Bud Coxhead and Bill Warren designed the El Toro. For months several members had been looking for a good dinghy that would do double duty as a sailing skiff to keep the kids occupied while mum and dad loafed on deck in a snug harbor. When* Rudder *came out with an eight-foot punt called the Sabot, they put it through a redesigning process.*

The leeboards were scratched and a centerboard was added, a rudder replaced the steering oar and a long stick replaced he folding mast. A little deck and splash boards were placed on the bow so the tiny ship wouldn't scoop up water rowing ashore at Paradise Cove... wondering what the offspring should be called... "For all the bull thrown around here tonight it should be the El Toro," Bill Warren replied. Not being able to draw a recognizable bull, they settled for a shovel in the throwing position. They found a trench shovel and traced it for the logo on the sail. The original shovel is still proudly displayed at the Richmond Yacht Club Rudder's *editor gave permission to build the El Toro that they had stolen from the Sabot and published The plans with the result that thousands were eventually built.*

Third, a junior boat that is responsible for bringing literally thousands of young persons into the sport is the Optimist, conceived after World War II to meet the need for an inexpensive junior boat on the West Coast of Florida. When Clark Mills crafted the first one in 1948 out of a 4-foot by 8-foot piece of plywood, it was not predictable that this would lead to the formation of a class in which junior teams compete annually on an international level and introduced literally thousands of young persons to the sport.

THE SEARS CUP - U.S. JUNIOR SAILING CHAMPIONSHIP

Junior sailing as a North America championship had its start in 1921 when Herbert Sears, Commodore of the Eastern Yacht Club of Marblehead established the Sears Cup. In the first year it was restricted to clubs in Massachusetts, but the following year it was made an open event for juniors of any yacht club. After managing the event for a decade, Eastern deeded the cup to NAYRU in 1931, in the belief that NAYRU was in a better position to make it a truly national event. Nonetheless, the NAYRU Trustees limited venues to clubs on the Atlantic coast north of Sandy Hook. While that implied some parochialism, perhaps the principal reason was that in those days youngsters were not able to travel at will with the freedom that they can today. The limitation was lifted in 1951.

In 1984, three hundred of the world's best sailors arrived in Long Beach, California, for the XXIII Olympiad. It was an event that had dominated their thoughts if not their lives for years. Yet of that elite number one group would emerge preeminent —the members of the United States Sailing Team.
In a remarkable performance, American sailors took medals in all seven classes. Gold for Star, Soling, and Flying Dutchman; Silver for Tornado, Windglider, Finn, and 470.
Since then, American sailors have continued to dominate world competitions. And, in the heated scramble for berths on the American team that goes to South Korea, they have put together an outstanding win record with more than forty medals at the Goodwill and Pan American Games, The Olympic Practice Regatta, and world championships.
Gold Medals for Star, Soling, Flying Dutchman.
The U.S. Sailing Team: Racing in a sea of Silver and Gold.
It's a remarkable record achieved by sailors whose skills were honed by the most rigorous programs of the Olympic Yachting Committee of the United States Yacht Racing Union.
1984 Olympics. Soling Gold Medalists Rod Davis, Ed Trevelyan, Robbie Haines.
Rolex proudly supports both the USYRU and its Team because precision, endurance, and excellence are as inherent in a Rolex timepiece as they are in championship sailing.
ROLEX
Oyster Perpetual Lady Datejust and Oyster Perpetual Datejust, both in stainless steel with 18kt white gold bezel and stainless steel Jubilee bracelet.
Write for brochure. Rolex Watch U.S.A., Inc., Dept. 612, Rolex Building, 665 Fifth Avenue, New York, New York 10022-5383.
© 1988 Rolex Watch U.S.A., Inc.
The amateur sailors who appear in this ad do so with the consent and for the benefit of the U.S. Sailing Team. Rolex, Oyster Perpetual, Lady Datejust, Datejust and Jubilee are trademarks.

67

CHAPTER VII

YACHT CLUBS

BAY HEAD YACHT CLUB[1]

Barnegat Bay is sheltered from the Atlantic Ocean by a long sandy spit of land that dangles from the coast of New Jersey, beginning about 30 miles south of Sandy Hook and Lower New York Bay. The spit runs about 40 miles (with a narrow inlet from the ocean about half way down) almost to Atlantic City. In geological terms it is a barrier island, or two, created by erosion of the coastline by wave action over centuries that deposited the eroded sand off-shore. Barnegat Bay itself is less than five miles wide at its widest point. At the head of the Bay is the town of, appropriately, Bay Head where the Bay Head Yacht Club is situated.

Some yacht clubs are fortunate enough to have had archivists and/or chroniclers. The BHYC had none. For much of its history it was a turnkey operation; the clubhouse contained only practical things like oars and sails and foul-weather gear, and there was no room for collections of documents. In addition, it was a wholly summer operation. All its members lived elsewhere nine or ten months of the year.

Until the nineteenth century the area around the Bay was almost totally uninhabited; access to it from Philadelphia or New York or anywhere else was almost impossible. The first known building was a lodge built in 1811 for amateur hunters and fishermen who sailed down from the New York area. In 1851 one could take a train from New York to Princeton, but from there it was cross-country by stagecoach to the shore, another jolting 40 miles.

Barnegat Bay is shallow throughout so the summer residents, as they began to arrive, followed the example of the few year-rounders: fishermen who used very shoal draft boats for their fishing, clamming, and oystering. As a result, two native types of boats have evolved: the flat-bottomed, scow-like garvey and the sneakbox or duck boat, which ultimately became a sailboat.

The first formal, or semi-formal races, on the Bay took place in 1864 among a few locals. In 1871 they, "the captains," decided to hold a Toms River Challenge Cup each year for the championship of Barnegat Bay, and they even went up to New York City to buy a silver trophy for it. By then, with better railroad connections from Philadelphia and New York, people were beginning to build summer homes around the Bay at Bay Head, Mantoloking, and Point Pleasant. The Challenge Cup became an event for both locals and summer people.

By 1888 the time seemed right to think of establishing a yacht club, and the necessary steps were taken with dispatch. The stated purpose was "to promote yachting and to foster athletic sports on the water... and to promote the general prosperity of Bay Head." The writer expressed some doubt respecting the order of these priorities since two of the founding officers were a local house builder and a boat builder. By the next summer a small clubhouse had been built, a simple structure with rooms for changing from wet clothes to dry, storage lockers, toilets and a balcony on top for viewing races. The cost was a modest $375. It was built on pilings, and access to it was across a series of catwalks over the marsh.

During the early years the boats used by the club were catboats and sneakboxes. To avoid the nuisance of handicapping the former were divided into four classes: up to 16 feet LWL, up to 18, up to 21, and up to 25 feet LWL. Each class was level raced. The sneakboxes were a different matter. In converting duck boats to sailboats, many different ideas of speed and stability developed (in any fresh wind, they required sand bags). This made level racing a dubious test of skill so they raced with handicaps for a number of years. In 1901, since the 20-foot LWL catboat had proved the most popular, a one-design to that length was created, and nine were built.

The original clubhouse soon became inadequate, and a second was built beside the first in 1898. At two stories, 24 x 40 feet on the first and 24 x 24 on the second, it was about four times larger and included a 190 foot dock. It was financed by bonds issued to the members. A few years later, a shed was built to house about 40 canoes. And in 1909, after government dredging to open up a silting channel which provided fill for the marshes near the club, there was room for four tennis courts.

Another one-design that came along about the time of the tennis courts was the Bay Head One-Designs, which were a close copy of the old Swampscott (MA) Dories. They were gaff-headed sloops with a club-footed jib, and they were raced hard until they finally wore out about 1930. Until the 1930's it was a yacht club very much ahead of the times, since it encouraged women and juniors to sail, e.g. the 1914 BHYC racing schedule provided that each Saturday the women raced at ten and the men at two. (Presumably, the raucous Bay wind was tamer in the morning.) The juniors raced on Mondays and Wednesdays, and junior sailing was co-ed.

By the end of World War I the Sneakboxes, mostly of the 20-foot LWL type but others very different, were still sailing under handicap, but a group of 15-foot one-designs suddenly appeared, which gave rise to the question, "Why aren't all boats this small one-designs?" Answer, "They were fast becoming so." By 1930 there were three classes of cats, two of 15-foot Sneakboxes (of which there were now more than 1,000 along the east coast), Class 'E' Scows, and Stars. The 15-footers became the junior boat of the 1920's. While they capsized easily and frequently, no one minded, for the water was shallow and warm and the boats easily righted.

From the beginning of yacht racing all races had been sailed over fixed courses regardless of wind direction. Unless the wind blew from a certain direction, even a long race could be without a single beat. During the 1930's the winter frostbiters of Western Long Island Sound and New England began changing this procedure with their multiple short races and insistence on the first leg being a beat to windward. Note, however, that the Barnegat Bay clubs did not give up their custom of starting and finishing races in front of the club until the 1950's. The reasons were simple enough: the people racing were fathers and mothers, brothers and sisters; the family wanted to watch; and, to boot, it eased the job of the race committee.

If the youngsters on Barnegat Bay were learning to sail before junior programs were common practice, who taught them? Sailing instructors were not part of most yacht clubs' staffs until the 1930's. They taught each other mostly, with occasional comments and suggestions from adults. They also crewed for their mothers and fathers.

While yachting in Barnegat Bay seems to have been a bit parochial at the outset, in 1925 two members of the BHYC sailed their 12-foot sneakboxes, equipped with small outboard motors, from New York to Miami. At that time the Inter-coastal Waterway existed, in good part, only on paper. The feat brought them and the Bay instant and widespread fame. From 1926 to 1932, the club held home-and-home team racing events with the Royal St. Lawrence Yacht Club in Montreal in Class 'E' Scows at home and a different form of scow at the RSLYC. While the 'E' Scow opened the club to racing on a continental scale, it effectively killed the 20-foot Sneakbox Class.

By 1927 the club had once again outgrown its clubhouse, and the membership, having said "No" most emphatically three years earlier, voted $54,000 in member bonds for the construction of a new one. With some overruns and extras that had not been foreseen, the final bill came to $74,000, which required $20,000 more in bonds. But 1928 was a great time to build a clubhouse. The delay of another year would have made it impossible.

One comes away from *100 Years at the Head of the Bay* with the feeling that Bay Head thoroughly enjoyed its first 50 years. The pleasure in remembrance of them shines through on almost every page. It was a wonderful foundation for the second half-century. The BHYC is idyllic of what a yacht club should be.

BISCAYNE BAY YACHT CLUB[2]

The Biscayne Bay Yacht Club was founded by a New Yorker. In 1877 the east coast of Florida consisted of only two communities of any size – St. Augustine and Key West. In that year, Ralph Middleton Munroe learned of a small "settlement" on Biscayne Bay called Coconut Grove. Munroe, a native of Staten Island, was an architect, boat designer, respected natural scientist of the first rank, and great grandson of the owner of Munroe's Tavern (now a museum) in Lexington, MA during the Revolutionary War. He was then running a successful oyster "planting" business.

Ralph Middleton Munroe,
the founding Commodore of the Biscayne Bay Yacht Club
Photo Historical Association of Southern Florida,
Ralph Monroe Collection

Enchanted by tales of Biscayne Bay, the western limit of the trade winds, in 1874 he determined to go there. To do so, he had to take passage on a vessel going to Key West and there find a smaller boat that could take him back some 150 miles to the shallow bay. The Bay had been named for Pedro Vizcaino, a Spaniard who had lived many years before on the principal island (Key Biscayne) sheltering the Bay.

Munroe was not disappointed. Five years later, when his wife contracted tuberculosis, he took her there in the hope that the climate would improve her condition. Unfortunately, she died shortly after their arrival, but Munroe continued to come back, sailing his own boat down every winter. It was a ketch of his own design, a 33-foot adaptation of the flat-bottomed New Haven Sharpie, that could handle the November storms of the east coast and still not run aground on Biscayne Bay. He also designed several round-bilge sharpies for people he had talked into becoming winter visitors at Coconut Grove. (If they wished to come, it had to be by boat, for there was no railroad, indeed no road of any kind.) As described in *The Commodore's Story – Ralph Middleton Munroe*,[3] this particular sharpie had more stability than the New Haven flat-bottomed version and did not pound in a seaway. About 25 were built, and a comment of an owner, L.D. Sampsell, at the Southern Yacht Club in New Orleans provides an insight into the caliber of the designs of Monroe who later became a close friend and host of Nathanael G. Herreshoff:

> *This work of yours of 1885, Commodore, was more than a third of a century ahead of her time, when, we consider what the designers should now be coming to – an easily driven, light draft, lightly ballasted, sweet-lined hull, with reasonably narrow beam, the right free-board, and the properly placed large heavy centerboard, which can be driven with a light, easily handle sail-spread, or by the less cumbersome engines. Shallow draft is most convenient for more than 75 percent of our coast from Nova Scotia to Mexico. I do not believe that the smallish deep boat with ponderous ballast on a short keel is the safest and fastest vessel for any kind of deep-water use, anywhere, anytime in any weather.*

When he arrived in the late fall of 1886, Ralph Munroe was introduced to a new resident named Kirk Munroe, no relation. The two instantly became friends. Kirk, most noted as a writer of adventure books for boys, had founded American Sailing Canoe Association. He was also to build the first tennis court and organize the first baseball team in the area.

The tiny population of Coconut Grove consisted of farmers, fishermen, Indian traders, and winter visitors. All, of course, had boats. In February of 1887, Ralph and Kirk Munroe decided to sponsor a regatta to celebrate Washington's Birthday. Their efforts produced 15 entries: six dinghies, six boats under 35 feet, and three larger. Encouraged, they decided to form a yacht club, so Kirk nominated Ralph as commodore, and Ralph responded by nominating Kirk as secretary. A formal meeting to organize would have to await the return of the winter visitors. The Club continues to celebrate Washington's birthday with a cruise and chowder party on the real anniversary – February 22.

When the meeting took place with 14 founding members, it quickly elected the two Munroes to their new positions and ratified the constitution and by-laws they had written. The new club then leased, for $1 per year for five years, a disused lighthouse at the south end of Key Biscayne. Thus, for a time at least, it could boast that it had the tallest clubhouse in the country - 150 feet high.

When Ralph Munroe left for Staten Island to wind up his affairs and prepare to become a citizen of Coconut Grove after the winter of 1888-89, he left plans for the construction of a two-story building. The lower floor would be for the use of the Club – storage of gear and repair and maintenance equipment. The Commodore was to live on the second floor. When he returned that fall, it had been completed, and he moved in.

The lighthouse proved to be inconvenient as a clubhouse, so most meetings of the Biscayne Bay Yacht Club were held in the commodious home of Kirk Munroe. It is worth noting that, at the meeting to plan the Washington's Birthday regatta of 1892, Kirk's house guests at the time were a Seminole Indian leader and his wife. At that same meeting, a club burgee was adopted. It was simply the numerals '25' superimposed over the letter 'N,' standing for 25 degrees North latitude, the location of the lighthouse, and signifying the southern-most yacht club in the United States.

Meanwhile, a man named Henry Flagler, an original investor in Standard Oil, was building railroads down both coasts of Florida and buying land as he went. By 1896, he had reached the Miami River. He then incorporated the land north of it as the City of Miami, which his people ran as his personal satrapy for many years. Coconut Grove, south of the river, was absorbed by Miami in 1925. The new City of Miami had a dramatic and almost immediate effect on the Club. By 1898 Kirk Munroe's home, no longer being large enough to hold the quiet Washington's Birthday after-race party – now elevated to a ball, was moved to Flagler's opulent new Royal Palm Hotel on the north bank of the river. By 1905 the club had 100 members and 76 yachts, many too large for the Coconut Grove house and docks.

In 1898 the Commodore built his first 'flying proa' patterned after the South Pacific proas with a long, canoe-like hull supported by an outrigger to windward and driven by a lateen sail. From *The Commodore's Story:*

> *Coming about was a queer upheaval of precedent. Instead of luffing, they bore sharp off, slacking away the sheet. One man brailed up the sail (tricing the boom to the lateen yard) to spill the wind out of it, jumped to the tack-lanyard, cast it off, and ran to the opposite end of the boat, passing the tack (the junction of the yard and the boom) to leeward of the mast (which was stayed only to windward) and immediately bowsing it down in its new position at what had been the stern, but was now to be the bow. Meanwhile the steersman had carried his oar in the other direction, and as the sheet was trimmed in (at the new stern) the boat gathered way, headed up and was off on the new tack. The way the strange machine crabbed to windward was certainly far beyond the performance of any other small boats.*

In addition the two dagger boards amidships had to be interchanged when tacking, and the crew would move in and out on the outrigger to keep it flying five to ten feet above the water. A proa could attain speeds of over 20 knots.

The following year, 1910, Ralph Munroe retired after 23 years as commodore. He was not happy with what had happened to his club, but he had the satisfaction of having brought it, with Kirk's help, through the early years, a time when many a new club had foundered. It had come to the point where it could build two new clubhouses in four years without going into debt. Kirk Munroe stayed on as secretary for ten more years.

By 1914, the membership list had become quite different form the earlier years. It contained names like William J. Matheson (Allied Chemical), Charles Deering (International Harvester), Andrew Carnegie, Marshall Field, Charles Armour, and Glenn Curtiss. Most were northerners, and their yachts were large, the largest 277 feet, and 95 percent power. Few sailors were left. One,

Proa designed by Wirth Munroe and sailed by headmaster and students of the Adirondack-Florida School on Biscayne Bay ca. 1937
Photo Ransom Everglades School

who had already come and gone, is worthy of special note: "Tootie" McGregor, a very wealthy woman who sailed a 63-foot schooner. She applied for membership in 1896 and was accepted as a full member, a status very possibly unique in the United States at the time. When she died, alas, the club declared the precedent null and void.

The club continued to be affected by the Miami environment, one of intense, almost frenzied investment in land and development. During the early years of the 20's, a large percentage of members were real estate developers. In one startling instance in 1924, a development company took a large tract of land it had bought, divided it into small lots and auctioned them off. In two hours it took in $43 million. Five days later, when the company was able to get its books settled, it discovered that the land had been oversold by one-third and had to return $11 million!

In 1926 the bubble burst and after Miami was struck by two "killer" hurricanes, in which 342 people lost their lives, the financial collapse was irrevocable. Among the property losses was Ralph Munroe's boathouse/apartment, although the second (1905) BBYC clubhouse survived, and several years later was barged up the Miami River to become a member's private home.

In 1929 came the stock-market crash, and the wealthy northerners who had survived the '26 collapse departed. Membership in 1930 was down to 75. Slowly, as most other clubs did, it recovered. In 1932, the club decided to return to its origins at Coconut Grove. At the same time, it vowed to restore the custom of serving at the after-race party on Washington's Birthday a simple but copious fish chowder. It had been the honored way of celebrating that race in the earliest years.

The son of William Matheson agreed to pay for a new clubhouse. It was designed with a weather eye on hurricanes: the ground floor was an open structure of stone arches with the main quarters on the floors above. Twenty-three years later the design received its first real test. The hurricane of 1945 poured seven feet of water through those arches for several hours, but the structure held firm. During the intervening years, a bar, called the Rathskeller, had been built on the ground floor. It was, of course, destroyed but quickly rebuilt and dubbed 'The Bilge.' The sturdy 1932 clubhouse still stands firm today.

Before the Southern Ocean Racing Circuit was started the Club ran what for many years was the 'anchor race' for the Circuit – the Miami-Nassau Race, and until the formation of the Coral Reef Yacht Club next door (next door to which is the US Olympic Sailing Center), it conducted the principal around-the-buoys events on the Bay.

Probably because of its geographical location, the history of the Biscayne Bay Yacht Club does not mention the North American Yacht Racing Union either at its inception in 1897 or its revival in 1925.

THE BOSTON YACHT CLUB[4]

While Boston and New England cherish the 'oldest' designation in much of their cultural, economic, and social achievements, yacht racing is not among them. By 1830, there was easily enough wealth, which brings with it leisure, in Boston to permit the area to begin the establishment of formal yacht racing, i.e., yacht clubs. There were, indeed, yachts in the area, and they did race but on an ad hoc basis, assembling from their own docks in the North Shore to hold races. A Boston Yacht Club was started in 1834 but lapsed four years later; a yacht club did not seem to be needed.

In 1844, John P. Stevens in New York wrote to his friend Robert Bennet Forbes in Boston with news of the formation of the New York Yacht Club and its plan for a cruise to Newport in August. Forbes, one of the finest American sailors of the 19th Century, replied that he would "round up some of the Boston Fleet" and sail down to join in the celebration. That he did, and a dozen Boston yachts sailed down around Cape Cod, through the Nantucket and Vineyard Sounds, and across Rhode Island Sound to Newport, a considerable voyage even today. It was an impressive demonstration of enthusiasm for yachting and yacht racing. There was one race held during the historic meeting, incidentally. It was around Conanicut Island, and it was won by Forbes, with Commodore Stevens second.

Yet, it was not until 1866, the year after the Civil War ended, that the Boston Yacht Club was formed. It was triggered by a Fourth of July race in Boston Harbor. The yachts were all large, and the experience made plain that it is impossible to conduct yachts races without race committees and without rules, if serious risk to life and limb was to be avoided. Thus, 15 men met to consider founding a club. By November, the groundwork had been completed, and 90 men assembled to elect officers, approve a constitution and by-laws, and to sign on as members. The constitution cited, as its purpose, encouraging yacht building and naval architecture and the cultivation of nautical science.

One of the new members was a youngster who was a freshman at MIT. His name was Nathaniel Greene Herreshoff. While looked upon as the club mascot, young Nat had already designed his first major yacht (aside from *Meteor*, a small craft designed and built by him and brother John when they were barely teenagers). He raced the newly launched *Violet* that summer against his father, who was sailing a yacht of his own design. The father won, and the son was devastated. "Why, Nat," said the father, "*Violet*'s not broken in yet; give her a chance." Nonetheless, young Nat took an axe to his carved model for the yacht and smashed it to pieces. As a result, it is probably the only yacht Capt. Nat ever designed that is not represented by a model in the Herreshoff Maritime Museum at Bristol, RI.

He could not destroy the yacht itself, however, for she had already been sold to a founding member of the Boston Yacht Club, Eben Denton, who won many races with her over the next two decades. Nat's father had been right, and the experience taught him the difficult lesson of patience.

The next year something happened that illustrated, as much as anything could, the genius of N.G. Herreshoff. The Boston Yacht Club was in need of a measurement rule for handicapping disparate yachts. The New York Yacht Club had already tried and discarded three measurement rules, and a fourth was in the process of failing. The experience of the Royal Yacht Squadron in England was similar. So the club turned to the young MIT student. Promptly, young Herreshoff worked out the simplest and most sensible measurement rule that had yet to be seen.

All of the measurement rules that had been adopted thus far, and all that would be created for many years, incorporated two, three or more factors. Herreshoff used only one. He reasoned that, while beam or draft or both might be increased to permit more sail area, the potential increase in speed by doing so would be offset or even cancelled by increased hull friction. Conversely, to shrink beam or draft or both would require decreasing sail area, lest a yacht be over-canvassed. To leave those three factors out of account would lead to safer yachts with beam, length, and sail area appropriate for their length and yachts able to sail most efficiently in a variety of wind and sea conditions, which is what all sailors encounter over time. Thus, length was his only factor.

By using long observed maximum speeds of vessels of various lengths, from eight-foot dinghies (five knots) to 216-foot clipper ships (17 knots), Herreshoff worked out the following formula: M (speed in knots) = 3 x cube root of L (LOA + 2 x LWL) -1. (LOA for overall length and LWL for waterline length.) Since all yachts sail much of the time at less than maximum potential speed for lack of sufficient wind, and large yachts suffer more than smaller ones in that circumstance, he made an adjustment to the formula: M = 2.5 x cube root of L. Herreshoff argued that the adjusted formula would affect all yachts, large and small, proportionally in winds strong, medium, and light. He was right. It worked, and what could be simpler! Moreover, it was a 'direct reading' measurement rule coupled with tables of time allowances in minutes and seconds per mile thereby eliminating complex calculations.

Seven years later, the world-famous British physicist William Froude validated N. G. Herreshoff's parameter for determining speed potential. By 1870, the British Navy had converted entirely to steam power and had commissioned Froude to advise it on hull design to obtain maximum speeds in order to minimize the tonage of coal required. In 1874 Froude produced the results of his study. In it, he observed that the principal factor of speed in any hull was waterline length, and maximum potential speed potential was 1.3 x square root of LWL. To go faster than that, a ship would have to climb its own bow wave, which would require an enormous increase in engine power and fuel. That rule applied, of course, only to displacement sailboats.

Another observation Froude made was that, while naval vessels travel upright so that their immersed waterline remains constant, yachts under sail do not. When heeling going to windward yachts extend their effective waterline. There was a lesson that would affect the thinking of naval architects for generations! At the time, Herreshoff was working with the U.S. Navy, designing and building vessels that sailed upright – torpedo boats. When he returned to designing yachts, he remembered the lesson. In 1891, he designed *Gloriana*, 70 feet overall with a nominal waterline of 45 feet. Her hull was shaped with overhangs fore and aft to minimize wetted surface and drag when she was sailing upright. But when she was beating, her effective waterline increased to 50 feet. *Gloriana* was unbeatable and became the standard for yachts for three generations of designers. Capt. Nat was an amazing man – a genius both as a naval architect and a civil engineer.

To return to the Boston Yacht Club's development, its first order of business in 1867 was to apply for a charter from the Massachusetts legislature. The petition came back refused. The grounds were, "such an organization might lead to immoral and ungentlemanly conduct, detrimental to the public interest." The officers were dumbfounded.

Was it because the club had been organized for pleasure rather than service? While the famed Puritan ethic had reached its zenith many years before and had been in decline ever since, enough of it remained that it could have been the reason. Or, was the legislators' vision of sailors bound up with the waterfront and its saloons and bawdy houses? Or, did they think that a yacht club would lower the stature of the other gentlemen's clubs in the city? Most of the legislators belonged to at least one of these clubs, the reputations of which were deemed as important as their churches. In any event, the misunderstanding was eventually straightened out by a number of discrete and earnest conversations in important quarters.

By June of that year the membership of the club had doubled, and the first "Review of the Club Squadron" took place. It was not a regatta but a parade around the harbor. A steamer with a band on board was hired to carry the non-yacht-owning members to the rendezvous point in Hull. The next week the club held its first regatta in which 16 of the club's yachts raced. A week later the Squadron was asked to escort the vessel carrying President Andrew Johnson into the harbor. The Boston Yacht Club was brilliantly on its way.

It was not to last, however. Dissension, jealousies, and schisms soon arose. There were several reasons. One was that some members had been embarrassed by the legislature's charter refusal, which had been issued publicly, of course. Another was that the club had achieved instant glamour, thus attracting many people who did not sail and had no intention of acquiring a boat. The sailing members feared that this group and their wives would monopolize the club's quarters in Pemberton Square. A third was the objection of some to the club's policy of requiring no minimum size of yacht; to them, nothing short of 30 feet should be considered a yacht. Finally, and ironically, the very creation of the BYC opened a long-delayed gate; there had been enough latent interest to support four or five yacht clubs in the Boston area, and many members lived more conveniently to the proposed sites for them. (Boston proper was then very small in area – only about ten square miles.)

The club nearly foundered. Members drifted away in droves. In 1870, no meeting, executive or annual, contained more than nine men. No one wanted to be commodore, and the treasurer had to fill the position. With no quarters, meetings were held in his downtown office. Meanwhile, five new yacht clubs were created, among which was the Eastern Yacht Club founded by the 30-foot-minimum group.

The remaining members determined to hang on. In the fall of 1871 the most determined and resolute of them, Benjamin Dean, accepted the position of commodore. He and the effect of competition spurred the club, and it turned the corner only a year later. In 1873 it purchased land at City Point (within the harbor but well out of the main shipping lanes), and a clubhouse was built and opened the following year. It was a commodious building, 70 feet by 70 feet, two and a half stories, built partially over water on pilings, with porches, kitchen and dining room.

The celebratory regatta that year had 20 entries, including six schooners, the largest being 108 feet on deck. Adding greatly to the scene was the yacht *America* serving as the committee boat.

After three years at the helm Benjamin Dean declined to stand for re-election. In his final report to the club he urged it to strive for innovation, to hold to its egalitarian principles and to be sparing in the award of prizes (prizes commonly included money). He wrote:

> *It is not the prize money the yachtsman seeks. It is the pleasure and excitement of honorable contest with his fellow yachtsmen, and of the contest with the elements.*

Another yacht to add luster to the Boston Yacht Club was *Shadow*, owned by member Dr. John Bryant. N.G. Herreshoff built her in 1877.[5] With a conventional sail plan, but a hull very different from any yacht previously delivered from the Herreshoff yard, she was an extraordinary vessel. She won a 126 races out of the 150 or so in which Bryant entered her.

In 1881 another extraordinary yacht appeared on the American scene. She was *Madge*, a 40-footer designed and built by George Watson of Scotland for a Scot and considered to be the finest yacht in Great Britain. She spent the summer in America wiping out every boat of her size that she raced in the New York area but had not yet had a match with *Shadow*. In October the two finally met in Newport and sailed two races. *Shadow* won the first handily, in part because *Madge* lost her starboard spreader at the leeward mark before the beat; *Madge* won the second by nine minutes with a three-minute handicap in her favor.

The significance of *Madge*'s success was that it came in the midst of what was called the sloop vs. cutter controversy. Many years later L. Francis Herreshoff (N.G.'s grandson) observed that, since what the Americans term a sloop and the British a cutter had identical rigs (except for the double head rig often found on the British yachts), the controversy should have been called the "beamy" vs. "narrow" controversy. For some years American and British designs had been moving in opposite directions (partly due to differences in their respective measurement rules). American yachts were becoming beamier and shallower, while British yachts were becoming narrower and deeper. *Madge* helped convince American yachtsmen that they were moving toward an extreme that was fast becoming inimical to both safety and pleasure; the two yachts were years ahead of their time.

In 1882 a most unusual thing happened at the Boston; it elected, and then re-elected four more times, Jacob Pfaff as commodore. Pfaff was not a Yankee but an immigrant from Bavaria. Since he had come to this country as a young adult, we can assume that he spoke with a strong German accent. Moreover, he was a Roman Catholic. Beyond that, he did not have a "proper" business background: he owned a brewery! It is doubtful that any other major yacht club in the 19th Century would have done such a thing.

In 1885, 1886 and 1887 the Boston Yacht Club distinguished itself in another way: three-straight successful defenses of the America's Cup. The campaigns were organized by member Gen. Charles Paine to challenge yachts of the New York Yacht Club for the honor of defending the Cup. The three yachts were designed by member Edward Burgess, and two of them were built by member George Lawley. After the victory by *Volunteer*, following those by *Puritan* and *Mayflower*, the City of Boston celebrated the achievements of the three men at a gala in Faneuil Hall. Mayor Hugh O'Brien invited every prominent citizen of Boston to the event, and most came to honor them. One who could not, Oliver Wendell Holmes, wrote his regrets to the Mayor, saying that: "General Paine is the only commander I ever heard of who made himself illustrious by running away from all his competitors."

Note that member N.G. Herreshoff, who was Rear Commodore of the Boston for three years, took over from Edward Burgess (who died at an early age in 1891) and designed the next six America's Cup defenders. Another member of note was Charles Francis Adams II, a direct descendant of John and John Quincy Adams, and a member for 72 years; he had joined the BYC two years before entering Harvard. "Charlie," as he was known by everyone, was considered by his peers during the first four decades of this century, to be one of the three best sailors they ever competed with, the other two being Harold S. Vanderbilt and C. Sherman Hoyt. Paine, Burgess, Adams, and Vanderbilt were all members of the Eastern and New York Yacht Clubs as well.

The 1890's began another decline of the Boston YC. There were two reasons: one was that the City Point clubhouse had been hemmed in by an unattractive and noisy commercial development; the other was the beginning of out-migration of Boston citizens to what are now called the suburbs where new yacht clubs were built. The result was that the Boston area temporarily had more clubs than it needed.

That situation was ultimately solved by mergers. By 1903 the BYC had six stations, including one at Marblehead and one at Five Islands, ME. One of the four within Boston Harbor was at Rowes Wharf. That was not satisfactory for yachts, because it was in the very midst of traffic by commercial vessels, but it did provide a fine little three-story brick building for members, convenient to downtown and to commuting ferries, and situated picturesquely in a cobble-stoned alley within the wharf property. The yearbook of 1910 listed almost 800 members and 362 yachts, of which 19, sail and power, exceeded 100 feet in length.

At that time member Roger Upton decided to form an informal power division within the club. For a year and a half he steered 36 power boat owners through a series of courses on navigation, boat handling and safety precautions that he either developed himself or borrowed from the U. S. Navy. His work paid off, not only for the power boaters but for the club's sailors as well. The annual cruises headed down east in July 1912 with 40 sail and 20 power. On the first day's run, from Marblehead to Portland, a sudden and furious storm arose that dismasted half the sailing fleet and left many sailors injured, including broken arms and legs. Through the valiant efforts of the competent and well-drilled power division, not a life was lost, and each of the 20 had a sail yacht in tow when they finally reached Portland. That fall the BYC formally established its Power Squadron.

The following year the Boston invited delegates from seventy yacht clubs that had power boats on their yacht lists to a meeting at the New York Yacht Club. From that meeting it was only a short step to the formation of the United States Power Squadron. Meanwhile, Roger Upton was busy with another project – finding a vessel he could buy that was capable of being converted into a floating machine shop and had enough power to be able to tow any yacht of the club. His idea was to have it accompany the annual cruises down east. He did just that.

The 1920's decade was one of continued growth for yacht clubs, indeed clubs of any kind. It also marked the beginning of democratization of yachting generally. In 1921 Commodore Herbert Sears of the Eastern Yacht offered a cup for juniors. Within three years, it had come to represent the junior national championship. In 1930, Sears, satisfied apparently that the North American Yacht Racing Union was finally a going concern, deeded the Sears Cup to NAYRU. Meanwhile, Commodore James Hodder of the Boston offered the Hodder Cup for women. It was first sailed for in 1924, and Hodder believed it to be the first women's championship sailed anywhere in the world. Surviving sailing instructions for a regatta held by the Boston in 1927 show starts being provided for an astonishing number of 19 classes of yachts of less than 20 feet!

Today, the Boston Yacht Club exists only in Marblehead. By 1920, it was clear that the Hull station (originally the Hull Yacht Club) was becoming a losing proposition. But there was now an independent Hull Yacht Club that did not need additional space, and a yacht club is hard to sell. It took nine years to do that. Meanwhile, the Dorchester station reverted to what it originally was – the Dorchester Yacht Club. In 1962 the club sold the City Point station to a new organization, the Boston Harbor Yacht Club.

That left two stations. The BYC had had a station in Marblehead since 1902. By 1955 it had become totally inadequate so the club bought a small waterfront hotel, which is its present clubhouse. For years the Rowes Wharf station had been primarily a luncheon club and a meeting place, not just for the club but for all manner of nautical organizations. In 1965, however, the Boston Redevelopment Authority razed the aging Rowes Wharf and with it the Boston's handsome little brick building, leaving Boston Marblehead as its sole location.

CAROLINA YACHT CLUB - 1853[6]

"On Sunday, April 24, 1853, seven men who loved sailing founded the Carolina Yacht Club[7] and elected Richard Bradley III its first Commodore. The first clubhouse was located on 'The Banks' – currently Wrightsville Beach, North Carolina. Its claim as "the third oldest yacht club to be formed in the United States (preceded only by the New York Yacht Club and the Southern Yacht Club of New Orleans)" overlooks the earliest club to conduct a sailing regatta, the Detroit Boat Club.[8]

In the early days members often raced on the Cape Fear River where the port and town of Wilmington is located – a favorite stopping place on the Inland Waterway route from Norfolk to Key West. An article in the July 21, 1852 edition of the *Wilmington Herald*, *'A Racy Affair'* describes the complexities of racing in those waters:

> *... attempted to navigate the small channels and outlets of that uncertain body of water which forms communication between the Sounds in question, who knew the rapid departure of the current, and the agreeable and inevitable duty of propelling boats by dragging them along the prominent rifts of sand or oyster beds on the eve of the emergence, with a July sun blazing upon the face of the navigator from the shining water ebbing noiselessly away, and an occasional inroad by those energetic and blood-sucking occupiers of the marshes, 'sandflies'...*

The type of boats being raced before the Civil War is described in an 1854 edition of the *Herald*:

> *... it was whispered that Mr. Bradley would soon have something to 'clean up' the Sound waters. This rumor proved true. Mr. Joseph Flanner bought the new boat and presented it to Mr. Bradley. Though but 18½ feet long she cost $700. She was built in New York by Bob Fish[9] ... in everything she differed widely from all other boats of her day, having the then unusual beam of 7½ feet – the greatest width being near her stern. She bore resemblance to a great smoothing iron. Moreover, she had a bowsprit hanging 12 feet over the cut-water. Such form and rig created much comment, and as she had beaten every boat of reputation in and about New York, she was severely criticized by the knowing ones on account of the very sharp, lean bow and that it was so ugly, for they were destined to see that part of her in every contest. She was called the Princess and was never beaten.*

The War Between the States, the Spanish-American War, the two World Wars and the frequency of equinoctial gales and hurricanes caused repeated lulls in yacht racing and often severe damage to boats and facilities. Nonetheless, "The end of the nineteenth century saw a greater participation in yachting by the wives and daughters of members," and in 1899 prizes were put up for The Ladies' Race on July 21.

Yachts were customarily handicapped according to length, but in 1910 T. P. Hammer introduced the 'flying start'[10] and handicaps were based on the combination of LWL and square root of sail area.

In 1913 a fleet of nine New York Fifties, designed and built by Nathanial[11] Herreshoff for $17,000 with sails, was introduced. They had a crew of captain, two sailors and a steward. An indication that members traveled extensively to compete was the awarding by the New York Yacht Club of its Astor Cup in 1884 to Commodore Pembroke Jones for a race off Newport, RI.

In 1920 a dozen Class 'A' catboats built to the same specifications:

> *Were purchased by individual members who wished seamanship to be the deciding factor in races... During the 1920's folks rode the trolley to the Yacht Club disembarking at Station Four with their beach bags and picnic baskets to stroll the covered walkway from the streetcar to the CYC front porch. In the 1930's Moths, Snipes and National One-Designs joined the Class 'A' through Class 'D' boats in the South Atlantic Yacht Racing Association regattas... SAYRA included Carolina Yacht Club of Charleston, the Charleston, the Mount Pleasant, the Sea Island , the Beaufort and the Savannah Yacht Clubs.*

An indication that Inland Lake Scows had proliferated in the SAYRA was the purchase by William Emerson of the *Mischief* in Savannah. Note that Class 'A' and 'E' Scows raced on Lake Murray outside of Columbia after WW II; the 'A's were usually trailed to Wisconsin for summer competition.[12]

World War II severely curtailed racing leaving only teenagers competing in Moths. It brought the war close to home as periscopes of enemy submarines could be seen from the beach, and members participated in armed horse patrols.

> *"The Great Storm of 1954 was more furious in its wrath than its predecessor, the Great Storm of 1899, requiring the Club to be rebuilt a second time."*

In the 1960's a full-time sailing instructor was added along with Windmills and Optimist Prams. Also the Y-Flyer Class was begun. In 1966 the Carolina Yacht Club sponsored the initial ocean race for cruising boats, and "in 1976 members of the Carolina Yacht Club bought the first six Solings sold in the United States." These were raced on Olympic courses laid in the ocean.

In 1972 the Club held the Fireball World Championships; Commodore of the Class was Herb McKim. The event was repeated in 1992 with entries coming from as far away as Australia, Japan and South Africa. As a sign that more and more women were competing, Charlotte Sprunt Murchison became the first woman to serve on the Board of Governors.

THE CHICAGO YACHT CLUB[13]

Lake sailing was beginning to develop in Chicago after the Civil War, and there is a record of the first yacht race for a prize having been held in 1871. The Great Chicago Fire later that year, however, set back all sports activity and recreation severely for several years. By 1875 sailing had picked up again, and the Chicago Yacht Club was formed late that summer. It chose as its first Commodore John Prindiville, a retired captain of cargo vessels, both sail and steam, who had arrived in Chicago in 1833 from Ireland as a child. Many members were also members of the Board of Trade, by which the sailing vessels that carried grain were chartered, so there was a close association of yachtsmen and commercial sail.

The first activity was a match series the following summer between the Commodore's yacht and one from Toronto. The ante for the match was $1,000 for each. Out of the second race came a protest concerning proper finishing procedure, "an old argument that arose many times before the present rule was adopted." Since the protest decision refers to the "winning stake-boat" and "rounding" it, we could guess that there was only one finishing mark, and that the "present" rule was to have two finishing marks between which yachts passed to finish. In any event, the Toronto yacht was disqualified and later sued under the 'Gambling Act' to recover the $1,000.

Somehow, according to the story, the matter was referred on appeal to the New York Yacht Club, which ruled in his favor. This is the first recorded instance of the NYYC serving as an appeals body for an outside club. Then, and for many years thereafter, any appeal within the club was heard and decided by the full membership at the annual meeting.

In 1883 the club made a cruise to Milwaukee (about 90 miles). The next year, after a recommendation that the club use the New York Yacht Club's measurement rule was turned down, the club ended up with two rules so incompatible that they would certainly produce different numbers. Apparently neither of the two camps would give in.

In 1896 the Yacht Racing Union of the Great Lakes was created by a group of clubs, including the CYC. Three years later, after creating a common measurement rule for all the member clubs, it appointed a measurer to measure all yachts in the Union. The handicapping, it turned out, was to be applied by starting all yachts separately, according to their handicaps.

> *It was an unwieldy system and difficult to keep the records accurately; so, in an era of large wagers and strong tempers, the result was often chaotic, and questionable gentlemanly conduct ensued.*

Meanwhile, the club was having membership difficulties, and it went as far as applying to the Chicago Athletic Club to be taken in as its "yachting branch." That fell through, but the crisis was soon over, and by 1898 the CYC was determined to build a new clubhouse. A problem arose with the City of Chicago over a small piece of city-owned land at the foot of Monroe Street. When that was cleared up, construction proceeded, and the new clubhouse was opened in 1902. It was an imposing, two-story structure with wrap-around porches on both levels.

In 1896 neighboring Columbia Yacht Club sponsored a race to Michigan City which became a fixture. Two years later the first Mackinac Race was held in which five yachts – two sloops and three schooners – competed without handicap. (Notably, this was eight years before the Bermuda Race on the East Coast and the Transpac on the West Coast.) By then interest seemed to have turned toward distance racing and away from racing around the buoys. In 1902 the Columbia Yacht Club began a race up the coast to Waukegan, and the CYC instituted a similar one to Kenosha.

It was also in 1896 when the Lincoln Park Yacht Club (later to be merged with the CYC) challenged the Royal Canadian Yacht Club to a series of races for a cup. The challenge was met by Æmelius Jarvis, probably the best known sailor of Canada and one of the main movers in founding NAYRU the next year. He sailed a yacht named *Canada*, and the match was sailed in "neutral" waters off Toledo. *Canada* won, whereupon Jarvis deeded his cup to the Yacht Racing Union of the Great Lakes for competition within the Union. Since called the 'Canada's Cup,' it is still sailed for, although for years it was primarily a Lake Ontario event.

In 1905 there were two races to Mackinac, a small island atop the Lower Michigan Peninsula where Lakes Michigan and Huron meet. Mackinac lies some 300 miles almost straight up Lake Michigan from Chicago, and that was the first race. The second was from Port Huron to Mackinac, and it was sponsored by the Detroit Country Club "under the auspices of the Chicago Yacht Club, and in conjunction with the Chicago-Mackinac Race."

The other big feature of that 1905 races to Mackinac was the yacht *Lady Eileen*. She was sailed by Miss Evelyn Wright, a flag officer of the CYC, and her all-female crew! Can any club anywhere top that, only four years after the death of Queen Victoria? This was not a one-time caper; she sailed it again three years later. Also, in 1912 and 1913 a combined Chicago/Columbia crew raced a women's crew from the Royal Canadian Yacht Club of Toronto. Word of women's sailing from then through the 1930's was sporadic.

The year 1908 marked the 13th running of the Columbia Yacht Club's race to Michigan City. Heretofore open only to Columbia members, this year it was open to all and drew more than 100 entries. It was also the year in which the Lake Michigan Yachting Association banned the use of professionals in any race under its jurisdiction, and the Mackinac Race was sailed solely by amateurs, presumably for the first time.

In 1910 the Lake Michigan Yachting Association adopted the Universal Rule, and all the yachts entering the Mackinac Race the next year were rated under it. The race was won by *Amorita* in 31:14:30, a course record which stood until 1987 when ten boats bettered it; *Pied Piper*, a 68-foot ultralight sloop set a new elapsed record of 25:50:44, which has not yet been beaten. The Mackinac was cancelled in 1917 due to WW I and did not resume until 1921. In 1924 an 'R' boat, *Sari*, was the smallest among the entries. She not only won on handicap time but won boat for boat, an amazing feat in a long race in which many of the yachts were twice her size.

In 1920 the CYC merged with the Lincoln Park Yacht Club at Belmont Harbor (it is not really a harbor but one of several anchorages foresightedly built by the city along the lakeshore after WW I). One of the congratulatory messages received was a wireless from explorer Donald MacMillan, a member of the club, transmitting from the schooner *Bowdoin* at Lat. 70.30 North and Long. 72.30 West. That would have put him in the very upper reaches of Baffin Bay. Three years later the Club built a specially designed steel scow, 150 feet by 50 feet, with two decks, for its floating clubhouse which has ever since been moored in Belmont Harbor on Chicago's North Side.

As for one-designs and restricted classes (boats built to the Universal Rule), the first one-design was a small knockabout called the Pup. Four were built in 1901, and they were club-owned. The method for their use is interesting. When members wished to race them, their names would be put into a hat. The first name drawn would be the skipper of Pup No. 1; the second and third would be his crew; and so on until the four boats were filled. After each race the three crews in each boat would receive the same points according to their finishing position. These points would accumulate during the season and thus determine the year's class champion. This is an early instance of giving recognition to crew members, those who pull the strings, serve as lookouts, and do the dog work. A person could, for example, be skipper in three races, crew in six, and become the club champion – a novel concept not practiced currently.

In 1902 came the 15-foot class; in 1912 a boat designed by B.B. Crowinshield, 20 feet 4 inches overall, came into being, and the fleet lasted until WW II. The first 'R' arrived at the club from the east coast in 1914, and the fleet became the dominant class during the 1920's. In 1922 the Great Lakes Challenge Cup, originated for the 'P' class and now known as the Richardson Cup, was transferred to the 'R' class. In 1930 it was reported that, while Eastern Yacht Club sailors had begun to leave the 'R' for the 30 and 40 Square Metres (Swedish designed), the R's were still going strong on Lake Michigan. While the 'R's reached a high level of popularity on both coasts and on the Great Lakes, nowhere were they as popular, nor did they last as long, as at Chicago.

Stars arrived on Lake Michigan in the early 1920's, not at CYC but north of Chicago in Wilmette. Next was the Eagle Class locally designed to the 'S' classification of the Universal Rule. It appears to be the only other boat designed to that classification level, aside from N.G. Herreshoff's one-design of 1919 which he called simply the 'S' boat. The fate of the Eagle Class is not given, but the 'S' boats are still proudly sailing.

In 1933 a temper-testing incident arose that fairly illustrates the problems often created by measurement rules. The CYC had again changed its rules:

> *It was very confusing and, when you consider that, in 1933, the [new] Lake Michigan Yachting Association rule was used by the Jackson Park and Columbia Yacht Clubs in their races, the NYYC rule was used for all other Mackinac Race, and the [new] CYC rule was used for all other CYC-sponsored cruising [offshore] races, one can appreciate the chaos of figuring out the finishes after each race.*
>
> *The owners fumed over the situation, too, as every time the rules were revised (annually), they had to have their yachts re-measured in order to qualify to race. Finally, in 1935, except where specifically announced, it was decided that the LMYA measurement and racing rules were to govern all CYC races. With the other major clubs already being governed by these rules, the problem was virtually eliminated.*

– at least temporarily. Note that the Race Committee reserved the right to change the rules whenever it wished and also the reference to racing rules. The re-incarnated NAYRU was now seven years old. Did the LMYA still not conform entirely to its rules. Apparently it did not. It would appear that the district associations of this part of North America – the Inland Lake Yachting Association, the Lake Michigan Yachting Association, and the Inter-Lake Yachting Association – took stronger hold and exercised more leadership than their sister associations elsewhere. It seemed that they could bang heads together and get away with it.

THE CRUISING CLUB OF AMERICA[14]

The Cruising Club of America was launched in the winter of 1921-22 by a group of yachtsmen interested in cruising and the development of the cruising type of yacht. It was felt that this branch of the sport never had attained the position it deserves in a country so rich in sea-going tradition and whose natural advantages are so peculiarly favorable to cruising, possibly because of the fact that there never had been any concerted action by cruising enthusiasts.

The yacht clubs of the country had made racing a large part of their activities and there were several inter-club associations devoted to the advancement of this branch of yachting, but there never had been in this country an organization comparable, for example, to the Royal Cruising Club, which, in the 40 years preceding the formation of our Cruising Club had done so much toward making cruising a national institution in Great Britain.

Two yachts from Baddeck, Cape Breton (Nova Scotia) played a role in the founding of the Cruising Club of America – *Elsie*[15] built in 1917 by Dr. Alexander Graham Bell at his Beinn Breagh (Gaelic for 'beautiful mountain') laboratory as a gift to his son-in-law, Gilbert H. Grosvenor, and the *Typhoon* built in 1920 at the laboratory for William Washburn Nutting, our first Commodore.

In 1919 aboard the *Elsie* on a cruise to Boulaceet Harbor (currently known as Maskell's Harbour) Nutting. F. W. (Casey) Baldwin and Grosvenor discussed the concept of forming a cruising club. The next year Nutting, Baldwin and Jim Dorsett sailed *Typhoon* to England where they were welcomed by officers of the Royal Cruising Club and became even more enthusiastic over forming a similar organization in America.

On returning home Nutting, using the Royal Cruising Club as a prototype, persuaded a group of yachtsmen to launch the Cruising Club of America. Shortly thereafter, Henry A. Wise Wood, a charter member, was requested to formulate ideas on the objectives and scope of the activities of our Club. The following are excerpts from his report:

> *We have chosen the title, Cruising Club of America. In choosing this title did we mean to imply that we are the Cruising Club of the United States? or of the United States and Canada? or of all the America's?*
>
> *... As those to the north of us are our intimate friends, of our own sealoving stock, it would seem to be too narrow a view of our field did we rate ourselves only a national organization. As we are an offshore club, composed of blue-water men whose playground lies well beyond the Volstead line,[16] I suggest that we use in our title the word America, in its geographical and not its political sense. To do this should result in drawing into close relationship all the deep-water amateur sailormen of our hemisphere. This, I assume, is what we wish to do...[17]*
>
> *... Let us refuse stoutly to accumulate an on-shore contingent; let membership in the Club be a mark of achievement. This policy will give us a standing at home and abroad such as no American yacht club ever has had... Thus we shall become an active force influencing others to make adventurous use of the sea.*

The Club is best known worldwide for its staging of the Bermuda Race and the Onion Patch Trophy – an international team race series, including the Race itself, similar to the Fastnet Race cum Admiral's Cup series and the Sydney-Hobart Race cum Southern Cross series.

In 1923, with no Bermuda Race having been held since its fifth in 1910, there was interest in reviving it. *Yachting* magazine rounded up five volunteers, including its editor, Herbert L. Stone,[18] who agreed to form a committee that would create an organization without the help of any yacht clubs. The Royal Bermuda Yacht Club agreed to handle the finish, but everything else was dealt with by the committee. The next year the New Rochelle Yacht Club (Long Island Sound) offered its Race Committee to start the race at New London, while the RBYC handled the entries, communications and other administrative details.

Before the 1926 race the Cruising Club of America had become active and was asked to take over the Race. Since this was coincident with its mission of promoting offshore passages, it promptly agreed. Subsequently it sponsored several transatlantic races, e.g. one from Newport to Plymouth, England in 1931, from Newport to Norway in 1935 and from Bermuda to Spain in 1972.

The role of the CCA and its rating rule are related in *Chapter IX – Ratings Rules, Time Allowances and Classification of Yachts.* The above credo did not anticipate that the club would eventually develop and administer, what for several decades served as the foremost measurement and rating rule for offshore racing yachts in North America, its CCA Rule; especially since its own focus has been on organizing cruising events on the continent and some far-flung parts of the globe.

DUXBURY YACHT CLUB[19]

The town of Duxbury, about 35 miles south of Boston, is one of the most charming villages in New England, with a main street lined with handsome homes, many of which date from the 1700's. Its yacht club sits on the edge of a shallow bay that Duxbury shares with the towns of Kingston and Plymouth to the south. The Club's history says that it was "inspired" in 1874 and formed in 1875. The original record book, long lost but discovered in 1994, indicates that the inspiration was three races held by the townspeople in 1874. That was great fun; let's form a club!

It is described as an unpretentious, family-oriented club. It is indeed unpretentious; its present clubhouse, built at about the turn of this century, consists mainly of one large room with a stage at one end and a narrow porch out front. And there is a ramp leading to a small float. No dining room, no bar, no locker rooms, no parking area – none of the amenities that most clubs would think absolutely necessary. The members of Larchmont, Grosse Pointe, Southern, and St. Francis would wonder at the Spartan facilities.

The bay at the Duxbury end is so shallow that even dinghy races have to be scheduled according to the tides. Out in front of the club and the adjacent town pier there is a dredged anchorage area that cannot be more than one hundred yards square. This writer recalls having fetched the basin one day during the low of a spring tide. Aside from the basin itself, the only water left in the bay was a long, narrow, meandering channel, and the mussel beds were at chest level when standing in the cockpit of a Malabar Junior.

The Duxbury Yacht Club was, and is, unusual in other ways, too. In 1900 it laid out a golf course so that, if one wanted to play golf in Duxbury, he belonged to the yacht club; same with tennis, since 1927. It was common in so-called 'resort towns' in Maine, Cape Cod, 'The Islands' and elsewhere for clubs to have family memberships vis-à-vis more cosmopolitan clubs such as Eastern and the Boston. Thus the by-laws of the Duxbury Yacht Club, almost from the beginning; stated:

> *A family membership shall consist of a husband and wife with the unmarried sons and daughters residing with them.*

Early on in 1905 Duxbury had its own club one-design, the DYC 15-foot Class of which 15 were built. Later it became the DYC 18-foot Class. Length was expressed as waterline length, LWL. In 1920 as a service to his club, the famed John Alden designed a junior boat called the Duxbury Duck. More than 90 were built, and by 1928 there were 45 or more of them at the club. They lasted well beyond the end of WW II.

In the history is a discussion of the first lawn (grass) tennis court built in the United States, commonly thought to have been either on Staten Island or in Newport, RI. In 1927, however, William Appleton Lawrence, retired Episcopal Bishop of Massachusetts, wrote his memoirs. In them he presented persuasive evidence (his own first-hand knowledge) that the first grass court had indeed been built in 1874 in Nahant, one of Boston's early summer resorts, although the dimensions of courts varied widely and were not standardized until the national lawn tennis association was formed. The inventor of tennis, Major Wingfield, was an Englishman who had patented the game six years before.

By 1913 there was ladies racing one day a week. By 1919 there was a junior sailing program, and Duxbury lads won the Sears Cup three times in its first six years – 1923, 1925, and 1926. In the first two of those events, the Duxbury helmsman was C. Raymond Hunt, who later went on to display his genius at boat design (Bertrams, Boston Whalers, the 110 and the 210, the Concordia yawl, etc.). During those early years, boys were required to wear caps, shirts, neckties, and jackets while sailing! That really was not so odd, come to think of it; their fathers all dressed that way for sailing – witness a film taken aboard the schooner *Mistress* in the 1930 Trans-Atlantic Race depicting C. Sherman Hoyt wearing a business suit and fedora. The junior program also included girls, which was most rare during the 1920's; they, of course, wore dresses. Out of the program came young women who competed every year for the Adams Cup and were runners up seven times in the first two decades of that competition, which began in 1925, until finally winning it in 1971.

Finally, if ever visiting Duxbury, take care not to set the natives' teeth on edge; it is pronounced 'dux-bree', not 'ducks-berry'.

EDGARTOWN YACHT CLUB

SAILORS' RIOTOUS NIGHT ASHORE OR THE FOUNDING OF THE EDGARTOWN YACHT CLUB[20]

"As in many other New England ports, yachting at Edgartown [Martha's Vineyard, MA] was inspired by a few retired mariners who, finding sojourning ashore somewhat insipid, turned back to the sea for a pastime, rather than a livelihood, and took the youngsters with them.

"So we must regard Captain Jared Fisher, with his *Ripple*, the first island-owned craft maintained solely for pleasure, and his old whaling rival and crony, Captain Oliver Norton, with his *Minnie*, as the founders of the sport inside Chappaquiddick in the early 1880's. Twenty-five years later, one of the boys whom these old sea dogs trained off Cape Poge, Jared Bliss, a grandson of Captain Fisher, came back home to help organize, the Edgartown Yacht Club, from the leadership of which he has just retired after many years of service, although not until he had hauled the club out of the doldrums, quadrupled the membership, and built a clubhouse for its fleet of more than 70 sailboats.

"Yet, tall yachts with fluttering pennants, brass cannon, and uniformed tars were not uncommon at Edgartown even in the earlier days of the sport in New England, and on the bridge deck of the new clubhouse are a dozen settees from the vestry of the Baptist church, which are cherished as souvenirs of the visit of the New York Yacht Club fleet in its cruise of 1858. Driven out of Holmes Hole, now Vineyard Haven, by a stiff nor'easter, the yachts found a snug anchorage in the old whaling port, and that Saturday night the yachtsmen, with their band, went ashore, hired the town hall, and gave a dance. When the Edgartown girls learned that the Selectmen had charged two dollars for the hall, double the usual price, they sought to make amends by inviting their yachting friends to a "Sing" in the vestry the next night. And there, under the glimmering beams of sperm oil lamps, the [members of the cruising fleet] and the rest held hymn books and sang "Coronation" and other tunes with the fairest of Edgartown's daughters.

"Thousands of yachts have rounded the little harbor light that first shot forth its beams a little more than a century ago since that early yachting call, and each year visitors have found in the harbor an increasing number of pleasure craft. High water mark for racing boats was reached last August when 143 yachts from half a score of clubs in southeastern Massachusetts started in Edgartown's fifth annual regatta, which proved the incentive for the formation of a new yacht racing association [the Southern Massachusetts Yacht Racing Association], which is now a member of the North American Yacht Racing Union.

"In addition to pointing with pride to the Vineyard Haven Interclub Class, which now numbers 20 boats at Edgartown, Vineyard Haven, and Nantucket [some still exist], yachtsmen in the whaling port enjoy breezes that blow from the southwest almost with trade-wind regularity, while racing facilities are such that, when conditions are too strong in Nantucket Sound, there is landlocked Katama Bay in which to race."

SAILING AND CLUBS IN HAWAII[21]

Racing in Hawaii during the 1850's and 1860's was informal and conducted by trading vessels and vessels that moved cargo and passengers between the islands. These were schooners in the range of 70 to 85 feet. Prizes were occasionally as high as $1,000. The first account of such a race appearing in the *Pacific Commercial Advertiser* is dated April 20, 1846 and involved two schooners

The Honolulu Yacht Club was founded in 1869. The first race of that year was between two flat-bottomed, center-board sloops, the *Cara Belle* and the *Dauntless*, both 24-feet LOA, 7-feet beam. The start was between the bow and stern of a schooner *Active* lying at Market Wharf and positions drawn for by lot. The course was triangular, seven-to-eight miles in length, which was covered in one hour and 16 minutes. It was not close; *Cara Belle* won by six minutes.

In the second race, held three months later, the two were joined by a third yacht, winner undetermined. There is no record of any racing in 1870. In 1871 there were two races, one conducted by the Honolulu Yacht Club in which six yachts competed for a silver cup valued at $25. One of the six was from the deck of a visiting British ship. The second race is known because it was advertised in the Honolulu newspaper. It was described as the "Mechanics Regatta" to be held on his Majesty's birthday. It was open to all with a time allowance of 30 seconds per ton, sails to be used to be declared before the start.

The Honolulu Yacht Club did not survive, but how long it existed is not known. In 1885 two clubs were founded, the Hawaii Rowing and Yachting Association with King Kalakaua as its President, and the Honolulu Yachting and Boating Club with Governor Dominis as its first Commodore. Neither organization survived, and the latter lasted only five years. In 1901 the Hawaii Yacht Club was organized and located itself at Pearl Harbor. It advertised for members "of a minimum age of 16, with good moral character and an interest in yachts." In 1924 two other clubs began life, the Pearl Harbor Yacht Club and the Kaneohe Yacht Club. The former was disbanded during WW II, but the latter is still going and is the oldest continuously operating yacht club in Hawaii.

Extant is the first, and apparently only, page of the sailing instructions for the first race of the new Hawaii Yacht Club in 1901. The winner in each of the four classes was to receive a club pennant. In describing the course there was something unique: one of the turning marks would be an anchored stake boat with a flag. All yachts were to keep twenty-five feet from it while rounding – a condition set by the nervous gentleman who agreed to undertake that perilous duty? At the bottom of the page was:

> *At 6 o'clock, a luau will be served to the yachtsmen and their guests, after which the Entertainment Committee will give the boys a feast of music and wit.*

Where the luau was to be served was not divulged, but it was not the clubhouse, for there was as yet none. An accompanying article and picture from the *Pacific Commercial Advertiser* of May 1903 tells of a clubhouse about to be constructed. It was to be two stories with a porch ('lanai' in Hawaiian) on each level, "with such accommodations as will guarantee the peace and security of yachtsmen and their clothing and supplies." On the lower level there were to be a kitchen and dining room, lockers, showers, and dressing rooms.

> *Above stairs will be one great club room, mosquito proof, and so arranged that it will be available for the placing of cots for the accommodation of those who may wish to spend the night.*

Total size: 26 x 50 x 2 feet. Total cost, less furniture and dock facilities: $1,300.

Clippings from a Honolulu newspaper ca. 1937[22] tell of races in that city sailed by "three little flat bottom, centerboard, sloop-rigged boats" under the auspices of the Honolulu Yacht Club in 1869 for a prize of $100. Two years later the fleet had been augmented by two similar boats, one newly built and the other an import from Plymouth, MA, brought on the deck of a ship and sold at Honolulu. For the annual regatta of 1871 they were joined by a sixth, an entry from a British vessel in port. In 1874 King Kalakaua, a sailing enthusiast, became ruler of Hawaii, but the next mention of racing was not until a regatta held to celebrate his birthday in 1881.

In 1885 the Hawaiian Rowing and Yachting Association was formed, with King Kalakaua as its first president. It was still in existence (as of 1937), and the fleet of 'S' boats at Pearl Harbor were still racing for one of its trophies. The club's most impressive trophy, however, was a huge, binnacle-shaped object officially called the HR & Y Challenge trophy. It was first raced for in 1889 and, to his delight, the King won it. He promptly filled it with champagne and passed it around as a loving cup. That started a tradition for what promptly became known as the Kalakaua Cup, of the winner filling it with champagne. It was raced for by the Star Class until its demise and currently by offshore yachts in a three-day series held over the Fourth of July.

After the King died the fervor for sailing somehow declined precipitously so that by 1903 there was very little of the sport seen in the Islands.

The first one-design in Hawaii may have been the Sparrow Class. It came from England via Singapore in 1914. It was a 15-foot, gaff-rigged, centerboard sloop. A Honolulu resident had seen a fleet of them racing at Singapore and brought the plans for the boat home with him. The following year he and some friends had seven of them built. Since Honolulu Harbor was crowded with commercial traffic, they obtained permission of the Navy to sail them in Pearl Harbor. Their activity and yachting in general was curtailed by WW I and did not recover until 1924, when another group of sailors engaged prolific designer Charles D. Mower, apparently semi-retired from Boston to Honolulu, to design a slightly larger sloop of 18 feet LWL. Seven of those were built, and their owners formed the Pearl Harbor Yacht Club.

The role of Hawaiian Clubs in conducting the Transpacific Race and after WW II becoming the Mecca for one of the world's most popular offshore racing series, the Kenwood Cup – Hawaii International Ocean Racing Series – appears elsewhere in this *History*. Although the first NAYRU Constitution in its listing of the original Member Associations included among "other" "...and Hawaiian Islands Districts," and there had been several attempts to form an Hawaii Yachting Racing Association, the YRA was not officially established until 1966. The first Commodore was Cy Gillette who later in 1985 became the first Commodore of the Royal Hawaiian Ocean Racing Club.

LAKE GENEVA YACHT CLUB[23]

Lake Geneva lies about 40 miles northwest of Chicago just over the Wisconsin line. It is about nine miles long and a mile wide with the town of Lake Geneva at its eastern end. The lake became a summer resort for wealthy Chicagoans when a railroad that ran through the town was built, and, for some, their summer homes were their only homes for a year or two after the Chicago fire of 1871.

Some clubs in publishing their centennial histories have fudged the beginning date a wee bit. A group of people meet in December to consider their mutual interests in establishing a yacht club. The next summer they hold a semi-formal regatta, perhaps only a single race, and meet again before Labor Day to approve a constitution and by-laws that a committee has drawn up and decide about dues for next year. But the founding date is always cited as December of the previous year. The Lake Geneva Yacht Club may hold the record for back-dating.

During the summer of 1874 three sailing races were held on Lake Geneva. The first was to celebrate the Fourth of July and included seven boats. The second, in mid-August, was to celebrate the arrival on the lake of a new boat built in New Haven and designed after the very fast Connecticut Sharpie used by the oystermen on Long Island Sound. She was 33 feet LOA, 26 feet LWL and rigged as a cat-ketch. The third was to celebrate the arrival of Civil War hero General Philip Sheridan who was coming to visit a friend. Hastily a race to honor him was arranged for the last day of August, and $100 was subscribed for purchasing a trophy to be called the Sheridan Prize.

The Sheridan Prize, 1874, Lake Geneva Yacht Club, an example of a sandbagger
Photo courtesy of Lake Geneva Yacht Club

The race was held, but the winner did not receive the prize: it had not yet been made. It was crafted later that winter by a Chicago silversmith as a beautiful model of one of the sloops on the lake named *Nettie*. It was available for the 1875 race, but General Sheridan was unfortunately not able to be there to present it. The year 1876 would be the country's centennial, and big plans were afoot, as they were in all sailing centers, to celebrate it with a major Fourth of July regatta of two classes – one for boats that "belonged on the lake" and one for "residents of the lake." The distinction was apparently to keep the summer people, with their deeper pockets, out of the latter class.

One part of the planning was to establish a yacht club, and that was done in April of 1876. After the custom of the day, once the business of a constitution and by-laws was completed, 18 yachts were enrolled in the club, and then their owners were admitted as members. Nonetheless, the Lake Geneva Yacht Club dates itself from 1874, the year in which the Sheridan Prize, although not yet cast, was put in competition. In short, for two years the Sheridan Prize, first as an idea and then as a silver trophy, was the diadem in the crown of the Lake Geneva Yacht Club.

By the Fourth of July about 40 more people who were not boat owners were admitted. The town's and the club's celebration was rather dampened by the news, three days earlier, of the disaster at Little Big Horn. (General Sheridan was commander of the Department of the Missouri, and Colonel Custer was under his command.) The day also brought very light winds, and the course for the races took five hours to sail. As a result, the sailors missed the parade and the chase for the greased pig, but they were in time for the evening's fireworks.

During the rest of the summer scrub races were held each Saturday. On the 31st of August, the race for the Sheridan Prize was sponsored by the new yacht club, replacing the local hotel, whose owner, now the club secretary, had sponsored it the first two years. The winner was *Nettie*, and her owner, another Civil War general, had her replica presented to him by General Sheridan.

For the rest of the decade and during the 1880's the level of racing was about the same: Fourth of July, Saturday races, and the Sheridan Prize on the last day of August (unless it was a Sunday). In 1886 a new trophy appeared that illustrated the dichotomy in attitude of many American clubs about professional vs. amateur sailors. For example, the Boston and Seawanhaka Yacht Clubs were founded on the principle of amateurism, struggled to remain so and were successful. New York and Eastern Yacht Clubs, on the other hand, had such large yachts that they could not compete without professionals, including helmsmen, and this mode lasted well into this century. Lake Geneva's new trophy specified that helmsmen had to be the owners, and those tending sheets had to be amateurs. That probably reflected the fact that the club had begun using sandbaggers, boats popular on Long Island Sound and Narragansett Bay. Three men could tend the helm and the sheets, but up to seven more were necessary to keep sandbaggers on their feet, such was the enormous spread of canvas they carried.

Three other aspects of nineteenth century yacht racing that can be seen in Lake Geneva's history were cash prizes (along with trophies), side-betting among owners and betting by the public. All three customs were common in Great Britain and had migrated to North America. Cash prizes, of little interest to wealthy owners, were usually distributed to the paid crews. As for the general public, until yacht racing began to develop rapidly after the Civil War, it had only horse racing and prize fights on which to bet. Yacht racing added a third avenue.

Cape Cod catboats soon joined the sandbaggers on the lake, and the latter were adapted so they could be rigged either as sloops or catboats. The earliest of the catboats were built in New England or New York, but a builder on the lake began building them for local purchasers, and it was not long before the catboats crowded the sandbaggers out. In 1892 an interesting thing happened. Three of the fastest sloops on the lake were built by a man named Cornwall of Port Washington, NY. They had serially won the Sheridan three years in a row, so a club member ordered a fourth. He expected essentially a copy of the first three, but when it arrived, he and everyone else were astonished. The first three, all five years old or more, had plumb stems and sternposts. The new one, however, had pronounced overhangs fore and aft with a spoon bow. What had happened in the interim was the appearance of *Gloriana*, designed by N.G. Herreshoff to the Seawanhaka Rule. She had revolutionized American yacht design almost overnight.

By 1895 ten of the 44 yachts in the fleet resembled *Gloriana* to some degree, and it was causing a problem. The club's sole measurement for handicapping was "sailing length" or waterline. The boats with plumb stems and sterns could be measured once and that was it: the waterline remained the same regardless of how many crew or how much ballast they carried; not so with the boats with overhangs. Their waterlines increased according to the weight aboard, and a footnote many times longer than the rule itself had to be added. It meant that such yachts had to be measured after each race, with all crew and ballast still aboard. LWL is a difficult measurement to make and having to do it after each race was a pain in the neck.

Lake Geneva seems to have lagged, at least in contrast with eastern clubs, in getting rid of another pain - one in the back from shifting ballast. With sandbaggers in decline on the lake, however, a new class was created in 1896 called the 18-foot fixed-ballast class. Any boat whose waterline qualified her could join simply by stowing her sandbags under the floorboards and leaving them there, but the crews of the other classes could continue shifting ballast until their backs gave out. The club also abandoned the outmoded method of allowing yachts five minutes to start and taking their times as they started. Now the starting time for all was the starting gun. Also, the club finally adopted the Seawanhaka Rule, which then had only seven more years to live.

When the North American Yacht Racing Union was initially founded in 1897, the prime movers were five regional associations, the Yacht Racing Association of Massachusetts, the Yacht Racing Union of Long Island Sound, the Lake Yacht Racing Association, the Pacific Inter-Club Yachting Association and the Inter-Lake Yachting Association. The usefulness of such organizations was the first lesson learned by delegates from other regions, and several more district associations were formed in the three or four years following. The first of these was the Inland Lake Yachting Association formed the very next year. The prime movers in that venture were three men respectively from the Great Bear Yacht

Club in Minnesota, the Oshkosh Yacht Club and the Lake Geneva Yacht Club. They arranged for a meeting in Milwaukee to which representatives of 18 clubs were drawn from four states – Minnesota, Wisconsin, Illinois, and Indiana. Thus was the ILYA born.

The first task to which the ILYA addressed itself was the abolition of handicaps. To do so it established two official classes – the 20 and 17-foot (LWL) Scow classes under the Seawanhaka Rule It also forbade deadweight ballast, limited crew weight and established a reasonable and rational maximum sail area. This was not 'simon pure' one-design racing in today's sense, but it was the first class racing in the region conducted without handicaps. The Scows were boats of unusual shape: square bow, square stern, flat deck, long overhangs, and very shoal draft to suit the many shallow lakes of which Geneva was an exception. Scows, derided by many as "floating platforms" and "sidewalk boats," fitted that region, by reason of their shoal draft.

Within three years the ILYA made two changes. The first was to abandon LWL for LOA, one reason being that minor changes in trim dramatically affected LWL to the bane of the measurers. The other was to specify minimum scantlings, so that the scows would not break up after two or three races in a good breeze, as some were already doing. While intelligent and progressive, these actions almost brought disaster to Lake Geneva. The members had thought they were sending their representative to Milwaukee to help promote interlake competition. Instead, they found most of their best little yachts made instantly obsolete by the direction taken toward scows by the new ILYA. That was the second blow the club had sustained in two years. The first had been the establishment of the Lake Geneva Country Club, one of the earliest golf clubs in the midwest and an instant success. Within a year most of the members of the LGYC had become members of the LGCC, and it was off to the links they went. Many of the club's boats sat at their moorings most of the summer. Said the author of *LGYC 100th Year*, "Never again was yacht racing quite the same."

Lake Geneva was offered the opportunity to host the third Inland Lake Yachting Association regatta in 1900 and grabbed it. Town and club together raised $4,000 to cover the expense involved, which included providing tents with wood floors and electric lights in the town's Library Park for visiting competitors. The event chairman also wangled free transportation for boats from the Chicago & Northwestern Railway and half fares for their crews. The regatta, as it was to be for almost two decades, was limited to one boat per club in each of the two classes. It was a success and gave a much needed shot in the arm to the club's fortunes.

Until 1902 the members had not given much thought to the idea of having a clubhouse, probably because most of the members' homes were on the shorefront at the east end of the lake. In that year, however, the LGYC merged with the West End Yacht Club formed only seven years earlier. This meant that the club now had members at both ends of the lake and some in the middle. A clubhouse became a useful idea. Eventually, a plot of land was leased, and a simple building was erected and open for business in 1906.

By this time the club's boats consisted mainly of scows in the two classes mandated by the ILYA and a form of catboat that was close to, but not quite, a one-design: 24 feet LOA, minimum beam of seven feet, minimum freeboard of 14 inches – and a pointed bow. The scows had evolved to the point of having twin rudders and twin bilge boards. The club had come to accept the scows fully; its problem with the ILYA was with the policy of one boat per club per class and a decision to hold all regattas at Oshkosh. So the Lake Geneva Yacht Club and seven of its closest neighbors, without defecting, set up a subsidiary association to race the ILYA 'A' and 'B' scows and a new class of scows 18 feet in length. Its first regatta on Lake Geneva in 1906 drew over 50 boats, by far the largest event ever on the lake. It was not meant to compete with the ILYA, but it effectively did, and the rift that caused lasted for ten years.

In time it also affected the club's own Saturday races. By 1913 one might see six or seven 'A' scows at the line and three or four cats. The 'B' Class Scows were dead. Then came World War I. In 1916 the club was chagrined to learn that its land lease would not be renewed (real estate developers were knocking on the owner's door). Worse yet, the lease specified that no trees were to be removed, and it was impossible to move the clubhouse without cutting down several trees – impasse. In 1918 only the Sheridan Prize event was sailed, and the club's 'clubhouse' was literally the Lake Geneva Country Club. The Yacht Club was at a very low ebb.

After the war ended the club recovered but slowly. In 1922 the ILYA offered the club another opportunity to host its annual regatta, and once again that was a much needed shot in the arm. It was equally successful, not the least of the reasons being the grand ball hosted by the club's commodore at his sumptuous home. Another boost for the whole ILYA area, with its many small lakes and small clubs, was an industrial development: automobiles powerful enough to trail a boat. The 38-foot 'A' Class Scows needed a four-wheeler that looked like a farm wagon without sides, but the new and smaller 'E' Class Scows could do with a two-wheeler. There were no trailer manufacturers, of course, so these trailers were all made locally out of whatever materials were at hand. Their construction usually began with parts from a wrecked or worn-out Model-T Ford. They provided much greater mobility for yacht owners of the area.

In 1925 the club hosted the ILYA regatta once again. One of its noteworthy aspects, as reported in the press, was that several boats in the 'E' Class Scow and catboat class were sailed by girls. In this respect the ILYA was at least a decade ahead of most of the country. By the end of the regatta it had become apparent that it made no sense for a sailing club to be operating out of a golf club. Also, for eight years the club had depended on the kindness of the commodore and his predecessor for the use of their piers. In the process of looking for a location the search committee found a piece of shorefront land with a small house on it; the club bought both, and the building with a few alterations and improvements lasted the club for forty years.

An interesting story involves the club's third oldest trophy, the Expert Trophy, given to the club in 1892 as a challenge trophy. The deed specified that any yacht (not owner) winning it could be challenged after two weeks' possession by another yacht. It had last been raced for in 1897 and won by a sandbagger named *Sphinx*. At that point sandbaggers were in steep decline, and *Sphinx* was never challenged. In 1926 the club tracked down her current owner and politely wrote to him, asking that he return the trophy. The man refused. "Splendid," wrote the commodore, "get your boat ready. You will have our written challenge in the mail shortly." He then went to examine an old sandbagger that had been sheltered in a local barn for many years. It needed a lot of work, he concluded. Apparently, the other fellow examined *Sphinx* and came to the same conclusion: he returned the trophy. The sandbagger in the Lake Geneva barn was ultimately restored to sailing condition, but that was not done until 1947.

Another story illustrates the answer to a question that may arise in the minds of those who have never sailed a scow. One of the entrants in the Sheridan Prize race in 1931 was Henry Porter who had first won it in a sandbagger in 1892 and had won it five more times in the intervening 38 years. He announced that it was to be his last Sheridan. On the day of the race, it was blowing like stink, and several 'A' Scow owners decided that it was too much for them. That left six prepared to risk it.

One capsized before reaching the starting area. Two more went over still short of the starting line a second or two after the gun. A fourth flipped a minute or so later. That left only Henry Porter's *Viking* and Commodore Schmidt's boat still racing. As they approached the windward mark, a violent gust knocked both of them over simultaneously. The Commodore's boat turned turtle; the *Viking* did not. The *Viking* was not ready to quit, however. With great effort the crew got the mainsail down. They tied lines to one end of the spinnaker pole, wedged the other into the bilgeboard slot where the board protrudes from the underside of the boat and guyed the pole by securing the lines to cleats on the fore and aft decks. The heaviest man in the crew went hand over hand up the pole to the end and chinned himself, the boat popped upright. The crew climbed aboard, doused the jib, put a triple reef in the main and finished the race. As they crossed the finishing line, a launch came by holding out a large thermos jug on the end of the boat hook.

The decade of the 1920's was the best and healthiest of the Lake Geneva Yacht Club's history thus far. Its reach did not exceed its grasp, its operating budget was modest, even Spartan, and the club was able to sail through the Great Depression with ease. A final note: during World War II only the junior sailing program remained in operation. The club, however, had the Sheridan Prize, which had been raced for every year without fail since 1874 and may well be the oldest such trophy in the United States. The club made certain, until the war was over, that at least two qualified boats were in the water in late August to race for the Sheridan on the 31st. The record remained intact.

Righting *Viking* and reefed down on Lake Geneva
Photo Lake Geneva Yacht Club

1972 Olympic Gold medalist crew in the Soling Class – 'Buddy' Melges, Bill Allen and Bill Bentsen
Photo courtesy of Harry and Gloria Melges

LONG BEACH YACHT CLUB – THE CONGRESSIONAL CUP[24]

In 1963 some members of the Long Beach Yacht Club, CA who were interested in match racing mulled over the traditional method of holding such races. In the past, in a series such as the America's Cup and the Seawanhaka Cup, there had always been challenger vs. defender – two yachts match racing once or three or five times and usually in restricted or open-design classes. They queried why not an invitational regatta in which, say, ten skippers and crews would sail a round-robin using a matched set of boats? And why not make it an annual event? Those questions led to the creation of the Congressional Cup.

Commodore of the Club, William T. Dalessi, and others solicited the advice of various distinguished yachtsmen around the country, including Arthur Knapp, Jr. of the Larchmont and New York Yacht Clubs, and in concert the reaction was, "A fine idea." Originally the concept was to ask the President of the United States to sponsor a cup for what started out to be a North American event, and inasmuch as precedent at the White House for Presidential sponsorship required that the event be international, the plan was switched to sponsorship by Congress, thanks to the Representative Craig Hosmer and Senator Thomas Kuchel picking up the baton. The Cup is believed to be uniquely the only sports trophy ever sponsored by Congress. One of the terms of the deed was that the silver bowl, engraved with the Congressional Seal, was to remain permanently at the club regardless of the winner's yacht club affiliation.

The first event took place in 1965 in which all the competitors were American. The winner was Gerry Driscoll of the San Diego Yacht Club who won every race. Since then the event has become international in scope with some of the winners being noted sailors from overseas such as Harold Cudmore, Peter Gilmour and Chris Dixon. It has also been won by such distinguished American sailors as Barney Flam, Ted Turner, Bill Ficker, Dennis Conner and David Perry.

The yachts used the first year were borrowed Cal 40's designed by Bill Lapworh. Subsequently various classes of yachts have been used, and no attempt during the first decade or so was made to equalize them, other than to require that all meet the class rules. In later years a special effort has been made to equalize the yachts as much as possible, and sets of sails were purchased for use exclusively in the series. In 1993 the manufacturer of the Catalina 37 donated 11 to a foundation to be used annually for the Congressional Cup. In 1988 judges were replaced by on-the-water umpires under the guidance of Thomas F. Ehman, Jr.[25] – a procedure that quickly became standard with all important match races. The conduct of the Congressional Cup is handled by several hundred volunteers, and the ambiance and hospitality coupled with its 'amateur' aspect, similar to the Seawanhaka Cup, make it a singular international match racing event.

For a number of years the Congressional Cup was an event unique to the Long Beach Yacht Club. Its success, however, ultimately led other yacht clubs around the world to adopt the same, or similar format. As a result, a World Match Race Conference has evolved which includes the Congressional Cup, and the International Sailing Federation (then IYRU) created a World Match Sailing Committee Advisory Board to monitor rankings of skippers for the Omega Champion's Award.

Two features that remain unique with the Congressional Cup are the award to the winning skipper of The Crimson Blazer and to the last-place skipper a copy of *Race Your Boat Right* which author, Arthur Knapp, Jr. used to award in person.

LOS ANGELES TO NEWPORT HARBOR[26]

Name changes, mergers and moves tend to be confusing and chronologically occurred as follows:

1901 on December 5 the South Coast Yacht Club was founded.

1910 the Los Angeles Motor Boat Club and Sunset Yacht Club were organized.

1920 South Coast Yacht Club changed its name to the Los Angeles Yacht Club.

1922 the Motor Boat and Los Angeles Clubs consolidated and moved into the facility of the California Yacht Club (no connection with the club of same name in San Francisco 1893-1920).

1927 the LAYC separated from the California Yacht Club and moved to Fish Harbor.

> *Yachting in Southern California grew slowly from the 1860's...sailing dory enthusiasts... a number of large schooners and fairly fast sloops.*

The focal point was Terminal Island where the Southern Pacific and Salt Lake railroads terminated.

The impetus for forming a yacht club at San Pedro was the practice of the local sailors of competing in races held by the San Diego Yacht Club (founded 1889) and the Santa Barbara Yacht Club (initially founded 1872). After the formation of the South Coast Yacht Club, it conducted its first race to the whistle buoy off Point Fermin for sloops and large schooners.

The South Coast Yacht Club registered its pennant in June 1910 with the U.S. Commissioner and Navigation. Next to its clubhouse (a shed) was the space of the Catalina Yacht Club formed in 1893 at Avalon by Hancock Banning (it disappeared by 1903 when the Sophia Yacht Club was formed which ceased after the great Avalon fire in 1915).

As early as 1903 there began to be complaints about the extreme racing machines built under the Seawanhaka Rule, e.g. Alex J. Mitchel's *Columbine* 46 feet LOA and 24 feet LWL. Both San Diego and South Coast YC's adopted the Universal Rule created by Nathanael G. Herreshoff to which the 'P's, 'R's, Nicholas Potter designed California 32's, 'Q's and the Gold Plater 'M' and 'N' classes were built. An example of the schism within the club caused by the adherents to the two rules was the resignation of Alex J. Mitchel, who took advocates of the Seawanhaka Rule with him to form the Sunset Yacht Club at Long Beach (it later changed its name and then dissolved when most of the members joined the South Coast Yacht Club).

TRANSPAC RACE TO HONOLULU

In 1906 South Coast Yacht Club fell heir, by reason of the earthquake aborting the start at San Francisco, to staging the first Honolulu Race. South Coast Yacht Club Commodore H.H. Sinclair competed in his 86-foot schooner, *Lurline*, against C. Clarence McFarlane's 48-foot schooner, *Paloma*, (from Hawaii) and Charles L. Tutt's ketch, *Anemone* and won. The SCYC (later Los Angeles Yacht Club) has participated in every race since, and has been a host club for most of the race starts and, also, for many of the races to Tahiti.

The Honolulu and Bermuda Races both started in 1906 and share the distinction of being, "the two oldest, regularly-scheduled 'blue water' races in North America." The respective distances of the races are 625 and 2,225 nautical miles of which 2,000 of the latter consist of reaching and running. Note, however, although Lake Michigan being 'fresh water' strictly speaking might not qualify as a 'blue water' event, the Chicago-Mackinac Race predates the above two having started in 1898. The first four Transpac races started from San Pedro, and following World War I the starts circulated between Santa Barbara, San Pedro, Newport-Balboa, Santa Monica and San Francisco after which they settled at San Pedro. The settlement came after fierce debating, and was militated by the nature of the Pacific High and the difficulty of yachts from the south beating to a start in the north.

The race had its genesis in an invitation issued in 1886 from King Kalakaua of Hawaii to the Commodore of the Pacific Yacht Club in San Francisco to attend his fiftieth birthday celebration. By way of inducing yachts to visit the Islands, the King offered to put up prizes. While there were no takers, one of the trophies turned up years later and is designated the King Kalakaua Trophy for First Overall. In the summer of 1905 Commodore Sinclair of the South Coast Yacht Club met with Clarence MacFarlane and other yachtsmen of the Hawaii Yacht Club while in Honolulu with his schooner, *Lurline*. The result was the formation of a committee to stage a race in 1906 from San Francisco to Honolulu, and MacFarlane agreed to sail his schooner, *La Paloma*, there for the start. As above-mentioned, she arrived in San Francisco to find the City in ruins from the earthquake and after communicating with San Pedro, diverted to the new starting point.

As author, Jack Smock, points out:

> *Prior to 1905 all long distance ocean races, both here and abroad, were sailed on a boat-for-boat basis. In the summer of 1905 the Brooklyn Yacht Club cruise from New York to Norfolk introduced the concept of time allowances. The club's rating system was simple: an hour for each foot of length – length to be determined by 'LWL plus one-half the total of overhang'. After studying the effect of such an allowance on the results of the 1905 Emperor's Cup (Trans-Atlantic) Race, Commodore Sinclair proposed to Commodore Holborn of the Hawaii Yacht Club a time allowance of 30 minutes per foot of LWL.*

Smock observes that the introduction of time allowances was a 'landmark' innovation destined profoundly to affect yacht racing. Thenceforth systems of handicapping for the Transpac ran the gamut from the Universal Rule in 1928 to the Seawanhaka Rule in 1930 and to introducing a factor into the IOR rule to rein in the ULDB's (ultra light displacement boats). In 1936 the Sparkman & Stephens 52-foot yawl, *Dorade* (winner of the 1931 Transatlantic Race), which had been acquired by James Flood, of San Francisco and had Myron Spaulding aboard as skipper, was first in elapsed time, winner overall and first in Class 'B' on corrected time:

> *... demonstrating that properly designed smaller boats could whip the big, professionally-manned seagoing craft that had dominated long distance racing... since yachting began.*

LOS ANGELES YACHT CLUB AND NEWPORT HARBOR YACHT CLUB

South Coast Yacht Club established Station 'A' at Balboa (Newport Harbor):

> *...leasing the 'Pavilion', after previously lending support to the Newport Beach Chamber of Commerce for dredging and developing the bay area. The general advocates of this station were Dr. Albert Soiland, Charles E. W. Hubbell, Benjamin P. Weston, Warren D. Wood, Dan Laubershiemer and others.*

The long sail around from San Pedro, waves breaking over the bar at the entrance and the shifting mud flats had deterred sailing in the Harbor. Members were accepted from Newport and Balboa, and in 1916 this nucleus formed the Newport Harbor Yacht Club of which Dr. Soiland became first Commodore. The history of the club, *Newport Harbor Yacht Club, 75 Years*, is dedicated to him:

> *Dr. Albert Soiland, founder of the Newport Harbor Yacht Club. A man of vision, enthusiasm, and determination, he was a pioneer and driving force in southern California yachting. He led the movement to form the Southern California Yachting Association, helped to form the Pacific Yachting Association, and organized the Transpacific Yacht Club... He served as Commodore of the South Coast Yacht Club in 1915, and one year later he founded the Newport Harbor Yacht Club.*

In one of his memoirs[27] Commodore Soiland describes how a group of sailors from San Pedro took the P.E. Railroad to Newport Beach on, "a drizzly Sunday Morning in February, 1903,[28]... and first discovered Newport Bay." They crossed the Bay in a boat provided by the East Newport Town Company to Old Newport. Soiland and others bought some lots and subsequently Station 'A' was established and became the forerunner of the Newport Harbor Yacht Club. His description of navigating his 35-foot motor cruiser, *Viking II*, through the inlet into Newport Bay illustrates the difficulty of introducing yachting to the area:

> *The yacht laid outside (the Inlet) until several big breakers had spent their force, then started in. We were lucky. We bumped over a few sand bars but with an incoming tide were soon safe inside the peninsula and made our way carefully up to the Balboa Pavilion and anchored. This was the first time a sizable yacht had been in the Bay.*

March 3, 1920 the South Coast Yacht Club changed its name to the Los Angeles Yacht Club. The next year the Southern California Yachting Association was formed under sponsorship of the Newport Harbor and Los Angeles Yacht Clubs and held its first regatta at Santa Barbara. In 1922 the San Diego and Santa Barbara Yacht Clubs and the Los Angeles Motor Club signed the Articles.

The first Southern California Yachting Association regatta to be held in the Bay took place in 1922 by which time jetties had been built facilitating passage through the Inlet. It was not, however, until 1936 as a result of a depression-era work project that the Army Engineers completed a major dredging of the Bay (Harbor).

In the same year LAYC and Los Angeles Motor Boat Club combined using name of LAYC, and, following the incorporation of the California Yacht Club, LAYC signed an agreement with the CYC to join the two clubs but keep LAYC's sailing and social identity. The combination proved to be popular and attracted a sizable fleet of large yachts during the next decade.

In the early 1920's the Star was introduced by Owen Churchill, Ben Weston and E. Nordhoff. An LAYC team of Jim Cowie and his brother Gordon won the Star Class World's in 1940. LAYC member George Fleitz repeated the feat when the Club held the 1941 World's.

In the 1940's the Luders 16's became popular, and Robert Ziegler won the Internationals at New Orleans in 1949. Also the Ray Hunt '110' caught on.

Thirteen years after Six-Metres were raced in the 1915 Exposition in San Francisco Bay, the first four Sixes were shipped on a Mallory Line steamer to Southern California for the Mid-winter Regatta of March, 1928, and were purchased by LAYC skippers. The Universal Rule 'R's raced concurrently with the Sixes, but eventually both classes were phased out by strictly one-design and lighter displacement classes such as the PC from San Diego.

Other classes racing at the Club were Eight-Metres, which included Owen Churchill's 1932 Olympic gold medal winner, *Angelita* (it was restored and featured in the opening ceremonies at the 1984 Olympic Games at Los Angeles).

In 1936 LAYC separated from the California Yacht Club and moved to Fish Harbor, and ten years later the Club leased property at Dimick's Cove at Howland's Landing.

One of the Club's most popular and prestigious races is the International Race to Mexico which started in 1960 and is sailed on even years.

Finally, pollution problems at Fish Harbor militated a move in the mid-1990's to Cabrillo Marina.

NEW YORK YACHT CLUB, 1844 - 1900[29]

Probably more has been written about the New York Yacht Club than any ten clubs in North America. This chapter attempts illumination of only the highlights of that extraordinary organization taken from the history of the club by member John S. Parkinson, Jr.

1844 TO U.S. CENTENNIAL

1844 In the year in which the club was founded John Tyler was President of a country that contained 26 states, only three of which lay west of the Mississippi River. The Cunard line, using ships powered by both sail and steam, had been in business only four years. While transportation along the east coast was still almost entirely by ship and stagecoach, the new Pennsylvania Railroad was in the midst of laying track between New York and Philadelphia. New York City occupied only the lower quarter of Manhattan Island, its northwest point being Madison Square where Fifth Avenue and Broadway converged. All beyond was forest and farmland. Brooklyn on the east and Staten Island to the southwest were separate communities. The club held its first regatta in Narragansett Bay off Newport.

1845 Commodore John C. Stevens builds and gives to the club a clubhouse on land he owns across the Hudson River in an almost vacant area called the Elysian Fields (now in Hoboken). The Club holds its first 'annual regatta' racing to a government mark off Sandy Hook and return thereby establishing a precedent for a perennial annual perhaps unmatched by any other club in North America. Location of start and finish is still a subject of debate inasmuch as the Club Racing Records, press accounts and those of historians are in conflict.

1846 The Club conducts the "First Amateur Corinthian Regatta... October 6... None but members to sail and handle their yachts. The allowance of time on this occasion was reduced to 45 seconds per ton Custom House measurement."

1847 It holds the "Second Amateur Corinthian Regatta... Over the New York Yacht Club Course (from off the clubhouse in Hoboken to and around a buoy off Sandy Hook)... the yachts to be manned and sailed exclusively by members, allowing each boat 'yacht' a pilot."

1848 Mainly through the efforts of Stevens, the Secretary of the Navy under an Act passed by Congress authorizes the Club to design a burgee – the 'yacht ensign' – enabling yachts as non-commercial vessels to go from

FIRST AMATEUR CORINTHIAN REGATTA

OF THE

NEW YORK YACHT CLUB

OCTOBER 6, 1846

For a Cup subscribed for by members of the New York Yacht Club. None but members to sail and handle their yachts. The allowance of time on this occasion was reduced to 45 seconds per ton Custom House measurement.

The course was from a stake boat (the 'Gimcrack') anchored off the Club House, Elysian Fields; thence to and around a stake boat anchored off Fort Washington Point; thence to and around a stake boat anchored in the Narrows (off Fort Hamilton), turning it from the eastward and return to the place of starting. Whole distance 40 miles.

SECOND AMATEUR CORINTHIAN REGATTA

OF THE

NEW YORK YACHT CLUB

OCTOBER 12, 1847

Over the New York Yacht Club Course

By a resolution passed at the second general meeting, July 13, 1847, it was decided by members, not yacht-owners, that on the second Tuesday in October, a regatta should take place for a prize made by their subscription, the yachts to be manned and sailed exclusively by members, allowing each boat 'yacht' a pilot.

The following gentlemen were appointed a committee to regulate the regatta, with full power to postpone if the weather should prove unfavourable.

EDWARD CEUTER.
LEWIS M. RUTHERFURD.
NATHANIEL P. HOSSACK.

Lewis Herreshoff article in *The Badminton Library* 1901 © Longmans, Green and Co.

port to port in domestic waters without clearing customs.[30]

1851 The club holds a dinner to celebrate the victory of the schooner *America* at Cowes. Notably absent are her designer, George Steers, and her builder, William H. Brown. While criticized roundly by the press for the grievous slight, the club did not apologize. The reason for not including them was simple enough: they were not members.

1853 A significant change in the by-laws is made. All voting is to be done by a roll call of the yachts in the club rather than of their owners. This was to insure that control of the club would remain in the hands of sailors and not be taken over by social or non-sailing members – a practice followed today by many clubs with contingents of swimming, tennis, golf, etc. members.

1856 The minimum size of a yacht eligible for membership is raised from 15 to 25 tons, Custom House Measurement, which would be approximately 45 feet LOA.

1857 Highly detailed Uniform Regulations for the dress of members and paid crews while afloat are voted into the by-laws. Also, since some of the members are not as experienced as the old guard, each yacht is to carry a professional pilot to avoid the shoals around the perimeter of the harbor and commercial traffic in channels.

1858 The club holds its first ocean race: a start off the Elysian Fields clubhouse and down through the Narrows, along the southern shore of Long Island, around Montauk Point at its eastern end, back through Long Island Sound and finishing at Throg's Neck.[31] One New York paper considered that rather daring.

1861 The Civil War has begun, and the club urges its members to make their yachts available to the U. S. Government. Only two did, one being James Gordon Bennett, Sr., in order to gain a commission in the Navy for his 20-year-old son. There were no cruises during the war, and the annual regattas were held either in New York Harbor or western Long Island Sound.

1865 The club is incorporated, and a seal is adopted with the motto "Nos Agimur Tumidis Velis" (let us go with billowing sails).[32] With the end of the war comes an influx of new and very wealthy members, who quickly outnumber the older members. Numerous new yachts exceeding 100 feet in length were ordered; as historian Parkinson observes, so many that some must have been on order before the war – no doubt evidence of the new wealth generated from the expanding industrial revolution.

1866 An extraordinary event: a winter ocean race from Sandy Hook to the Isle of Wight, UK. The club had long suffered jibes about its timidity in sailing its huge yachts only in protected waters. James Gordon Bennett, Jr. and two other members decided to answer the critics. One October evening, apparently well served, they challenged each other to a race across the Atlantic, not next spring, but as soon as preparations could be made. Each put up $30,000 for the kitty. Bennett then spent another $10,000 to hire the best coastal captain he could find, Samuel 'Bully' Samuels a former clipper ship skipper, to command his 105-foot *Henrietta*. While it is difficult meaningfully to equate $30,000 with current dollars, laborers were then living on wages of less than a dollar a day; few would earn half that sum in their lifetimes.

Three schooners, *Fleetwing* and *Vesta* being the other two, almost identical in size, with only Bennett among the owners aboard, set forth on the 11th of December. It was a rough and cruel passage; the yachts were buffeted by storms, gales and mountainous seas and burdened by swirling snow and the formation of ice. One yacht lost six men when a wave smashed across her entire deck and swept them overboard. Yet, all three made it. Bennett won, arriving at the Isle of Wight on Christmas day, after a passage of 13 days, 21 hours and 55 minutes and pocketed the $90,000. His opponents trailed him by only four and nine hours respectively.

1868 The club moves from the Elysian Fields to Staten Island. This became necessary because of the great congestion of commercial traffic in New York Harbor. The new location provided a handy sailing area in the Lower Bay. Upon moving the club sold its clubhouse to the newly formed Hoboken Yacht Club composed of members residing across the river from Manhattan.

1870 On the occasion of the first challenge for the America's Cup a familiar yacht re-appears. In 1861 the Confederate Navy had bought the *America* from her British owner and put her to work on tasks for which her great speed was well suited, principally as a blockade runner. On once occasion, however, she was chased into St. John River, FL by Union vessels. Trapped in shoal water, she was scuttled to avoid capture. When the war was over, the U.S. Navy raised her and commissioned her. In 1870, nominally under charter to a New York Yacht Club member, she was one of the 17 yachts[33] sailing against *Cambria*, the British challenger. With her navy crew she finished fourth.

Further about the *America*: in 1873 she was sold to Benjamin Butler who managed to induce the Navy to spend $5,000 refitting her. Butler, described by historian Samuel Eliot Morrison as "a rogue, a rascal and one of the four most incompetent generals in the entire war," nonetheless, was a capable sailor. He sailed the yacht skillfully out of Marblehead for 20 years and then gave her to his nephew, Butler Ames, who continued to race her, albeit with a greatly altered rig, until 1901. She then lay abandoned until 1921 when a group of Boston yachtsmen restored her over a period of six years.

In 1927 she was towed to Annapolis with symbolic crews from many different yacht clubs aboard each leg of the journey. On the first leg, Marblehead to Boston, she carried youngsters of the all-junior Pleon Yacht Club. At Annapolis she was presented as a gift to the U.S. Naval Academy. Unfortunately, the Navy on short budget rations had no alternative but to haul her and place her in a shed. In March of 1942 the weight of snow from a severe blizzard collapsed the roof of the shed crushing her, at age 91, beyond repair.

The same year James Gordon Bennett, Jr. raced across the Atlantic on a course the reverse of the race of 1866, i.e. from east to west, against the British yacht *Cambria*. By reason of her being the first challenger for the America's Cup the race created intense interest along the East coast. In spite of Bennett having again selected Samuels as skipper, after 2,900 miles she lost to *Cambria*, although by only 1 hour 43 minutes

1872 The club now has a city clubhouse on Madison Avenue at 27th Street shared with the American Jockey Club. The Regatta Committee's sailing instructions have already incorporated the 'flying start'[34] that was introduced in England only last year by the Prince of Wales.

During the New York Yacht Club cruise:

> *... there was a handicap race over the regular Block Island course, which is important, as showing how the yachts of that time were rated. I think the clubs of both countries will finally come to this as the fairest way of sailing yacht races. Certain it is, no system of measurement has ever been satisfactory, and probably never will be.*[35]

It sounds as though time allowances were arbitrarily assigned, or perhaps assigned on purely relative LOA or LWL.

1873 At the annual meeting the Commodore announces that a committee has been formed to design a club badge to be worn on social occasions and to be made by Tiffany & Co. Stated he:

> *Badges have become a necessity to all clubs, both in the United States and in England. The New York Yacht Club in its personal, financial and social status outranks any other club or society in the City.*

The Harlem and Jersey Yacht Clubs were coming into prominence.

1874 One day of the Annual Regatta is to be designated as Ladies' Day. The race that day will be sailed in cruising trim with the wives of members aboard as non-participating guests – a status for which the racing and/or class rules would soon contain a provision for many decades for the purpose of exempting them from the crew quota requirements.

1875 The club has just completed a new clubhouse on Staten Island much larger than the previous one – two stories with a verandah on three sides and a long, commodious pier. The North Shore Ferry Co. had been engaged to run a ferry from Manhattan to the club for members and the public, the latter to be deposited on the street via a separate exit. The fare: five cents.

Up until then William Vanderbilt's Staten Island Railroad Co. had had a monopoly on ferry service to the island charging ten cents a head. Not willing to take this new competition lying down, Vanderbilt instructed his lawyers to go to court to obtain an injunction. Impatient at the legal delay, he sent two of his tugs over to knock down the club pier. They were fought off by the determined and combined efforts of North Shore employees, club members and the Staten Island Fire Department. North Shore's services continued unmolested.

In the same year one of the club's yachts appeared flying a spinnaker, the first seen in North America. The spinnaker boom measured 45 feet on a yacht only 76 feet LOA. This development followed England by almost ten years; the yacht *Sphinx* sported one at Cowes in 1866 – hence the origin of the name.

CENTENNIAL TO 1905

1876 The year of the United States Centennial during which the club sponsors a race for large yachts on the first day, an offshore race on the third and on the day in between the City of New York sponsors a race for smaller yachts. Owing to their LWL being less than 20 feet, yachts in the latter did not qualify for enrollment in the Club nor as entries in its regattas. In the City of New York race, for which several members assisted the race committee, there were several sandbaggers and the catamaran, *Amaryllis*, designed and sailed by Nathanael G. Herreshoff and his brother who won handily. Several catamarans had been built previously, but they quickly broke apart from wracking. Herreshoff's use of the ball-and-socket joint to connect the two hulls as a solution to this problem, indigenous to multihulls, is described by his blind brother, Lewis, in a log[56] that he kept of a cruise up the Hudson River the next year in another Herreshoff catamaran, *Tarantella*:

> *In* The Spirit *of May 26th, Mr. Meigs has much to say about the comparative merits of the flexible joint system, used in the connections of my catamaran, and the rigid or partly rigid plan which he pursues. For illustration, he makes use of a most happy simile, which, I think, serves my purpose better than it does his. 'Twas that of two drunken brothers, wending their way through the streets, arm-in-arm. So long as they keep walking on a smooth, level plain, their connections are undisturbed, but if, in their erratic course, one of them would step off the curbstone into the gutter, the other one, if he undertook to keep his brother on the same plane as himself, would find it very irksome, and after several repetitions of that sort of thing, I think they would be glad to part company.*
>
> *But the laws of nature, which Mr Meigs talks about, have made most admirable provisions for this emergency. She has placed in the shoulder of each brother a perfect ball-and-socket joint, which allows one to raise himself over an obstacle, or sink into a depression, without disturbing their union, or laying out of any strength on either side, which would tend at last to make the bond irksome and injurious.*

96

N.G. Herreshoff patented aspects of seven of the catamarans built in 1876-79 that featured stability without shifting ballast. Unlike today's catamarans, they were designed to sail with the weather hull rarely lifting clear of the water.

As an indication of the proliferation of the sport in the greater New York region, Clubs participating in the Centennial Races were: New York, Atlantic (Brooklyn), Brooklyn, Seawanhaka Corinthian, Long Island, Williamsburgh, Central Hudson, Columbia, Manhattan, Pavonia, Hudson River, Bayonne, Mohican, Jersey City, Red Bank, Perth Amboy and Providence.

In the same year Benjamin Butler, a founding member of the Boston Yacht Club, sailed the *America* up from Marblehead for the club's ocean race. She won it beating the favored yacht, *Alarm*, the flagship of the NYYC's fleet. While in New York Butler applied for membership in the club but was blackballed – "not considered eligible for membership" in the jargon of club language. Nonetheless, he participated in numerous club cruises without his yacht's finishing position being officially recorded.

As an indication of how the preeminence of the New York Yacht Club would in the next decade be diminished by the surge in yachting activity elsewhere on the East Coast, Coffin[57] quotes a writer in one of the dailies referring to the year 1876:

> *There are clubs in and around Boston with numerous yachts; but their fastest ones, with the exception of the America, are second-class vessels which have been purchased from the New York clubs.*

Coffin comments:

> *This was correct in 1876, but in 1886 the Eastern Club of Boston has the* Fortuna, *probably the fastest schooner in the world; the* Mayflower *and* Puritan, *center-board sloops, that are superior to anything in the New York Yacht Club, and a fleet of smaller yachts that are unrivaled in their respective classes. While the conservative and eminently respectable New York Yacht Club has been standing still, and living on its past, its sister organizations, the Atlantic, the Eastern, the American, the Seawanhaka Corinthian and the Larchmont have been ahead with spinnakers pulling.*

Catamaran ***Amaryllis II***
Photo Herreshoff Marine Museum, Bristol, RI

1882 The club now has 23 steam yachts, including the first of J. P. Morgan's *Corsairs*, a mere 175-feet LOA. The annual meeting decides that the club's uniform is too ostentatious and votes a sharp reduction in the amount of gold braid and the number of gold buttons. Five years earlier the annual cruise sailed as far as Edgartown. This year the cruise went around Cape Cod to Marblehead to race with the Eastern Yacht Club establishing a long-term relationship between the two clubs.

1883 Another prominent blackball – Jay Gould, the flamboyant and hugely wealthy financier for whom the term 'robber baron' was coined. He has a new steam and sail yacht, a three-masted schooner 230 feet with bunkers that carry 170 tons of coal. Unfortunately he had not just stepped, but had trampled, on the toes of a number of members. As a consequence, Gould led a group in forming the American Yacht Club at Rye, New York.

1886 The club leases two piers, one at 26th Street on the East River and the other at 23rd Street on the North (Hudson) River. They are to accommodate club members who wish to commute to their offices by steam yacht. Commodore Elbridge Gerry, grandson of the Massachusetts Governor whose name made its way into the dictionary as 'gerrymandering,' has taken delivery of a new steam yacht. It is not only lighted by electricity but has an electric ice-making machine. It is described as palatial.

1887 Rufus T. Bush, who two years before had launched the 133-foot schooner *Coronet*, put up a $10,000 challenge to race across the Atlantic from Sandy Hook to Queenstown (Cork), Ireland. Another member, Caldwell H. Colt, son of the founder of the Colt Arms Mfg., who owned James Gordon Bennett's former *Dauntless*, accepted. He hired out of retirement Bennett's former skipper, Samuel 'Bully' Samuels, to serve as skipper, and the race started in March. The yachts encountered spring gales which opened up seams in the aging *Dauntless* necessitating pumping 100 strokes an hour and reducing canvas. The newer *Coronet* finished some 30 hours ahead of her. On one day *Dauntless* logged 328 miles.

Coronet today is the oldest registered yacht in North America and renown for having belonged to Commodore Arthur Curtiss James and later to The Kingdom, a missionary society at Gloucester, MA. She is due for restoration by the International Yacht Restoration School in Newport, RI. Respecting Colt, he died at young age while Commodore of the Larchmont Yacht Club.

1888 The Regatta Committee adopts Code Flag 'B' as the protest flag. Edward Burgess, the brilliant Boston designer with three consecutive America's Cup defenders to his credit, has designed a 40-foot class for the club. It is what today would be called a development class, but it is the nearest approach to a one-design class among larger yachts so far seen in North America.

1890 A station and pier have been built in Newport. It signals a major re-orientation of the club. Thirteen years earlier the club gave up its Staten Island headquarters after only three years of use. Traffic had made racing even in the Lower Harbor simply too unpleasant, and most of the racing was now being done during the annual cruise. Without a waterfront clubhouse the members had to join other clubs, mostly on Long Island Sound, for mooring and docking facilities for their yachts. Lack of facilities along the eastern seaboard for putting in to port and re-supplying, changing afterguard, etc. led to the practice of building, or acquiring, stations. Because the best cruising areas were to east at Newport, Buzzards Bay, Martha's Vineyard and Nantucket, the preponderance of the club stations, which by 1906 numbered 11, were established in those waters.

The cruise that year consisted of a flotilla of 120 yachts, including many of the club's 71 steam yachts (triple the number only eight years before). When they were joined at Newport by a fleet almost as large from the Eastern Yacht Club, the harbor must have been a sight to behold.

1891 A former Commodore offers the club the use of land at Glen Cove on Long Island with a pier, float and small building which became Station No. 10. Burgess's 40-foot class has been joined by a 46-foot class, also based on the Seawanhaka Rule (the club had given up its own rule four years before). Burgess, James Fife of Scotland and N.G. Herreshoff have all designed yachts for club members to parameters of the class. Capt. Nat's contribution was the *Gloriana* whose overwhelming success discouraged the class the year after it was born. No other yacht in the fleet could compete with her.

1893 The membership exceeds 1,000 for the first time. The annual dues, which were raised from $10 to $25 after the Civil War, remain $25. Nine steam and sail yachts of the club have left on an around-the-world cruise.

1894 On the club's 50th anniversary a woman applies for membership. She is the widow of a former member who was the brother of Andrew Carnegie. There is precedent for this: for a number of years British clubs have been admitting women as associates, and Seawanhaka Corinthian Yacht Club recently followed suit. The flag officers propose that the applicant be admitted, provided that she has a yacht suitable for enrollment, and be permitted to fly the club burgee, register her private signal with the club and use the club docks and stations. The vote of the membership was a resounding 'negative'. Nonetheless, the club later became one of the first to admit lady members, albeit with limited privileges.

1895 This was a year of travail and bitterness. It was caused by the charge by America's Cup challenger *Valkyrie III*, owned by Lord Dunraven, that the NYYC had cheated by adding illegal ballast to *Defender* under cover of darkness. Controversy had already erupted in the first race easily won by *Defender*. Disadvantaged by a spectator steamer during pre-start maneuvering, *Valkyrie III* was somewhat ahead and to windward as the two yachts luffed up towards the committee boat to avoid being over early. As they came close to it, *Valkyrie III*, in order to kill more time, bore away across *Defender*'s bow. When she found that she could not , she luffed to keep clear, but, as her stern swung, the end of her overhanging boom swept the other's weather rail and snapped her topmast shroud. *Defender* hoisted her protest flag and attempted to jury-rig the broken shroud before starting, but thus handicapped lost the race by two minutes.

The Regatta Committee properly disqualified *Valkyrie III*. Oliver Iselin, head of the NYYC syndicate, wrote a note to Lord Dunraven offering to re-sail the race. The reply was polite and short: while Dunraven disagreed with the Committee's reasoning, it had made its decision, and that should be the end of it.

The next issue was a complaint by Dunraven requesting that a race in which the yachts were interfered with by the spectator fleet be abandoned. The Committee replied that it would do its best to keep the starting line clear, but that it believed it was unable to monitor the course to prevent both yachts from possibly being affected by chop and wash caused by steam vessels. After crossing the starting line that day *Valkyrie III* headed straight back into New York Harbor, and Dunraven boarded a ship for Liverpool.

Two months later the club learned that Dunraven had published an article in the magazine *London Field* in which he made his charge for the first time concerning illegal addition of ballast. The club, in consternation, immediately called a special meeting. J. P. Morgan and two other members were appointed to serve on a board of inquiry. To fill out the board Morgan appointed two impeccably disinterested outsiders, Captain Alfred Thayer Mahan[38] as secretary, and Edwin Phelps as chairman, recently Ambassador to the Court of St. James.

Feeling ran so high that when Dunraven returned to New York for the hearing the Police Department provided around-the-clock protection, and he was removed from his hotel and put up in the remote home of a club member. The inquiry occupied five days, and the testimony was published in the 556-page volume *Report of the Special Committee of the New York Yacht Club.*[39]

The best evidence that Lord Dunraven could muster was that it had appeared to him *Defender* after a night of work on her was sitting lower in the water based on the positions of a water-drain outlet and her bobstay. The night of work consisted of unloading lead pigs that had been added to compensate for the removal of several bulkheads and below-deck fittings – four tons of items that were absent on *Valkyrie III.* The pigs supplied had been too long to fit between the frames and had been transferred to a tender to be cut in two. The next morning both yachts were remeasured and came within one-eighth and one-sixteenth inches respectively of their original measurements, i.e. considered within allowable tolerances.

The unanimous decision of the Special Committee was that no impropriety had been proved and that all actions had been satisfactorily explained. The report referred to Dunraven's departure after giving testimony, and gave him an easy out by stating:

> *... the Committee is not willing to doubt that, if Lord Dunraven remained present throughout the investigation, so as to have heard all of the evidence that was introduced, he would have of his own motion withdrawn a charge that was so plainly founded on mistakes...*

It is noteworthy that the Royal Yacht Squadron was invited to take part in the inquiry but declined; also, what comment there was by the British press gave Dunraven no support.

1897 The by-laws have been changed to extend membership to owners of yachts of less than 25 tons (cubic contents) but without voting rights. This came about because of the presence of a one-design class, the Newport 30's, designed by N.G. Herreshoff, of which there were already 14 in the club. The sailing instructions were also changed to permit yachts to carry non-participating guests aboard while racing.

1898 There was no cruise this year owing to the Spanish-American war. Twenty-one yachts of the club were on loan to the Navy and in service as gunboats.

1899 Club makes plans to raise $150,000 to buy three plots on West 44th Street on which to build a new clubhouse. Commodore J. P. Morgan solves the problem by buying them himself and presenting them to the club. Morgan, deprecatory of the proliferation of Georgian revival style clubhouses in the City, was instrumental in engaging young, innovative architect, Whitney Warren. Warren conceived of the eclectic clubhouse that continues to be the home of the club's fabled model collection in its 'great hall' of classic proportions.

1900 There is a new class in the club, the New York 70's, a.k.a. Newport 70's, designed by N.G. Herreshoff. The figure refers to LWL rather than LOA.[40] Only four were built, and in their first race out of Newport they almost foundered in a heavy blow and steep seas. Thereafter they leaked severely and proved unwieldy to crew and handle. At the end of the season they were reinforced with steel trusses but continued to have problems. The ultimate in 'skimming dishes,' they were the final proof that the Seawanhaka Rule lacked sufficient controls to prevent excesses in design; the Rule had become terminal.

1901 The new clubhouse officially opened, and "ladies were invited to be present, a precedent that was not to be repeated for many years."[41]

1905 Edward VII presents the club with the King's Cup open to yachts of any recognized yacht club – a traditional race that continues to this day, although currently as the Queen's Cup. Also, Emperor Wilhelm presents the Emperor's Cup for Transatlantic racing – the cup purportedly of solid gold turned out to be pewter thinly veiled with gold plate. The first race is from Sandy Hook to the Lizard, England. Entries consist of eight from the NYYC, two from England and one from Germany. This was the race in which the 189-foot, three-masted schooner *Atlantic*, designed by William Gardner, set a record of 12 days, four hours, one minute and 19 seconds that will not be broken for decades. Her skipper Charlie Barr (the Scot who drove *Columbia* and *Reliance* to America's Cup victories) when cautioned by the owner, Wilson Marshall, at the height of a storm to shorten sail responded, "You hired me, sir, to win this race, and, by God, that is what I am going to do" upon which he ordered Marshall below.

1997 The Club revives the past and sponsors the Atlantic Challenge Cup: the Ultimate Race Against Time for a run at the record established by the *Atlantic* open to yachts 85 feet in length or greater .

ROCHESTER YACHT CLUB[42]

The Rochester Yacht Club is situated on the Genesee River which empties into Lake Ontario. It is near the river's mouth in the town of Summerville about six miles north of downtown Rochester. There was a short-lived predecessor on the river – the Genesee Yacht Club, which was born in 1874 and died abruptly in 1876. The following year, the RYC was founded with only one member from the prior club. Perhaps taking what they perceived to be a lesson from the GYC, the RYC members insisted on building a clubhouse immediately. Fifteen hundred dollars was raised for the purpose, a member donated a parcel of land, and a substantial, two-story building, 85 by 25 feet, was erected. It was finished, save for painting, in 30 days during the spring of 1877.

During the open house in June, more than 500 people visited the new club, enjoyed a catered dinner and danced to the music of a local orchestra. A special train was detailed to take the guests home. Said Rochester's principal newspaper:

> *A place of this kind has long been needed... and it will no doubt meet with the greatest success. There is no reason to doubt that the directors fully understand how to manage the club and preside over its destinies in the most satisfactory manner.*

Only it was not to be. The club's first regatta[43] was scheduled for July. Summerville had become a resort town, and a railroad, a spur of the New York Central, connected it to Rochester. On the day of the race two very full trains totaling 17 cars brought hundreds of spectators from the city to watch. Perhaps as a portent of the future, the race began with very light wind. Halfway around the 12-mile course it failed altogether, and none of the eight entries finished within the time limit or for several hours thereafter.

The next ten years are an almost complete blank. All that is known is that the clubhouse burned down in 1881, and the owner of the land, who had neglected to deed it to the club, decided to use it for real estate development. The club was "moribund." When it was reactivated in 1887, the members started all over again – new constitution, by-laws, officers, and directors. (Apparently, no records from 1877 could be found.) Also, the club had 46 "charter members" who, among them, owned 15 yachts. The re-birth, while not nearly as grandiose as the original, was on much more solid ground. Under the auspices of the Lake Yacht Racing Association it held another first regatta which was "a decided success with many of the representative yachts of the different clubs on the lake taking part." The RYC was back to stay this time.

The emphasis on developing yacht racing was so intense that it was two years before the club began to think about another clubhouse. The site selected was not on the river but on the lakefront. It was, in one sense, not an ideal location, since it was bounded on one side by a blast furnace of a steel company and on the other by an amusement park with a roller coaster right next to the property. This one, 45 by 62 feet with three stories, cost $2,500 to build and furnish.

By 1892 the club had 157 members and a yacht list of 29 sailboats, the largest being a 63-footer, and seven steam and naptha powerboats, the largest at 98 feet. One of the sailing yachts was *Madge*, which had emigrated from Scotland in 1881. Designed by George Watson, one of the two most famous yacht designers in Scotland (the other was James Fife), *Madge* supplied the climax to the often acrimonious controversy over what a yacht's shape should be. It was called the sloop vs. cutter controversy. That was a misnomer, for a cutter was simply the British term for what the French, Dutch, Canadians, and Americans called a sloop. The main differences were the steep deadrise, narrow beam and divided head rig of the cutter vis-à-vis overhangs, wide beam and single headsail of the American sloop. L. Francis Herreshoff once said that it might better have been called the narrow vs. beamy controversy.

In 1881 *Madge*'s Scottish owner sent her over to race American yachts, after having wiped out most of the fastest British yachts. Consider her dimensions: 46 feet LOA, 32 feet LWL, and only 7 feet, 8 inches in beam, a length beam ratio of 6:1. She carried ten tons of lead attached to her deep keel. A number of match races (best two of three) were arranged for her, and she won them all easily – until she met *Shadow* at the end of the summer at Newport. *Shadow* was designed by N.G. Herreshoff at age 21.[44] The two boats split their first two races. Why they did not sail a decisive third we do not know.

In any event, *Madge*'s performance that summer and the capsize at her mooring during a line squall of *Mohawk*, the largest yacht in the New York Yacht Club's fleet, gave Americans reason to reconsider their derision of the British "lead mines" and to question the direction in which American yacht design had been going. It was to be another 20 years, however, before a new measurement rule was created to prevent the building of "skimming dishes." Meanwhile, *Madge* was sold to an American owner in 1892 after which she raced on Lake Ontario for the rest of her career. In 1907 as she lay abandoned in a marsh at the mouth of the Genesee, Aemilius Jarvis, the great Canadian sailor, bought her mast as a memento and installed it as a flagpole on his lawn in Toronto.

As an observation of the lifestyle of the 1890's, the house rules of the RYC in 1892 provide insight:

- *No intoxicating liquors shall be drunk on the club premises.*
- *No intoxicated person will be permitted in or about the clubhouse.*
- *Steward will report violation of this rule to the Executive Committee. Repetition will be ground for expulsion.*
- *No gambling of any kind will be allowed on the club premises.*
- *No game of any sort will be allowed on the club premises on Sunday.*
- *The Ladies Parlor is for the ladies' exclusive use; positively no gentleman allowed therein.*
- *Children will not be allowed on the club premises unless accompanied by adults.*

From then on the RYC prospered, not least because the club concentrated on racing; everything else was secondary. There was handicap racing among the larger yachts, and soon there was a fleet of one-design club dinghies for level racing. There was the annual Lake Yacht Racing Association regatta for distance races and around-the-buoys races. There also was the Canada's Cup, named not for the country but a yacht. It was a challenge trophy to be raced for by one Canadian and one American club. The Chicago Yacht Club was the first challenger (against the Royal Canadian Yacht Club) in 1899, but a Rochester boat won the trials for it, represented Chicago, and won. In 1903 Rochester won it on their own, and the next four spirited and exciting series were between Rochester and the Royal Canadian Yacht Clubs. After the 1907 event an unfortunate and often bitter disagreement arose between the two clubs, and the Canada's Cup was not raced for again until 1930.

Circa 1902 the club built a second clubhouse on the opposite side of the river's mouth but facing the lake. It contained a dining room and bar and became the club's social center, leaving the building on the west side for boating activities. As a next step, the club dredged its way into a small pond south of the new building for use of a mooring basin. That arrangement lasted until 1914, when the club sold the newer facility to a Rochester brewery, which used it for many years as a retail outlet.

Meanwhile, the club had begun to go into decline for reasons that remain obscure. The membership dropped from 400 in 1910 to less than 250 within four or five years. Interest in racing declined. Perhaps having a social clubhouse had not been a good idea. Perhaps the membership came to have interests other than sailing, or new members came into the club with other interests. In 1912 the club merged with the Columbia Rifle Club because it had a downtown clubhouse. The marriage ended in divorce two years later. In 1915 the earlier clubhouse on the river was sold, too, leaving the club with none. It was reduced to holding its meetings at the Rochester Whist Club, and dues were reduced from $5 a quarter to $3.

The decline, however, lasted only six or seven years. Perhaps it was the establishment of a Star Class fleet that helped to turn the tide. The record is too scanty to be sure what did, but the RYC's fortunes improved to the extent that by 1920 it was ready to begin plans for a new clubhouse. By the spring of 1922, after a subscription drive that raised $17,000, construction was underway, and the June meeting of the Directors admitted 98 new members. The building finished in September was more modest than any of its three predecessors. The first floor contained locker rooms, showers and the steward's quarters, and the second, with wide overhangs fore and aft, contained a combined club and dining room, kitchen, a large fireplace and a screened porch. In front of the club a 250-foot dock was built. With little change this building served the needs of the club until 1933, when it was remodeled and enlarged. The year 1922 ended with 421 members, almost double the low point only seven years before.

In 1925 the 'R' class came to Rochester and was to become the backbone of the racing fleet until World War II. The very next year the RYC was said to have the largest number, seven, of 'R's of any yacht club in the country. The 'R's were built to the Universal Rule and would have been 34-38 feet LOA.

Life on a lake has one advantage: no tides to contend with. It also has disadvantages: high water in the spring and low water in late summer and fall. The Rochester Yacht Club is on low ground with marshy land around it. After years of having the lower floor of the club inundated by water each spring, the building finally had to be raised three feet to eliminate the problem. Also, during the decade of the 1930's Lake Ontario was low the entire time. That increased the silting near the mouth of the river, and the yacht basin had to be dredged every year, which was a heavy expense.

There was also another problem, the seiche, which is a fairly common occurrence on large lakes and bays. It was not until 1925, however, that the RYC experienced one severe enough to cause damage. On that occasion, a drop in atmospheric pressure sucked all the water out of the river-mouth area, including the yacht basin. When it returned, it came back as a great wave, slamming most of the club's boats up against the dock and depositing several of them on it.

A seiche is cyclonic in nature and sometimes tornadic in intensity. It is caused by a wave of extremely low pressure passing over a body of water, which reduces the atmospheric pressure on the water surface as much as a half-million tons per square mile. Since the area beyond the perimeter of the seiche is under higher pressure, water is sucked from all sides, causing a 'bulging' of the lake's surface. When the trough of low pressure dissipates or passes beyond the lake, the water is released to flow back to its original locations which creates a wave that can be destructive to low-lying land areas.

The decade of the 1920's was, among other things, the decade of the "great experiment" – Prohibition. Yacht clubs near the U.S./Canadian border, such as the Seattle and the Royal Victoria Yacht Clubs, had many a tale to tell of the movement of liquor from north to south, but the Rochester Yacht Club history is more reticent of the subject; its history contains but one story.

After racing at Toronto, a Rochester 'R' boat left for home carrying 21 cases of Scotch whisky stowed in the bow. Her course took her well off-shore from the Coast Guard station at Olcutt, west of the Genesee, which was renowned for its harsh treatment of bootleggers. The course ran her into rough seas that caused the ill-loaded boat to hobby-horse so badly that most of the cache had to be transferred to the cockpit. They reached port undetected and docked in the yacht basin in the middle of the night astern of a power vessel. Two girl friends were called to bring a car, and the 21 cases were unloaded into it. The next morning, coming down to clear up their boat, the crew discovered that the vessel next to it was a Coast Guard cutter from Olcutt. They had carried the whiskey right past it within four or five feet!

In 1929 Eight-Metre's came to Rochester. Metre yachts were built to the International Rule, created in London in 1907 by representatives from 11 European nations. While they were there, they also created the International Yacht Racing Union to manage the rule and oversee international racing. Most of the yachts built to the rule thereafter were the Six, Eight, Ten and Twelve-Metres. The Eights ranged in length from 46 to 50 feet LOA, which meant that they were expensive. Since the end of the year brought the onset of the Great Depression, it became necessary to form syndicates in order to buy and maintain them. It was worth it, however, for the Royal Canadian Yacht Club had Eight's, too, and they raced for the Canada's Cup in 1930, 1932 and 1934. The Eight's, beautiful racing machines, seemed to personify yacht racing, and they helped maintain the spirit of the RYC through some very lean years. They were superseded on the lake by the Six-Metres in the late 1930's, although the Club continued from time to time to host the Eight-Metre world championships. The Sixes, which ranged in length from 35 to 39 feet and were much less expensive, became very popular on Lake Ontario, Long Island Sound, the west coast, and in Europe. Eleven countries entered Sixes in the 1936 Olympics.

As it did to all yacht clubs, not to mention millions of hapless citizens, the Great Depression caused serious financial hardship to the Rochester Yacht Club. By 1932 there was a significant drop in membership, which had numbered in the four-hundreds during the 1920's. It was necessary to drop the annual dues from $50 to $25 and to waive the initiation fee. But racing persisted, helped considerably by the development of a Star Class fleet, and membership climbed in 1936 from a dismal level to 243. It would not be until after World War II, however, that the membership would reach the 400 level again. The RYC had plenty of company, of course; almost every club in the United States could tell the same story.

THE ROYAL CANADIAN YACHT CLUB[45]

The Royal Canadian Yacht Club's role has been pivotal to Canadian and North American Yachting involving leadership in the Canadian Yachting Association (CYA), the Lake Yacht Racing and the Lake Skiff Sailing Associations (LYRA and LSSA), the Yacht Racing Union Of The Great Lakes (YRU) and NAYRU. It is significant that Paul Henderson, current President of the International Sailing Federation (ISAF) is one of many RCYC members who have been involved in such organizations and have participated in Olympic and other international competitions.

The seven founders of the modest Toronto Boat Club in 1852 soon renamed it the Toronto Yacht Club[46] presaging its major focus. The designation "Royal" authorized by Queen Victoria in 1854 oriented the club to British naval traditions. The adoption of the burgee carrying in its cantons a crown and a beaver, derived from Toronto's coat of arms, symbolized a strong link with the city.

Until Canada's adoption of the national "Maple Leaf" flag, from 1878 club yachts proudly flew the Blue Ensign associated with British naval auxiliary vessels. During the American Civil War many members were part of a

Naval Pilot Brigade formed to offset possible infringement of Canadian security on Lake Ontario. It was further active during the "Riel Rebellion".

Club activities were sharply curtailed during the World Wars. Many racing yachts were shorn of their lead ballast for bullets and nearly 1,000 members served in the Canadian forces. A unique bronze and granite capstan/sundial memorial, dedicated in 1926 by "Governor-General Baron Byng of Vimy," now bears the names of 72 members who gave the ultimate sacrifice for their country.

In 1980 RCYC celebrated 100 years on Toronto Island which, within commuting distance by club ferries, forms Toronto Bay. The Club fleet, now numbering over 500, still participates in a myriad on the "Bay" and nearby Lake Ontario, fronted by the spectacular city skyline. The current island clubhouse dedicated in 1919 by the Prince of Wales (later, King Edward VIII), which opened in 1922, replaced two earlier island structures destroyed by fire (along with priceless records) in 1904 and 1918.

Earlier club quarters were on the city waterfront. The first, a structure of two stories built on a leaky scow, served from 1853 until its replacement in 1855 by the retired steamer, *Provincial*, acquired in Buffalo. She would often part her moorings, once sank, was refloated and used until the winter of 1869 when she drifted into the ice of Toronto Bay and was destroyed "as a hazard to navigation."

The Club's *Annals* contain a revealing insight into the early development of the Marconi/Bermudian rig in the form of a painting titled "Toronto Boat Club Coming into the Harbour" dated July 30, 1853. Among the boats in the painting is a sloop with such a rig and caption explaining, "it was then called leg-o-mutton sail." Coincidentally a painting dated 1857 at the Royal Nova Scotia Yacht Squadron shows eight out of 13 yachts with Bermudian rigs.

The first island clubhouses opened in 1881 and 1906, and their present successor has been the heart of the club's summer activities since 1922. Up to 1906 various city quarters maintained 12-month operations. The resumption of year-round activities occurred in 1974 following the merger with a badminton/squash club. The present spacious city clubhouse, built a decade later, provides for social gatherings, racquet sports, swimming, fitness facilities, all which supplement the summer recreations of the island.

Apart from the implied allegiance 'to the Crown,' RCYC objectives are to:

> *Encourage members to become proficient in handling their yachts, to promote yacht architecture, building and sailing in Canadian waters and excellence in competitive sailing.*

Proficiency and excellence have been demonstrated by its members from the outset in Canadian and foreign waters. Commodore George Gooderham, patriarch of a family that still adds to the club's laurels, set an example in 1888 when his 87-foot schooner *Oriole II* cruised a 1,000 mile round trip to win the Mackinac Cup, defeating a Chicago America's Cup candidate *Idler* by 7½ minutes on elapsed time and over 24 minutes on corrected time. RCYC sailors continued to build a fine record in later Mackinac events as well as in Olympic and Pan American Games, LYRA and other association classics. They have competed in the Bermuda Race(s), the Southern Ocean Racing Circuit (SORC), Onion Patch Series, and Admirals Cup series in which *Magistri* skippered by "Chuck" Bentley was 18th among the 41 surviving finishers in the disastrous 1979 Fastnet Race.

Ill-advised challenges for the America's Cup (*Countess of Dufferin* in 1878 and *Atalanta* in 1881) were redeemed by *Canada I*, *True North* and *Canada II* in 1983 and *Australia* in 1986. *Canada I* reached the semi-finals skippered by Olympic medalist Terry McLaughlin, now regarded as one of the finest match racing skippers on the continent.

The Prince Of Wales Cup, considered "the oldest yachting objective on fresh water" is the premier of many RCYC trophies. A challenge cup, it was presented by Prince Albert Edward, (later King Edward the VII) and raced for since his visit in 1861 when he became the first of many royal patrons (H.R.H. Prince Philip, Duke of Edinburgh, is the present incumbent).

Second in importance to the Prince of Wales Cup, the Queen's Cup was donated by Queen Victoria in 1891.

The 1896 victory of Commodore Aemilius Jarvis with *Canada* in a series of match races in Toledo against Chicago's *Vencedor*, began the era of Canadian/American Great Lakes rivalry for the Canada's Cup. Seventeen contests to date have been sailed first in the lordly 'cutters,' then Eight-Metres, and followed to this day in sloops.

Another Commodore, Norman Gooderham, scored numerous victories (comparable to those by the American Charles Francis Adams and Addison Hanna) three of which gained the YRU Richardson Cup, the last at Toledo in 1926 sailing the Canadian designed and built 'R' class *Eleanor*. His son, N.W. (Bill) Gooderham's, record included competing in the Six-Metre Class in the Olympics, North American championships and the Seawanhaka Cup aboard *Titia* on Oyster Bay versus the storied Herman F. (Swede) Whiton's *Goose*. Bill's son, Bryan, is a world champion of the revitalized Eight-Metre fleet. RCYC sailors have triumphed in such other classes as Dragons, Stars, 5.5's, Sharks, Finns, Flying Dutchmen, Lasers and the International Fourteen.

Dinghy racing is covered elsewhere in this history. Suffice it to say that RCYC has led in developing the Fourteen through the skills of 'Charlie' Bourke and a new generation of designers.

In yacht design Commodore Jarvis led the way with a number of innovative racers from the yacht *Whistlewing* to "one of the first and fastest fin keels ever built – a 30 foot 'skimming dish' oddity with a 9½-foot overhang and 525 pound bulb keel." Such was his stature in yacht racing (Canada's win at Toledo in 1896 was just one of over 300 in his career) that he was Sir Thomas Lipton's navigator on *Shamrock III*, the trial horse for her successor's America's Cup challenge.

G. Herrick Duggan, engineer and bridge builder, designed 142 craft, notably the series of skiffs (scows) commencing with the first *Glencairn*, winner of the 1888 Seawanhaka Cup, which he successfully defended for nine years running. 'Byng' Benson, designer of two champion 'R's, *Eleanor* and *Nayada*, in 1924 created the 25-foot LOA, raised-deck 'C' Class which was very popular on Lake Ontario and beyond for over two decades.

In the post World War II period RCYC's George Cuthbertson became "the dean of Canadian yacht designers." Not only did he produce the 40-foot *Red Jacket*, the first non-American yacht to sweep the Southern Ocean Racing ircuit, but his C&C Yachts Limited formed with an early associate, George Cassian, expanded to include boat building affiliates at Oakville, Niagara and Kingston and later became the continent's largest yacht building company. C&C produced 18 lines of racers from Sharks to C&C 41's and have gained world-wide recognition. Cuthbertson's custom designs include several Canada's Cup champions, the 61-foot *Helisara* for Herbert Von Karijan, the conductor of the Berlin Philharmonic Orchestra and the 67-foot Phantom for trucking magnate Ralph Ryder.

A recent unique design, the unstayed, cat-rigged Nonsuch, now numbering around 1,000 in a variety of sizes and concentrated on the lower Great Lakes and Southern New England, was designed and produced by club member Mark Ellis, also designer of a number of custom racing cruisers.

Since 1924 the club has stressed youth instruction and for three of the past four years the RCYC Junior Club, long co-educational, has topped the Ontario and Canadian field. Commodore Paul Phelan, a top Dragon skipper and owner of *Red Jacket*, was the first chairman of the International Yacht Racing Union Youth Committee. His continuing input to the sport of sailing at all levels earned him the IYRU's highest award, the Beppe Croce Trophy placing him in the ranks of former winners – the Kings of Spain and Norway, the legendary Olympian Paul Elvström, and the great U.S. yachtsman and designer Olin J. Stephens, II.

RCYC dedicated 1995 as *Hiawatha*'s year in recognition of the Toronto-built steel-hulled club ferry, that for the past 100 years, along with the newer *Kwasind*, have faithfully transported members, guests and royalty (one of the latest, Prince Charles) to and from the city and island. Considered to be one of the world's oldest still in-daily-service vessels of her kind, she has undergone renovations and motors from original steam power, through gas to diesel. In many ways the success and longevity of her career epitomizes RCYC's fine heritage.

ROYAL NOVA SCOTIA YACHT SQUADRON[47]

The earliest regatta held in North America by a yacht club[48] for which sailing instructions exist is for the REGATTA held at Halifax on August 17, 1836 – a year before the formation of the Halifax Yacht Club. It separated the "sailing boats" into "First, Second and Third Classes" approximately according to length; at least the entry list records lengths in First Class running from 34 to 24 feet, in the Second from 29 to 14 feet and in the Third from 18 to 13 feet. Whether the overlap in size was by reason of another parameter such as rig is not recorded, but a possible explanation is the provision:

> *Boats belonging to Fishermen (there was a separate Fisherman's Class), except the winners of the First Fisherman's Prize, will be allowed on application to the Umpires, to contend or the other prizes appropriated for the classes to which, if not previously classed, the Umpires shall decide such boats belong.*

The distinction between 'amateur' and 'professional' stems from a British practice attributed on the one hand to a genuine concern over the advantage acquired by someone whose profession provided a training experience not available to the casual competitor and on the other hand to the desire to obviate gentry having to compete with commoners. The names of five umpires appear on the regatta instructions; it would be interesting to know to what extent their role resembles that of current day International Umpires. No mention is made of time allowances.

> *From the time of the First Regatta, the activities of the Royal Yacht Squadron and the presence of the Royal Navy and Army in Halifax greatly influenced the development of yacht racing here. The Royal Yacht Squadron provided the pattern upon which the Regatta was planned, since it was to "be conducted on the principle of the Grand Annual Regatta, held at Cowes in the Isle of Wight." The festivities of the day were concluded by a Ball on board* HMS Jupiter.

Several features of the Regatta were, however, novel, e.g. a special class for fishermen "(the beginning of a custom that led to the International Fishermen's Races of the 20th century and the legend of the *Bluenose*)" and a race for Indians in canoes.

For the next ten years following the 1826 races,

> *regattas were held sporadically. The one held on August 17, 1836 was such a success ... that at a meeting was held on July 27, 1837, to decide 'That a club be formed to be called the Halifax Yacht [sic] Club...*
>
> *At the time there were only ten such clubs in the world, none of them in North America. There had been a small club named the Knickerbocker Boat Club in New York in 1811, but it survived only a few months. Shortly after that what is today the Beaconsfield Yacht Club house in Quebec was built, though it was not intended for that purpose and no record of a club exists from that time.*
>
> *In Boston a few years before the formation of the Halifax Yacht Club there had been what was called the Boat Club, but it was certainly not a yacht club... and by 1837 the idea had been abandoned.*

By 1844 rivalry between Dartmouth (across Halifax Harbour from Halifax) and Halifax boat-builders kept interest so high that the *Halifax Times* considered the regatta "among the standard recreations of a Halifax population."

The Squadron also has a copy of the Notice of Regatta for 1860 in which year its guest of honor was Albert, Prince of Wales. As from the beginning, the HYC's sponsors were the Governor of the Province and the Admiral in charge of the British Naval Station at Halifax. By 1860 a third sponsor had been added: His Lordship, the Mayor of Halifax. Similar to the notice of 1836, it divided the sailing competitors into the following groups:

> *3) First Class Fishing Sailboats* ***first prize $20***
>
> *4) Second Class Fishing Sailboats, under 25 ft overall* ***first prize $50***
>
> *10) Decked vessels (Fishing and Coasting) of 60 tons N.M. (net measurement or under)* ***Provincial Prize $150***
>
> *14) First Class Yachts, 5 tons and upwards* ***first prize $60***
>
> *15) Second Class Yachts, under 5 tons* ***first prize $40***

Classes not above listed consisted of Fishing Flats, Fishing Whalers, Gigs open, pulled by mechanics and pulled by young men under 20 years of age, Canoes paddled by Indians, Canoes paddled by squaws, different classes of Man-of-War pulling boats and Wherries and Square-Sterned Boats pulled by amateurs.

Elsewhere this history of NAYRU discusses the evolution of the Bermudian, or Marconi, rig. It is significant that a painting by John O'Brien titled "Mystery: 'Yacht Race, Halifax' 1850" shows a yacht with Bermudian rig racing against a couple of schooners with the same rig. The Club History after recounting the reorganization of the Halifax Yacht Club into a "more structured and nautical way" reports:

> *The 1857 fleet totalled 13 boats, eight of which were Bermudian-rigged, a rig virtually unknown in racing in Europe and America until the next century. It was truly an advanced design for the time, bearing more resemblance to modern racers than any other boats. A Bermudian, or 'Mudian' as it was sometimes locally called, was usually a sloop, its single tall mast carrying a three-sided 'leg o' mutton' mainsail... The Americans later called it the Marconi rig, because of the tall mast with its complex of stays reminded them of radio towers.*

The history notes that Bermuda had many close ties with Nova Scotia, especially through the military. In this respect there hangs in the National Maritime Museum at Greenwich, England a painting by John Lynn captioned, "1834 A Bermuda Schooner," which carries 'Mudian' mainsails on her three masts.

In 1861 Queen Victoria granted permission to use the word 'Royal' as part of the Club's name, but not until 1862 did the Club receive "its first Admiralty Warrant, which permitted an enrolled yacht to display the blue ensign; because it was classified as a man-of-war without cargo, a yacht possessing a Warrant had privileges such as exemption from harbour dues."

One of the Club's most prestigious trophies is The Prince of Wales Cup presented in 1861 by the Prince of Wales. Because the race for the Cup was open to all yachts belonging to members of the Royal Halifax, a time allowance, "perhaps overly simple" was instituted and caused difficulty many years later. When in 1874 the function of drawing up a new rule setting a standard time allowance formula for inter-class races was delegated to the Sailing Committee the History notes, "They proceeded to select the wrong rule by the wrong method, and to choose the wrong time to test it." As the brouha over the rule intensified a member suggested, "that the Club collect from other clubs in Canada, the United States and England, information about their systems." All the systems were summarily dismissed because they, "did not make provision for the increased allowance that must necessarily be given when larger classes are contending with the smaller." The tack they took contained elements of the theory of the PHRF rule, ie. "they assembled a chart that showed how many times a first class yacht had won the race for the POW (12), and how many times a second class yacht had won (one)..." and concluded that a time allowance of two and one-half minutes per ton was "if anything, too little." To increase the time allowance for the benefit of the second class raised a howl of protest from owners of the more expensive first class yachts. The result was a stalemate, and by 1875 the situation had deteriorated as epitomized in a letter to the editor of the *Morning Chronicle* signed, "Your Obediant Servant ALL IN A FOG."

On November 25, 1875 yacht owning members revolted and formed the Nova Scotia Yacht Squadron making it the second oldest and one of seven yacht squadrons in the world.[49] Patterned after the Rules of the Yacht Racing Association of Great Britain, voting power rested in the hands of yacht owners, and virtually all the yachts of the Royal Halifax Yacht Club had been assimilated into the Nova Scotia Yacht Squadron. It was not until November, 1880 that the Admiralty recognized that the Halifax Yacht Club had "almost entirely merged "into the NSYS and granted the Squadron's request for a warrant.

With the advent of the 1887 Jubilee Races yachts from American clubs in Boston and New York were invited with the exhortation:

> *There are no more enthusiastic yachtsmen in the world than those who live among the Bluenoses. The yachting craze is as predominant in Halifax as it is in Boston, and the successes of the sloops owned in your city are familiar to almost every resident of the city I come from.*

By 1890 the RNSYS was in danger of becoming a social club so house rules were adopted prohibiting gambling and games of chance.

> *One very real problem was money. A few wealthy yacht owners could keep pursuing new designs that pushed the limits of speed while still conforming to changing measurement rules. They introduced costly innovations – lead keels, manganese bronze fins, and double planking over steel frames.*

This led to the concept of a relatively small one-design boats, a class of 'Knockabouts' (after a similar Boston class by that name). Designed by Mr. McLeod and built at Joshua Mader's boat yard, they were drawn for by lots:

> *to settle who would take delivery of the first boat... Knockabout races quickly became a very popular spectator sport, particularly since the owners had a habit of pairing off in dueling contests, so that watching the lead boats was only part of the entertainment.*

In 1898 "the handful of members left in the Royal Halifax Yacht Club decided to let old wounds fade and be united with RNSYS." They were all made honorary members of the Squadron, and they brought with them the Prince of Wales Cup.

In 1904/5 the Eastern Yacht Club, reasoning that "Halifax, under the British flag, is to us as much a foreign port as Malta or Gibraltar" decided "it would be pleasant to fraternize with our Provincial cousins across the Gulf of Maine." This set the stage for a race from Marblehead to Halifax. Eastern offered a silver cup, and RSNYS offered their Prince of Wales Cup in open competition for the first time while visiting yachts were in port. The start was scheduled for August 21, 1905, and the largest yacht was the schooner *Elmina* from the New York Yacht Club. The RNSYS History characterizes the race as the first ocean race in North America[50] having preceded the Bermuda and Honolulu Races by a year. It was not until 1939, however, that there would be a second Marblehead-Halifax Race. Through the efforts of several yachtsmen, the persuasion of Herbert L. Stone, editor of *Yachting* and renewed interest on the part of the Boston Yacht Club the race was revived.

After the turn-of-the-century ladies became more active in the club, especially as a result of a 1906 provision in the constitution of the Squadron:

> *allowing a woman who owned a yacht or dinghy to become a member, although not a regular member. As long as she owned a boat, a woman was eligible to become a Flag Member… If she sold her boat, however, she lost her membership. The only privilege this membership gave her over other ladies was that she was allowed to compete in Squadron races; she was still restricted in the areas and times she was allowed to use the club-house.*

In 1922 Stars were delivered at the Squadron in an effort to expand interest in racing through the medium of one-designs. One-design racing received a further boost in 1946 when, at the insistence of Armdale Yacht Club (above the RNSYS on the Northwest Arm), Bill Roue (designer of the famed racing schooner *Bluenose*) was given the green light to proceed with the Bluenose Class – a 23-foot keelboat sloop. To quote a 37-year-old Halifax stockbroker:

> *It's a racing boat, part of a large fleet, but it can be a nice day sailing boat as well. And it's an unbelievable boat to sail with a very sensitive helm. It can turn on a dime and it can really handle a blow.*

The Class has been perpetuated in GRP.

THE ROYAL ST. LAWRENCE YACHT CLUB[51]

In 1888 Canada as a country was only 21 years old, its first transcontinental railroad had been completed just two years before and the population of Montreal was approximately 225,000.

The founding of the St. Lawrence Yacht Club came about through a newspaper notice inviting interested parties to attend a meeting to consider establishing a sailing club. The meeting attracted 47 people. The "consideration" lasted only a few minutes. Within six weeks, a constitution, by-laws, and a burgee were approved, officers were elected, and the club held its first regatta. By June the membership rose to 110. There were, at the time, four other boat clubs in the area, but most of their activities involved canoe and rowing matches. The St. Lawrence Yacht Club was interested solely in sailing.

It is amusing to note that the club's first race in May with nine entries was delayed by a protest. It was alleged that one of the yachts had a crew member who was a paid hand. The allegation was heard and proved to be true. Since the yachts were all waiting at the starting line, the embarrassed Race Committee agreed that the paid hand could stay aboard for the race but never again. Meanwhile, the Committee would see to it that a new by-law would forbid such a thing.

The sailing seasons of 1888 and 1889 passed with the club homeless and not yet incorporated. Much time was spent in 1890 in finding and acquiring property on which to build a clubhouse. Montreal lies north of a wide section of the St. Lawrence River that is called Lac St. Louis. and it was east of the city where the property was located, in a cove in Dorval. One of the requirements in site location was access to it by rail from the city. By the next year the clubhouse was finished, but its use was limited until a basin could be dredged for mooring boats.

In 1894 the club became Royal upon the issuance of a warrant by the British Admiralty upon the instruction of Queen Victoria. That not only changed the club's name but enabled its members to fly the blue ensign of H.M.'s Fleet. Queen Victoria designated yacht clubs as 'Royal' rather liberally; yacht clubs, more than any other kinds of institutions, received the designation, eight in all in Canada.

By 1894 the dredged mooring basin had not only been completed but a 65-foot channel out to deeper water had also been dredged, and a 500-foot pier had been constructed. Membership had increased to 430, and the club had a stable and coach house for transportation to and from the Dorval rail station. A substantial addition to the clubhouse was planned along with two tennis courts. The plan changed to a completely new building, which was ready for use in 1897, including a copious number of small bedrooms for members' weekend use. It was to serve the club until 1961.

In 1896 the Royal St. Lawrence entered international competition with a challenge to the Seawanhaka Corinthian Yacht Club on Long Island, New York for what came to be called the Seawanhaka Cup. The story of that competition is to be found in the section of this Chapter dealing with the Seawanhaka Corinthian Yacht Club. Three years later the club did something unique for its day in yacht club history: it formed a subsidiary called the St. Lawrence Yacht Company. Its sole asset was a boat building and repair shed on the club property which was leased to a professional boat builder.

The next step was to provide a downtown clubhouse for use by members during the long Canadian winter. Most of the members lived and worked in the city, so the club leased the second floor of the building that housed a bookstore on the street floor. To establish a presence in Montreal it created, in conjunction with the St. George's Snowshoe Club, a winter ball held at the new and elegant Windsor Hotel. It became one of the premier social events of the year for many years.

The Royal St. Lawrence Yacht Club's centennial history devotes, justifiably, an entire chapter to the competition for the Seawanhaka Cup. The Club's great victory in the first year was most remarkable. In all of Canada at that time there was not a single professional yacht designer, and it was competing with an American club that had the legendary N.G. Herreshoff and Clinton Crane as its designers. The Club's designer was an amateur member, G. Herrick Duggan. Within a short time the names of the yachts he designed, first as a challenger and then as defender, were as well known in North America as the names of NHL hockey stars are today. A member as well of the Royal Canadian Yacht Club, he was made an honorary member of the RCYC in 1897 and described in *The Annals* of the Club as:

> *His great talent was not confined to designing skimming dishes. In a period extending over 47 years he designed and sailed various deep draught units of the RCYC fleet running from 30 to 60 feet LWL.*

The boats used for the Seawanhaka Cup competition were variously known as 'half raters' (a British term) and the 15-foot class – today they would be considered 'scows.' The Canadian crew won its challenge in the waters of Oyster Bay in 1896 and defended it successfully seven times, until the cup was finally wrested from the Royal St. Lawrence Yacht Club by the tiny Manchester Yacht Club in Massachusetts. As the author of the Club History concludes, "It remains the outstanding moment in Canadian sailing history."

The concerted effort to defend the Seawanhaka Cup took its toll. The club seemed exhausted by it, and competition declined during the next few years and during the period of the Great War (1914-18), when almost one-third of the members were fighting in Europe. It was not until 1921 that the club created a trophy, the Royal St. Lawrence Challenge Cup donated by George H. Duggan, to be raced for against the White Bear Yacht Club of White Bear Lake, Minnesota, a club with which it had developed close relations during the days of the Seawanhaka Cup.

Interest was reviving. The ladies had their own clubhouse, a home on adjacent property bought during the war. The club had purchased a dozen dinghies for the training of juniors. And it was the year in which headlines in the Canadian newspapers told of the races between Nova Scotia's *Bluenose* and the fishing schooners of Gloucester, MA. *White Bear* won the series and the Challenge Cup, and racing regained the fervor of the earlier days.

In 1929 the Royal St. Lawrence Yacht Club joined the North American Yacht Racing Union and became a founding member of the new Canadian Yachting Association. The year ended with the onset of the Great Depression, which the club seems to have survived better than most in North America. Perhaps it was due to the fact that from the beginning the Royal St. Lawrence concentrated on scows and dinghies, less costly to build and maintain than the vessels of other clubs. As an example, both the New York Yacht Club and the Boston Yacht Club during the 1890's had enrolled more schooners and sloops, several of which in each were more than 100 feet in length. But cost was not the major determination of the size of the classes: The shoal waters of Lac St. Louis governed the types of boats suitable for the conditions.

The women of the club, who had their own clubhouse after World War I, were not members. Men could visit their clubhouse at any time, but women could enter the men's building only during the dinner hour and on special occasions. It was not until 1928 that women could be elected as associate members. That entitled them to compete with men, but paradoxically they could not win any of the club's trophies, since they were reserved for full members only – men.

The 1947 club directory indicates that nothing had changed in those two decades. It was not until 1961 when, perhaps prophetically, the ladies clubhouse had been torn down to make room for a new clubhouse – the club's present quarters – that women became eligible for full membership. It was eight years later when a woman athlete, a member of Canada's Olympic Ski Team, became the club's overall champion.

A woman of 92, who had been associated with the club since about 1910, related that the women in the early days did not feel especially alienated: that was the way things were, and they accepted it. During the 1920's a few women began to crew for their husbands or fathers, but some of those gave it up after a few experiences. The dowager remarked:

> *Perhaps those were the times of gentlemen and chivalry, but I can tell you that chivalry died once we were on the water. They shouted at us just as they'd shout at another man. I remember more than one woman coming ashore in tears, saying "he can't shout at me like that," and vowing never to go on the water again.*

As for juniors, there is an early reference to a Junior Squadron in 1888, but it did not last, as a later reference makes clear. In 1919, however, the club sponsored what was probably the first Sea Scout troop, whose members trained in a variety of boats ranging from a 46-foot cutter to a navy gig. In 1930, it sponsored schoolboy racing for the Bluenose Trophy and, in 1936 when intercollegiate sailing began, the club became the home for McGill University's sailing team. The Junior Squadron began in earnest in 1947 with three cat-rigged dinghies and two 14-foot scows, later called the Mount Royal Class.

ROYAL VICTORIA YACHT CLUB[52]

Most of the yacht clubs founded during the 19th Century were established by successful, deep-pocketed men. They may have been small in the beginning, but they grew steadily, if slowly, into the next century. Not so the Victoria Yacht Club. For its first 50 years it lived on the constant edge of disaster. Victoria, BC – the capital of the Province – is on the southeast corner of Vancouver Island about 40 miles south of the latitude of the Canadian/U.S. boundary of the state of Washington. It borders on the entrance to the Strait of Juan de Fuca leading to the Pacific Ocean and gets its worst weather in storms from the southeast across the Strait.

Founded as a fur trade fort and later becoming a rough gold-rush town, Victoria was oriented toward the sea. All of its major streets ended at the water's edge, and its principal industries were all marine related. In 1892 its population was only 17,000. Early on, a custom of a two-day celebration of the Queen's Birthday developed in which the entire town turned out to participate in, or watch, cricket matches, baseball and lacrosse games, tug-of-war contests, and bicycle, canoe, and rowing races. Eventually, sailboat races were included, and 14 boats, all small, turned out for the event in 1891. The time seemed to be ripe for an expansion of sailing.

The following year a notice appeared in the daily paper inviting interested persons to a meeting to consider the possibility of forming a yacht club. It attracted 47 men, mostly young and full of enthusiasm. Only 31, however, actually paid the five-dollar entrance fee and became official members. At the same time the five or six clubs in the state of Washington scheduled a meeting to consider formation of an association. The new Victoria Yacht Club sent two delegates which enabled the new organization to christen itself the NIYA (Northwest International Yachting Association). Its first regatta was held in Seattle, and the Victoria Yacht Club sent the only boat that seemed capable of competing with the American clubs.

The 1893 regatta was to be held in Victoria. One problem with that was the lack of a clubhouse. The club had been using a boat livery building that rented canoes and rowboats, but it was unsuitable for hosting all the American yachts that were expected. Hence, the club borrowed the Canoe Club's quarters for the event, which was to be part of the Queen's Birthday celebration. The second problem was money. The VYC's treasury contained only a little more than $100. The club, after much pleading, managed to extract $475 from the Celebration Committee, an amount that was about 15 percent of its budget for all events. Of 18 yachts entered, 14 were American, and a Seattle boat won the race over a course of 25 miles, several times around a small course close to shore. Compared with the other events, a disproportionate number of citizens watched the sailing, from shore and from boat, and it was the highlight of the celebration. The VYC was on its way!

Vancouver with a smaller population than Victoria became the terminus for the Canadian Pacific Railway's trancontinental railroad and was destined to grow much faster. By 1894, it was competing strongly with Victoria for industry, and the railroad was the principal reason. But the new VYC Commodore, George Kirk, had a vision – to make Victoria the Cowes of the Pacific. On a trip to England that year he attended Cowes Week, after which he wrote a letter to the Lords Commissioners of the Admiralty, asking that his club be designated Royal and its members be permitted to fly the blue ensign of H.M.'s Fleet. The Commissioner responded by asking that the club furnish a list of its yachts, their tonnage, their owners, and "their positions in the Colony." Commodore Kirk sent the reply to the club Secretary, asking him to comply promptly. The Secretary just shook his head; the club had fewer than 20 yachts, of which Kirk's own at 40 feet was by far the largest, and few of the members could claim any particular distinction. He just filed the request.

In 1895 the NIYA regatta was again to be held at Victoria, but the club still did not have a clubhouse. Commodore Kirk sought to solve that in time for the regatta by creating a corporation that would build a clubhouse and rent it to the club for $50 a year. The corporation issued $2,000 of capital stock in shares of $10 each. He then turned to the members to buy them. He sold exactly 28 and had to buy the remaining 172 himself. Nonetheless, the clubhouse was built. Since it was to occupy foreshore space on a property in a central, convenient part of the harbor, it was built on pontoons to an attractive design by a club member who was an architect. Not only that, it was built on time and for less than the anticipated outlay.

The yacht race was to be the centerpiece of the Queen's Birthday celebration. Thirty yachts were entered, five from Victoria, and the spectator fleet and shore watchers were numerous. But there was not a breath of wind. Nor was there any the next day. The wind returned nicely on Monday, but the burghers of Victoria had all gone back to work, and there was no one to watch. Worse, the club's treasury was totally exhausted by the hospitality extended to the visiting yachtsmen during the two extra days.

Worse yet, the new clubhouse proved to be in almost too convenient a location: right next to one of the harbor's commercial wharves. In December, a freight and passenger steamer from Puget Sound, while sidling in to dock, struck the clubhouse, knocked it off the pontoons, and sank it. No sooner was it restored to its pontoons and repaired than a winter storm in gale strength came along and sank it again! It took until May this time to rebuild it in time for the 1896 Queen's Birthday. So fierce was the wind that of the 27 boats entered only 19 started and only two finished. Several were badly damaged and one sank. It need hardly be said that there was no spectator fleet, and the spectators on Beacon Hill, the best vantage point on shore, were all forced to flee the wind.

Later that day, a grossly overloaded trolley car, while crossing a bridge at the end of the harbor, fell into the water when the center span gave way, and 55 people, including a number of children, were drowned. During the following winter, one of the founding members, a ship captain, was lost at sea. At the General Meeting the next March, with only 19 members present, the mood was somber indeed. The Treasurer announced a treasury balance of $2.75 and reported that, of 87 members, 44 had yet to pay last year's dues (which were then $5 per year). He then announced his resignation.

The following winter another storm sank the clubhouse for the third time. In July of 1897, a further problem arose for the VYC (and several other clubs). A steamer arrived in Seattle from Alaska and off-loaded two tons of gold. Within hours, the word got out that gold had been discovered in the Klondike region of the Yukon Territory. "Ho for the Klondike!" Almost overnight, both Vancouver and Victoria were filled with men on their way north to make themselves rich. In the excitement yacht racing was all but forgotten. For the 1898 NIYA regatta at Victoria only five yachts entered of which three were from the VYC. The General Meeting of the club had to be postponed three times that year for the lack of a quorum of 15.

The Klondike fever did not last long, but when it was over, only two clubs, Seattle and Victoria, had enough interest in the NIYA series to make the effort. They agreed to hold the regattas at Port Townsend, about halfway between the two. But the new venue did not help much; only Seattle and Victoria showed up. Meanwhile, two good things finally happened to the VYC. One was to elect as treasurer a retired army sergeant-major, who was used to having his orders obeyed. In one year he put the club's finances in order and even made the first $50 rental payment, which past Commodore Kirk had been patiently awaiting for six years. The other was building a small fleet of one-designs the first on the west coast. From a design by Charles D. Mower published in *Rudder* magazine, they were 23-foot keelboats or 'knockabouts' as such designs were called on the east coast. One feature of the knockabouts was their stubby little bowsprits or none at all; another was that they were small enough to be sailed by three or four men. Easily able to carry on in 30-knot winds, they became an instant hit.

In 1903 a second British Columbia club was born - the Vancouver Yacht Club. Its birth had been delayed by the Klondike fever. The members of the Victoria Yacht Club took the news with pleasure, but that soon turned to dismay. The Vancouverites were so impatient to go sailing that, rather than wait for boats to be built, they began buying Victoria's boats at a price the older club's members could not resist. For a while it looked like the Vancouver people would strip every sailing yacht from Victoria Harbor. Then came a most bitter pill. In 1906, after only three years, the Vancouver club became the Royal Vancouver Yacht Club.

Not only had the Victoria lost most of its yachts, it was losing people. The new blood that any club depends upon for growth and stability was lacking. Men who wished to be on the water were turning to powerboats – runabouts and launches. Membership at the Victoria was down to 30, the lowest in its history. Moreover, the lease on the foreshore property was running out and would not be renewed. The limited frontage on the harbor was becoming too valuable for use by an indigent yacht club. Members were beginning to talk seriously of the possibility of having to disband.

Once again came a reprieve in two forms. One was the membership of James Dunsmuir, the richest man in western Canada (coal mines on Vancouver Island). This was a morale booster. The other was the decision to admit powerboat owners to club membership. This was a big financial boost since they joined in droves; so many, in fact, that they soon began to dominate the club. The influx of new funds enabled the club to build another clubhouse. The site was not the best that might have been found, however, inasmuch as it was located in a more remote area of Victoria Harbor adjacent to a pungent paint factory in one direction and an even more pungent chemical factory in the other. The move was foredoomed to failure.

Another step Mr. Dunsmuir took was to offer a handsome cup, which he called the Alexandra Cup, after one of his mines, to the Royal Vancouver Yacht Club to further the dream of its commodore to establish a west coast America's Cup type of match racing between one American member of the NIYA and one Canadian member, i.e. comparable to the Canada's Cup competition on the Great Lakes. To show that the Royal Vancouver Yacht Club was going first class, the commodore engaged the famous designer James Fife, of Scotland, to design a challenger to the 29-foot LWL agreed upon. When it arrived, it was said to be the most beautiful yacht ever seen on the west coast. After two or three trial races against the fastest of the club's yachts and wiping them all out, the *Alexandra* was pronounced ready to go and sat awaiting the match.

Meanwhile the Seattle Yacht Club was also building a yacht, *Spirit*, designed by one of its younger members, Ted Geary, who was to skipper it. He spent the entire month of June drilling his crew on her almost daily.. The practice paid off, and *Alexandra*, despite being the better boat, lost two races to one because of inferior crew work. The following year, 1908, *Spirit* won, again, two races to one. Members of the VYC bought *Spirit*, not to race her for the Alexandra Cup, for she had been designed in and built in the U.S., but solely to race her against the *Alexandra*. A match between the two was arranged and it created great interest. But when the day came to sail it, there was no wind.

So *Alexandra* sailed on down to Seattle for the 1909 Alexandra Cup and to race the new Seattle boat, *Spirit II*. A measure of the intensity of the competition is the following report:

> *Every known trick was used to assure maximum speed potential, e.g. black lead (graphite) and burnishing bottoms between races.*

After they had split the first two races, a furor erupted. It seemed the Seattle boat had been measured by placing considerable weight in her bow ends to raise her stern. This was done to shorten her waterline. Had she been measured level, she would not have qualified as 29-feet LWL. In high dudgeon the Vancouver skipper refused to race, the Seattle boat sailed the course alone, and claimed the Cup. The RVYC commodore refused to present it, took it back home, and thus caused the temporary termination of the west coast 'America's Cup' – shades of what happened between the Royal St. Lawrence Yacht Club and the Seawanhaka Corinthian Yacht Club over the Seawanhaka Cup.

In 1911 the Victoria Yacht Club applied for Royal status. This time the requirements included having a fleet aggregating 2,000 tons. Fortunately, James Dunsmuir had just purchased a Clyde-built steam yacht of 238 tons, and a new resident from eastern Canada had brought with him an auxiliary ketch of 118 tons boosting the fleet total to meet the requirement. The rest of the application went easily, and finally the Victoria Yacht Club was Royal.

It also had become clear that Victoria Harbor was no place for a yacht club. Commercial traffic was increasing rapidly and was a danger for moored yachts. Moreover, the neighborhood was becoming increasingly pungent. A search began for a new site. Recently, the Hudson Bay Company had sold a 1,000-acre farm on Cadboro Bay, four miles from the center of Victoria, to a group of Winnipeg investors. Their intent was to create an exclusive suburban sub-division, and they had hired the landscape firm founded by Frederic Law Olmsted of Boston to lay it out for them. They were delighted at the thought of having a yacht club as part of it and offered the club an acre of choice property at a low price. After a year of indecision between that site and several others, the Royal Victoria Yacht Club accepted the offer and built a new clubhouse which is still there today. The only disadvantage of the site was being exposed to the winter winds from the southeast. That would be cured half a century later by a breakwater that made the anchorage and marina a year-round in-the-water operation.

The next two years were happy and productive ones, but in August of 1914 World War I began. It was expected to be over by Christmas, but it dragged on for four years. A quarter of the membership were in the military, little new blood came in, and the spirit drained from the notion of racing. When it was finally over, some men did not come home at all, some came home crippled and some returned only to find the adjustment almost more than they could handle. Moreover, the area was in a state of economic depression for several years. In 1919 the membership was down from pre-war strength of 325 to merely 168, and it would be a long, slow climb back.

When the soldiers and sailors of British Columbia returned, they discovered that by a vote by ballot their province had become dry. That was not what they had fought for! In 1920 prohibition was decisively defeated at the very time that the U.S. had embarked on its "noble experiment." Almost immediately Victoria became a center for supplying the lower west coast with liquor, and not without economic benefit to the club. Scotch, landed for a $1.40 a bottle in Victoria, could be sold for $4 everywhere along the coast of Washington, Oregon, and California. It was an immensely profitable business, and the clubhouse's lower floor was often stacked to the ceiling with cases of scotch, which, it was rumored, belonged to members involved with a rum running cooperative of distillers and distributors.

Despite that, the club reached the end of the 1920's still in precarious position, and the stock market crash of 1929 just about finished it. Some people found that their membership in it was a social liability. Said one:

> *The club had such a bad reputation around town for not paying its bills that you really did not want to admit that you were a member.*

All yacht clubs in North America suffered from the Great Depression to a greater or lesser degree, but the Royal Victoria, which had suffered from ill health from birth, apparently had become inured to it. We can take pleasure and relief from learning, in the latter half of the club's history, that its second half-century contained far less travail and woe that the first. Indeed, today it is one of the principal yacht clubs of Canadian yachting.

One of the roles that the Club assumed was organizing the Swiftsure Lightship Race the course for which was out the Strait of Juan de Fuca, around the lightship and return. When the Seattle Yacht Club decided to sponsor the Swiftsure Lightship Race in 1930, RCYC had no entry, but the next year it was represented by Harry Barnes' *Minerva*. For some years after World War II the start of the race was moved around until 1951 when RVYC took it on, and thenceforth the start has been from Victoria.

ST. FRANCIS YACHT CLUB AND SAGA OF THE YACHT *BARUNA*[53]

By 1926 the San Francisco Yacht Club had found its site at Sausalito no longer tenable by reason of heavy ferry traffic interfering with boating and causing damage at the moorings. A schism developed among the members respecting whether to move to Belvedere across the Bay from San Francisco or to the San Francisco Marina near the City. A block of 49 members, largely the more affluent, opted for the latter site where they founded a club the next year which became the St. Francis Yacht Club. At a location readily accessible to racing waters, it assumed a major role in the conduct of its own and of Yacht Racing Association of San Francisco Bay events. Exchanging privileges with the New York and Royal Thames Yacht Clubs, it was active in international Six-Metre racing and established a match race trophy jointly with the Royal Prince Alfred Yacht Club at Pittwater, New South Wales, Australia. For many years member, Charles Langlais, was on the NAYRU Board, and when he retired, was succeeded by James Michael – later President of NAYRU.

While this monograph concentrates on a magnificent yacht, it is equally the story of its designer, Olin J. Stephens, II who gained national prominence with his yawl *Dorade*. This revolutionary 53-first raced in the Trans-Atlantic Race from Newport to Plymouth in 1930 with Olin and brother Roderick, Jr. on board. She was first to finish and beat several larger yachts by more than two days. While in England she won the Fastnet Race. Upon her return to New York, her crew was given a ticker-tape parade up Broadway and presented with the keys to the city.

In 1932 she won in the most competitive class, 'B', in the Bermuda Race. 'Rod' Stephens sailed *Dorade* back to England in 1933 and won the Fastnet again – four trans-Atlantic passages, incidentally, without an engine. *Dorade* was followed by *Edlu*, a 56-foot sloop that won the 1934 Bermuda Race. 1935 was the launching of *Stormy Weather*, a 55-foot yawl that won both the Trans-Atlantic Race and the Fastnet that year with Stephens at the helm. Out of the amazing success of those three boats in four years was born the firm of Sparkman and Stephens – the 'Sparkman' being Drake who managed the firm and its brokerage department.

By late 1936, with the U.S. slowly making its way out the Great Depression, interest among deep-pocketed

Baruna **in front of St. Francis Yacht Club, 1955**
Photo Commodore Robert C. Keefe

Americans centered on the 1938 Bermuda Race, which was to be the biggest yet. The sponsoring Cruising Club of America had set a maximum length of 73 feet LOA for the race, and sights were set on that figure. Three of the major yacht designers of the country had boats abuilding. The Quincy Adams yard in Massachusetts was building L. Francis Herreshoff's *Tioga*, later and better known as *Ticonderoga*. The Herreshoff yard in Bristol was building John Alden's *Royono*, and Luders in Stamford was building Philip Rhodes's *Escapade*. All had been designed to the maximum length.

Henry C. Taylor, of the New York, Seawanhaka Corinthian and Cold Spring Harbor Yacht Clubs, had already commissioned Olin Stephens to build a similar boat, but the availability of a yard capable of building it was doubtful. The three mentioned were up to their ears in work. Fortunately, a contract with Quincy Adams to build a duplicate of *Tioga* was canceled, and it suddenly had building time. Thus, it took on the job of building *Baruna*.

At 72 feet and yawl-rigged, *Baruna* was the largest yacht that Stephens had yet attempted. With a waterline of 50 feet and a draft of 9 feet 6 inches, she carried an 1,100-pound bronze centerboard that increased draft to 14 feet. She had hollow spruce spars, the mast being 106 feet above deck, a measured sail plan of 2,300 square feet, two sets of running backstays and three sets of spreaders. The upper jib headstay was seven-eights. "Her rig was every bit as advanced as her hull design, which was not always the case in this period of design transition." Aluminum spars were considered, but there was only one company that could supply them, and the concept was new. (In 1934, Vanderbilt's America's Cup defender, *Rainbow*, had an duraluminum mast, but it was made up of 12,000 riveted plates and was built in an aircraft factory.)

Baruna's sail inventory, supplied by Ratsey & Lapthorn, included two mainsails, a mizzen, three genoas, three jib topsails, two mizzen staysails, four spinnakers, a staysail, a drifter, a ballooner and one set of storm sails: a total of 20. Made of cotton, the #1 mainsail was of 13-ounce Egyptian duck, hand sewn and triple stitched, with 1 inch four-strand manila bolt-rope all the way around. The running rigging was a mixture of cotton, linen, and manila line, with all guys, sheets, and halyards of one-quarter inch plough-steel wire spliced into rope tails.

> *Her winch package was also most complete for the time. Merriman #6 bronze winches covered the yacht for use as sheet, guy, and halyard winches. Aft, on the counter under the mizzen boom, she had a two-speed, chain-driven pedestal winch, designed by Rod Stephens and hand-built at the Nevins yard in City Island, NY. This 'grinder' handled the genoa, topsail sheets, and after guys. It was rated to pull about 3,000 pounds, which was the maximum sheet load that could develop on the yacht. Loads exceeding that strain would destroy the clews of her various headsails.*

Below decks *Baruna* was not stripped out, as most racers are today. Taylor intended her to be used, and she was, for extensive cruising, so her accommodations were appropriately designed. For example, her galley, aft of the mainmast, extended the full width of the boat, and the stove included an oven. Aft of the galley in the main cabin the gimballed dining table seated ten. In the cabin was a small soapstone fireplace for warmth against the night chill of the Maine coast. The wood used for the interior of the yacht was natural butternut, which provided a light and airy atmosphere. Lockers were everywhere, and all sails not bent on the booms could be stowed out of sight.

A ladder led up from the main cabin to a very large deckhouse with windows on all sides and seating for ten. Below the floorboards there was access to the engine and all the mechanical equipment. Aside from the deckhouse, the deck was flush with a fine sheer line. She had a spoon bow and a long-ended counter with a small transom. Her topsides were painted a gleaming black.

> Baruna*'s deckhouse, aft stateroom, and main cabin were truly spectacular in design and finish. They were of a yacht standard and quality never again equaled on a large racing yacht.*

In his 1960 history of the Cruising Club of America John Parkinson wrote, "[She] was the greatest big boat of her type in the history of the sport." Extraordinary praise, but could she sail?

The answer was soon to come. It was a struggle to get her fitted out in time for the 1938 Bermuda Race, and there was no time for practice racing, just a few shakedown runs. Nonetheless, she was at the starting line on time with Olin Stephens as navigator. The wind ranged from 15-20 knots and was on the nose until she crossed the Gulf Stream. From there, it was a close reach to the island. *Baruna* finished in three days and 19 hours plus, eight hours before the next finisher. First to finish, first in Class 'A' and first overall in a fleet of 38 boats. Indeed, she could sail, and beating in moderate to strong winds was her forte. Owing to her great weight – a designed displacement of 102,000 pounds – she would be more vulnerable downwind and in light air.

World War II broke out in September 1939, and war in Europe meant war in the Atlantic Ocean and cancellation of the 1940 Bermuda Race. The Transpac, however, was sailed, and two Stephens designs were shipped to the west coast to race in it. One was the 55-foot *Blitzen*, which *Baruna* had beaten in the 1938 race by more than two hours on corrected time. The other was *Chubasco*, very similar to *Baruna* but a bit smaller at 67 feet. *Blitzen* won the race to Honolulu handily, and Chubasco was second in Class A and fifth overall. These boats not only enhanced the reputation of Olin Stephens but demonstrated the quality of *Baruna*.

In 1940 the CCA substituted a more inland course for the exposed Bermuda course: from Block Island around the Nantucket Lightship, down east to Mt. Desert Island and finish at Gloucester. Seventeen yachts started the 455-mile race in a northeast wind that turned into a full gale with heavy rain squalls. *Baruna*, which spent 1939 cruising and collecting trophies in the racing on the NYYC cruise, was the favorite, and she had a beat both ways. When she reached the turning mark at Mt. Desert, the storm ceased, the wind filled in from the southwest, and it was a 140-mile beat back to Gloucester. She left all the others miles behind.

Baruna was laid up that fall and remained so until the end of WW II, since Henry Taylor and his eldest sons were in military service for the duration. Many yachts were given, sold to or commandeered by the Navy and Coast Guard to augment coastal patrol boats on both coasts. Sailing vessels were particularly useful for anti-submarine warfare inasmuch as they could patrol under sail without being detected by subs, had good station-keeping characteristics and, not needing refueling, could stay at sea for weeks at a time. They had a hard life in this role, however, and many of them had their sailing careers either ended, or drastically shortened, by war's end. *Baruna* was spared that fate.

The Bermuda Race resumed in 1946 but with a fleet of only 34 entries. It was also a light-air race that took *Baruna* 29 hours longer to finish than it had in 1938. Nonetheless, she was first to finish, first in Class 'A', and third overall. The rest of the year was spent cruising and competing on the New York Yacht Club cruise, including winning the King's Cup, the club's most prestigious trophy. In 1947 she won the Newport to Annapolis Race,[54] another light-air affair, in which she finished first but corrected out to third overall.

Big-time racers were looking forward to the 1948 Bermuda Race, by which time everything should be back to normal. It would be the first big post-war test for the east coast's ocean-racing fleet. It turned out that the number of entries was disappointing – only 36 – but *Baruna* was enjoying the strong northeast winds and finished first, four hours faster than her 1938 time; again first in Class 'A' and first overall. When she found the right spot to cross the Gulf Stream, she was so far to the west that she sailed around Bermuda and approached the finishing line from the south. No winning yacht has done it that way since.

In 1949 *Baruna* won the Newport-Annapolis Race again. She also had a worthy competitor for the first time, *Bolero*, a yacht built with several purposes in mind, the foremost of which was to beat *Baruna*. Another design of S&S and built for John Nicholas Brown (Vice Commodore of the New York Yacht Club), she was likewise designed to the 72-foot LOA maximum. Painted black and very similar in profile, it was difficult to tell one from the other from a distance. They were not sister ships, however, for Olin Stephens had been on a learning curve for 13 years since designing *Baruna*. They met for the first time during the NYYC cruise. It was a draw: each won a cup in two tries.

In the 1950 Bermuda Race the major factor in the outcome was the Gulf Stream. The boat that finished first, indeed, had finished last in Class 'A' two years before. *Bolero* finished three hours ahead of *Baruna* and corrected out second overall. *Baruna* was seventh. A story told by H. Stillman (Stilly) Taylor, son of Henry C., illustrates how close was the rivalry between the two yachts. Night had fallen, and it was essential tactically that *Baruna* not lose track of *Bolero* whom she was trailing . Suddenly Taylor hailed the watch to tack in order to follow *Bolero*, out of sight in the dark. When asked, afterwards, how he could tell that she had tacked, he said that he had seen a mess of garbage streaming at right angles to *Baruna*'s course containing artichoke leaves, and that only a yacht such as *Bolero* would be serving artichokes on an ocean race.

In 1951 the two yachts met several times, including the Matinecock-Port Jefferson Race, which *Baruna* won by 39 seconds. The Newport-Annapolis Race, however, was the thriller. It started on a beat in a smoky sou'wester, that turned to a drenching thunderstorm, then to fog and a calm, followed by a light southwesterly. During the storm, *Baruna*'s mainsail was torn, and it was taken down for several hours for repair. She caught up when they reached the Chesapeake Lightship which they rounded overlapped. Then the wind freshened, and they charged up the Bay in a 160-mile luffing match, overlapped most of the way. *Bolero* crossed the finishing line 22 seconds ahead, but *Baruna*'s tiny handicap advantage was just enough to make her first on corrected time. The subheading of an article in the *New York Times* read: "Sea Duel a Once-in-a-Lifetime Race."

After the 1952 season *Baruna* switched oceans, moving from the Atlantic to the Pacific, having been sold to prominent San Francisco yachtsman James Michael[55] who was to own her for 16 years. Michael, who had grown up sailing a Bird and then a Star, had bought *Dorade* in 1940 at age 21. After sailing her for three years, he was called to service in the Navy and sold her. When the war was over, he was looking for another boat. An Olin Stephens design was what he really wanted, and his opportunity came in 1953. Henry Taylor was ready to sell *Baruna*, but he was reluctant, understandably, to sell her to anyone on the east coast. Thus, she made the voyage via the Panama Canal to San Francisco.

Baruna found the waters of San Francisco Bay, where a boat has to be able to sail well to windward in a breeze to win, and the waters offshore, where races often involved rounding the Farallon Islands in rough seas, to her liking. She even did well in the Transpacs, although downwind was far from her best point of sail. Thus, she began a successful second career in the Pacific which included an episode worth telling.

The 1955 Transpac was the "year of the big wind." It blew hard all the way to Diamond Head, and winches were breaking down throughout the race. (The same was occurring in heavy wind races outside of the Golden Gate). The use of aluminum masts, fiberglass construction, dacron and nylon sails, and dacron lines were fast becoming standard. Previously, when the strain grew too great, sails blew out or sheets broke; now, winches were collapsing. The Merriman winches, standard equipment on yachts for years, were no longer up to the tasks required of them. *Baruna* and *Orient*, an S&S design built in Hong Kong in 1938, along with almost every other boat, reached Honolulu that year with hardly a winch still functioning. The owner of *Orient*, Tim Moseley, was an engineer, so he and Michael (a lawyer) contacted the Merriman Co. about the problem. Since it had not yet become a problem on the east coast, the Merriman people saw no reason to take action. But Moseley did, and the result of his efforts was a new kind of winch, and the company that Moseley and Michael created to manufacture and market it was named Barient. Two decades later, the Merriman Co. no longer existed.

Of the two 'B's *Bolero* has fared better than *Baruna* and having undergone a thorough rehabilitation is cruising in the Caribbean.

SAN DIEGO YACHT CLUB[56]

Until 1885 San Diego was little more than a fishing and whale-oil producing village. In that year the Santa Fe Railroad arrived, and the town grew rapidly - from 6,000 to 24,000 in one year. The following year the San Diego Rowing Club and the San Diego Yacht Club were both founded at the same organizational meeting. The commodore who elected to head the latter was the only yacht owner in the group.

The boom that caused four-fold population increase apparently petered out. The SDYC almost did, too. By 1891 the club had 46 members, but it seems to have been almost moribund for the next decade; at least there is no record of its activity. In 1902 the commodore, exasperated at his inability to move the club to action, quit and founded the Corinthian Yacht Club. He seems to have taken many of the yacht-owning members with him. In addition, a dozen or so younger men founded a third club, the Phoenicia Yacht Club, which took as quarters a disused schooner, abandoned and berthed at one of the town's piers (it merged with the Corinthian in 1917).

The commodore's defection seems finally to have stirred the club to action. In 1903 twelve members met to reorganize the club and to lay plans for buying land and building a clubhouse. That was done, and a clubhouse was erected the following year. It was sold, however, for delinquent taxes, amounting to $9.21 including penalties, in 1909. In 1903 Sir Thomas Lipton put up a handsome silver cup for use as a challenge cup (how many Lipton Cups he scattered among North American yacht clubs over the years is not known, but there must be well over two dozen). That stimulated yachting interest greatly, and the SDYC won the first challenge in the 47½-foot racing machine, *Detroit,* imported from the Great Lakes against a local challenger and two from the South Coast Yacht Club of San Pedro (vic. Los Angeles Harbor). The competition began the tradition of interclub competition in Southern California and thus eventuated the Southern California Yachting Association to which the Club deeded the trophy in 1933. San Pedro Yacht Club wrested it away in the second match. The Lipton race continued to be sailed in San Diego until 1921, and it was the yachting event of the year.

Other than the Lipton events, most of the races of the San Diego and Corinthian clubs were sailed in catboats rented from two boat liveries in the bay. Both were poor and in debt, supported only by entrance fees of $10 and dues of 50 cents per month. In 1905 the two clubs gave up their separate lives and merged, keeping the San Diego Yacht Club's name but, since it was engraved on the Lipton Cup, Corinthian's burgee. Corinthian's clubhouse was retained and San Diego's rented. Next, the risky step of doubling the dues to $1 per month was taken. The negative reaction was small, and the club soon retired its combined total debt of $988.

This put the club on the road to full recovery, and it began to attract members men with yachts of significant size, a couple as large as 35 feet. By 1908 a member had built himself a 68-foot ketch in order to race in the Honolulu race (today's Transpac). It required several amateur musicals to raise money for rigging and outfitting her, and the twelve members of the crew were required to pay $35 each for their own food during the voyage out and back. The *Lady Maud* with the owner's wife and another woman aboard distinguished herself and the SDYC by coming in third of four yachts, edging out the favored yacht from Hawaii on corrected time.

Chula-Vista one-design, ***Nereid***
Captain C.D. Bolte of Chula Vista
Photo John Willett

Joseph E. Jessop at 92 and Jack Sutphen sailing a nine-foot Dyer 'Dink' in San Diego Harbor
Photo Bob Couarnubias

Also, in 1908 member Dr. E.W. Gahan founded the Junior Yacht Club, a separate organization with separate quarters for the sole purpose of training juniors for racing – the fourth such instance in North America. Gahan received two rich dividends from his investment: with junior crews, he won the Lipton Cup in 1909 and 1910. Then, he persuaded the SDYC to adopt the junior club formally. That step, taken rather reluctantly (it was said that Gahan threatened to resign if it was refused), would provide the club with many dividends in the future. It was a very forward-looking step for that time, perhaps too much so, for the program was discontinued and had to be re-started some years later.

In 1910, the club had its first one-design, very shoal-draft 27-footers – the Chula Vista.[57] The class was started by the Chula Vista Yacht Club located at the town of same name in the Southeast section of the Bay where the water was not as shoal as it is today. Built to uniform specifications and measurements with a gaff rig and short bowsprit, the class was one of the earliest one-designs on the Pacific Coast. The club was washed away by floodwaters when in 1916 the dam at the head of the valley (the major source of lemons for the U.S.) broke and silted up the Bay.

In 1910 SDYC had to look for a new home because of a landfill project in the face of which the clubhouse was smack in the way. That emergency was met by buying a disused ferry that had been a dance hall for several years. It was bought for $1,000, and San Diego's mayor donated $1,000 to furnish it. At the same time, the initiation fee was raised to $20 and the monthly dues, to $2. That enabled the club to raise the salary of the club manager from $35 to $40 a month. In addition to being keeper of the clubhouse, he had other duties: to run races, to tow stranded yachts home, to pull boats off the mud flats, and to run the club launch. The club then had 76 boats in its squadron, but only 17 were sailboats.

In 1914 the old ferry had to be moved again: more construction going on in the rapidly growing community. A gas-powered bilge pump was put aboard, and the old girl creaked and clanked her way across the bay to Coronado. That location was disadvantageous, for, although the bay is not very wide, it meant a ferry ride to get to the club. Nevertheless, the racing schedule between late May and mid-September grew to 23 events, and soon there was a regatta on New Year's Day and Washington's Birthday.

As it did to many clubs, World War I almost caused San Diego's demise. By the end of 1918, with many of the most active racers in the club gone for two years, and with the ferry having deteriorated beyond repair, the club was once again almost moribund. The ferry was dismantled, and the club arranged for temporary quarters with the Navy Sailing Club. It took three years to restore membership and a sustaining income. The first post-war regatta took place in 1920 with only ten boats, five from Los Angeles.

The matter of replacing the defunct clubhouse was addressed by a drive to obtain one hundred new members at an initiation fee of $100, to be converted, as an option, to club construction bonds. The arrangement was contingent on $10,000 being raised in this manner. The goal was met, and a new clubhouse was contracted for in that amount. Note that prices ratcheted up rapidly after the war, caused by world-wide inflation during 1919 and 1920. The clubhouse was well built and later (1934) readily survived being barged to pilings off Roseville Pier which is the site of the club's present home, approximately halfway between the City and Point Loma. It not only survived the trio but lasted until 1963 when it was replaced with a larger structure. In addition, the club acquired a second pier and building on the City side of the Bay for only $3,000 that it called Roseville – Station #2.

The San Diego Yacht Club hosted in 1924 the Southern California Yachting Association regatta and the second Pacific Coast Yachting Association regatta drawing 127 yachts, some all the way from Vancouver, Seattle, and San Francisco. A remarkable turnaround! Membership in the club at the end of that year stood at 174, the highest by far in its history. The next year member, Joe Jessop, won the Star Internationals on Long Island Sound, and that inaugurated a long tenure of the Star Class in San Diego Bay. The previous year the 'On to Ensenada' Committee had been formed to launch what became the popular race to Ensenada. There was also a major power-boat race, and the author of the Club History speculates on the possibility that the rapid advance in powerboat speed during the decade of the 1920's was sparked by the rum runners of the prohibition era. The remaining years of the decade represented continued growth and sailing successes over a widening horizon of competition far from home. The main clubhouse, still in Coronado, had to be enlarged to accommodate everyone.

Lacking a program for the juniors after the demise of the Junior Yacht Club, several youngsters approached the Commodore in 1928 to request that a junior sailing program be re-instituted. Once again, there was grumbling about "having kids under foot," but its proponents prevailed, and thanks to the leadership of Joe Jessop a junior program became part of the club's regular operation. This is really when the dividends began to accrue, and the SDYC's junior program has been the foundation of many of the championships the club has reaped since then. The Juniors started off in the Flapper, a 16-foot gaff-rigged class which did not catch on at the clubs on the Bay. The next year, however, an 18-year-old junior from the Southwestern Yacht Club, Joe Ruski, designed the appropriately-named Starlet which was built by George Kettenburg, Jr. It was a small edition of the Star, 16 feet 14 inches LOA, costing $70, including sails, if home-built, or $125 if built from a kit. While it caught on in the Bay, a proposal to have it adopted by the SCYA by the Junior Divisions of its member clubs on the grounds that,

> *The one-design feature is essential so that if boys (and girls) are unable to ship boats to a regatta site, local boats of the class will be available,*

failed. Coincidentally, a college student, John Lindeman, at the Encinal Yacht Club, Alameda, San Francisco Bay designed a similar boat 17 feet LOA for the same purpose known as the Junior or Baby Star. Either the San Francisco or the San Diego boat could have become national and international in scope inasmuch as they served the same purpose as the Snipe, i.e. an inexpensive and more easily handled version of the Star, but neither enjoyed the promotional boost given the Snipe by the yachting media a year later.

1930 was a banner year for another class that affected sailing on the West Coast and remains highly competitve today – the PC conceived by Joe Jessop, Sr. and George Kettenburg, Jr. and built at the latter's boatyard. Although sailed as one-designs, they rated very close to the Universal Rule 'S' Class which prompted the next year a team race with the 'S' fleet at Honolulu. The US Navy was persuaded to ship boats and crews to Hawaii for six weeks of team racing against the local fleet at the end of which the final score was 106 to 100 in favor of the PC's. The San Diego fleet was sold in Honolulu and eventually supplanted the 'S's. According to Joe Jessop, so many of the crews worked in San Diego banks that some of them closed their doors for the period. Family names such as Jessop, Kettenburg, Trepke, Driscoll, Scripps, etc. span several generations of yachting on the Bay and also Mission Bay where the Mission Bay YC was founded by Austen T. Bowen and his brother-in-law, Thomas O. Scripps whose uncle was Alonzo de Jessop, father of Joseph E.

The Great Depression affected the SDYC as it did all North American clubs, but seemingly less so than most. Perhaps that was because Southern California was the

San Diego PC 32-foot *Minx*, belonging to Jack Sutphen
Photo courtesy of the owner

fastest growing part of the country. By 1932, more of the club's boats were moored at Station #2 than at the Coronado clubhouse, for the majority of club members lived on Point Loma and in Mission Hills. Consequently plans were made to move the Coronado clubhouse to Station #2, and this was done, by barges, in 1934. It was a tricky job. Pilings had been installed in front of the existing pier, and the two barges were pushed in between them at high tide. When the building was exactly in place over the pilings, it was held there until the tide went down, setting the clubhouse neatly on the piles. The barges then were pulled out, attached to other pilings to become floats and a new veranda was built to overlook the bay.

The next year the club was host to the annual SCYA regatta in which 400 boats participated, 60 from Los Angeles. It was also the year in which the club enrolled its first woman member. Total membership passed the 200 mark, and tennis courts were built. Most important was a federal/state project to dredge a 200-foot channel 20 feet deep into the bay from the ocean, passing right in front of the club. Much of the dredge material was dumped on Shelter Island to the south, giving much needed protection from strong winds from that direction. The club was surviving the Depression very well.

THE SAN FRANCISCO YACHT CLUB[58]

The San Francisco Yacht Club was founded in 1869. The city was then only 20 years old as a formal community and only a decade away from having been a shanty town. The newcomers from the east, drawn by the discovery of gold in the vicinity, had a more important purpose than building proper houses. They also had little time for pleasure boating, if indeed many of them knew how to sail. Nevertheless, every ship bringing passengers "around the Horn" carried on deck one or more smaller boats that could be used either as working boats or yachts.

In 1860 the *Daily Alta* devoted the front page of one issue to recounting sailing activity on San Francisco Bay. Surprisingly there was enough to fill the entire page in the very small print that newspapers then used. There was record of two or three match races sailed in 1852 and during the next two years. In 1855 a group that called itself the San Francisco Yacht Club held an annual regatta in which six boats competed (and one man drowned when the boat he was on capsized). The next year its regatta had 13 entries. The same year, another group, calling itself the Pacific Yacht Club, held two races. The prizes for the second one, incidentally, were $50 for first place and a new suit of sails for second place, with the winner having the option of choosing which prize to claim. There was also mention of a Pioneer Club. None of the three clubs survived.

Thus, the 1869 SFYC ranks itself as the first *permanent* yacht club west of the Mississippi and as fifteenth on the continent before the advent of NAYRU that is extant. The Portland (ME) and Savannah (GA) Yacht Clubs were founded the same year on April 26 and June 14 respectively. One race was held by the SFYC that year, but the date is uncertain; it may have been in August, or it may have been in October. The only surviving account of it was written almost 20 years later. There were six boats in the race, three sloops and three schooners. The race was about 26 miles long. Starting near Mission Rock, the yachts sailed to a stakeboat off Hunters Point, to another across the Bay near Oakland and to a third stakeboat near the Golden Gate. After rounding the latter, they reversed course and sailed back around the first two marks to the finish line.

In that year, or the next, a small clubhouse was built on a railroad bridge that spanned a small inlet on the east side of the city. The second year another race was sailed, again with six boats of which two bore different names from those in the first, so the club apparently had eight yachts. The race was ordered abandoned by the judges when one of the yachts broke her jib stay! It was re-sailed a week later. A third race was held in 1871.

There were none for the next four years, in part due to the panic of 1872, during which mining stocks took a nosedive, and "almost every San Franciscan speculated in them." An old-time member writing many years later of the early days about the club, said:

> *[It] had a few sailing men and more who liked to go near the water and 'talk' yachts... A great many persons went to the clubhouse on Saturdays and Sundays to eat chowder.*

At some point the railroad bought the clubhouse, apparently somehow having sufficient leverage over the club to do so. Where they went after does not seem to be a matter of record. It may be that it found some space near the new Palace Hotel, for the club held its meetings in that monumental rococo 300-room structure. Also, a handbook published by the club in 1877 includes a table of distances, and many of them began at a nearby Front Street wharf. By 1876 racing had resumed, and there were two races, one with 29 entries. Among them were a small class of Plungers, centerboard catboats used by San Francisco oystermen but often converted for pleasure use. Their name suggests the motion of a boat in the Bay's celebrated steep chop.

Next year there were two more races. It would appear that every race sailed thus far had been around the same three stakeboats in the same locations; after the first race, the owner of one boat lodged a protest against the first mark having been moved to a new location, which he duly lost. During these years racing turned into "vendettas among the larger yachts, backed by large bets and attracting large spectator crowds." Apparently sportsmanship was not the paramount characteristic of races in which high stakes were involved; cf. the account in *Chapter I* of early racing in New York Harbor.

Before the year was over a committee of five was appointed to find a site for a new clubhouse. As the New York and Boston Yacht Clubs had already found, racing in a busy commercial harbor is not fun. The search led the committee to Sausalito, but the members disagreed over two sites. One was in Sausalito proper, and the other was in a district called New Sausalito. The members, owners of the largest yachts in the club, who carried paid crew to race, preferred the first site, the Corinthian contingent preferred the other. That created a fine row resulting in the big-boat members walking out, forming a new Pacific Yacht Club and building a clubhouse on the first site, while the remaining SFYC members built on the other. The latter proved to be the better location, although the clubhouse had to be built on pilings. Pacific's was in a more exposed area. While real estate developers later tried to re-name it as Shelter Bay, yachtsmen even today refer to it as Hurricane Gulch. Also, the SFYC's new home was only a short walk from the landing for a ferry across to the city.

Did the Corinthians remain loyal? In 1880 the club planned a race in which all skippers and crew had to be amateurs. Only four yachts turned out for it. But the very next year, four of the big-boat owners organized an open regatta for small boats in four classes ranging from 15 to 35 feet LOA. The four men formed their own race committee, banned money prizes, and bought a lot of silver to hand out as prizes. The event, called the Mosquito Regatta, a term used on both the west and east coasts for open racing in small centerboarders, was an instant success and became an annual event. Indeed, it was so successful that after five years those who came to compete in it decided to form a Corinthian Yacht Club, the constitution of which specified that no yacht more than 45 feet on deck was eligible for membership. The CYC is today in nearby Tiburon.

As the years rolled on, the club prospered as did San Francisco, where most of the members lived and worked. By 1890 the city's population had reached almost 300,000, and the next year it had its first skyscraper, the ten-story *Chronicle* building. The club contained many of the city's movers and shakers, but it was an unwritten rule of the club that politics and religion were not to be discussed within its walls. The rule changes were made, however, that gave the 'armchair admirals' of the club something to discuss and complain about. One was to require display of a flag in the rigging for a protest to be valid. The other was an increase in the time allowances from 45 seconds per foot of waterline to 60 seconds. Some wished to make it 75 seconds, which was commonly used on the east coast, but they had to settle for a compromise figure.

In 1895 several prominent yachtsmen of San Francisco Bay, some from SFYC, banded together to purchase a trophy designated as the San Francisco Perpetual Challenge Trophy. Initially it was deeded to the Encinal YC on the Bay at Alameda on the basis that it was to be for a match race challenge competition open to any club on the Pacific Coast. The SFYC challenged for it immediately, but Encinal defended it successfully that year and the next. Corinthian took it away in the third match. After one year with no challenge a San Francisco boat beat Corinthian's on corrected time. It seems strange, in the light of today's match race format, that such a match would not extend to at least three races.

In 1896 the Pacific Inter-Club Yacht Association was formed. It was, in fact, a protest against San Francisco's domination of the Bay. Its courses, its racing rules, and its sailing regulations were used by all the clubs in the bay, and several of the newer clubs wanted more say in how things were done. It was a matter of size exercising influence: all 57 of the largest yachts in the Bay were enrolled in the SFYC. Despite the underlying purpose of the movement, the SFYC supported it. For some reason, however, the new organization did not take hold and exercise its potential influence for a full decade.

By that time the earthquake of 1906 had occurred. It heavily damaged the city but left Sausalito untouched. Ironically, the quake launched the classic schooner *Yankee* on her own as she lay in her cradle poised on the way – she still sails on the Bay. For two months in the spring the club was a storehouse for the Red Cross supplies used to help the refuges from San Francisco. Nonetheless, the club opened on schedule in June. Up until about that time all racing had been done in the Bay, but after the first race to Honolulu, and on the east coast the first to Bermuda, interest in off-shore racing increased enormously. The commodore offered a cup for an open race to, around and back from the Farallon Islands, which lie 30 miles offshore. The race became popular and is still being run.

In 1915 a notable yacht, the 'N' class *Westward*, designed by William Gardner and sailed by John Hanify, won the King George IV Cup. Whereas a number of the larger 'M' boats raced in Long Island Sound waters, some of which migrated to the West coast, and the smaller 'Q's became popular on both coasts and on the Great Lakes, the 'N' is recorded as having been sparsely represented only on San Francisco Bay, Southern California, and Lake Michigan.

In 1925 the race to Tahiti was inaugurated thereby pioneering the world's longest ocean race. The following year, when the Club was faced with the alternatives of either relocating at Belvedere or at the San Francisco Marina near the City, a group of members favoring the latter broke off and founded the St. Francis Yacht Club.

Until after World War I, the club had been "basically a male retreat and domain." That began to change – very slowly – as women began playing a more visible role and children were given "more than a glazed glance." The movement received a push one day. There were a couple of dozen Sausalito kids, whose parents were members, who hung around the club after school and during the summer. No activity had ever been planned for them, but they amused themselves in various ways. One cold, foggy day in 1921, however, they built a fire in a bucket in the attic of the club to keep warm, and the smoke from the fire startled some members, who thought surely the club itself was on fire. It shook the Board of Directors, too. They held a meeting on the kid problem and decided to put them in the charge of the caretaker, a crusty old bos'n who had retired from the British Navy. First, he had them do yard work. Then he taught them how to paint. Next, he taught them knots, how to splice, and how to use a palm and needle. Then he taught them how to row. By the time he had done that, the Board had bought some Cub boats, an 18-foot John Alden design, so he taught them how to sail. That is a novel way to start a junior program, and although not the conventional way, it worked.

The club owes its survival through the 1929 depression years and the building of a clubhouse at its new Belvedere Cove site to Commodore Clifford Smith, the indefatigable man who had developed the Star fleet in the Bay in 1923 and who almost literally held the club together during the worst of the depression years. The clubhouse was small; in fact, the original floor area is now the dance floor of the dining room. The labors of building it, however, had a strong therapeutic effect on the club. Every hammer blow increased the spirit and determination of those who worked on it, which was almost every member, including their wives and children. The task was finished in 1934.

While the clubhouse was going up, a venerable and cherished yacht of the club was going down. That was the 53-foot sloop *Annie*. Built in New Jersey in 1861, she had a most impressive racing career on the east coast before being sold, at age 19, to a member of the SFYC. She continued to win races in San Francisco Bay for many years, but ultimately she grew frail with age. In 1935 her subsequent owner had to conclude that there was little that could be done to save her. Hence, with club members in solemn attendance, *Annie* was set afire and burned. Not, however, until her mast had been taken out to become the club's flagpole.

As a final note, we have seen how the club had twice been decimated by the departure en masse of dissident members. In 1941 the opposite happened. Five years earlier a group of young, small-boat sailors had established the Richardson Bay Yacht Club and optimistically bought the hulk of a disused barkentine, beached at

Sausalito, as a clubhouse. That soon proved to be a mistake, for the old windjammer was literally beginning to fall apart. After they burned her, they rented the San Francisco Yacht Club's Sausalito clubhouse for $25 a month. By 1941, with one hundred fifty members and thirty sailboats, but with WW II on the horizon and most of its members of draft age, the club's future suddenly became uncertain. "It was a great relief," said member Roger Eldridge, "when the San Francisco Yacht Club agreed to take us in, lock, stock, and barrel... It was as though we ran into their sheltering arms."

THE SEATTLE YACHT CLUB[59]

Seattle lies on the eastern shore of Puget Sound, which extends some ninety miles from its southern terminus at Olympia to its northern terminus at Port Townsend from which it is another 90 miles westward out the Strait of Juan de Fuca past Victoria on Vancouver Island to the Pacific Ocean or 80 miles north to the port of Vancouver. The Strait was named by an early Spanish explorer and the Sound in 1792 by George Vancouver who had been navigator for Captain James Cook. Considering the distances it is remarkable that the yacht clubs in British Columbia and the State of Washington have been able to compete jointly for over a century.

There were no settlements on Puget Sound, however, until the 1850's, and their growth was slow. The census of 1880 showed only some 3,500 residents of Seattle. Real growth would not begin until 1893 when the tracks of the Great Northern Railway reached the town. What little leisure time the residents had was spent mostly on hunting and fishing. Nonetheless, a few sailboats existed, and six raced in a regatta in 1875 on Elliot Bay, an elbow of the Sound that serves as Seattle's harbor. The next year was the country's centennial year, and 15 boats signed up for the regatta that was part of the celebrations.

Boat races seem to have become a custom for the Fourth of July celebrations, and a Seattle newspaper mentioned a Seattle Yacht Club in 1879, but no other record was ever found. If it existed, it was very informal and was intermittently mentioned in the reports of Fourth of July festivities. An 1890 report refers to the club being 'founded' and lists names of the 22 members with dues at 50 cents a month and a proposed schedule of events. Yet, in 1892 it was 'founded again', and the club regards that as its official beginning point, since it was solidly functional from that date on.

That it was solidly functional is attested to by the fact that, during the 1890's the population of Seattle almost doubled, reaching 81,000 by 1900. That meant job opportunities were increasing steadily, and money was being made by the business community. The city also had a maritime background, inasmuch as all the early citizens had arrived by sea, and Puget Sound was Seattle's only 'highway' to and from the outside world for many years. Another factor, perhaps, was the migration of a number of yachtsmen from East Coast cities to Seattle. They were shocked at how little this marvelous sailing area was used, and one such person urged that the club take in members who knew nothing about sailing and teach them at club expense.

If the 1892 founding went well, the compilation of the centennial history for 1992 did not. During the 1960's, in preparation for some renovation work, someone threw out much of the records of 70 years' activity. A member took home what was left with the intention of writing a history. He promptly died, however, and his widow inadvertently threw out all that he had rescued. Thus, the entire job of research for the first 20 years, and much for the next 50, had to be done with outside records, which made it far more difficult.

It was summer when the 1892 organizational meetings took place, and two priorities were established. The first was to find a site for a clubhouse and begin building one. The second was the reason for the urgency of the first: the newly formed Northwest International Yachting Association decided to hold its first annual regatta in Seattle in October to honor the newest club in these western Canadian/American waters.

A site was soon found in West Seattle. A real estate development company agreed to lease the club a generous piece of land there for $1 a year, and construction began immediately. It was financed by three methods: first, dues ($1 per month) were collected for a year in advance; second, two hundred corporate shares at $5 a piece were issued; third, as a carrot, the first 200 people to pay the initiation fee ($5) and dues would be designated as charter members.

The building was not finished in time, but it turned out that it didn't make much difference. The regatta had to be canceled after two days of no wind and one of dense fog. A worse blow was that members very quickly became disinclined to use the clubhouse. One of the reasons for selecting the site was that a ferry from downtown had a West Seattle dock nearby. Yet, members asserted that it was inconveniently located and within a few years it stood vacant.

Two years later another club was founded in Seattle calling itself the Elliot Bay Yacht Club. Its members appear either to have been men who did not feel able to afford the Seattle Yacht Club or potential members who did not want to go out to West Seattle. By mooring their boats downtown and nearer their homes, they could keep an eye on them more easily during bad weather. (Actually, most of the SYC members moored their boats there, too.) For quarters the club rented a room in a building on one of the downtown piers. For the most part their boats were smaller than those of the SYC, but to judge from the vocations of its four commodores over 11 years, who were successively a manufacturer of jewelry, a dentist, a towboat company president, and a shipbuilder, it had a distinguished membership.

It cannot be said that the racing activity of either club was non-stop. The SYC had its Fourth of July Regatta, and the EBYC had its Labor Day regatta. All else were scrub races, sometimes with only two boats. There is no evidence of a rivalry between the two, nor even any competition between them, unless it occurred on an informal basis during those scrub races.

Most of the information about the early years came from microfilm records of the *Seattle Post-Intelligencer.* Its yachting reporter faithfully recorded the yachts in a race, their owners, the course sailed, the wind conditions, the order of finish, and the enthusiasm of spectators. But he gave no evidence of knowing anything about boats and racing (once referring to a new, up-to-date yacht, he mentioned that her facilities included a toilet room).

As a result it is difficult to visualize much about the boats that were sailing in and around Seattle. We do know that the largest yacht in the area was a 63-foot yawl, owned by the richest man in Seattle and the next commodore of the SYC. There was also an "up-to-date knockabout," and "about 20 of the smallest class." Many years later a member who grew up during the period wrote of "skipjacks," boats whose hulls resembled today's Snipe but were larger, carrying crews of three or four. There were perhaps half a dozen of them. He also mentioned a schooner, whose owner installed a four-horsepower gasoline engine in her in 1899, making her "the first auxiliary sailboat in the northwest."

During the first decade of the new century most of the formal racing activity in Seattle still amounted to the Fourth of July Regatta of the SYC and the Labor Day Regatta of the EBYC. When twice asked to host the Northwest International YA Regatta, the SYC had to seek help from the EBYC in managing it. There were distractions, or deterrents, to racing from two directions. One was cruising. Puget Sound had many attractive gunkholes, and the waters to the north had more islands than one could visit in a lifetime.

The other was powerboats, both naptha and gasoline, which had become very popular almost overnight. They raced on the above-mentioned Lake Washington East of Seattle at speeds that sometimes exceeded 20 knots. They also cruised on the Sound at a much more sedate velocity. In 1907 during a celebratory evening parade with illuminated paper lanterns, almost one hundred powerboats chugged around the harbor.

The Seattle Yacht Club was sinking rapidly into a moribund state. This was despite continuing rapid growth of the city, whose population increased from 81,000 in 1900 to 237,000 in 1910. Many years later, a member wrote that, in 1907, the club consisted of "a little shanty perched on a cedar float." The Elliot Bay Yacht Club also ran into trouble when its lease on a downtown pier was cancelled in 1904. Despite the setback it negotiated a long-term lease of waterfront land from the city and had its own clubhouse, not far from the SYC's original building, by 1907.

Merger was inevitable, and it occurred two years later with the tail wagging the dog. They became the Seattle Yacht Club, but the EBYC officers would run it, and its flag would be the burgee. The SYC's only contribution to the merger was its single asset: $1,260 in its treasury. When the merger took place, the EBYC's first yearbook was about to go to press. A brief notice of the merger was hastily inserted, but there was not time for anything more. The yearbook contained pictures of the EBYC's flag officers, past and present, but those of the SYC were absent.

In 1909 and 1910 two incidents, unfortunately, soured international relations in the area. The first was the Alexandra Cup – a match racing challenge cup. The East Coast had its Seawanhaka cup and Lake Ontario its Canada's cup; in the same vein the Vancouver Yacht Club (soon to become 'Royal') offered a challenge cup, named for the yacht *Alexandra* that would defend against any challenge, best two of three races. The Seattle Yacht Club challenged, and it was agreed to hold the match at its venue during two weeks of racing in celebration of the Alaska-Yukon-Pacific Exposition.

The Seattle yacht, Ted Geary's *Spirit II*, won the first race, but Vancouver insisted that she be re-measured. A dispute arose over the measurement, and the Vancouver's yacht, *Alexandra*, pulled up stakes and departed home, alleging that she had been measured with her gaff and boom hoisted vertically against her mast and with an anchor stowed in her bow. These actions depressed her bow and raised her stern, thus reducing her waterline and improving her rating. The *Spirit II* completed a sail-over, was declared the winner, and claimed the Cup. The Vancouver Yacht Club refused to deliver it, and that summarily ended the international challenge for several years. This led, in Ted Geary's words, "to strained relations with good friends across the border which lasted four years."

The second incident was the Northwest International Yachting Association Regatta of 1910 held at Victoria. The club did such a splendid job that the NIYA board awarded Victoria the event for the next three years, and the other member clubs were to chip in to cover expenses. Seattle, for one, was assessed $100. Apparently, the member clubs considered this to have been in a high-handed manner, for none of them paid their assessments. As a result, the 1911 event was cancelled, and the NIYA became a thing of the past.

When Vancouver and Seattle yachts were measured for the Alexandra Cup in 1909, under what rule was it done? It was the International Rule (under which the 'metre' classes were measured) that had been adopted by the new IYRU in London in 1907. Three years earlier a consortium of New York and Boston clubs, led by the NYYC, had adopted a rule devised for them by N.G. Herreshoff. Initially called the Herreshoff Rule, it soon became the Universal Rule, a misnomer since it was never adopted overseas, and spread across the continent supplanting the Seawanhaka Rule as it went. This meant there were two rules in the Northwest, and inasmuch as the preponderance of numbers, both in yachts and yacht clubs was heavily on the American side, the Canadians ultimately agreed that the joint rule should be the Universal Rule, although reserving the International Rule for certain events or classes.

In 1912 Sir Thomas Lipton, while on a ship's cruise, visited Seattle and became a guest of the Seattle Yacht Club. Upon learning of the strained relations resulting from the aborted Alexandra Cup Challenge, he offered to present another challenge cup, obviously to be called the Lipton Cup. How many cups the famous tea merchant and super salesman brought, or later sent, to the U.S. is unknown. A few years ago, a Lipton Cup was discovered in a dark corner of a vault in a Quincy, MA bank, where it had been sitting in a box for, possibly, as many as 75 years. It is again being raced for. Sir Thomas did not do it on the cheap; the Seattle cup cost him $3,000 in pre-WW I U.S. dollars.

The SYC decided that the appropriate boat for the cup would be the 'R' Class under the Universal Rule. Member Ted Geary immediately called a friend at the Vancouver with the news and asked for a challenge, which was given then and there. He then set to work designing and having built, with the help of a syndicate, an 'R' to defend against Vancouver's challenge. Geary when a lad had built his first sailboat himself, and he had already designed his first winning yacht before going off to Cambridge to study marine architecture at MIT. Upon his return, he became one of the leading yacht designers of both sail and power in the northwest. It was *Spirit II* designed by him, incidentally, that allegedly had been measured in such a bizarre manner during the Alexandra Cup. Geary never answered that allegation but replied only to a second charge that boarded on the trivial.

Ted Geary called the new yacht *Sir Tom* and successfully defended the Lipton Cup against Vancouver in 1914. *Sir Tom* (38 feet LOA, 23 feet LWL, and 8 feet beam) went on to become the most famous yacht in the history of the SYC and in the class on the Pacific coast. She either won, or successfully defended, the Lipton Cup four more times. She won the Pacific International Yachting Association 'R' class championship for 16 straight years. (The PIYA was successor to the Northwest International Yachting Association) She won the Pacific Coast 'R' class championship five times, on four occasions sailing all the way down to Southern California to San Diego to compete. Geary after every victory sent a clipping to Sir Thomas until the old man died. *Sir Tom* outlived her namesake by many years; she was 43 when she finally had to be broken up.

The Seattle Yacht Club entered 1913 with 371 members and 88 boats, both sail and power. Among the boats were ten small one-designs, bought by the club for the encouragement of young men who might want to learn to sail and become interested enough in the sport to buy their own boats and "enjoy to the full the joys of yachting and cruising on Puget Sound." As often was the case with junior programs, especially during the 1930 depression years, it was also intended to be a source of new members. The current membership reflected not only the vigor of the club and the prosperity of Seattle but also its population. There were now more than a quarter-million residents, due in good part to the opening of the Panama Canal.

Notably the club had a greatly expanded schedule of racing and cruising events. This reflected not only the spirited interest of the members but also the climate of Puget Sound. While Seattle is five degrees of latitude north of Chicago and Boston, it has a much milder winter climate than both. Yachting could begin in March and continue through October, whereas on the Great

Lakes and in New England north of Cape Cod it was, and continued to be for many years, strictly a Fourth of July to Labor Day activity.

In 1912 the SYC established its first outstation on nearby Bainbridge Island. It also celebrated its 20th anniversary with a dinner at a local hotel, where the tables in the banquet hall were laid out in the shape of an 'H', with the sailors on one side, the powerboat men on the other, and the officers and guests in the middle. In 1916 a new club, the Queen City Yacht Club, was established solely for powerboats. It was perhaps one of the first, if not the first, such club in the country. It still exists, its premises presumably undefiled by the presence of sailboats.

In 1918 the U.S. government did the SYC a huge favor: it took the West Seattle clubhouse and property, little used since it was built, off its hands to create a training center for prospective merchant marine sailors. In the prior year the project of six years duration – connecting Lake Washington with Puget Sound had been completed. This required a short canal from the Lake to Portage Bay and a long one from Lake Union west to the Sound. With the proceeds of the sale the club purchased property on Portage Bay where it built its current clubhouse. While it is still the club's main base, a SYC member today may use any of 11 outstations ranging from lat 47° 20' N in South Puget Sound to lat 50° 3.3' N in the area of Desolation Sound in British Columbia; four are manned. Many members are also members of the Corinthian Yacht Club situated on Shileshole Bay near the exit of the Canal to the Sound.

The big news of 1920 was the establishment of the Pacific International Yachting Association (PIYA). World War I, which had engaged the Canadians far longer than the Americans, was finally over, and the rift that had occurred well before it began was healed by the new organization. The custom of issuing honorary memberships had been initiated by the New York and Eastern Yacht Clubs. In 1900 for example, they both listed the Prince of Wales, King Alfonso of Spain, the President of the United States, the Secretary of the Navy, and several others as honorary members. It was partly a public relations gesture and partly the expression of social prowess. By 1921 the SYC had a very long list, ranging from Sir Thomas Lipton to the Inspectors of Steam Engines for Puget Sound to the city's Chief of Police (most politic to have those gentlemen on one's side)

In 1921 there were two departures from standard activities. First, the club bought an eight-oared shell with which members raced the University of Washington and the Portland Rowing Club. The other was the development of a junior program for the children of senior members. The boats used were small catboats, a local boat called a "flattie" because of its completely flat bottom, and later Star boats. The junior club was unusual in that its members could remain such until they became 26. Their clubhouse was a room in the basement of the club.

The 1920's were the decade of the great experiment: prohibition. It was less a problem in Seattle than in many other localities. It was only 100 miles to Vancouver, and a former Seattle police lieutenant developed a thriving import business, using a fleet of several fast powerboats to provide dockside delivery of whiskey to parched citizens, including club members. He came a cropper, however, in 1929, when he was convicted of smuggling and sent to jail. In 1933, when prohibition was repealed, he was pardoned by President Roosevelt.

It was also a period of continuous growth – of members, of boats, both sail and power, of racing, and of property. This ended with the stock market crash of October, 1929. For two or three years, the club's survival was in doubt, and the few members who remained were reduced to providing the club's maintenance and repairs themselves. For the Opening Day celebration in 1931 only 40 sailboats turned out on Lake Washington, far fewer than had been out there two years before.

In 1931 the Club sponsored an ocean going race, the Swiftsure Lightship Race, over a 160-mile course from Cadboro Bay, through the Strait of Juan de Fuca, 18 miles into the Pacific, around the Swiftsure Lightship and return. Intermittent for the next decade or two, it became a very popular race involving swift currents, fog and a wide range of weather conditions. In 1951 the start was moved to Victoria, and Royal Victoria Yacht Club assumed responsibility for conducting the Race.

The Star boat, in great favor during the early '20's, made a comeback, since it fitted better the straitened bank accounts of the members. Other inexpensive one-designs in Puget Sound during the decade were the Knockabout (essentially a Star with a cabin), the "flattie," the Lightning, the Penguin, the El Toro, and the International Fourteen.

Recovery was slow throughout the '30's, and the SYC resorted to a "hard sell" to attract new members, even offering free parking as an inducement. Annual dues had to be kept low and, at $25, they were little more than they had been at the beginning, when adjusted for inflation. The year 1940, with war impending, made Seattle a "boom town" almost overnight, and the club's fortunes turned abruptly upward where they have been ever since.

'R' boat *Sir Tom* under her original rig,
Ted Geary designer and helmsman
Photo from the Seattle Yacht Club Historical Files

THE SEAWANHAKA CORINTHIAN YACHT CLUB[60]

Oyster Bay on the north shore of Long Island is about 35 miles from the island of Manhattan and one of the few ports of the island that pre-dats the American Revolution. In 1871 there were only two ways to get to Oyster Bay. One was by ferry across the East River, then by a train drawn by a wood-burning engine, with the final five miles by carriage. The other was by steam vessel, a three-hour trip up the river and along Long Island Sound.

Yet, the yacht club was founded in that sleepy fishing village in 1871 by a dozen New Yorkers who had summer homes there. It was called Seawanhaka, the Indian name for Long Island, meaning land of seashells. Its primary purpose was to encourage Corinthian sailing and racing. When the New York Yacht Club was founded in 1844, that has been its purpose, too. The club soon discovered, however, that most of the new members it had attracted could not race and maintain their yachts without the assistance of professional captains and usually some crew. Other clubs had the same experience.

Seawanhaka's first Sailing Regulations contained two items that would make major contributions to yachting: 1) in all regattas, the owner (or another club member) must steer each competing yacht: 2) no yacht, after taking her position, shall start water or ballast, no shifting of ballast, no booming-out of ballast, and she shall "bring home" the same ballast with which she started. The second regulation was intended to halt the long-standing custom of disposing of ballast, when the wind went light or the final leg was a run, and constantly moving ballast to the new windward side after tacking on a beat. The practice was not only pernicious, requiring additional crew to do only that back-breaking work, but dangerous, for it encouraged unsafe designs. Indeed, the grossly over-rigged 30-foot sandbaggers, prevalent in that part of Long Island Sound, could not sail without ten crew and their 50-pound bags of sand.

Seawanhaka took a ribbing over its Corinthian fetish from Historian Captain R. F. Coffin[61] who lampooned it in 1887:

> *There has been some little boasting on the part of the Seawanhaka Club over a claim that they were the first to introduce 'Corinthian' racing, and so fearful have its members been that their superiority in this respect would be lost sight of in the now almost general adoption of this method, either in whole or in part, that some years ago they tacked the word 'Corinthian' on to their originally beautiful Indian name 'Seawanhaka', making it a clumsy and cumbersome title out of their first extremely appropriate name; I suppose few, if any, of these young gentlemen are aware that on the 6th day of October, 1846, the New York Yacht Club sailed a match for a cup subscribed for by members, the rule being – "none but club members allowed to sail or handle the boats, but each yacht may carry a pilot."*

Captain Coffin never reported that the New York Yacht Club match was repeated only once – in 1847 – and would not become a feature of the club's racing until decades later.

In the early years meetings were held in summer aboard Commodore William L. Swan's yacht[62] and in winter at Delmonico's, a famous restaurant in lower Manhattan. The club's closest association was with the Atlantic Yacht Club of South Brooklyn, which was much nearer to the members' homes than Oyster Bay.

Despite its remote location, Seawanhaka grew steadily holding two or three regattas a year, beginning on the Fourth of July. It was unable, however, to accept the invitation of Atlantic to joint its 1874 cruise, for it had only two ocean-going vessels. Notwithstanding, it sponsored an important race at Newport, an open Corinthian race for schooners – and the right people came to sail as amateurs: from Seawanhaka (2 entries), New York (2), Eastern (2), Boston (1), Atlantic (1), and Brooklyn (2). The Race Committee was composed of the Commodores of Seawanhaka, New York, and Eastern. The start was under the new "flying start" system (as opposed to being at anchor until the starting gun), conceived in England two years before: two starting signals, ten minutes apart, yachts to be timed as they crossed the line.

The race was won by *Idler* out of Seawanhaka, which took the $500 silver prize.[63] It had demonstrated that amateurs could handle large vessels competently. While successful, the news of this approach to the sport was not received favorably in many quarters. Indeed, one newspaper observed that it could not understand "how gentlemen could demean themselves by performing the work which they paid their servants to do." The professional captains and crewmen were, of course, dismayed.

The next year, the club wound up leasing a pier on Staten Island, then an independent community. With the lease came sufficient land on which to build a small clubhouse just large enough to provide locker and storage space. The reason for doing so was that most of the club's members lived and worked in Manhattan, and Oyster Bay was an inconvenient location. The club was not walking away from any property investment, but it was walking away from the small fraction of the membership who lived there. The abandoned members then regretfully formed the Oyster Bay Yacht Club.

The actual Seawanhaka clubhouse was still Delmonico's restaurant, where all meetings were held. These meetings came presently to include a lecture series, open to all, and conducted by professionals who came to instruct amateur yachtsmen on the subjects of racing tactics, sail handling, and yacht design. The last was considered the most important, for members were sorely deficient in knowledge of what a boat's hull should look like, why, and how it moves.

As was reflected in the chapter on the New York Yacht Club, the designs of yachts had become increasingly troublesome or – to use a word commonplace at the time – unwholesome. Yachts were wet, uncomfortable, lacking in cabin space, and, worst of all, unsafe. The young Seawanhaka club took that as a challenge and enlisted the cooperation of the New York Yacht Club to find a solution. It suggested consideration of an idea by a British designer, Dixon Kemp, who believed that a wholesome yacht could be achieved by a measurement rule that encouraged a balance between waterline length and sail area. The two clubs agreed on principle but disagreed on what seemed a minor point but was, in fact, a major difference. So each adopted its own version of the principle in 1876. Seawanhaka's, called the Seawanhaka Rule, was simply LWL + square root of SA divided by 2.

The rule was quickly adopted in North America, even by the Boston clubs, which had used successfully for two decades a very simple version of the 'Herreshoff Rule' (see the section on the Boston Yacht Club). The Rule worked because everyone understood the purpose of the formula: the two elements were intended to be of equal weight. New yachts coming down the ways had more freeboard, more draft, less beam and smaller sail plans. The rule worked so well that five years later Dixon Kemp persuaded the Yacht Racing Association of Great Britain to adopt it. But sail area soon began increasing and LWL, decreasing. In 1891 N.G. Herreshoff sealed the doom of the Seawanhaka Rule. He realized that when a yacht is heeled over on the wind the immersed length of the hull, rather than the measured LWL, became the effective LWL. With this in mind, he designed Gloriana with 60-feet LOA and 45 feet LWL and a hull shaped so that when heeled her effective LWL increased to 50 feet! Every foot that the rule credited to her LWL, Capt. Nat used to gain more sail area. *Gloriana* was simply unbeatable. In one year she wiped out the New York Yacht Club's vaunted new 46-foot class, thereby ending its career.

To return briefly to portable ballast. It was not only most onerous work to shift bags of iron shot or pigs of iron or sand, but it was self-defeating. Until all the ballast had been shifted to the new windward side after a tack, a yacht was either lugging along or sailing beyond her lines. British clubs had banned it in 1856; the Boston-area clubs banned it in 1871. Seawanhaka's first rules banned it in 1872, but clubs in New York were slow to follow suit. A technological development pushed them along. Lead as ballast was five to ten times as expensive as iron, but increasing affluence in Great Britain and America made its use affordable. At first there was a mixture of the two, and the lead was placed lowest in the hull; then it was all lead but inside the hull; and ultimately some outside, some inside. The problem with outside ballast was the difficulty of securely fastening it and the concern that it might be knocked off by grounding. In 1860 George Watson of Scotland solved the problem when he designed and built three yachts on which all the lead ballast was securely fastened outside to the bottom of the keel. The issue of shifting ballast became moot.

In 1886 Seawanhaka, successful in so many of its efforts thus far, was forced to retrench on amateurism. The sailing regulations were changed by the annual meeting to say: "Professional crews shall be allowed on schooners and first and second class sloops and yawls." American yachtsmen were still not able to accept simon-pure Corinthian racing. Also, while many were wealthy enough to purchase large yachts, finding enough amateurs to crew them and maintain them was not feasible. This continued to be the case into the next century in the case of the larger classes such as NY 30's, Twelve-Metres and offshore yachts.

In 1887 the club at its last meeting at Delmonico's, voted to lease a residence on 32nd Street as a city clubhouse. It also voted to continue its lecture series, still open to all at a modest fee, and to include basic and celestial navigation. At the same time, it established a committee to work with other clubs to solve the problem of classification, the system for which was chaotic. When entering an open regatta at one club, a yacht would be assigned to a given class. The next week at a different club she would be assigned to yet another class. The method of classification was random and made many owners most unhappy.

From their inception the Boston Yacht Club (1866) and Seawanhaka Corinthian Yacht Club (1871) had been the most progressive in the Northeast. Both also strongly supported Corinthian sailing. In its first year SCYC banned the shifting of ballast during a race, a step that was soon followed by most of the yachting community, notably excepting the Sandbaggers. Five years later it sponsored a new measurement rule. Immediately called the Seawanhaka Rule, it temporarily leveled out the extremes on which yacht design was foundering. In 1888 the minutes of the annual meeting record a paper read by an officer of the club on the pressing need for a national yachting organization and adoption of the following resolution:

> *Resolved, that the present Committee on Yachting Interests... is hereby requested to consider the expediency of the formation of a general yacht racing association, or of one to include the principal clubs of the Atlantic Coast, such formation to include ... a uniform classification, a uniform system of measurement and uniform racing rules; they are hereby authorized... to represent this club officially at all meetings with representatives of other clubs, and to do any and all things that may become necessary to accomplish the object in view.*

In prior years several smaller and less influential clubs and groups of clubs had issued similar calls, but this was the first time that it had been attempted by one of the large clubs. It would be eight years before such an organization would be formed, and when NAYRU was established in 1897, Oliver Cromwell of Seawanhaka was elected its President.

The leased land on Staten Island, because of club growth, had become greatly overcrowded, and the club began to seek land for a permanent location. Several sites were considered, but in the end it was voted to return to Oyster Bay. There were several reasons for that. First, racing in New York Bay, Upper or Lower, was becoming increasingly unsatisfactory because of heavy ship traffic and commercial development along its shores. Second, rail service to Long Island had improved dramatically and had been extended to Oyster Bay. Third, there were now a number of yacht clubs at the western end of the Sound, notably Larchmont and the American at Rye. There was also the Oyster Bay Yacht Club formed by its deserted members who had waited patiently for their parent club to come home.

The site chosen was unsettled Centre Island which protected the harbor of Oyster Bay from the Sound. The purchase was made in June 1891, and a commodious clubhouse was erected and opened 12 months later, complete with piers, docks, and tennis courts. A nine-hole golf course, the first course on Long Island, soon followed, and the remainder of the purchased land was put up for sale to members. While construction of the clubhouse was in progress, access had to be considered. Centre Island was virtually an island connected to the mainland on the north side of the Bay by a man-made causeway. Access to it was via a tedious and uncomfortable trip by horse and buggy from the railroad station on the south side of the Bay. Hence the club purchased a 50-foot steam launch for the two-mile run to and from the townside pier, and in keeping with the societal proprieties of the day, it acquired a smaller naptha launch for the club's employees. During the opening-day ceremonies, the happy amalgamation of the Oyster Bay Yacht Club and the Seawanhaka Corinthian Yacht Club was announced.

In 1895 the final tie to New York City was severed by a decision not to renew the lease on the city house on 32nd Street. Before the club departed, however, it sponsored three meetings with representatives of 15 of the 20 yacht clubs then existing on the Sound. The meetings resulted in the formation of the Yacht Racing Union of Long Island Sound, to the presidency of which Seawanhaka member and prime mover Oliver Cromwell was elected. That made eight regional yachting associations, the Lake Yachting Association (Lake Ontario), Inter-Lake Yachting Association (Lake Erie), Newport Yacht Racing Association (Narragansett Bay), British Columbia Yacht Racing Association, Northwest International Yacht Racing Association, Yacht Racing Association of Massachusetts Bay and Lake Michigan Yacht Racing Association as well as Yacht Racing Union of the Great Lakes as an umbrella organization.

In 1896 Seawanhaka reached out to wider waters by establishing the Seawanhaka Corinthian International Challenge Cup (for Small Yachts). Under the deed the definition of "Small Yacht" was one that, "shall not exceed the maximum limit of the so-called 'Twenty-five-foot Racing Length Class' or fall below the minimum limit of the so-called 'Fifteen-foot Racing Class' of the Seawanhaka Club [i.e. Rule]... All matches shall be sailed between a single yacht on behalf of the challenging club and a single yacht on behalf of the challenged club." The second challenge was by the Royal St. Lawrence Yacht Club of Montreal. By agreement the '97 match was to be sailed in the 20-foot Racing Length class rather than the 15-foot previously used. Since the Rule over 20 years had been bent out of all recognition of its original purpose, the yachts were most extreme with as much, or more overhangs than LWL and so little freeboard that, "... it was common practice when running in rough seas or a crew member to lie thwartships just forward of the cockpit to prevent the boat from filling when she dove under a wave." As an indication of improvisations being used to add sail area, there was a prohibition against rigging the spinnaker pole as a bowsprit.

Seawanhaka triumphed in the first event but lost the cup to the Royal St. Lawrence in the second. It would be a number of years before it came back to the U.S. and then it would be to the Manchester Yacht Club (MA). It was, however, another example of Seawanhaka's progressive and innovative approach to yacht racing. At the 1897 annual meeting the Club took one step forward and one backward. First, it created a 'B' class of membership for men under 30 with no initiation fee and annual dues of $15 (Class 'A' members paid $50). Patently, it was to attract more younger members, and it worked. By the end of the year there were so many new 'B' members that the limit of club membership of 400 was reached.

The second step was to reduce the length of yachts permitted to carry one professional from 25-foot LWL to 20. Clearly it was to accommodate the smaller classes that were being raced by younger members rather than a reversion to the era of professionals in charge and wagers being laid. At clubs in general, as the Boston Yacht Club was finding, the concept of the entire crew being amateur was still having tough going. Yet, a close reading of the Seawanhaka history suggests that the younger members believed they did not need such a concession in order to compete; the rosters of crews of the smaller yachts seemed to contain only members and their friends. Lest we think, however, that the 400 members of Seawanhaka produced a great amount of racing, Parkinson notes that in 1897 there were only 15 racing days, four of which were the trials for the Seawanhaka Cup. At the annual regatta, 33 yachts competed in 14 classes, ranging from 95-foot schooners to the 20-foot Seawanhaka Cup class, and there were four sailovers by single entries. This is consistent with what would have been found at most of the major clubs at that time.

In 1898 Seawanhaka commissioned the construction of twenty-two small cabin sloops of 21-foot LWL called 'knockabouts'. The term was never officially defined, but it was originally applied to fishing schooners without bowsprits and in the case of yachts generally referred to smaller classes – sloops 30 feet LWL and less – without bowsprits. Knockabouts originated in the Boston area but soon spread to Buzzards Bay, Narragansett Bay, Long Island Sound and a few as far south as New Orleans. Their popularity lasted for several decades and laid the basis for the tradition of intra-club racing in one-designs without time allowances that could be ordered in quantity at a reduced cost. In effect, younger members not only could afford to acquire them, but also the small number of crew obviated the expense of professionals.

By 1896, the Yacht Racing Association of Great Britain had found that the measurement rule it had adopted from America had become a disaster and replaced it. In North America similar misgivings were arising about the Seawanhaka Rule. John Parkinson said of the yachts then being built: "They were disgraceful examples of marine architecture." With very little underbodies, exaggerated overhangs, and excessive sail plans, they were an expensive and dangerous parody of what a 'wholesome' yacht should look like.

It is difficult when reading the histories of the New York and Seawanhaka Corinthian Yacht Clubs to decide which club was the most responsible for phasing out the Seawanhaka Rule. The difficulty is compounded by the fact that most of the principal players were members of both; indeed, the histories of both were written by the same person. On the strength, however, of Seawanhaka's refusal to accept the British rule adopted by NAYRU (see *Chapter III – YRAs – Long Island Sound*), it is reasonable to assume that the NYYC assumed the pre-eminent role. For the story of how the Universal Rule replaced the Seawanhaka Rule see *'R' and Six-Metre Classes Chapter VIII* and *Chapter IX – Rating Rules*.

Not only were the technically-minded men involved in measurement rules members of both clubs, but about one-third of the members of each held dual membership. The same opulent yachts, from sloops of 90 feet to a schooner of more than 200 feet and steam yachts exceeding 300 feet, appear on the rosters of both clubs and are convincing testimony that the turn-of-the-century represented the golden era of yachting – one never to be repeated. In 1905 a suggestion was made to merge the two clubs. That would have benefited New York, whose only station near New York City was a very small structure at Glen Cove (approximately half way by water between Oyster Bay and Manhattan). It would also have benefited Seawanhaka by giving its members access to the new and magnificent New York Yacht Club quarters in the city on West 44th St. It is doubtful that the idea ever received serious consideration.

On a page devoted to the activities of 1907 Parkinson states: "The Ladies Race was won by the 15-footer *Bobs*, sailed by Mrs. W. A.W. Stewart." Nothing more. Was that a first-time event for women? By then the 15-foot class (23 feet LOA) had supplanted the knockabouts, and more racing appeared to have been taking place at Seawanhaka in that class than in any others. In 1910 there is another reference to the Ladies Race, and in 1911 Alice Landon is recorded as having "sailed the 15-footer *Imp* to victory over the men." Whether or not 1907 marked the first racing by women at Seawanhaka, it was surely among the leaders, if not the sole leader, in providing that opportunity to women.

In the spring regatta of 1916 there were, in addition to one handicap class, 13 one-design classes, including the Star Class which was in its fifth year. They ranged from the Fifty-foot Class to the dinghies that were 15 feet overall. It would appear that one-designs predominated at Seawanhaka.

Just ahead was United States involvement in World War I, and many Seawanhaka members who owned suitable power yachts offered them to the U.S. Navy, as did members of yacht clubs up and down the east coast. These were used as patrol boats on the lookout for German ships, particularly at the entrances to significant shipping harbors. The arrangement was that the owners could command them until a formal declaration of war with Germany was declared. After that Navy personnel would take over, but many owners remained at the helm throughout the war. Indeed, several Seawanhaka members actually had a few appropriate vessels built just for that purpose. New York and Seawanhaka member J.P. Morgan's *Corsair III* (304 feet) and other large yachts did anti-submarine duty in the English Channel and along the French coast.

In 1916 a new Fish class by N.G. Herreshoff , 16 feet LWL and all named after a fish, appeared and promptly took over from the 15-foot class. During the war they were the only class racing, and still were the only class during the recovery year of 1919. By the next year class racing on the Sound had revived, joined by the new Victory Class (31 feet LOA, 21 feet LWL) designed by William Gardner. It sported an innovation, a masthead mainsail – the Marconi/Bermudian rig. The Star Class, which had already tested it before the Victory appeared, would officially convert in 1921.

In 1920, also, the one-design 'S' boat by N. G. Herreshoff with the new Marconi rig, first appeared at Seawanhaka. None of the three classes, however, was the first to use it. Two yachtsmen on the Sound had experimented with it individually in 1916 and 1917. In 1919 George Nichols made a pragmatic experiment by match-racing two New York Fifty's, one gaff-rigged, the other Marconi-rigged. After a series of races, swapping skippers and crews after each race, he was satisfied that the Marconi rig was the faster on all points of sail except dead downwind. That settled the question; within six or seven years, almost all racing yachts were converted to the triangular mainsail. One of the few exceptions was the New York Thirty class, which decided that it was doing very well with the gaff rig.

In 1896, as noted above, the Yacht Racing Association of Great Britain, after a disastrous experience with a version of the Seawanhaka Rule, created a new rule that had the same objective as the Universal Rule here: to create yachts with larger underbodies that would increase stability and provide decent cabin accommodations. The product of the imaginative formula was a number in feet. After making several adjustments during the next decade, the YRA presented the rule to the yachting countries of Europe at a meeting convened in Paris in 1906, as means of promoting an International Yacht Racing Union (representatives of several major American clubs were invited to attend but declined). The only change to the proposed British idea was to change feet to metres. Otherwise, the idea was readily accepted, and the International Rule was born and the International Yacht Racing Union founded.

In 1920 Seawanhaka ventured again into international waters, seeking the agreement of several British clubs for an annual team race to be held alternately in the Solent and Long Island Sound. It was agreed, and each side split the cost of 125 pounds to acquire a trophy called the British-American Cup. It was Seawanhaka's wish to have the yachts used to alternate between the Six-Metre overseas and the 'R' here, since the two were very similar in size and each carried a crew of four. The British objected, saying that a yacht built to the Universal Rule could not be sold in Great Britain. The opposite argument might have been made since yachts built to the International Rule were in very limited use in the US, but Seawanhaka agreed to the Six-Metre for all competition. As it turned out their concern was groundless. By the spring of 1922 fourteen had been built, several by members of clubs along the Connecticut shore and two in Boston. That made a healthy start for the U.S. Six-Metre Class the first of which had been built in San Francisco Bay to race in the 1915 International Exposition regatta.

The first series of six races held in the Solent in 1921 resulted in an easy British victory. The next summer, however, there were 14 Sixes with which to hold trials, and two were chosen from Seawanhaka and one each from Manchester (MA) and Indian Harbor (CT) Yacht Clubs. A rip-roaring series ensued. In the first race the American boats came in one, two, three and four leaving the British behind by 16 points. The British recovered four in the second race, lost eight in the third, recovered three in the fourth, two in the fifth and eight in the last. The final score was U.S. 111, Great Britain 104. The top scorers were tied: Seawanhaka's *Lea*, designed by Henry J. Gielow and sailed by C. Sherman Hoyt, soon to become an American sailing legend, with two wins and 35 points; and *Coila III* out of the Royal Northern Yacht Club (Scotland), which came in first, second, and first in the last three races. American sailors were now fascinated with Six-Metres.

Meanwhile, the Seawanhaka International Challenge Cup, which despite a change in the Declaration of Trust in 1922 to permit challenges by domestic clubs still lay dormant, was finally challenged for by the Royal Northern Yacht Club. The Manchester Yacht Club agreed to defend with a Six-Metre, and John Stephens, owner and amateur designer of *Coila III*, stayed here for the challenge the next month. He won three straight races and took the Cup to Scotland.

By this time competition for the Cup had already exerted a profound influence on the direction in which yachting in North America was headed. Unwittingly, the unlimited excesses of yachts designed under the Seawanhaka Rule for the Cup matches had accelerated the demand for a new rule with more comprehensive controls; it had stimulated inter-club competition among clubs in the East, Midwest and Eastern Canada; it had paved the way for international competition on a continental scale as well as overseas. In these respects it became a factor in generating an awareness of the need for an overall administrative body, i.e. a union of clubs and associations in North America.

Since the 1923 team racing for the British-American Cup was to be held at Cowes, Seawanhaka immediately challenged the Royal Northern for the Seawanhaka Cup nominating Sherman Hoyt to compete. The first British-American series had rejuvenated racing at Cowes, still in a slow recovery stage after World War I, and the spectator fleet was very large. There was even a Royal Navy battleship escorting the royal yacht aboard which white-tie balls were held in the evenings. The British drubbed the Americans again. After the racing and more parties, Hoyt and the rest of the team went to Scotland for the Seawanhaka Cup and informal racing with the Scots beforehand. During the best-of-five series, the spectator fleet was the largest in 30 years. It was *Coila III* v. *Lea* again.

The 1924 British-American series was again at Oyster Bay. This year the spectator fleet was so large that the U.S. Navy sent three destroyers to help control it! The scoring was changed to the best four out of seven races, and it was tied three to three after six races. The British, having won the match for the third time, took permanent possession of the Cup. In the same year a Norwegian club challenged for the Seawanhaka Cup but was defeated in three races by the champion Scottish yacht *Coila III*.

The next year, with the British-American Cup gone, Seawanhaka created a syndicate to concentrate on recovering the Seawanhaka Cup. Before doing so, it bought a yacht designed by William Fife, the Scottish designer who had designed most of the British Sixes that they had so far encountered. After studying her and taking off her lines, Clinton Crane designed *Lanai*, to be sailed by Sherman Hoyt. Crane obviously had learned something from Fife, for Hoyt beat the vaunted *Coila III* three races to one. Finally, after twenty-nine years, the Seawanhaka International Challenge Cup was back at Oyster Bay.

In 1925 the Scandinavian Yacht Racing Association wrote to Seawanhaka offering to bring to Oyster Bay a team of Sixes to race for a cup they would carry over with them, the Scandinavian-American Cup. The club accepted and quickly organized trials among 11 boats from which to select a team. This time the team turned out to be all-Seawanhaka, two of them being the veterans *Lea*, with Sherman Hoyt at the helm, and Crane's *Lanai*, with Dick Boardman, a Bostonian and another veteran of the British-American series, steering her. The four boats and crews from Scandinavia contained one each from Sweden, Norway, Finland and Denmark. The American team won, four races to two.

That retired the cup, but there was another, the Scandinavian Gold Cup, which had been raced for in Six-Metres since 1919. Herman F. Whiton, who now owned *Lanai*, challenged for it in 1926. He and his crew, all of whom had just been graduated from Princeton, were an anomaly to the Scandinavians at Hanko, for they were the youngest crew ever to have been seen at such a high-level event. The conditions for the Cup permitted one entry each from any country, and Holland entered along with Norway as defender. Whiton, despite having a crew as raw as a cabbage, beat them both.

The next year (1927) Norway challenged for both the Seawanhaka and the Scandinavian Gold Cups. Competing for the latter were Sixes and crews from Sweden, Finland, Denmark, Great Britain, Holland, and Italy. Five new American boats were built to face this invasion, making 11 in all for the Cup trials. Norway won the Seawanhaka Cup three races out of five. In the Gold Cup series, the first three races were eliminations for the top three, which then sailed four more races. Norway, Sweden, and Finland survived the cut, and Sweden took the Gold Cup by one point over Finland. The Swedish helmsman was the renown sailor Sven Salen, who unveiled his new weapon, a close-winded overlapping jib that he called a Genoa, since he first used it in Italy. Another claim to early use of an overlapping jib is documented in a letter from 'Sis' (Hovey) Morss appearing in the Museum of Yachting's (Newport, RI) magazine, *Spinnaker* Sept/Oct 1993:

> *... [L.] Francis Herreshoff... when he designed both of my* Orioles *[Thirty Square Metres], and he actually invented the roller-reefing gear, ventilated spinnaker, and Genoa jib – which were used for the first time on* Oriole *when I took her to Kiel, Germany and afterwards in Sweden for team racing in 1930. Our jib was known as the 'biggest, biggest' and was copied in Italy, and we called it the 'Genoa jib'.*

All in all, the two events demonstrated that Americans still had a bit more to learn about designing and building Six-Metre yachts.

There are more stories about the Sixes, but the foregoing surely suffices to illustrate what a shot in the arm they were to both continental and international racing. They sailed on through the 1930's with an impact that was more important than the America's Cup, because they involved more sailors and more nations. By the 1960's both the Seawanhaka and British-American Cups had switched to the 5.5 Metre Class so that activity in the Sixes was relegated to a fleet in Puget Sound sailing domestically and to the St. Francis Yacht Club (San Francisco) competing in European waters and match racing against the Royal Prince Alfred Yacht Club down the coast from Sydney, Australia. In 1927 a fleet of 14 Ten-Metres, designed by Starling Burgess and built in Germany, began racing on Long Island Sound. Then came Eight-Metres, designed by Burgess, and during the 1930's, a dozen Twelve-Metres were built, six of them one-designs by Burgess. The latter were outclassed after the mid-1930's by Clinton Crane's *Seven Seas* and *Gleam* and Olin Stephens' *Northern Light, Nyala* and *Vim* designed for members of Seawanhaka. Competition was held in some of these classes at the Eastern Yacht Club as early as 1928. Delivery of the foreign-built yachts was to Halifax, NS from where they were sailed to Long Island Sound. In this way they could be entered into the U.S. as 'used' merchandise at lower duty.

In closing this chapter it is fitting to mention the organization, in 1936, of the Seawanhaka Corinthian Junior Yacht Club, whose first Commodore was Henry H. Anderson, Jr. A junior sailing program had existed since about 1915, but the new club had its own quarters, as well as its own boats and instructors. As a program and a club, it was second only to the junior Pleon Yacht Club in Marblehead, which had been formed before 1900.

It would be most difficult, if not impossible, to name a yacht club in this country that has contributed more to the development of sail racing and corinthianism than Seawanhaka Corinthian!

SEVERN SAILING ASSOCIATION[64]

The August 20, 1960 edition of *The Sun, Baltimore* in describing the role that the Severn Sailing Association was about to assume as host for the North American Women's Sailing Championship for the Mrs. Charles Francis Adams Cup epitomizes what the Club stands for:

> *One of the youngest, smallest sailing clubs on the Chesapeake Bay, yet strong enough to support an international reputation and the chance to do the honors as host for the first national sailing championship races ever held on the Bay, does not follow conventional lines.*

An indication that it is a purist sailing organization is the provision that no one is permitted to join who harbors the idea of using it for power boating. There is no bar, and it is renown for its strong junior program. The program was initiated by Mrs. John H. Donald (a sister of past NAYRU President, Robert N. Bavier, Jr.); guided for many years by Dr. Stuart H. Walker and conducted in its early days by George (Stovey) Brown. Dr. Walker also was responsible for reviving the International Fourteen Class, and the Association Fleet hosts international events attracting competitors from Bermuda, Canada and other parts of North America. Among other classes sponsored by the Association are the Penguin, Comet, Severn One-Design, National One-Design, Hampton, Lightning and Soling.

The Association was incorporated in 1954, held its first annual regatta in 1956, but did not acquire its present location at Sycamore Point off the confluence of Spa Creek and the Severn River until 1957. It has always been a hands-on, bootstrap operation where member work parties did the major portion of landfilling and bulkheading to develop one of the finest facilities on the Bay in 1859. The formation of the Ladies Auxiliary, known as 'Sanddollars,' traditionally has appointed the clubhouse and furnished meals.

The Association became a Mecca for centerboard class championships, hosting the Alantic Coast Thistle Class in 1960, the Mobjack Nationals in 1960, the International Fourteen Nationals in 1962 and in 1963 hosting the NAYRU Mallory Cup Series, Lightning Class Dixie Districts and the North American Cadet Championships. That year was the sixth time that Dr. Walker was elected Commodore, and when he stepped down the next year, he took his Fourteen to England and became the first American to win the Prince of Wales Trophy.

In 1965 the Junior Instruction Program enrolled 147 students and replaced the Gannets (a George O'Day version in GRP of a Fourteen tailored to club use) with the international 420, the class adopted by the Chesapeake Bay YRA. The next year they were used for frostbiting and for the NAYRU Singlehanded Championships for the O'Day Trophy. The same year the clubhouse burned to the ground resulting in the loss of records and photographs.

The Association was well represented at home and abroad in championships; for example, in 1968 junior teams competed in the 420 Worlds in England, won the 420 Nationals in New York, won three of eight races in the Sears Cup finals in San Francisco, the Mobjack Nationals and Dr. Walker crewed for Gardner Cox in the 5.5 Metre in the Olympics.

In 1970 Solings were introduced; the Comet Internationals were held; and in 1971 the Snipe National Championships and international team racing in the Fourteens. The following year Samuel V. Merrick, known for his leadership in the 'E' Class Scow and the Soling class, was elected Commodore.

Perhaps the key to the success of the Association has been, again to cite *The Sun, Baltimore*, that early in its history the membership, because of overdemand, was:

> *...closed unless an applicant can persuade the admissions committee that he can't live without sailing.*

THE SOUTHERN YACHT CLUB[65]

During the 1840's and 1850's New Orleans was a very prosperous place. Cotton was king, the city rivaled New York as a port and banking center, and money was plentiful. Wealth, fashion, and the art of good living made it one of the most cosmopolitan areas in the country. To its north lay Lake Pontchartrain, 40 miles long and 24 miles wide, a lake that was potentially a great place to sail.

Yet, New Orleans was not a healthful place in summer because of the scourge of yellow fever and malaria. All those who could went elsewhere to escape the diseases, and the favorite place was Pass Christian, Mississippi, 65 miles to the east on the Gulf Coast. It was there that the Southern Yacht Club was formed in 1849. The name was chosen as a compromise because, although most of the founding members were from New Orleans, some came from Pass Christian. Eighteen yachts, ranging from 12 to 39 feet in 'keel length,' competed in an 18-mile race that began and ended in front of the town's principal hotel. The handicap used was simply 45 seconds per foot of keel length, which meant that the largest gave the smallest only 13 minutes for a race that lasted well over four hours for the most of the fleet. The hotel, incidentally, put up the prize, the Hotel Pitcher trophy.

The second regatta was held two weeks later, for which occasion the ladies of the town were prompted to provide another prize called the Ladies of Pass Christian Pitcher. The trophy had an interesting career. During the Civil War Union General Benjamin J. Butler, in charge of the occupation of New Orleans, commandeered it, along with much of the silver looted by his soldiers from deserted homes. "Silver Spoon" Butler he was called by the local citizens. What became of it after that is unknown, but it turned up in 1933 in a pawn shop in New York, where it was redeemed by a friend of the Commodore of the SYC and returned to the club.

During the summer of 1849 the club held ten regattas, most at Pass Christian but also at Bay St. Louis, Biloxi,[66] and on Lake Pontchartrain. Very few clubs came even close to that many races in their first season. Apparently most of the yachts remained on the lake during the winter, for in the summer of 1850 the first regatta was a long-distance race of 65 miles from the lake to Pass Christian. One of the persistent aspects of yacht racing during the nineteenth century, both in England and the U.S., was betting on races, both by the general public and by competitors. The Southern Yacht Club sought to curb that at the outset by adopting a by-law that forbade betting by competing owners. History does not record that it had much effect.

By 1852 a railroad had been built to cover the six miles from downtown New Orleans to the lake thereby opening up the south shore of the lake to the development of amusement parks, hotels, restaurants, and parks from which to watch rowing matches and yacht races. As a result, the SYC began using the lake more often for its racing, except during the hottest summer months. The good judgment of repairing to Pass Christian was verified in 1853. During that summer 8,000 inhabitants of New Orleans died of yellow fever.

The minutes of the 1856 annual meeting noted that "the first regatta of the season was forced to be postponed for want of stake boats. All of the craft used for buoys were out fishing." It seems to have been necessary to hire fishermen to sail out to specified locations and anchor as turning marks. In 1858 the club inaugurated a Junior Division of "young men," age limits not specified, as a means of encouraging a continuing flow of new blood. At the annual meeting of 1860 a committee was appointed to study the by-laws, to consider revisions, and to report at the next meeting. That next meeting was not held until 1878.

The Southern Yacht Club was moribund during the Civil War and almost so for 12 years thereafter. The only record found of those years is a report of a race in 1870 – of only three yachts. But New Orleans was slowly recovering, Mardi Gras was back as a result of legislation enacted in 1872 declaring it a legal holiday in Louisiana. Finally, the club came back to life in 1878 after a meeting at which it was determined to build a clubhouse on the lake. The club had 300 members, all of whom had been screened to guard against the admission of purely social members, and dues were $12, double what they were antebellum. An elaborate dress code was voted upon and adopted.

The club was incorporated, the raising of money accelerated, plans were drawn and construction of the first clubhouse proceeded. It was a two-story structure with a cupola next to the entrance of the New Basin Canal. The city deeded to the club land behind the club and land behind the lake levee for the creation of the yacht harbor. The opening was held in June 1879; the Southern Yacht Club was finally back in business. So was the whole lakefront on both sides of the club, with more hotels, restaurants, bath houses, Ferris wheels, a carousel – and a noisy roller coaster right behind it.

In 1880 the club welcomed a distinguished visitor, former Commanding General of the Union Army and former President of the United States Ulysses S. Grant, with a 21-gun salute.

Readers in the northeast familiar with the early sandbaggers of western Long Island Sound and Narragansett Bay will be surprised to learn that sandbaggers also existed on Lake Pontchartrain during the 1880's. In fact, the club issued a challenge in 1880 to a New York group, which responded by sending one of its best boats and crews down to race against four SYC sandbaggers. The race was for a purse of $1,500, a princely sum for those freaky little boats. The Yankee boat did not win, but she was impressive enough for a SYC member to buy her on the spot. In that same year the club made a sound investment, the purchase of a small schooner for the training of people who could not yet afford a yacht but wanted to sail and were prospective yacht owners. The club ended the year with 433 members, which probably made it third in size in the country; only the New York and Boston Yacht Clubs would have been larger.

With respect to New York and Boston, several yacht owners from those areas had their boats sent down (either sailed ahead by their professional crews or transported on the decks of ships) to match race against local boats on the Gulf Coast from Mobile to New Orleans. In addition, Gulf sailors were buying boats designed and built in New York and Boston.

Hurricanes have been unwelcome visitors to the Gulf Coast over the years. In 1856 there had been a monster hurricane, and several others had occurred during the next four decades. In 1893 another monster arrived and came ashore east of New Orleans at Pass Christian, Gulfport and Biloxi, MS. Offshore from the ports lay Ship Island which had numerous marine facilities, a hospital, a quarantine station, several warehouses and Fort Massachusetts. When the wind finally abated, not a single structure remained, most of the low-lying islands had disappeared, and none of the people living and working on them survived. The total loss of life on that island, nearby Cat Island, the mainland, and numerous ships and schooners coming and going was never determined, but it was in the thousands.

The membership of 1880 appears to have been the high-water mark, as numbers occasionally cited after that date were lower. Nonetheless, the club remained healthy, and it was joined toward the end of the century by new clubs: Bay-Waveland and Biloxi (MS), Mobile (AL), Pensacola (FL) and Galveston (TX). In 1898 the clubhouse was in jeopardy from the rotting pilings supporting it and had to be demolished. It was quickly replaced with a second building that was much like the first but of more elegant appearance. It was one of the ornaments of New Orleans, still the most important and largest city of the south, with a population in 1900 of 216,000.

In 1901 the Southern Gulf Coast Yachting Association (which became the present Gulf Yachting Association in 1920) was formed, and its earliest efforts at promoting regional racing appear to have been "circuit" races, in which each member club entered one club-owned boat. During the prior 30 years, the pre-eminent yacht was the *Suzie B.* (built in New Jersey), which won every race in which she was entered for 11 years. During the next season, her owner arranged a match race with another owner for serious stakes: $1,000 and the hand of a woman they had both been courting. Neither yacht finished, but the lady choose *Suzie B.*'s owner nonetheless. A few weeks later, the two met on the street, a duel ensued, and the prospective groom lay dead on the sidewalk.

For 20 more years under six different owners *Suzie B.* continued to win races one after the other. Finally, five boats were built with the primary purpose of beating *Suzie B.* Four of them were designed (one by Edward Burgess) and built in Boston, the other in Biloxi. Eventually all five managed to beat her, but it took a lot of money and effort, and she was 33 years old at the time.

Another yacht that still has a place in New Orleans history was the *Nydia* built during the 1890's. In 1904 she was bought by A. Baldwin Wood, the ingenious engineer who designed the system that still keeps New Orleans, which is lower than the Mississippi River, from drowning. It is a series of canals, underground drains, and pumps to collect water from upstream of the City and pump it into Lake Pontchartrain. For 52 years Wood sailed *Nydia*, competitively and for pleasure, until his death from a heart attack while sailing her alone with his dog aboard. In his will Wood left one million dollars and his yacht to Tulane University with the provision that she be preserved for at least 99 years. She sits there today under glass in the patio of the student center.

There were other noteworthy events in 1904. The SYC, which now had 125 vessels, including steam yachts and naphtha launches, held its 55th annual regatta (not in terms of events but of years elapsed). The feature of this event was a new fleet of Skates, which were essentially scows – shallow draft, wide beam, dual leeboards and rudders, clouds of canvas and the need for a crew of twenty or more men in a blow. They could exceed 20 knots in such a breeze.

The second happening of note involved women. In 1897, after some heavy arm-twisting by the then Commodore, the board voted "to permit ladies to all parts of the clubhouse." In 1904, however, the club actually sponsored an "all girls" regatta: one race with five knockabouts and crews of three. Not many yacht clubs preceded the SYC in such a venture. They still have 'skipperette' races to this day.

In 1906 the Southern went out of the Lake and the Gulf to compete for the first time. The Kiel Yacht Club had invited Americans to select a yacht of the Sonderklasse (a German design) to compete for a trophy offered by Kaiser Wilhelm. $3,500 was raised within the club to have a Sonder (30 feet LOA, 20 feet LWL, 7 feet beam) designed and built in Boston, since the eliminations were to be held at Marblehead. Upon arriving in Boston the selected crew of New Orleans found that their appointed helmsman, the Vice-Commodore of the SYC, was not eligible to compete in the eliminations. Although he had lived in Louisiana for all but the first three years of his life, he was not an American citizen. Thus, the club was forced to substitute a man of inferior skills but one who had been born of less careless parents. Between that mishap and a broken mast in the second race of the series for the Roosevelt Cup, donated by President Roosevelt, New Orleans came in seventh in a class of nine. The winner, to the surprise of no one in the northeast, was Charles Francis Adams II.

In 1918 the clubhouse was evacuated altogether for use as a convalescent hospital for soldiers during the horrendous, almost nation-wide influenza epidemic. Once World War I was over the club was re-energized. The board had plans for a major club expansion, and the power boats were raring to race and cruise, but where were the sailboats? It would appear from club history that the numerous and vigorous sailors of earlier years had grown old without replacement by younger blood. The answer lay in a huge (for 1920) $250,000 investment in remodeling and additions to the club and the creation of a small new sloop called the Fish class designed by Rathbone de Buys. Sir Thomas Lipton, who "during his boyhood days worked in New Orleans at a streetcar barn", provided a handsome trophy. One of the additions, incidentally, was a wing that provided the SYC with the largest dance floor in New Orleans; the club had become the social Mecca of the city, and its membership rose to 2,500.

A second class, simply called the 21-footers (LWL presumably, since they had cabins, which would put them in the 30-foot LOA range) was resuscitated and with the Fish gave the club two popular boats on which to rebuild the sailing program. The boats of the Fish class were all club-owned, which made them a significant attraction to young men who could not yet afford to purchase one. In 1924 the club obtained a charter to establish a Star class fleet, and 12 members immediately placed orders for Stars. By 1925 sailing had regained its normal place in club operations. Indeed, the winner, Earl Blouin, of the Star elimination's went to New York to compete in the Star Nationals on Long Island Sound and finished fourth out of fifteen.

Within a year there were 36 Stars at the SYC and other clubs in the SYC/Gulf fleet, and 1927 saw the SYC win the Bacardi Cup at the Star mid-winters held in Havana (its permanent site from 1925 until the U. S. boycott). In December of that year Sir Thomas Lipton returned to New Orleans and on his departure promised yet another Lipton Cup for the SYC Star fleet. In 1928 the winner of the cup, Prentice Edrington, Jr., with his crew, Gilbert T. Gray, also won the Star International Championship at Newport Beach, California, and the club became the host for next year's event for which there were a record 20 entries. The event was held one week before the Stock Market crash of October 29, 1929.

The Southern Yacht Club was in danger of foreclosure and narrowly avoided it, mainly because one of the two banks that held its mortgages forgave the remaining balance. The next five years paralleled the familiar stories of other clubs during the Great Depression. The SYC plodded on doggedly, however, despite reduced participation in racing. One prescient move that would help insure a better future was the creation of a junior sailing program. Another fortunate factor was the winning of the Star Class gold medal at the Los Angeles Olympics in 1932 by the SYC team of Gilbert Gray and Andrew Libano. The club was now not just a regional but a national institution in the world of yachting.

The Southern Yacht Club was fortunate to have several families, some of Olympic and world championship calibre, who provided leadership over two or three generations. Among them was Ernest Lee Jahncke, Commodore 1914-16 and a member of the NAYRU Executive Committee. Commodore Gilbert Scheib of the Gulf Yachting Association succeeded Jahncke both as Commodore of SCYC and as a member of the NAYRU Executive Committee where he served for eleven years. Scheib was very active in bringing the Mallory, Adams and Sears national championships to the southern and Gulf Coast areas. He was replaced on the Executive Committee by Commodore G. Shelby Friedrichs, whose son G. Shelby (Buddy), Jr. in turn succeeded his father at NAYRU. 'Buddy' also was a Gold Medalist in the Dragon Class in the 1968 Olympic Games with Barton W.B. Jahncke and Gerald Click Schreck as crew thereby simulating the feat of Gold Medalist Gilbert T. Gray in the Star Class in 1932 with Andrew J. Libano as crew.

1968 Gold Medalists in the Dragon Class – Barton W.B. Jahncke, G. Shelby Friedrichs, Jr and Gerald Click Schreck
Photo: Southern Yacht Club

TOMS RIVER CHALLENGE CUP[67]

The date of William W. Robinson's article is significant. It marked the centennial of the birth – 1871 – of the Toms River Yacht Club and of the trophy put up by the members, all summer residents of the town. The members had a brand new club, but none of the few members who owned sailboats had ever raced them. To compensate the local professionals on the river and Barnegat Bay were invited to compete, and eight accepted the challenge. The Challenge Cup was a graceful double-handle ewer 14 inches tall, designed by a member, whose son-in-law ran a jewelry shop in New York called Tiffany & Co. Members donated $179 to pay for it, and the design was sent to Tiffany for execution in coin silver.

All of the yachts were working catboats ranging from 24 to 26 feet, of a design common to the Bay for almost a century. They were gaff-rigged with plumb stems, low freeboard, counter sterns with a fairly long overhang and boxy cabins. In overall appearance, they were quite different from the familiar beamy New York and Cape Cod catboats. Two of the owners were engaged in freight hauling around Barnegat Bay (reflecting the lack of roads in the area), and the others were fishermen and oystermen.

The prospect of a race, the first formal one ever seen on the Bay, generated great interest, not only in watching it but in betting on it. When the day finally came, everything that could float was out on the river filled with people, and the shore at the mouth of the river, where the starting and finishing areas were set, was lined with more people. As was the standard procedure until the mid-1870's, the race was started from anchor with each boat positioned between stakes sunk into the shallow bottom 50 feet apart on the starting line. After dropping anchor between the stakes, the boats fell back about two boat lengths. (Apparently this was a windward start.) At the preparatory signal the crews were to draw up within 25 feet of the line. The next gun was the start, which the boats made without tripping anchors, leaving them on the bottom to be recovered later. The method guaranteed that there would be no premature starters.

There had been some discussion of staggered starts, according to handicaps, but the idea was dropped. How the handicaps were figured is not recorded. The race was ten miles long, and the marks laid out for it were also stakes driven into the bottom. The wind was light at the start and then died, but a good sou'wester came in at noon, and the crowd was treated to a rousing finish, with the first boat only a length or so ahead of the second. The latter won on corrected time.

The race was so successful that a second race was held in October, after the summer folks had gone home and was just for the locals. That procedure held for several years. Meanwhile, the betting escalated until it became serious money. In one race it became obvious to the crew that the skipper was not about to win if he could possibly avoid it, although he was sailing the favorite. A quick crew mutiny with some force applied made him realize that, whatever bets he had made, he had better not throw the race. In 1875 it was discovered after the Cup race that someone had nailed blocks of wood to the bottom of one boat. The next year men with shotguns took turns guarding the boats during the night before the race.

As the years passed members began buying similar boats built by local builders purely as yachts. The race for the Toms River Challenge Cup gradually changed its character, still as intense but Corinthian in character. The catboats became the predominant racing yachts on the bay as other clubs were formed there and adopted the same general design.

After World War I, during which the Cup was not raced for, catboats began to proliferate even more. In 1923 four Toms River Yacht Club members had Charles D. Mower work up a new design a good deal larger at 36 feet LOA, with 55-foot Marconi rigs and 650 square feet of sail. These were called the Class 'A' catboats, and the four originals were still racing in 1971. Each had been through several owners over almost half a century, and each had been refurbished and even rebuilt several times. Not only were they still being raced but the names of one or another of them were engraved on the Challenge Cup as winners in every year since 1923 but one – and, of course, the four years of WW II.

TRED AVON YACHT CLUB[68]

In June, 1931 at Oxford on the Eastern Shore of Chesapeake Bay a sturdy bathhouse was built on the roof of which the Kap-Dun Club ('Association' per one source) was organized – the name deriving from the old English spelling of Cape and Dun meaning 'town'. The name changed to Tred Avon Yacht Club, but it is not clear whether in July or January, 1932 when ladies were accepted as non-voting members at same dues as men – 50 cents a month. Sailing began with two Barnegat Bay Sneak Boxes and a double-ended Knockabout. While swimming had been the principal sport at the boathouse, when "millions of pesky creatures known as sea nettles arrived" sailing quickly displaced it. The town of Oxford, however, as a seaport and sailing center goes back to the early 1600's.

Racing started in July on the Tred Avon River in boats 20-feet and under, two in crew, unlimited dead ballast and no keels. The entrance fee was ten cents per boat for the purpose of purchasing trophies. The next year limitations were placed on sailboats of 16 and 20 feet: no boards, ballast or keels and no more than one mast, mainsail and jibbon. The boats were log canoes – the traditional mode of travel of our forefathers – converted into sleek and beautiful racing craft. Later the Class 'E' Scows became stiff contenders for the canoe but did not survive.

It was not long before there were over 100 entries in the Club's regattas which started as free-for-alls in craft from 8-foot Moths to 100-foot cruising yachts. The Comet, designed by Gham & Lowndes Johnson at the request of Elliott Wheeler, who wanted a smaller version of the Star with a centerboard instead of the deep keel, and built by Ralph Wiley was introduced and called successively Crabs, Star Junior and ultimately Comet. In fact the first one was name *Zoea* (a stage in the development of a crab). Later Stars and Penguins appeared and more recently Lasers, Laser II's and Optimists.

In its early days it was not unusual for a thousand or more spectators to watch the racing from The Strand and bets being made and cash prizes offered by sponsors. Typical of the outstanding yachtsmen who raced at the Club was J. Graham Johnson who won local and national sailing honors and died at the tiller of his Star during a race. The Club enjoyed a close relationship with the Chesapeake Bay Yacht Club in Easton, and the two jointly sponsored racing the first season in 1932 – a practice that continues to this day. Another feature of the Club was junior sailing which started from its inception and was characterized by one member as:

> *The young people were so fortunate to learn sailing and small boat handling under such wholesome circumstances.*

Currently classes designed and built on Chesapeake Bay such as log canoes, Comets, Hamptons, Penguins and Chesapeake 20's race in the Chesapeake Bay Heritage Regatta. Well represented on the Eastern Shore in the early thirties was the Star Class racing at Betterton, Chestertown, the Raskob estate (currently a vacation home for the Russian Embassy) at Pioneer Point, St. Michaels, Oxford and Gibson Island. The Club has also held the National 5.5 Metre Championship which was once won there by R. E. (Ted) Turner, III.

28

CHAPTER VIII

CLASSES AND ONE-DESIGNS

OVERVIEW OF EARLY ONE-DESIGNS

'Classes' in the early phases of the evolution of the sport of yacht racing were a means of classifying, or grouping, yachts in order to provide relatively 'level' racing at their home club as well as when competing at other clubs or in other districts. Until the advent of a uniform system of measuring and rating, the parameters that were used were not adequate to insure the level playing field that today's class measurement rules, production molds, templates, etc. make possible. At the earliest regatta in North America for which sailing instructions are extant – Halifax Regatta held in Nova Scotia on August 17, 1836 – the classes were determined by length. While the "Regulations for Sailing Boats" governing the event does not provide the figures, the limiting lengths based on the description of the entries was approximately 22 feet and greater for "First Class," 18 - 22 feet for "Second Class" and 18 feet and under for "Third Class."

With the introduction in the mid-nineteenth century of the British Custom House Tonnage Rule, tonnage (cubic content of the hull) became the parameter, and in order to equalize yachts within classes, and for overall trophies, a time allowance of seconds per ton per mile were applied to times of finish. Later under the Seawanhaka Rule, which quickly spread from coast to coast, and the Universal and International Rules that succeeded it, classes were determined by ratings such as the 'R' Class which rated 20 under the Universal Rule and the Six-Metre for which the rating formula under the International Rule maximized at six meters. The exercise for a designer was to juggle the values for sail area, displacement, length, etc. to produce the fastest all around boat that measured to, or just under, the rating figure for the class. In today's parlance these would be termed 'restricted design' classes and, except for the larger Universal Rule classes, competed without handicaps.

Chapter IX – Rating Rules deals with the evolution of rating rules and how they affected class racing in more detail, whereas this Chapter focuses on how class racing achieved the level playing field by prescribing close specifications and measuring to tight tolerances tailored to the needs of each.

As noted in the Preface, three books covering one-design classes are *The History of Yachting – 1600 - 1815* by Arthur H. Clark published under the imprimatur of the New York Yacht Club, *Sailing Craft* by Edwin J. Schoettle[1] and *Early One-Design Sailboats* by Diana Eames Esterly.[2] The books constitute an invaluable checklist for what follows and are supplemented by the histories of numerous yacht clubs and classes and augmented with data obtained from files and interviews.

If one accepts the definition of 'one-design class' as one in which boats are built to uniform specifications close enough to insure level racing without time allowances, W. P. Stephens – the acknowledged 'dean' of American yachting history – who designed, built and raced them, would claim that the sailing canoes were the first one-designs. Notwithstanding, he is on solid ground when claiming the American Canoe Association, founded in 1880, was the the first racing association to have been

Idem on Upper St. Regis Lake, NY
Photo Michael Kahn

continental in scope. It preceded by four years the Lake Yacht Racing Association – oldest YRA in North America founded in 1884. The ACA by-laws contained Sailing Regulations of which Rule I stated:

> *... To compete under sail it must come within the limits of either Class 'A' or 'B' – 'A' being length not over 16 feet and beam 28 inches for that length and 'B' 17 feet with beam 28½ inches for that length (beam may be increased ⅛ inches. for each full inch of length decreased [as a means of ruling out long, slim speedsters].*

Further, both ends of all sailing canoes had to be pointed as distinct from other types.

> *In a chapter of* Canoe Handling, *1886* Forrest & Stream, *C. Bowyer Vaux on tactics advises: When passing an opponent, go to windward of him if you can. Do not try to retard him by getting directly [close] to windward of him, though, and thus taking the wind out of his sails. It is allowable to do this, but there is less satisfaction in beating a man when you have hampered him in his sailing. For this reason, do not blanket the canoe ahead of you running free – that is, steering directly behind him and covering his sails with your own, and taking the wind from them until you get up to him, when you must steer out. Blanketing is not against the rules, but it is jockeying, and jockeying is demoralizing in canoeing, just as it is in horse racing. Sail a fair, even generous race, and have the satisfaction when you finish of knowing that you won fairly.*

The philosophy of the American Canoe Association was déjà vu of that described by N.G. Herreshoff as being the practice on Narragansett Bay and in striking contrast to the advice on sailing tactics appearing in sailing magazines today. Nor did it jibe with the aggressive approach to sailboat racing in New York waters to judge from W.P. Stephen's comments in a letter to N.G. Herreshoff:[3]

> *The ethics of yacht racing seem to have been on a very much higher plane on Narragansett Bay than about New York, where a man often had to go ashore at a waterside 'hotel' after a race and fight for a prize before he got it. John Sawyer, who was a referee and stakeholder in many of the old sandbag races, once told me that they used to get him into a hack and to the railway station before his decision was publicly announced.*

An explanation for the seemingly polite rules for sailing-canoe racing may be that they were adapted from the rules for rowing events which to quote from the *Laws of Boat Racing Adopted by the California State Boat Club – Saturday, May 17th, 1873* provided:

> *5. Each boat shall keep its own water throughout the race, and any boat departing from its own water will do so at its peril. [This law contains the vital principal of the new code of boat racing rules which is that each competitor shall keep his own water and course... in contradistinction to the old plan of taking an adversary's water either for the purpose of obtaining a better position, or of washing and lathering him...]*

Sailing canoes, similar to catboats, were widely spread across the continent appearing on Chesapeake Bay as log canoes before 1840 around St. Michaels which today is still the center of the sport on the Chesapeake. It revived after the Civil War with the founding of the Chesapeake Bay Yacht Club in 1885, and one of the prolific builders was Robert Lambdin of St. Michaels who is credited with having built the first centerboard canoe in Maryland. Since rigs and hulls were hand-built and differed there was a handicap system so that first across the line took the cash prize and first on corrected time took the trophy – a combination of level and handicap racing. After 1900 competition suffered a lapse until the forming in 1924 of the Miles River Yacht Club. In 1933 the Chesapeake Bay Log Canoe Association was formed to regulate the sport, and much innovation in design and hull continues.

Elsewhere there were sailing canoe races at the Oakland Canoe Club on San Francisco Bay in the 1870's and at Camp Gardner (named after George W. Gardner) on Ballast Island, Lake Erie in the 1885 where the Western Canoe Association was formed as a division of the American Canoe Association.

Two other types of sailing craft appeared before 1840: the catboat and the sneakbox. Keel catboats existed in Narragansett Bay, Rhode Island, and there is record of a race held off Bristol in 1853. The story of the famous catboat *Una* shipped from Bayonne, New Jersey to England in 1852 bespeaks catboat racing activity prior thereto in New York waters, and in that year *Little Eva* appeared on Cape Cod waters where the Osterville cat sloops developed. Cats appeared on Massachusetts Bay before 1875; in San Diego Bay before 1900; the cat yawl was raced at the Nodaway Yacht Club, WI in 1894; and double-cats (ketches without jibs as distinguished from the cat yawls found at Nodaway on Lake Winnebago and in the east) at Mackinac, Lake Michigan. While the designs of the respective catboats were peculiar to the waters of each, inevitably racing of a one-design nature occurred at all these locations. Sandbaggers – so named for the portable ballast which was shifted by the crew at each tack – were racing at Mantoloking, NJ in the 1820's, and the sneakbox, which was a singular type of catboat with less draft and freeboard, appeared on Barnegat Bay as early as 1836 and in the hands of Howard Perrine became a formalized type of boat in New Jersey waters in the early 1900's. It was imported as far south as Biscayne Bay, FL where they were sailed in the 1930's.

The concept of boat-for-boat racing in similar types of craft developed in as far-flung locations as: racing in San Francisco Bay in the 1850's in Mosquito Fleets; the formation in 1888 of the Mosquito Fleet Yacht Club in South Boston to race boat-for-boat without handicaps; in 1893 the presence of a Mosquito Fleet at the Riverton Yacht Club in Delaware – a term used on both coasts for small, shallow-draft sailboats – in which boats from twenty to twenty-five feet raced on equal terms; in 1869 there was racing in a class of flatbottom centerboard sloops in Hawaii; a catamaran appeared at Encinal (San Francisco Bay) in 1876 – a year after Herreshoff launched his well-known catamaran, *Amaryllis*, and racing in catamarans subsequently developed for a brief period on the Bay. Sharpies which, similar to the catboats, evolved from types of boats used for commercial fishing as early as 1835 along the coast of Connecticut, were raced in New Haven Harbor in the 1880's, and a two-masted one-design version was built and shipped to Lake Champlain for racing enthusiasts – an early example of one-design racing.

Because the types of boats above-mentioned were often built by different carpenters, boat builders or amateurs, the classes fell short of meeting today's standards of strictly one-design. This may justify identifying the North Haven Dinghy, designed and built by William Weld in Maine in 1885, as the first truly 'one-design' in North America. Lloyd Ryland, Historian for the Pacific Inter-Club Yachting Association, raises the possibility that 15 foot one-design used in San Francisco Bay in 1897 was copied from the North Haven Dinghy. Two other early one-designs on the West Coast were the C.D. Mower 23 foot Knockabout at the Royal Victoria Yacht Club in 1901 and the Chula Vista One-Design on San Diego Bay in 1910. Two features of the North Haven Dinghy single it out as the pioneer 'one-design': first, the four initial boats were built to 'match' two existing local boats and successive boats were all built by a single builder, J.O. Brown Boatyard in North Haven; and second, the class is still actively racing with some boats made of glass reinforced plastic and the original spritsail rig changed to a gaff rig. Construction plans were drawn by John G. Alden in the 1920's which has helped perpetuate the one-design characteristic. Dimensions of the Dinghy are length 14 feet 5½ inches, beam 4 feet 11 inches, draft 13½ inches or 3 feet 10 inches with board down and 118 square feet of sail. That the sail of the catboat had no battens was in marked contrast to the transverse battens sported one year later on Nathaniel Herreshoff's *Clara* and on the mainsail eleven years later of the Seawanhaka's Cup aspirant, *Gnome*.

While there was no apparent connection between the North Haven Dinghy and the later International Fourteen Dinghy, it is interesting that only a few years after the launching of the former, the West of England Conference Dinghy (W.E.C.) – precursor to the International Fourteen – made its appearance in 1901. Respecting the North Haven Dinghy being the oldest class still racing in North America, on the world scene the Howth Sailing Club (vic. Dublin, Ireland) 17-Footer One-Design Class may well be the oldest class still racing one hundred percent in its original boats and rigs. Five boats were delivered in 1898 for the price of 90 pounds fully found and race today with the original rigs along with boats subsequently added to the class. The class in North America that can claim similar 'originals' is the gaff rigged centerboard Idem Class (for 'same' or 'identical' in Latin) designed by Clinton Crane in 1900 for the St. Regis Yacht Club[4] on Upper St. Regis Lake in the Adirondacks, NY, according to past Commodore John B. Trevor, Jr.[5] With a waterline of only 19 feet and an overall length of 32 feet resulting in the overhangs being 70 percent of LWL, a half a dozen of the original boats still race. Trevor maintains that "it is the oldest one-design class racing in the original boats," similar to the Howth Sailing Club fleet. Considering how overpowered the Idem is by reason of the large gaff-rigged mainsail, the main boom of which extended over the transom and had to be trimmed by a main sheet handler sitting in a special cockpit aft of the helmsman, and how unmanageable the helm becomes in a knockdown puff, the dedication of the owners and crews to the boat for close to a century is remarkable. Clinton Crane was notable for being among a generation of naval architects such as N.G. Herreshoff, Starling Burgess, C.D.Mower, John G. Alden, B.B. Crowninshield et alia who pioneered the early one-design classes. His designs ranged from a small self-bailing lifeboat for Arthur Curtiss James's *Coronet* to James's brigantine, *Aloha*.

The above classes were primarily local, or yacht club, in genesis, whereas one of the earliest examples of a district or yacht racing association introducing a one-design class was the Inland Lake Yachting Association adopting in 1897 two classes, 17 and 20-foot scows, partly as a result of exasperation over the expense and extremes to which boats were being designed under the Seawanhaka Rule and over the inequities of time allowances. According to *The History of the Neenah-Nodaway Yacht Club*[6] Lake Winnebago, Neenah, WI:

> *... before the advent of the one-class yacht, it (time allowances) often provoked tempers and aroused bitterness, (also the history of the scow is)... the search for a boat something smaller, lighter and less costly than the traditional yachts, a fast boat especially adapted to racing on a lake.*

In the same vein, earlier the Nodaway Yacht Club, founded as a Boat Club in 1894 under Commodore James C. Kimberly, approved a class 21 feet LOA, 15 feet 9 inches LWL, 5 feet 6 inches beam and 9 inches draught with board up. Rigged as catyawls the sail area was 250 square feet and size of spinnaker was open. The rationale for the move was the same:

> *They had also seen outbuilding force spiraling cost and inequalities on local racing... though general classes for racing craft had been acknowledged on the lake for some time, the idea of rigid class dimensions was new in the region.*

The next year the Club introduced a novel twist described as "well-nigh revolutionary" by providing that "no person who ever sailed a yacht for hire shall sail in the Nodaway Regattas a yacht whose sailing length is 35 feet or less."

The North Haven Dinghy, the Idem and the lake Scows were not, however, the earliest examples of the concept of racing similar boats as a class. Perhaps the first and most universal for its day was racing in Whitehalls. By the beginning of the nineteenth century the Whitehall[7] became the lightweight, oar-manned captain's gig, courier, shore shuttle, etc. for commercial sailing vessels to use when in port; also, for the 'runners,' agents for the chandlers servicing incoming vessels to place orders for supplies, arrange docking or lighters for unloading cargo, and so forth. To quote W. P. Stephens's *Old-Time Boat Building in New York*, 1936:

> *The first recorded rowing races occurred in 1811 using four pairs of sculls and a coxswain ... the boats were 28-30 feet, longer than the traditional Whitehall boats.*

Rowing races became a major sport drawing thousands of spectators along the banks of the Hudson (North) River, and private citizens were building special racing versions such as the John C. Stevens built in 1838 and named after the first Commodore of the New York Yacht Club and head of the yacht *America* syndicate.

While the *John C. Stevens* was four-oared, 30 feet in length, 4 inches in draft and weighed 140 pounds, Whitehalls usually were under 20 feet LOA, although to accommodate rougher seas in San Francisco Bay some were 28 to 30 feet In Boston ca. 1873 H.V. Partelow was building Whitehalls at Commercial Street, and in 1889 he turned out a 14-foot version. As racing developed among the boat clubs limitations were placed of not under 17 nor over 20 feet LOA, breadth not less than 4 feet and a minimum weight of 265 pounds – considerably heavier than the *John C. Stevens*. They were built of copper-fastened cedar planking with a top streak of oak and used for many utilitarian purposes: by Harbor Police and officials of the Ferry Department; by the Commodore of the Jeffries Point Yacht Club, et alia.[8] It is not certain when Whitehalls in New York Harbor became equipped with sails nor whether they were raced on a regular basis under sail, although W.P. Stephens implies so when discussing Whitehalls in New York, "... and a larger rig." In San Francisco, however, they were rigged with two masts, bow and stern, with gunter sprits and transported officers of ships, mail, couriers from chandleries, etc. to and fro from ship to shore.

The October 23, 1851 edition of the *Daily Alta California*, a Northern California newspaper founded in 1842, reports a match race under sail between a local Whitehall, *T.K. Batelle*, and a boat off a foreign vessel.[9] Numerous Whitehalls were built locally – some for personal use, and the archives of the John Porter Shaw Library[10] contain a photograph of several Whitehalls rigged as sloops with a gunter main racing in Bay circa 1900. An insight into the sometimes intense sailing competition in the small, sail-equipped work boats is the comment by John Gardner in *Whitehalls and Canoe: An Era Ends* that in the 1890's in Nahant (MA), "Fishermen were dory-mad racing them under sail". In the same decade C.D. Mower, whose yacht designs were popular from the Atlantic to the Pacific Coast, developed at Swampscott the 21-foot X Dory built by E. Gerry Emmons for sailing at the Swampscott Club and simultaneously a class of dories for the Riverside Yacht Club on Long Island Sound. Gradually at the turn of the century Dories in some areas succeeded Whitehalls.

Whitehalls racing on San Francisco Bay, estimated ca. 1900
Photo courtesy of San Francisco Maritime NHP, #B7.138 G

The Whitehall not only can be credited with the claim of having been the pioneer in class sailboat racing, but also can unequivocally be stated to have been the vehicle in which inter-collegiate rowing started. In 1843 William J. Weeks, a Junior at Yale University, bought a secondhand Whitehall and shipped it to New Haven naming her *Pioneer* and formed a club. She was 19 feet LOA with 4 feet beam built by W. & E. De La Montagne. Three more were bought by undergraduates thus establishing rowing as a sport at Yale 44 years before sailing. The next year students at Harvard University bought some Whitehalls.

As above recounted, the trend towards racing similar types of boats without time allowance was underway before the advent of the North Haven Dinghy and continued afterwards in many sections of North America.

(For a comprehensive listing of classes see *Appendix E.*) Classes built to specifications that permitted little or no variation in hull, rig and sail area so that they were virtually one-design began to proliferate as they attracted sailors seeking a level playing field, especially in club racing. As the process accelerated after the first quarter of the 19th century, the ranks of those racing restricted classes built to a specific rating under rules such as the Universal and International and imbued with the urge to excel through design and innovation severely diminished. An example of a strictly one-design is the 'S' Class of 1919 which quickly spread to Marblehead, Narragansett Bay, Long Island Sound, Hawaii, et alia. Rating 17 under the Universal Rule, the 'S' raced, nevertheless, on a boat-for-boat basis without time allowances, similar to the 'PC' (Pacific Coast) at San Diego, which by happenstance rated the same. An example, on the other hand, of an open, or restricted, design is the 'R' Class in which owners juggled the factors of length, displacement and sail area thereby producing boats of varying LOA and LWL – some as long as 46 feet – while staying within the class rating of 20. When Lee Wilson at Cleveland pulled a mold off the successful 'R', *Cotton Blossom*, in the 1960's to produce boats in GRP (glass reinforced plastic) the 'R', in effect, became truly one-design.

Most of the one-design classes by the turn-of-the-century were small – 30 feet or less overall – and they came into being on club by club basis for two reasons: they were inexpensive and fun to race. They, therefore, met the requirements of intra-club, and often inter-club, racing, and by 1900 there must have been more than 200 such designs.

'R' AND SIX-METRE CLASSES: UNIVERSAL RULE YIELDS TO THE INTERNATIONAL RULE

John Streeter recounts the history of the 'R' Class in a chapter in Schoettle's *Sailing Craft* and how sources and sizes of the 'R's varied. Clifford D. Mallory, President of NAYRU raced one of the largest R's, *Barbara*, designed by John Alden and built in Germany. They also varied depending on local conditions, e.g. 'R's in San Francisco Bay were more powerful than those on Long Island Sound. In contrast, for today's strictly one-design classes, e.g. the Shields, the only leeway permitted under class rules affecting performance is the selection of sails, and even so many classes make lump purchases of sails and distribute them by lot. Designers of R's in North America were legion including Charles Nicholson and William Fife from overseas and on the east coast of North America J.W. Roue of Nova Scotia, Herreshoff, Mower, W. S.Burgess, Anker, Gardner, Hoyts (Frederick M. and C. Sherman), Luders and Alden, in Toronto T.B.F. Bensen and in Vancouver/Seattle Ted Geary and E.B. Shock.

Six-Metres *Nordug IV* vs. *Lady Betty*, 1915 Panama-Pacific International Exposition Regatta
Photo from the Barneson Album, St. Francis Yacht Club

In terms of geographical distribution and longevity the 'R' Class merits the accolade of having been one of the most significant classes on the continent. Introduced in the early 1900's, it is still racing in a few locations on the Great Lakes. As Robert B. Meyer apologized at an annual meeting of NAYRU in the 1930's: "I keep mentioning and referring to the 'R' Class, because it is the only open class raced throughout the U.S."

Chronologically the 'R's started in Marblehead in 1906; were on Long Island Sound prior to 1913; at the Royal Vancouver Yacht Club in 1912 and the Royal Victoria Yacht Club a year later; at the Chicago Yacht Club in 1914 where they raced until 1972; in San Francisco Bay in 1913[11] and still racing in the late 1960's; at the Los Angeles Yacht Club in 1920 and San Diego Yacht Club in1922; in Hawaii in the 1930's as well as locations including Rochester, Royal Canadian Yacht Club, Cleveland Yacht Club and Sodus Point, NY where recently there were 'R's in GRP (glass reinforced plastic).

When Sir Thomas Lipton was visiting Vancouver in 1912 it was during the aftermath of a bitter rupture between Canada and the United States over the measurement under the Seawanhaka Rule of the Seattle Yacht Club entry, *Spirit II*, designed by Ted Geary for the 1908 match of the Alexandra Cup. Partly as a gesture to revive the international match race competition, Sir Thomas donated a $3,000 trophy which became the Sir Thomas Lipton Perpetual Challenge Trophy for which the 'R' was the designated class. The Seattle Yacht Club entered *Sir Tom* designed and sailed by Ted Geary, which won the Championship in a streak unbroken from 1914-1919 and went on to win in San Francisco Bay at the 1915 Panama-Pacific Exposition Regatta. The owner succeeding Geary continued the winning streak for a decade, and *Sir Tom* was "consigned to the scrap heap" in 1956. International racing in the 'R' Class, however, ceased in 1940, and after WW II the Six-Metre became the designated class, by which date a number of Six-Metres from Long Island Sound, where the class had peaked in the late 1930's, had migrated to Puget Sound.

Also, the 1915 Panama-Pacific International Exposition Regatta in San Francisco was the occasion of the first appearance of a Six-Metre in North America – the gaff-rigged *Lady Betty* (US 6/1) built for a member of the San Francisco Yacht Club at the W.F. Stone Yard to compete against *Nordug IV* from Denmark with a Marconi rig. It was the first large Marconi/Bermudian rig seen on the Bay to which her easy victory was attributed. The plan had been to have a number of Six-Metres come from Europe, but the outbreak of WW I intervened. Paradoxically, a Panama Yacht Club was formed in 1911 to herald the completion of the Canal but dissolved before the Canal went into operation.

As the 'R' Class expanded it became the designated class for the San Francisco (Perpetual) Challenge Cup established in 1895 for match racing on the west coast - claimed to be the oldest continuously raced for 'challenge' trophy in North America (note that the Seawanhaka International Challenge Cup was established the same year, although it has not been competed for on an annual basis). Perhaps an harbinger of the future, in 1929 and 1930 the Challenge Cup was conducted in the Six-Metre Class which succeeded the 'R' as the 'designated' class; by the late 1960's the 'R" had disbanded on the Bay. As reported in the January 1986 edition of *Latitude 38*,[12] an 'R', *Ace*, designed by Mower for Art Russo in 1925-26 outclassed the competition, similar to *Sir Tom* on Puget Sound, thereby hastening the eventual switch of dismayed owners from the Universal Rule classes to the International Six-Metre. She dominated the Perpetual Trophy from 1926 to 1928 and "was so good that she raced herself right out of competition." Fifty years of racing stands testimony to the longevity of the 'R', as was the case with 'R' fleets elsewhere.

'R' Class racing at the New York Yacht Club was episodic in contrast to the Chicago Yacht Club where it became a fixture for over half a century (1914-1972). At New York the New York Yacht Club Cup was put up for racing in the Universal Rule Classes, initially in the 'R' class in 1926 off Newport, and drew entries from the Corinthian and Eastern Yacht Clubs at Marblehead, Beverly Yacht Club, Seawanhaka Corinthian, Stamford, Capital, and New York Yacht Clubs – an indication of the spread of the class in lower New England. The primary reason for the lack of 'R' Class activity at the NYYC was the fact that many of its members were also members of clubs on Long Island Sound and raced Six-Metres at the Seawanhaka Corinthian Yacht Club in Oyster Bay. Until the ascendancy of the Sixes, however, NYYC members such as Junius Morgan, George Nichols, Robert Meyer, Sherman Hoyt, Philip R. and Clifford D. Mallory and James W. Alker raced 'R's on the Sound designed by N.G. and L. Francis Herreshoff, John Alden, Alfred E. Luders, Frederick M. Hoyt, W. S. Burgess, Charles D. Mower and William Fife (U.K.).

The *History* of the Chicago Yacht Club in conjunction with letters[13] from Herman T. Van Mell – one of the last owners of the highly successful 'R' *Ardelle* from 1945-1972 after which the class ceased racing – tell the story of the R Class at CYC.

> *Ogden McClurg started a class that would last for sixty years when he brought a new 'R' class, gaff-rigged sloop to Chicago in 1914. Though there was not to be class racing until 1920, the new 'R' won the last leg of the annual Triangular Race.* XXIX *was her name... and already there was talk of transferring the Lipton Cup to the new class. In 1917 Sam Dauchy, Commodore of the Lincoln Park Yacht Club, defended the Lipton Cup with his 'R',* Sari*" (38 feet 6 inches LOA, 25 feet 5 inches LWL, 7 feet 8 inches beam, 5 feet 9 inches draft).*

Sari, skippered by Benjamin Carter, after beating 330 miles won the Chicago-Mackinac Race in 1924 so decisively that the sponsor banned 'R's from future races. The class championship at the time involved eight races: three for the Lipton Cup and five for the Nutting Cup, all sailed without time allowance. Only when sailing in general club races where they would be scored against other classes were handicaps used.

> *The merger of the Lincoln Park Yacht Club into the Chicago Yacht Club in 1920 marked the beginning of the Roaring '20's and a great rise in racing activity (from the late 1920's until the late 1960's the 'R' Class was the preeminent racing class at the Chicago Yacht Club). The class was one of the first to try something ancient in origin (ca. sixteenth century in Holland) but new in the classes – the Marconi rig. On July 31, 1920 Railton and Kimbal's* Gossoon, *which had been sailed the year before by the winning America's Cup skipper Charles Francis Adams, drove upwind to a convincing victory in her first race under [this] rig.*

Note the gradual progression of the Marconi/Bermudian rig starting ca. 1850 at Halifax, at the Seawanhaka Corinthian Yacht Club in 1895 with W.P. Stephen's *Ethylwyn* Seawanhaka Cup entry and, as above-mentioned, in 1915 in San Francisco Bay with the Six-Metre *Nordug IV.*

Other fleets of 'R's' on the Great Lakes were at the Cleveland Yacht Club, Rochester Yacht Club and Royal Canadian Yacht Club at Toronto. In 1924 the RCYC shipped an 'R' to Chicago to challenge for the Richardson Cup, a match race series, and won. The Cup (a.k.a. Yacht Racing Union Great Lakes Challenge Cup) was regarded as the America's Cup of the Great Lakes and originally sailed for in the 'P' class, a Universal Rule boat two classifications larger. In 1914 Chicago had sent a 'P' to

Toronto to challenge, but World War I broke out the day after she arrived causing cancellation of the match.

The *History* goes on to recount that concurrently at the south end of the City the larger 'Q' class (approximately 50 ft) was getting started, one of which, the *Hope* designed by John Alden and built in 1929 is still sailing on Lake Michigan. According to Royce Foley of the Chicago-based Classic Yacht Association only about 27 'Q's were built – the first in 1906 and the last in 1930.

In 1922 the prestigious Richardson Cup was transferred to the 'R' class. The event had become international and was rotated among the Lake Michigan Yachting Association, Inter-Lake Yachting Association and Lake Yacht Racing Association drawing entries from fleets at Toronto, Rochester and Watertown. Noteworthy Chicago yachtsmen racing 'R's were Clare Udell, Harry Nye, Doc Potter, Hank Rubicam, Art King, Clark Wright, Eddie Schnabel, and Herman Van Mell to name a few. This format continued until World War II brought a halt to the series. After the War not only was transporting the boats too expensive, but also they were becoming too fragile to withstand such manhandling. For the 1941 - 1951 period, therefore, borrowed boats at host clubs were used. After the war the Royal Canadian Yacht Club was welcomed back, but the club was shifting from 'R's to Six-Metres, i.e. Universal to International Rule. In the meanwhile 'R's at Chicago continued to increase and reached apogee in 1950 at 17.

When the Richardson trophy competition resumed in 1952, 'R's remained the yacht of choice. They also raced out of the Club on overnight races to various points on Lake Michigan and were sailed hard and often. By the mid 1950's the major interest at the club turned to the Olympic classes – Stars, Flying Dutchmen, Finns and Solings. Thus, the aging fleet began to decline with boats often being sold to those who preferred restoring a 'classic' craft to racing. The last Richardson series held in the 'R' class was in 1966 by which time Lee Wilson of Cleveland had begun to mold 'R's in GRP using his successful 'R' class *Cotton Blossom* as the mold.

What does it take to maintain a wooden yacht beyond the age of 50? The saga of *Ardelle* is enlightening. Built in 1926 to a design by Charles D. Mower, she had a strong, rigid hull of double planking, the outer of mahogany and the inner white cedar. The outer planking was fastened to oak frames by countersunk, plugged brass screws and the inner liberally fastened to the outer by additional brass screws. Her first rehabilitation was in 1938, but that was not because of deterioration but to make her more competitive with newer yachts by which she had been out-designed. Principally, she was given a taller mast, a T-shaped boom (copied from the famous 'Fifth Avenue' boom on Harold S. Vanderbilt's *Rainbow* which enabled the foot of the mainsail to conform to the curve of the rest of the sail) and a number of stainless steel (new at that time) fittings to replace bronze ones. A self-bailing cockpit replaced the original, and she was given a number of new, or replacement, winches for the halyards, sheets and running backstays. When Van Mell, with a partner, Walter Bitter, whom he had bought out two years later, bought *Ardelle* in 1946, it took them and a professional carpenter three months to replace such of the oak frames and outer mahogany planking that had succumbed to dry rot during the war years. It was the last time this type of emergency work had to be done. The durable yacht, which had won many trophies in her racing days, was most fortunate to have last two owners give her meticulous attention every year. Preventative maintenance is the clue to keeping an old wooden boat alive. Today *Ardelle* is believed to be sailing on the Hudson River in her 70th year as a classic yacht.

The longevity of the 'R' class notwithstanding, this ubiquitous Universal Rule boat gradually yielded the playing field to the International Rule Six-Metre. Already noted was the presence of both classes at the San Francisco Exposition in 1915; of the 'R's in the early 1920's at the Newport Harbor Yacht Club in Southern California; and in San Diego Bay in 1928 – Ed Peterson's *Angela* having retrieved for the San Diego Yacht Club the Lipton Cup from Long Beach. In 1929 and 30 the San Francisco Cup went from the 'R's to the Sixes, and although it reverted to the 'R's afterwards, the local fleet had disbanded by 1960. In addition, the History of the Royal Vancouver Yacht Club[14] comments:

> *1940 marked the end of the international racing in the 'R' class on the Pacific Coast. After WW II the Lipton Cup was offered to the Six-Metre Class which by then had become an Olympic Class – a status never achieved by any of the Universal Rule Classes.*

The Seawanhaka Cup after WW II was first raced in the Six-Metre, but when it went overseas in 1922, open class racing revived on Long Island Sound in the 'R's, but only for a brief spell. At the Royal Canadian Yacht Club the 'R' likewise gave way to a strong Six-Metre fleet. On Lake Ontario in 1928 the International Rule went into effect at the Royal Canadian Yacht Club; but the Universal Rule 'P' Class was not affected since it continued to race at the top (rating) of the class.

Before the advent of today's 'simon-pure' one-design classes with International Status, the 'rating' or 'open' classes provided for many decades a commonality for competitive racing across North America. As an indication of the relative performance of yachts under the two

Six-Metre *Goose* in 1949 British-American Cup on the Solent skippered by George Nichols, Jr. and outstanding in the Class.
Photo: Beken & Sons, Cowes, I.O.W.

rules, related in the history of the Royal Canadian Yacht Club documents[15] is:

> *Further light to be expected from the International Rule was shed by the advent of the Six-Meter yacht* Merenneito, *the Finnish champion for the Scandinavian Gold Cup in 1927. Commodore Gooderham brought her to Lake Ontario for demonstration purposes (the next year). The yacht seemed too small to appeal to prospective builders but her speed was amazing. She was only raced twice: once against a fleet of 'R' boats, where she beat them boat for boat going to windward, and on time allowance off the wind; and once against the whole RCYC fleet, when she won the classic Prince of Wales Cup on time allowance. So impressed was the club with the possibilities of the new [International] rating rule that late in the year a challenge was prepared for the Canada's Cup and forwarded to the Rochester Yacht Club which had held the trophy since 1907.*

The above is a provocative insight demonstrating how the International Rule was producing not only a faster type boat for level racing than its Universal Rule counterpart, but also faster when racing under the Universal Rule under time allowance. Note that in approximate figures the International Rule Six, Eight and Ten-Metres, respectively, equate to the Universal Rule 'R's, 'Q's and 'P' classes (see chart in first section of *Chapter IX - Rating Rules*).

INTERNATIONAL FOURTEEN[16]

As detailed elsewhere, the first North American one-design was William Weld's North Haven Dinghy, 14 feet LOA, of 1885. Almost concurrently in 1887, an Irishman named Middletown designed, according to T.J. Vaughan (and others), the "earliest known one-design unballasted centerboard dinghy – the 13-foot open Dublin Bay 'Water Wags.'" The true predecessors of the International Fourteen, however, were the West of England Conference Dinghy (a long name for a short boat) of 1889, which was sloop rigged with a quadrilateral lug main, and the Norfolk Dinghy with a triangular lug sail. Both were 14-feet LOA and undecked. From the outset the Fourteen was a 'restricted' class with enough freedom for a variety of hull forms and rigs. Although international competition led to refinement and uniformity, and the granting in 1928 by IYRU of International Status, neither the Canadians nor the Antipodes conformed to the measurement and equipment rules in their entirety until the differences were finally resolved in 1996. The original rules of the Fourteen defined it as rating 0.3 under the old YRA (UK) rule. They stipulated:

> *Open boats not exceeding in length 14 feet, this measurement to be taken overall, instead of on the waterline, in determining the rating. The boats to be unsinkable. Draft not to exceed 12 inches with the centerboard housed and the crew on board. Centerboards, when housed, not to come above a batten placed across the boat from gunwale to gunwale. No bulbs on centerboards and no outside ballast allowed.*

The move to restricted classes, which was occurring both in the U.K. and North American, was primarily driven by dissatisfaction with rating and classification rules. In Canada the origin of Fourteen racing began with a design by I. Wilton Morse around 1897. It was adopted by the Lake Sailing Skiff Association (LSSA). Clinker built, these little yachts were limited by the Association to a minimum beam of five feet and a maximum of five feet 7½ inches. Bows were plumb and decking optional. They were raced in the Toronto and Hamilton areas. The competitors were entirely Canadian; on the other side of Lake Ontario Americans were pre-occupied with sailing canoes. Thus, it was a number of years before a Canadian versus American competition arose.

In 1914 a regatta was held on Lake Ontario for the Douglas Cup. Canada won it and held the Cup until 1921 when an American finally prevailed with a cat-rigged Bermudian/Marconi main. This began a trend away from gaff rigs in the class, which was also occurring in Great Britain where the principal action was located. The Star Class made the switch in the same year, and large yachts also began to convert to masthead rigs. By the end of the decade it was unusual in North America to see racing yachts of any size still sailing with gaff rigs. A few classes hold out until this day among which is the venerable Wianno Senior on Cape Cod. As is the case with most successful classes, one of the strengths of the Fourteen has been the quality and enthusiasm of its members. A notable early aficionado was Paul Phelan of Toronto for whom it reputedly was his first boat and who later twice served as President of the Canadian Yachting Association.

During the 1920's the design of Fourteens evolved under Morgan-Giles, Charles Nicholson and Uffa Fox at the Island Sailing Club at Cowes, Isle of Wight. On a royal tour H.R.H. The Prince of Wales was taken sailing in a Canadian Fourteen. Apparently even he (a life-long non-sailor to the disappointment of his father, George V) was impressed. When he returned to London, he presented a trophy to the National Fourteen Class. Although it was intended for the Class in the U.K., the Fourteen had by then become truly international in scope. The first regatta for the POW Trophy, which has become the most coveted trophy in the dinghy world, was held at Cowes in 1927.

Winners of the POW Trophy have been in the forefront of yachting worldwide, but it was not until 1954 that it was won by a team from the western hemisphere, and this was a Bermudian, rather than a mainland North American – de Forest (Shorty) Trimingham. The first American to win was Dr. Stuart H. Walker in 1964 from the Severn Sailing Association at Annapolis on Chesapeake Bay. Another American, Glen S. Foster was a close contender several times and won the POW

Week's Points Cup in 1963. The first Canadian to win was Ian Bruce in 1967 and 1968 and the next American was Steve Toschi sailing an American designed Benedict Fourteen in 1975.

Events in 1930 and 1932 provided a major boost in class activity in North America which had the effect of conforming the measurement rule and rigs of Fourteens on both sides of the Atlantic. In 1930 during the Canada Cup races at Port Charlotte, Lake Ontario, Clifford D. Mallory, President of the North American Yacht Racing Union, proposed and participated in a race in the Canadian cat-rigged Fourteens.[17] Having done so, he ordered a Fourteen from Charles Bourke of Toronto for his son and took it to Newport, RI during the America's Cup trials where it provoked heated discussion over the relative merits of British and North American Fourteens. This led to a team race held September 1933 at the Seawanhaka Corinthian Yacht Club, Oyster Bay, Long Island among teams from England, Toronto, Rochester and Oyster Bay – the latter using sloop-rigged Fourteen's brought over by the British. England won by a narrow margin over the Canadians and impressed all parties with their sloop-rigged boats. A subsequent match at the Royal Canadian Yacht Club off Toronto in 1934 served to convince the Canadians and Americans to adopt the IYRU measurement rule. A head-to-head testing of North American v. British designs occurred in 1936 in a match race on the Clyde for which Clifford Mallory put up a trophy. The same year an American team composed of George Ford, W. Tarr and Ed Pillsbury won against the Danish Fourteens and then lost to the British. While one of the earliest examples of international team racing occurred in the Sonder Class between the Eastern Yacht Club at Marblehead and a German team in 1906, it was the Fourteens and the Six-Metres that engendered the tradition of international team racing in North America.

In 1936 a Canadian boat appeared with the crew wearing a leather 'half vest' with a spring clip attached to it, to which he secured the jib sheet, thereby enabling him to hike more effectively by projecting his torso further outboard – and with less back strain. In the meanwhile Beecher Moore (of both American and British extraction) had developed 'The Bell Rope' on which the crew could hang by his hands. In the 1937 the Prince of Wales Trophy at Cowes, Peter Scott combined the two ideas by mounting a spring clip on a belt around his waist which may have effectively contributed to John Winter and Scott winning the Trophy. It, also, was the precursor of the trapeze which would not be approved by the class until 1969 – coincidentally while Scott was President of IYRU.

There are distinct 'virtues' in the concept of a 'restricted' class one of which is that it provides the opportunity for innovations that often improve the sport. For example, in 1938 Sandy Douglass turned out the first molded (plywood) Fourteen, perhaps the first molded boat in the world. Further, the Fourteen became the proving ground, as noted above, for the trapeze; for the kicking strap (boom vang) and halyard winches in 1932; the unballasted centerboard; extending the spinnaker pole to J + 25% to provide greater stability and drive; twin trapezes in the 1980's for helmsman and crew making the Fourteen "an ultimate watercraft;" fully battened mainsails and asymmetrical spinnakers; open transoms, roller furling jibs; hydraulic mast rams, tripod mast supports; and mid-boom travelers.

The Fourteen had another virtue the impact of which on US and Canadian sailors may not have been well appreciated. It introduced them to high performance sailing on an international level thereby providing a training medium for the post WW II Olympic classes to which they had had only limited exposure prior thereto.

It was Dr. Stuart Walker who received the accolade from T.J. Vaughan:

> *Who [Walker], it is fair to say, rebuilt and re-inspired the American Fourteen fleet during the 1950's and 1960's.*

Prior to World War II fleets were strong in Toronto led by sailors such as Paul Phelan and Paul McLaughlin; in Essex, CT by C. Eric Olsen; and in the Chesapeake, Vancouver, San Francisco Bay, Los Angeles and and Santa Barbara. After the War the revival of international fleet and team racing was championed by Canadian sailors Paul McLaughlin, his son Terry, Bruce Kirby, Ian Bruce and Buller who were producing the boat in GRP; U.S. sailors Ward McKimm, Steve Toschi, Glen Foster (NY), Dr. Stuart Walker (MD), Richard Fenton (Long Beach, CA); Richard Rose, Baird Bardarson, Tom Rosmond, Dennis Clark (all four Seattle, WA); Sandy Douglass who popularized a one-design version, and George O'Day (MA) in the US who produced a modified collegiate version in GRP; Bermudians J. Hartley Watlington, Dick Harris and Shorty Trimingham in Bermuda where 17 boats designed by Uffa Fox were delivered in 1947. In 1989 the World Championships were held at the St. Francis Yacht Club with 108 entries and were repeated on the Bay in 1997, hosted jointly by St. Francis and the Richmond Yacht Clubs. As above noted, 1997 was the first time that no longer were Great Britain, North America and New Zealand cum Australia at variance over the class measurement and equipment rules. Per the news release:

> *… the amalgamation of the Australian and New Zealand 14 skiff fleets into the International 14 World Council… [is] history almost being repeated as the International 14 Class itself was created over time through the joining of similar 14-foot development classes from several regions. In 1928 the regions of UK, America, Canada and Bermuda were brought together by the then IYRU to form the world's first dinghy to achieve International Status… "Fast – Fun – Forever – the Corinthian class for the thinking sailor."*

THISTLE CLASS

In recounting the history of the Inter-Lake Yachting Association[18] there was a reference to "a blaze of glory at I-LYA." This occurred at the 1945 regatta at Put-in-Bay, a group of islands in Lake Erie north of Sandusky, Ohio, to which Gordon K. 'Sandy' Douglass came with the prototype of his newly designed Thistle. It was an open boat of double-planked construction with light framing, as close an approximation as possible to what a molded boat would be (which it switched to in kit form and on reaching production stage). This was to be its first test. As people came around to inspect the newcomer, they shook their heads and muttered that she was no boat for Lake Erie's nasty seas. In effect, she was an enlarged International Fourteen requiring a helmsman and two crew.

Since she was one-of-a-kind, she was placed in the Universal Class, a catch-all for the bigger boats that did not fit into any of the various racing classes. They were handicapped under the Universal Rule. Said Douglass:

> *There we were, faced with the prospect of sailing the big-boat course, a fifteen-mile triangle out on open Lake Erie in winds estimated at forty miles an hour and higher in the gusts… Our competition consisted of a fair number of keel boats, the largest a big schooner, of which the best performer proved to be a 22 Square Metre. The 22's, coming from the leeward side of the Atlantic [Sweden], are designed for, and at the best in, strong winds. The little Thistle, less than half the size of the other boats, was given time by all of them. Under such circumstances, my hope was that we might complete the course creditably and perhaps save our time, if all went well. I myself did not know what she would do.*
>
> *We were given a windward start. Out of the corner of my eye, I noticed that a few of the other boats were smothered by the wind, and they were unable to get across the line on the first try. I was astounded to find that we not only were holding our own but soon were leading the fleet, footing as fast as the 22 and making good a full point higher. Just about every boat on the course was taking green seas aboard and plunging under solid water. The crews of some of the larger racing boats even formed bucket lines to stay afloat. We never once took solid water aboard; with a small tomato can, my wife occasionally dipped out what spray blew into the boat.*
>
> *By the time we reached the weather mark, the sail of the 22 was only a white dot in the distance behind us. Then came a wild, planing leg and a broad reach home in lightening wind. The race committee was astounded to see us coming, almost completely dry, more than 20 minutes ahead of the second boat and forty minutes ahead of the stragglers in the class.*
>
> *We also won the remaining two races in moderate to light winds, being the first boat in, never once calling on our handicap. But the old timers still mention "that race". It was the making of the Thistle Class, because it removed from the minds of those who were there any doubt of whether the Thistle could go out and take it. Now, light-weight planing centerboarders have demonstrated their abilities in convincing fashion in such events as the One-of-a-Kind 19 series that we know what to expect, but at that time they were almost unknown.*
>
> *Needless to say, I was kept busy after the regatta taking people sailing by the dozens. Everyone wanted to try out the Thistle. And that is why there were so many anxious Thistlers-to-be long before we were able to commence production.*

Later from the Douglass drawing board came the popular Highlander, although not as widespread as the Thistle, and the Flying Scot.

FINN CLASS

The Finn was born in 1952, the year in which the Olympic yachting games were held in Helsinki, Finland. A Swedish design by Rickard Sarby, it was selected by the Finnish Yachting Association[20] to replace the double-handed Firefly which had proven unwieldy when raced single-handed. At the Games 20-year old Paul Elvström of Denmark, who had won in 1948 in the Firefly, took his first, of five, gold medals in the Finn. No one else has ever accomplished this in a single sport, and probably no one ever will.

During the next Olympiad[21] Canada imported four Finns, but there were none in the U.S., so that their 1956 trials were sailed in Fireflies. The top four were then sent to Montreal to do some practicing in the real thing. Meanwhile, George O'Day imported a Finn, and he, as alternate, and John Marvin of Marblehead spent the next several months practicing in it. The familiarity with the boat won Marvin a bronze medal at Melbourne, Australia behind Elvström and Andre Nelis of Belgium.

In that year the Finn was accepted as an 'international class' by the International Yacht Racing Union, and the first Gold Cup championship was held in England. The Cup had been presented to the Class by Commodore 'Tiny' Mitchell of the Royal Corinthian Yacht Club and has served ever since as its World Championship. It was won by Nelis with Elvström second; the two sailors dominated the class for the next decade. By 1957 the U.S. and Canada both had Finn Class Associations which received a boost from two Finn sailors from overseas – Jack Knights of England and Colin Ryrie of Australia. The first North American championship was held at the Seawanhaka Corinthian Yacht Club at Oyster Bay, Long Island where the first U.S. fleet had been formed by many of the same sailors who had started the first fleet of Ravens in the early 1950's. It was followed quickly by fleets in Southern and Northern California and activity in the mid-west led by Peter Barrett. The first U.S. championship was held in 1959 by which time the Finn had become a feeder for those aspiring to make the Canadian or U.S. Olympic Yachting Team.

The Finn, coming into being just as cold-molded plywood of marine quality was being introduced, quickly went from pine to this lighter and stronger material. The unstayed wooden mast was shaved to suit the individual's need to be able to de-power the sail to match one's weight and build. During the 1960's most of the masts came from world champion Finn sailor, Joerg Bruder, of Brazil which has a native wood that was excellent for its bending characteristics. Over-shaving the wall thickness led to many a mast failure – a problem that eventually was overcome with the introduction of aluminum spars, and today in classes such as the 49'er by use of carbon fibre. In the same vein, GRP (glass reinforced plastic) soon replaced molded plywood for the hull.

With the advent of master molds certified by the IYRU and monitoring of construction under IYRU's Chief Measurer, the Class has maintained tight controls of its specifications. This, in conjunction with the durability and excellent seagoing qualities of the boat, has given the Finn an unusual longevity as an Olympic and international class. As a measure – perhaps somewhat over stated – of the Finn's sea prowess, Elvström was referring to the boat when he pronounced, "I'm as good in fifty-five as in five (knots)." Jack Knights once wrote about the boat:

> *The cult of the International Finn may seem strange to some people, uncomfortable, masochistically to others. But to us devotees there is nothing else remotely like it. The Finn probably offers the most purely athletic form of yacht racing and is therefore the most fundamentally competitive sailboat. The Finn gives thrills, frustration, and pleasures in roughly equal measure. It offers the rewarding opportunity of doing a difficult thing well. There are Lightnings and such for the rest; but there will always be those who aspire to be master of the Finn.*

FISH CLASS[22]

The Southern Yacht Club, given high marks by the City of New Orleans for its excellent work in housing ill and recuperating soldiers during the horrendous flu epidemic of 1918, came out of World War I in disrepair as a sailing club. Its recent heritage was primarily as a place for dinner dances rather than sailing. Rathbone de Buys, upon congratulating the 1919 Commodore on his taking office, advised him that yacht racing at the club was on the verge of collapse. There were only a few racing sloops plus a collection of this and that for which it was impossible to assign reasonable handicaps, even if the owners were interested in racing. He said, "You have a club of jelly beans and flappers."

Asked to make some recommendations, deBuys spat out several, among them the need for the Race Committee to control the racing, without interference or direction from the Commodore or the Board of Governors. Also, to appoint a Board of Appeal containing only experienced and knowledgeable sailors, since the Board of Governors contained few such people. The result was that the Commodore appointed him as Chairman of the Race Committee and granted him all his demands for authority and for making changes.

All that was not enough, he soon realized. What the club needed was a fleet of small one-designs, something that did not exist in his part of the world. Not only that, but to jump-start the operation the club would have to buy them and then charge members a fee for racing them and practice sailing during the week. After considering some one-designs of Long Island Sound and Massachusetts, he decided that a boat would have to be designed specifically for the shallow Lake Pontchartrain with its steep chop; being an architect, he designed it himself.

He had grown up on the Gulf Coast in Mississippi sailing a Biloxi Catboat, a little brute of 18½ feet with a sail hung on a gaff of 18 feet and a boom of 28 feet. It required fourteen sandbags of ballast and a crew of four. The Biloxi had been a popular boat before 1900 with a fleet of twenty or more sailing out of the port of the same name. Starting with the catboat, he incorporated features of the New England Sharpie and came up with the Fish (each boat to be named for a species of fish of the Gulf waters). With the straight lines and hard chines of a Sharpie and the beam and freeboard of a Catboat, to which he added a 'V' bottom, the Fish was 20 feet 6 inches LOA, 15 feet 10 inches LWL and 6 feet 8 inches beam. It had a lead keel of 220 pounds that added only six inches to the draft of three feet. He opted for a gaff rig, since it required more skill to handle, with a mainsail of 262 square feet and a small jib of 46 square feet. There would be a crew of three.

Fish Class sloop: designed by Rathbone de Buys, it was introduced by SYC and the first class indigenous to the Gulf Coast
Photo courtesy of the Southern Yacht Club

Thus, he had what he wanted: a small yacht that was safe for beginners, one that could develop a fair amount of speed, was economical to build and was sturdy thereby requiring a minimum amount of upkeep. The job then was to sell it to the Board of Governors. Reluctantly, after much grumbling, the Board agreed to buy six initially at a cost of $750 each. They were an almost immediate success. When they were delivered, only ten skippers stepped forward to rent them. Within two years there were 80 boats. Moreover, with the newly efficient control of racing (or "the iron hand of deBuys"?) boat owners who had lost interest in racing began to return. At the end of seven years, which marked the end of deBuys's tenure as R/C Chairman, there were more than 300 boats of which a fair number were sailed by women.

Although the number of Fish had tripled, supply was not able to meet demand, and many members were faced with the fact that, if they wished to sail, they would have to buy a boat. What could they buy? Well, there was the sporty yacht, born on Long Island Sound and sweeping across the continent, the Star. Also, within a few years, they could buy, or build for themselves, another smaller boat – the Snipe. This they did thereby widening the options within the club and enabling more avid members to find competition farther afield.

DeBuys had another idea that may or may not have been unique at the time. He divided the Fish sailors into four divisions. 'C' was for those who were beginners or yet had to win a race. Win one race in this division and be promoted to 'B' division; win two and advance to 'A'; win three races and be promoted to the Expert division. This provided two very useful attractions to the Fish class: it insured that everyone was racing against peers with comparable skills; and it was an incentive to learn and to improve one's skills.

DeBuys did not stop there; he began promoting the Fish at other clubs. The first to respond was the Pensacola Yacht Club (FL). While holding the first interclub regatta in years, he and the chairman at Pensacola put together the basic language for creating a regional association. The next year (1920) the five clubs that had

Fish Class fleets – Southern, Pensacola, Eastern Shore, Houston and Biloxi – formed the Gulf Yachting Association.[23] When writing his monograph in 1950, he noted that the Association then contained 12 clubs, and they all owned Fish Class fleets operated on a rental basis. Indeed, the Fish was the official class of the GYA since DeBuys had so stipulated in the class constitution. Further, he argued, somewhat tenuously, that the GYA actually owned the Fish. While the clubs bought and paid for the boats, maintained them and no individual could own one, the GYA only sponsored the class.

Just after the Fish class began Sir Thomas Lipton returned to New Orleans, where he had gotten his first job as a youth, and since had presented trophies liberally over North America. Happy boyhood memories, good friends among Southern Yacht Club members and an interest in fostering inter-club racing all motivated him to present a handsome cup to the Southern Yacht Club. Initially the club was planning to use it for the club's Fish class championship, but once the GYA was formed, deBuys talked the Board of Governors into deeding the Cup to the GYA to be used for a GYA Fish class championship.

At the end of the monograph de Buys offered some suggestions for the benefit and improvement of the sport. First, give keeper trophies, not just to skippers, but to their crews as well. "What skipper", he asked, "could win without a good crew." Second, the penalty of either retirement or full disqualification for infringing a rule during a race was far too harsh. Most such infringements were either minor matters and/or unintentional. A basketball team did not lose a game summarily because one of its members fouled an opponent. The penalty was either one or two free throws. Why could not the infringing sailor be given a lesser penalty and be able to continue as a legitimate competitor in the race? Third, the penalty for a premature start is similarly too harsh. In football a team that is 'off-side' at the snap is penalized a mere five yards. There must be a more reasonable penalty that can be applied to an off-side in yacht racing. He was prescient in his recommendations.

The fourth suggestion is rather curious. It is that yachting should not hold the racing rules as something cast in stone but make them amenable to change as the nature of the sport changes. By 1950 was he still active enough in the sport to have been aware that, under the leadership of Harold S. Vanderbilt, NAYRU had just made the most sweeping changes in the racing rules in the history of yachting? Nonetheless, Rathbone de Buys was a mover and a shaker. Without him yachting along the Gulf Coast might have remained as parochial as he had found it to be before the advent of the Fish Class.

OPEN CLASS RACING UNDER MULTIPLE RULES AT MARBLEHEAD[24]

By "open" class is meant in current terminology "restricted". In other words, a class in which the measurement rules specify limitations, either maximums or minimums, or fixed dimensions with tolerances, that control displacement, hull measurements and sail area. In the case of some classes these components become factors in a formula resulting in a specific number not to be exceeded. The International Fourteen is an example of the former; Metre boats under the International Rule are an example of the latter. All yachts in a class race boat for boat without time allowances.

During the period 1906 - 1940 there was more variety in open-class racing in Marblehead, MA than in any other site on the continent, but the numbers were not huge. The first such class was the Sonder of German origin.[25] Its sail area was limited to a maximum of 550 square feet. The sum of the LWL, beam and draft could not exceed 32 feet. A minimum displacement of 4,000 pounds was required, and there were minimum scantlings. Within those specifications a yacht designer could design any combination of hull and rig that he thought would be fast. 'Developmental' is also a term used for such a class; in fact it was the term used by N.G. Herreshoff.

The first Sonder built in North America was a yacht named *Uncle Sam*. In 1902 she was shipped to Germany to race at Kiel for the Emperor's Cup, which she won. After the series Emperor Wilhelm bought her and presented her to the German Navy. By 1906 there were eight Sonders racing at Marblehead – the highest number was 15 in both 1904 and 1909. Germany and Spain each challenged for the Emperor's Cup which was won by a U.S. boat, *Vim*. The following year three Sonders from Marblehead went to Kiel again and were overwhelmed, for, unlike the German boats, they had not been designed for the strong winds and seas encountered there. The German boats had low sail plans with flatter sails, narrow hulls, heavy keels and roller reefing. The American boats went to Spain where they lost again "under rather inconclusive sailing conditions."

The Germans came to Marblehead twice again, in 1909 and 1913, and lost both times. In the final contest the winner was Charles P. Curtis who at age 86 became the oldest man ever to win a class championship.

When the U.S. entered the War I, racing stopped. The clubhouse of the Eastern Yacht Club was turned over to the Navy for use in training seamen. After the War most of the Sonders were sold to members of the Eastern Point Yacht Club at Gloucester, but they returned to Marblehead each summer for Race Week. Six of them were still racing in 1932, but that was the end. One of the faults of the Sonder specifications was the inflexibility of the 32-foot limit. As the boats soaked up more and more water each year, their LWL and draft increased. This resulted in a heavy rating penalty thereby making the older boats less competitive with the newer ones, although under the Universal Rule the penalty would not have been as severe.

The Universal Rule involved three factors: .18 x (*LWL* + square root of sail area) divided by the cube root of *displacement* resulting in a rating number. While the formula looked simple enough, one of the drawbacks was that it required a good deal of care and ability to measure. Charles Lane Poor, Chairman of the New York Yacht Club Measurement Committee, who steered the rule into its final form, later said that when all the limitations on waterline and displacement were taken into account, it was actually nothing but a pure sail area rule.

Yachts under the Universal Rule were grouped (classified) in classes with a narrow range of ratings. The classes were assigned letters in descending order of size ranging in North America from the America's Cup yachts in the 'J' class to the next to the smallest class ever designed to the rule – N.G. Herreshoff's 'S' at 27 feet 6 inches LOA. Since Capt. Nat and his friend George Lawley in Boston built all of the 'S's, the class stayed one-design in the current sense of the term.

The first Universal yachts to appear in Marblehead were the 'Q' and 'P' classes in 1909 of which there were four of each. Yachts in the respective classes varied so little in dimensions that they dispensed with handicaps for weekend racing, as the Sonders had before them. Handicaps were used only for regattas involving several classes for which there were overall trophies. In such regattas other one-designs might race against them, if, when measured to the Universal Rule, they came within the number for the class. The best competition was in the 'P' class into which some of the most competitive sailors had graduated from the Sonders, including Charles Francis Adams and Charles P. Curtis. Neither class, however, ever had more than a dozen racing in any year. Part of the reason, particularly in the case of the 'P', which had an LWL of up to 37 feet, was that they required a crew of seven. The Boston and Corinthian Yacht Clubs had been strictly amateur from inception, and the day of hiring professionals as crew was gone at Eastern Yacht Club, too, except for the larger yachts. Seven may not seem a large crew today, but yachting had much more limited number of willing participants in those days.

As a consequence, several 'P' Class owners, including Adams, Curtis and B. Devereux Barker found buyers for their boats at the Royal Canadian Yacht Club at Toronto and went into the 'R' Class in 1912. The 'R', averaging about 37 feet LOA, underwent a great deal of experimentation and innovation, including leeboards, a cat rig sporting a tall Marconi mainsail of 56 feet on the luff, a swiveling mast to reduce wind resistance and such things as longitudinal framing, raised forward decks, T-shaped booms and tangs for attaching the stays and shrouds in lieu of eye splices.

Most of the innovations were created by local designers, e.g. George Owen and L. Francis Herreshoff. Among other notable designers of Universal yachts for Marblehead and elsewhere were John Alden and Starling Burgess. While the 'P' Class soon petered out, the 'R' Class continued, especially on the Great Lakes and West Coast – thirteen having been built for Marblehead sailors. Amply large enough for cruising, none of the yachts in the three classes was ever fitted with engines.

An additional class, the 30 Square Metre, was of Swedish origin. As its same suggests, it was primarily a sail area rule, the figure being the maximum area allowed in the mainsail and jib (30 metres is equivalent to 323 square feet). The area of the foretriangle was measured rather than the jib itself, despite the fact that the overlapping genoa jib had come into use by then. Like the Sonder, it had a number of limitations under the class rule, including two that the Sonder did not have. One was a freeboard requirement which was introduced under the International Rule to prevent the problem of 'skimming dishes' that had emerged under the Seawanhaka Rule. Another was a second beam measurement taken at the forward end of the waterline. In 1929 four were built in Marblehead in order to host a series including a Swedish and three German boats. In return, three raced in Sweden and Germany the next year.

Like the Universal Rule boats before them, the LWL of the Thirty Squares increased over time. In 1929 the average LWL of the three German boats was 25.3 feet compared with 23.2 for the American boats; ten years later four local boats averaged 28.4 feet. Both the Universal Rule designers and those for the Thirties had initially underestimated the size of boat that could be built under a given sail plan without inhibiting speed performance.

Comparison of the Thirty Squares with the 'R' Class, using boats built during the late 1930's, is rather startling. The former were 10 inches more on LWL, but the

'S' Boat *Clotho* off Oyster Bay, mid-1930's
Source unknown

latter carried mainsails almost twice as large. The reason was that the 'R's displaced 12,000 pounds whereas the Thirties displaced only 5,800. The Universal Rule resulted in heavy boats which inspired Howard Chapelle's remark that it had caused a great waste of good wood and lead. Under the Universal Rule the Thirties fell neatly into the 'R' Class, but the two could race competitively at Marblehead and on Buzzards Bay only in strong winds. During one year as many as 13 Thirty Squares were competing at the former location, one of which was raced by Charles Francis Adams.

Still another class, the International Rule Eight Metre which had become popular on Western Long Island Sound, appeared at Marblehead. Four were built by local sailors and four were imported from the Sound in 1930. The Eights were the maximum at Marblehead but sufficed for good exchange racing with owners on the Long Island Sound. The Eights were a little smaller than the 'Q' Class which usually could win in races between them, perhaps because of the difference in size.

Meanwhile, the Universal Rule yachts were losing favor. One reason was that their great weight made them expensive. Another was that New York Yacht Club had primarily racing on a boat-for-boat basis in yachts built to a class rating each of which came from a single builder. A third was that, despite its name, no yachts were ever built in Europe to the Rule, except for a few 'J' boats. Finally, the British, who had led in the development of the International Rule in 1906, considered that it was time for a change. After careful examination of the Universal Rule, however, they decided that it was inferior to what they had, so they made a few minor adjustments to the International Rule and kept it.

THE 'S' BOAT[26]

Nathanael Greene Herreshoff designed the 'S' Boat to the Universal Rule in 1919. It was 27-feet 6-inches LOA, 20-feet 6-inches LWL, 7-feet 2-inches beam and 4 feet 9 inches draft. Displacement was 6,750 pounds of which more than half was in the keel. It carried a large mainsail and a small, club-footed jib. The small cabin was essentially a cuddy. All Herreshoff's designs were graceful, but the 'S' may have been the most pleasing of his entire output. Two other yachts were designed to the 'S' category of the Rule, one on the east and one on the west coast, but neither raised much interest and both petered out. Thus, Herreshoff's design prevailed simply as the 'S' or 'S' Boat.

The concept for the design originated in a discussion about a new one-design between Herreshoff and a member of the Seawanhaka Corinthian Yacht Club, but the seven of the first ten built in the spring of 1920 went to the Eastern Yacht Club at Marblehead, MA. More went to both clubs by the end of the year. By 1924 Eastern and Seawanhaka were team racing in 'S's, and the Sears Cup was held in the class at Marblehead in 1926. By 1927 there were fleets at Bar Harbor (seventeen) and Northeast Harbor, MA, Quisset Yacht Club on Cape Cod, Ida Lewis Yacht Club in Newport, RI, and Pequot Yacht Club at Southport, CT. In 1928 a fleet was ordered by the Pearl Harbor Yacht Club in Hawaii. By then 94 'S' Boats had been built at Herreshoff Mfg. in Bristol, seven more by the Lawley Yard in Boston and two by the U.S. Navy in Hawaii.

World War II, as did World War I, had marked effect on many classes, fleets and clubs. It decimated the fleets at Ida Lewis, Quisset and the two clubs in Maine. Yet, they continued to flourish after the War on Long Island Sound. The years 1945-72 were called 'The Glory Years' for the class, and even as late as 1968 – 48 years after it began racing – only the Shields Class had more season series qualifiers among clubs of the YRA of Long Island Sound. Thereafter decline set in because of competition from a proliferation of classes built of GRP. Ultimately they became collectors' items because of their beauty, and ownership carried the cachet of 'classic yacht.' Fortunately, a few yards that wanted to stay with wood became havens for their restoration. Today the class is much healthier than it was two decades ago, and more then 60 'S's are sailing. In 1994 a fleet of 30 gathered at Bristol to celebrate the class's 75th birthday with a very competitive two days of racing.

Said Susan Buck of the Museum of Yachting in Newport, RI:

> *In many ways the Herreshoff 'S' Boat anticipated modern yacht design — the high ratio of sail area to wetted surface, the short, steep, heavy keel, the rather slack bilge, the mast curvature and an advanced hull shape – particularly the cropped stern and spoon bows. These features... are much in tune with the present... In light airs they can sometimes even overtake an Etchells or a J/24.*

Added Halsey Herreshoff:

> *They've worked out to be great for the strong southwest wind we get in Narragansett Bay and for Long Island Sound's relatively light airs too.*

THE SAN FRANCISCO BAY ONE-DESIGN KEEL-BOATS[27]

In 1922 a group at the Corinthian (Belvedere) and San Francisco Yacht Clubs commissioned John Alden's shop in Boston to take a local design, which had never been built, and adapt it to the strong winds and chop in the Bay. The result was the flush-decked Bird, 30 feet LOA, 7 feet 8 inches beam, 5 feet 3 inches draft with a 3,600 pound keel. It had small club jib but a very large Marconi/Bermudian mainsail with a relatively short mast but a long, overhanging boom. The rig required running backstays. Twenty-six were built, and they worked out extraordinarily well, and it could fairly be said they marked the start of one-design competition on the Bay. Obviously they were well built, since it was 35 years before the remaining 22 of the original fleet were outmoded and replaced by more modern designs. Although it has been suggested that the Bird resembled the Victory Class sailed on Long Island Sound, the Universal Rule 'S' Class was their parameter.

In 1928, since they were being sailed out of three clubs – St. Francis Yacht Club had bought ten, the owners formed the Bird Class Association of San Francisco Bay. The Association in conjunction with the yacht's durability created a cohesiveness that accounts for its long tenure as one of the outstanding classes in the Bay. The boats virtually became heirlooms within families.

Birds, which bore such names as *Kookabura*, *Oriole*, *Linnet*, *Robin* and *Curlew*, were both fast and close-winded. What made them legendary, however, was their ability to handle the strong winds and steep chop prevailing when the westerlies whistle at 20 knots or more through Golden Gate against an ebb tide. Not only could they handle the wind, but also they could barrel through the chop without hobby-horsing.

The legend survives; there are a few Birds left. As of 1990 the *Polly*, winner of more class championships than any other, was about to undergo restoration underwritten by $30,000 of contributions. "When completed, *Polly* will serve as a floating, touring tribute to the history of Bay sailing... and wooden yacht building techniques." Another, *Curlew*, has miraculously been kept in sailing condition, and a third, *Meadow Lark*, is under restoration in Oregon. The owner of *Oriole*, who has put thousands of hours of work on her, stated:

> *I have these eighty-year old people coming into my yard, bursting into tears, saying, "I learned to sail on that boat 55 years ago", and handing me a West Marine gift certificate. How can you quit after something like that ?*

A smaller version of the Bird was the Baby Bird, later called the Golden Gate. It was 25 feet LOA with the other dimensions reduced proportionately, including a keel of 2,200 pounds. The rigging was simplified by a small boomkin on the stern to which the backstay was fastened thereby keeping it clear of the overhanging boom. Boats in the class were owned by members of the Alameda and San Francisco Yacht Clubs.

Another one-design, started in 1935 and sponsored by the Pacific Inter-Club Yachting Association (and later by the Yacht Racing Association of San Francisco Bay), was the PIC (Pacific Inter-Club) – a 26-footer. The PICYA was seeking a boat with a simple rig and reasonable speed that would be within the means of the average sailor. The first of these were built and sailed in Los Angeles, but they were also used in the Bay.

Yet another was the Bear, also started in the 1930's. It was even smaller at 23 feet LOA. Like the PIC, it reflected the depression-era which militated inexpensive boats and cost about $1,300. The class was long-lived and in the mid-1950's was the largest one-design fleet in the Bay. One of the reasons was that in 1938 the designer-builder relinquished his rights to the plans which meant that individuals could build the boat themselves or buy a hull and take it from there. The other was that it was as tough as the Bird and could handle the wind and chop like a Bird. Similar to the Bird, it had almost 50 percent (2,100 pounds) of its displacement (4,400 pounds) in its cast-iron the keel. An article in an unidentified magazine of 1976 states that, while somewhat diminished in size, the fleet was still active.

INLAND LAKE SCOWS[28]

> *Shakespeare's famous line, "A rose by any other name would smell as sweet," singularly fails when applied to scows. I suffer still to say, "I sail scows." But add the words 'Inland Lake', then I marvel at those sailboats that have been part of my life since 1930.*

The term 'scow' is not precise, but these characteristics differentiate them from other sailing craft:

- *Light construction, like canoes (when fibreglass replaced wood in the 70's, weight was maintained unchanged);*
- *No keel, skeg or center protuberance to break a flat bottom;*
- *A cross-section generally rectangular but with rounded bilges;*
- *Bilgeboards in place of a centerboard;*
- *Double rudders, generally in line with the bilgeboards (exception single rudder for the 'C' and 'MC').*

Scows, unlike dinghies, go best when heeled and thus present a long, cigar-like form in the water. In doing so, wetted surface is kept to a minimum. Today there are six more or less one-design classes, mostly built by the Johnson and Melges Boat Works, the former in Minnesota, the latter in Wisconsin. The six, in order of their appearance and approximate numbers are:

'A'	38 ft.	Sail area 500 sq. ft.	20-30 active
'C'	20 ft.	216	700-1000 (cat-rigged)
'E'	28 ft.	323	300-400
'M'16	16 ft.	147	200-300
'M'20	20 ft.	176	150+
'MC'	16 ft.	135	n/a (cat-rigged)

The 'A', 'E' and 'M'20 classes carry spinnakers. The 'B' and 'D' classes have disappeared over the years.

The origin of this uniquely North American boat lies in the Seawanhaka International Cup for Small Yachts, offered by the Seawanhaka Corinthian Yacht Club in 1895. It was to be competed for by boats between 15 and 25 feet LWL. Under the Seawanhaka Rule, which intended that there be equality between (the factors) LWL and the square root of SA, a 15-footer could carry 225 square feet of sail. The first challenge came from England in the 15-foot category [as rated under the Rule], and the match was won by Seawanhaka using a yacht designed by member William P. Stephens.

The next contest in 1896 was more interesting. The challenge came from the Royal St. Lawrence Yacht Club of Montreal. To defend, 27 different yachts were designed and built:

> *An outpouring of activity that seemed to justify Seawanhaka's purpose in promoting small-boat racing by amateur sailors. These craft were designed by the cream of American design talent, including N.G. Herreshoff, Clinton Crane, William Gardner and Starling Burgess.*

Opposing them was a Canadian civil engineer named George Herrick Duggan, whose occupation was designing bridges. Duggan designed and built six yachts that were extensively tested by club members in races between all of them. All had been designed by taking advantage of the possibilities within the Seawanhaka Rule, in other words, to produce a boat that sailed fast but measured slow. He also took advantage of the hull shape that Herreshoff's revolutionary *Gloriana* had been given five years earlier – one that increased her effective waterline when heeled to her lines while on the wind. The shape included long overhangs and convex bows and counters. The design that was chosen to challenge was *Glencairn*, a name that reflected Duggan's Scottish heritage.

Glencairn did not make it as a 15-footer since she was only 12 feet on the waterline when sitting upright. Yet, when heeled, her waterline increased to 15 feet. Nonetheless, Seawanhaka accepted her, albeit reluctantly. Equally important, to minimize wetted surface her immersed width decreased from 5 feet 4 inches upright to 3 feet 11 inches heeled. The short LWL would have enabled her to have her sail area increased from 225 to 324 square feet without exceeding the number produced by the formula of '15 plus the square root of 225, divided by two = one,' but Duggan settled for 300 square feet.

Meanwhile, Seawanhaka was testing its 27 defenders in the same way, and the racing among them turned out to be more exciting than what followed. Clinton Crane's *El Hiere* (Arabic for racing camel a-propos of the pronounced 'hump' on her foredeck), was finally selected to defend against the Canadian challenger. It was no contest; *Glencairn* won three straight with ease, and America's best yacht designers had been humbled by a bridge builder.

Moreover, Seawanhaka's leaders were thoroughly alarmed by what they foresaw as disaster down the road – yachts that were as dangerous as the 'gravel wagons' (sandbaggers) that the Cup was intended to displace. Said W.P. Stephens:

> *Imagine the absurdity of having to keep these skimming dishes on their feet by getting on the windward rail – and having to weigh crew members like jockeys before a horse race.*

In those days only sandbagger crews sat on the rail and hiked out.

Before the 1897 defense at Lake St. Louis outside of Montreal (not really a lake but a wide, shallow confluence of the St. Lawrence and Ottawa Rivers) a 20-foot LWL was agreed upon and a limitation of 500 square feet was set for sail area. This was 25 percent more than the Seawanhaka Rule intended (*Glencairn*'s excess had been 33 percent), but it was hoped that the limitation would prevent extreme excesses. This time Duggan needed to make only four designs before deciding that he had it right. He named his choice *Glencairn II*. Meanwhile, Clinton Crane was having his *Momo* built in Canada where the technique of light construction was more advanced. *Glencairn II* easily defended the Cup, winning three straight again for the Royal St. Lawrence Yacht Club .

For the 1898 challenge Duggan designed three yachts that were minor variations of *Glencairn II* before deciding on a radical bet described by Duggan as "carrying to a logical conclusion" his earlier efforts. The result was *Dominion* which was something of a catamaran; indeed, Seawanhaka claimed that it was, and formally protested. The Royal St. Lawrence gave the protest to a

Canadian jury, its privilege under the deed of gift as the defending club, which dismissed it.

The cause of the protest was the shape of her hull. Between the rounded bilges the bottom was raised 2½ inches above the waterline to reduce the wetted surface when she was upright. In the meanwhile Clinton Crane was trying to exploit features of the first *Glencairn*, but it was not enough. *Dominion* with her 'tunnel' hull and peaked deck beat the challenger easily again, three to zero. By this time Herrick Duggan had gone a long way towards earning the reputation of being one of the pioneers in the creation of the 'scow'.

In the same year the Inland Lake Yachting Association, the progenitor of scows, was formed, and it adopted two classes under the Seawanhaka Rule – the 20-foot and the 17-foot (LWL) classes.

Immediately the rivalry began toward feather-weight construction and maximizing effective sailing length. Only three years later the ILYA was forced to adopt minimum scantlings and to regard length as overall length. The two classes thus became 38 and 32 feet LOA respectively. Class 'A' was limited to 500 square feet of sail area and Class 'B' to 350. The Association also adopted a rule that hulls were to be "no lower than their center point" and that "the gunwales must meet at the stem at an angle of not more than 35 degrees from the center line" as a means of outlawing tunnel hulls.

In 1899 the White Bear (Lake) Yacht Club challenged for the Seawanhaka Cup, but Seawanhaka pressured Royal St. Lawrence to accept the latter's challenge instead. It feared that if the Cup went to the 'remote hinterland' of Minnesota, that would be the end of it. The Royal St. Lawrence Yacht Club diplomatically offered White Bear a "special contest" in which the latter's boat would race against *Dominion*. White Bear's boat was *Yankee*, runner up to *Momo* two years before and no match for *Dominion*. The match for the Cup pitted Crane's *Constance* against Duggan's *Glencairn III*. Duggan won again, but the match went the full five races and ended in a controversy over the course for the last race. *Constance* went aground on shoals near the starting line and protested that the course failed to comply with the stipulation in the deed of gift that courses be laid out in waters of suitable depth for the competing yachts. The race became a sail over since Seawanhaka's representative forbade *Constance* to start, ordering her to protest instead. The protest was disallowed. Coupled with the hard feelings over permitting *Glencairn II* to race the previous year, Seawanhaka elected to stay on the sidelines for the next 24 years.

White Bear's challenge was accepted the next year, but its boat met the same fate (and same Duggan) that Seawanhaka had suffered four times straight. The next year a British club had no better luck. In 1902 the challenge came from the Bridgeport Yacht Club (CT), although the boat used was designed and built in Oskkosh and was sailed by a Wisconsin scow crew. When boat and crew arrived on Lake St. Louis, they found that their opponent would be *Trident*, a yacht with both bilgeboards and a centerboard. She was Duggan's last design for the Challenge Cup, and bilgeboards were his last contribution to the development of the scow. He stated that the three boxes (trunks) were the reason for the yacht's name, and that he had included the standard centerboard because bilgeboards might be considered not in the spirit of the deed of gift.

The bilgeboards were slanted about nineteen degrees from vertical, so that they would be vertical when the hull assumed its optimum racing angle. She took the series three straight. In next year's challenge appeared the last innovation on scows evolving from the Seawanhaka Cup – double rudders on the winning Royal St. Lawrence Yacht Club defender. Within a year all of the scows within ILYA had bilgeboards and double rudders.

Lake sailors of the ILYA had been sailing scows for only five years, but this is what *Rudder* magazine had to say about them:

> *It has been the custom to decry western yachting and to picture freshwater men as a lot of lubbers. But though they may be guilty of breeches of etiquette, hoist two flags on one string, fire guns on Sunday and wear the names of their boats on their hats, when it comes to racing scows they know more about the game in one minute than we Eastern people do in a month. It will be a bitter dose for the Easterner to swallow to have to go to the West to learn what he fondly considers is his own game. But if the West is to be beaten at scow racing, it can be done only by studying the freshwater man's methods.*

The ILYA undertook to manage the development of scows, and it did so intelligently, "like a careful horse breeder, encouraging and enhancing the good, eliminating the bad. The freaks; usually grandfathered, were allowed to die." Any proposed change was tested for a year before being adopted. Even bilgeboards were first given a year's testing.

In 1911 the 'C' scow came along, a smaller 20-footer that was cat-rigged. Then an even smaller 18-foot 'D' scow, also cat rigged, but it did not find favor and disappeared. In 1923 the ILYA created the 'E' scow, the first time that it had not just adopted an existing design. It was 28 feet LOA and was intended to be a family boat. It could be a family boat if the family contains good sailors, but it attracted too many top-flight sailors to remain so. The 'E' was slow to receive popular acceptance, since it substituted, for reasons of cost, a centerboard thus departing from what had become the traditional bilgeboards. In the 1930's the St. Regis Yacht Club in the Adirondacks, NY tried the same thing in order to simplify the job of the crew. The result in both cases was the same: as the boat heeled, too little of the centerboard was left immersed to provide lateral resistance and enough of a 'grip' in the water to prevent sudden capsizing. Consequently, in 1925 the ILYA switched back to bilgeboards, and the class took off. It was the same year in which nine 'E's were delivered to Barnegat Bay, NJ. All were built in scow country, and eight had square bows, since there had not yet been agreement on its configuration. As fleets of scows spread to places such as South Carolina, Lake Minnetonka, Barnegat Bay and elsewhere so did the jurisdiction of ILYA. Unlike the other District or Yacht Racing Associations of NAYRU, each of which represented yacht clubs and classes in a contiguous area, ILYA accepted membership from any club with a registered fleet of scows regardless of location. ILYA differed from the conventional procedures of NAYRU in another respect: for many years the racing rules were modified to provide a boat with spinnaker set right of way over others, including a boat on the wind, regardless of which tack she was on. The rationale was the difficulty of maneuvering and keeping a lookout by reason of the huge spinnakers carried by some of the scow classes.

Like catamarans, scows are more akin to racing machines than day sailers. Both 'A' and 'E' scows can exceed 20 knots in ideal conditions. They attain their best speeds when sailing under spinnakers at 45-50 degrees from dead downwind. Like catamarans, when on the wind their speed quickly draws the apparent wind forward requiring bearing off to keep the sails full. In addition the crew must be agile to keep the angle of heel as constant as possible on the fine line between minimizing wetted surface and obviating capsizing.

During the early years changes in hull design produced greater speed, and from the 1920's on, the bulk of the beam moved aft, headstays were no longer fixed on a bow plate and masts were moved farther aft. When the scows changed to GRP, incremental changes to the hull had to stop since it was much too expensive to alter molds to accommodate such experimentation. Once ILYA decided to require that GRP hulls meet the minimum weight of wooden hulls, they lost the advantage which catamarans have of using advanced technology to make lighter hulls.

Two persons in successive generations led the development of the scow: John O. Johnson, White Bear Lake boat builder, who patterned a single-hull version of the Dominion with twin bilgeboards in lieu of a centerboard and became the prime builder for the scow classes; and two generations of the Melges family of Zenda, WI who were both builders and sailmakers. It was Harry C. 'Buddy' Melges, Jr. – three-time winner of the Mallory Cup for the U.S. Men's Sailing Championship – who took the scow into the GRP era and also created such new classes as the 'M'20. Spectrum Nautical, Inc. provides the following profile:

> *... Buddy has won over sixty major national and international sailing and iceboating titles including the 1964 Olympic Bronze Medal in the Flying Dutchman Class and the Olympic Gold Medal in the Solings. He was also skipper of record for the 1987 Heart of America Cup Challenge in Fremantle, Australia. If sailing has a Babe Ruth, his first name is Buddy...*

INTERNATIONAL STAR CLASS[29]

One has only to skim through old Star Class *Logs* (yearbooks) to understand why this extraordinary class has had such staying power, enthusiasm, rigid enforcement of specifications and strength of organization. By 1933, for instance, the Association had standing committees: International Executive, Rules, Measurement, Development, Technical, Advisory and Isolated and Lost Stars. There also was a special one to "Suggest Revised Method of Sailing International Championships". In addition, there was an insurance officer, an advertising manager, a custodian of movie films and two editors – one for the *Log* and one for the *Starlights* (class publication).

The 1933 *Log* (the first edition was in 1922) states proudly, "The Largest Class of One-Design Yachts in the World". The title page lists in the border where fleets exist: U.S., England, Hawaii, Spain, Philippines, Denmark, Algeria, Switzerland, Sweden, Germany, Portugal, Bahamas, Italy, Venezuela, British West Indies, Cuba, Canada and France. On another page are listed 13 districts – six in the U.S. and one each in Vancouver, Honolulu, Havana, Paris, Cannes, Manila and Stockholm. Also listed are 31 certified class measurers including one in Barbados. Following that there is a list of 68 fleets worldwide.

Two pages are devoted to the insignia members are entitled to wear on the sleeves of their yachting coats and mess jackets consisting of various combinations of stars, bars (for skippers) and chevrons (for crew) indicating their highest attainment in district, national or international championships. The winner of the International (now World) Championship is entitled to carry a gold star on the mainsail in lieu of the class emblem. Members who have earned such awards are urged to wear them whenever in a nautical setting.

The Star Class dates back to 1911 when 27 had been built, or were a-building, most of them by Isaac E. Smith in Port Washington, NY. In 1933 *The New Yorker* magazine had this to say in its "Talk of the Town" section under the title of "First Cockroach":

> *The commodore of the largest one-design class organization in the world is George Arthur Corry. He is international head of the Star fleet. Though he is 71 now, he is no club-window commodore; he's out in all sorts of weather, as he has been for 50 years. He has five hundred trophies, most of which he won between 1900 and 1916 on Western Long Island Sound. He used to race 17-foot Bugs, the smallest keel boats of their day. They were thought too small to be called a yacht until one day in 1909 when a nor'easter came up. When Larchmont called off a regatta for large boats, Corry took out his Bug and, followed by three others, sailed over the course.*

It was in 1907 that noted yacht designer William Gardner had designed a small keelboat about 17-feet LOA that he called the Bug. Several were built, but they were too small for grown men. At the suggestion of Corry, who was to become the 'father of the Stars', Gardner enlarged the design by adding five feet to its length, making it 22 feet 7½ inches. That was the Star, just what Corry had in mind: a competitive yacht that could test the skills and endurance of capable adult sailors and one inexpensive enough for a person of modest means to afford (the first ones cost $250 at a time when a mug of beer was five cents and a hearty sandwich came with it).

The yacht had remarkably clean lines for its time; it had hard chines and a fin-and-bulb keel – an innovation by N.G. Herreshoff some 25 years earlier. It also had the traditional gaff rig with a boom that extended two feet or so beyond the transom. In 1911 33 Stars were launched and raced – 22 in Long Island Sound and 11 in Massachusetts Bay. By 1916 the class had a most ambitious plan which was to charter fleets all over North America and to hold fleet eliminations the winners of which would go to regional championships from which qualifiers would go on to the national championship. At a time when the farthest-flung fleet was four Stars on Lake Erie, this seemed not only ambitious but in the realm of a pipe dream.

The New Yorker continued:

> *In 1911 (when) the Star succeeded the Bug, Corry wanted to call them 'bugs' also, but Stuyvesant Wainwright asked him if, as Commodore, he wanted to wear a gold cockroach on his sleeve. He decided a star would look better. There are almost 1,000 Stars now, comprising 68 fleets in 18 nations. A tremendous European approval of this class has seen a great increase of Stars in the foreign yachting world.*

The plan to charter fleets all over the country could not be officially adopted until after World War I. By the end of 1921 the good skippers had switched to the Marconi rig, timely for the first National Championship which was held the next year on Long Island Sound with competitors from the Atlantic, Pacific and the Great Lakes regions. This and the next three were won by members of the Long Island Sound Fleet, but the trophy went, the fifth year, to Narragansett Bay and in 1927 to Newport Beach, CA. In six years the Star had become a national class, spanning the continent. Indeed, it had become an international class with 25 fleets in the U.S., two in British Columbia and one each in the Isle of Wight, Cuba, Barbados, Brazil, New Zealand and the U.S. possessions of the Philippines and Hawaii.

This was not only an amazing accomplishment but one that was emulated, but not quite matched, at the time only by the International Fourteen.

Concerning the switch to the Marconi/Bermudian rig, the Star, apparently, was one of the few classes that did not jump on the bandwagon promptly, and in fact the change was made spontaneously without any authority from the class inasmuch as the Star Class Yacht Racing Association was not formed until 1922. Tests made with the rig, however, had proved so conclusively that it was superior in speed and closer winded that a mandate was not necessary; owners just did it. The change cured the tendency of the Star to bury her bow in a seaway and made the boat, which originally was designed for use in the light airs on Long Island Sound, a better performer in heavy air and seas.

The next rig innovation was to modernize it by shortening the boom three feet and increasing the height of the mast five feet to provide a higher aspect ratio. In the

Official Specifications, Article I refers to the "new rig" that had been adopted in March 1930, effective as of January 1, 1931 for all championship racing. Individual fleets could decide for themselves whether or not to permit their yachts to use the old rig for fleet racing. *Article XIV, Spars*, specified the mast height from the gooseneck to the top of the sheave as 31 feet 9 inches and the boom length 14 feet 7 inches.

If George Corry was the 'father' of the Star, the noted New York designer, William Gardner was its 'genesis.' It was probably the smallest yacht that he ever designed, and it was a winner. When it proved so, the class bought the rights to the design which meant that builders' and sailmakers' royalties were thenceforth paid to the class. This, in turn, meant that if a builder or sailmaker did not adhere to the class specifications, any hull or sail out of tolerance could be denied approval by the class.

The class not only had a fine boat; it had George Elder, editor of its history. It was his salesmanship and enthusiasm that built the numbers so that within two decades there were Stars all over the world. The hull of the Star had been deliberately designed with hard chines so that it could be home-built more easily. Of the first 125, however, only four were. Nonetheless, it was the least expensive yacht above the size of a dinghy that was available, and Elder was promoting it hard. If yachting was looked upon as a sport for the wealthy, the Star was not in this category. While the class contained members of substantial means, the winner of the 1932 International was a bricklayer from Long Beach, Calif. When he entered his first championship in 1928 he had to work his way to New Orleans and back as a deck hand on a freighter.

The 1932 International was held at the Pequot Yacht Club in Southport, CT. At the time the world was in the depths of the Great Depression. Notwithstanding, there were 28 entries from all over the U.S. and from England, France, Germany, Sweden, Venezuela, Hawaii and the Philippines. It is noteworthy that the US Coast Guard provided seven vessels – a picket boat to serve as the committee vessel and six more to patrol the course. The courses were either windward-leeward or a triangle, both twice around, for a total distance of ten miles.

Each of the five races had a different winner, and the first 12 positions overall were held by American boats – the first three having been third, fourth and fifth in the same order the prior year. The thirteenth was a French boat which earned the 'Invader's Trophy' for the first foreign boat. In eighteenth place (with an eleven-year old girl from Chesapeake Bay at the helm) was the highest placing yacht entering for the first time, and she received the 'First Challenge Trophy.' All received medallions for competing – a good promotional practice for everyone to be recognized with something to take home.

In this regatta high-point scoring was used as was customary in all major regattas in that era. In club racing, however, in which a local fleet moved around from club to club with the result that the number of entries varied from race to race, percentage scoring was used, i.e. the percentage of yachts beaten out of the total number in each race. A yacht that sailed in three races with 17, 12 and 16 participants respectively and came in second in each had beaten 39 out of 42 other yachts – a winning percentage of 92.9 percent. The Yacht Racing Association of Long Island Sound later adopted a similar system for a season series co-created by one of its top sailors, William S. Cox, known as the Cox-Sprague Scoring System.

The editor noted the measurements of the top three boats which reveals how close they were to being identical – remarkable considering that Stars were then built by hand out of wood by at least 40 different builders: (maximum difference among the three expressed in inches)

4/16	LOA
1	Stem to L of mast
2 2/16	Stern to rudder post on deck
1	Stern to rudder post on bottom
1 11/16	Stern to keel
0	Height of Keel
0	Thickness of keel plate
0	Thickness of keel bulb
1	Rudder width
1 2/16	Rudder length
4/16	Beam on Deck sta. 3
14/16	Beam on Deck sta. 6
3/16	Beam on Deck sta. 8
7/16	Stern

The boats were built by different builders. Since all three owners belonged to fleets on Long Island Sound, however, the identical dimensions of the keels suggest that they were cast at the same foundry in the same mold.

In contrast to the 28 entries at the 1932 Star International, the Olympic Yachting Games at Los Angeles had only two Eight-Metres (Canada and the U.S.), three Six-Metres (Canada, U.S. and Sweden) and seven Stars – a total of 12 entries. The final point standing for the Stars after seven races was: U.S. 46, England 35, Sweden 27, Canada 27, France 26, Holland 16 and South Africa 7.

Aside from the International and the Olympics, the major events for the class were: the Mid-Winters and the Bacardi Cup, both held in Cuba at the spectacular Habana Yacht Club , after which there was team racing between the U.S. and Cuba; the Atlantic Coast championships; the Long Island Sound Championships which had been won by George Corry the first five years. Scattered around the country were 15 or so other championships, four of which raced for one of the plethora of Lipton Trophies. In addition, there was the Commodore Corry Cup. The Star was the first North American class to achieve 'International Status' under the International Yacht Racing Union, and a clue to its longevity, both as an International and an Olympic class, is to be found in Article XIV of the by-laws, titled "Outlawed Races":

> *The enforcement of class rules is essential for the protection of owners in a one-design class and is universally recognized. Members are required to report to the Association any race held for the Star class as such, wherein Class Rules are not respected and enforced by the organization conducting it or where entries of ineligible yachts are knowingly accepted. A member who makes himself a party to such practice by knowingly, and after due warning, entering into such outlawed events shall be subject to suspension.*

Displaced from the Olympics by the Tempest in 1972, the Class regained its Olympic status in 1980 until again displaced for the 2000 Games giving it the longest tenure of any Olympic class. In the 1934 *Log* is an editorial lamenting the tendency of newspapers and yachting magazines to lay more emphasis than necessary on fouls and disqualifications, "which hungry newshawks pounced on eagerly." Publicity has been very good for the sport, but negative publicity, "undermines the structure so diligently and painstakingly built." The cure for that, the anonymous writer went on to say, was for members of the Star Class to learn more fully and adhere more strictly to the rules. Then the, "inharmonious press cackling will die for the lack of nourishment." Not considered by the writer, and almost everyone else at the time, was that the problem had much less to do with sailors than with the rules themselves. They were not very good. This fact had not become critical heretofore by reason of the small numbers of competitors in any class. The more yachts that emerged on the starting line, the more the defects in the rules caused unavoidable fouls. The Stars were the first class to experience this. Revision of the rules, however, was still 14 years in the future.

In later years the Star class continued to obviate obsolescence by making such moves as adopting modern materials for the spars, but it remained unique, along with the Snipe, as a two-man class without a spinnaker.

Commodore Ralph M. Munroe and Captain Nathanael G. Herreshoff at Coconut Grove, FL, about 1925
Photo Herreshoff Marine Museum, Bristol RI

SUICIDE CLASS

The basic limitations of the Suicide Class are: 125 square feet of sail (a common denominator for all boats), 3½ - 5½ foot beam and minimum of 6 inches of freeboard. There was no limit on LOA (length seemed to settle on what performed best in particular waters); crew was fixed at two; and other regulations are minimal.

> *The Suicide Class was conceived around 1928 by several sailors from the Huntington Yacht Club at Huntington on the north shore of Long Island, NY who were challenged by the desire to build a 'different' kind of sailboat – a developmental (as N.G. Herreshoff termed it)[30] class that would be the fastest monohull afloat. Naval Architect William Atkin is thought by some to have been the 'father of the class,' though this is disputed by many who feel there is no 'father' and that Suicides are the composite contributions of all Suiciders.[31]*

166

Developmental Suicide designed by N.G. Herreshoff with single, double or triple-masted rig and sailed by George Nichols, Jr.
Photo: Ransom Everglades School

Naval architects attracted to the Class in addition to Atkins were N.G. Herreshoff, L. Francis Herreshoff, Olin J. Stephens, II, Seth Persson (responsible for a fleet at Old Lyme, CT) and Commodore Ralph Middleton Munroe of Coconut Grove on Biscayne Bay, FL. There was no primary builder. The Long Island fleet (14 - 21 feet LOA) numbered about 24 and was lost in the hurricane of 1938. The Florida Fleet was established at the Biscayne Bay Yacht Club in 1930 and ranged from 18 - 23 feet LOA. Later it migrated to the Miami Yacht Club on MacArthur Causeway. At its peak it numbered about 50 boats, became dormant in 1962 and began to revive in 1985.

The boats were unusual respecting their raked masts, wishbone booms and in many cases daggerboards instead of centerboards. Being planing hulls, they clocked between 22 and 30 mph; one reputedly planed under bare poles in a 55 mph blow. Creators of the Florida Fleet were, in addition to the Munroes, Pat Patterson, John Reid, Al Evans and C. Townsend Ludington. Harry Cates, a pioneer in the Moth Class was a noted builder of Suicides. Suicides were consistent winners in the Miami to Key Largo and Palatka to Jacksonville Mug Races.

Typical Suicide
designed by Wirth Munroe
Photo: Ransom Everglades School

Reasons for the attraction of the class varied with the individual. N.G. Herreshoff, for example, in his latter years wintered in Coconut Grove staying at the home of Commodore Monroe where the two designed and built boats and models. A dedicated believer in open – 'developmental' as he termed it – classes,[32] his exposure to the Suicide led to designing and building at the Herreshoff Mfg. Co. unique versions of Suicides with multiple rigs – sloop, two-masted and three-masted[33] – for two Long Island yachtsmen (future New York Yacht Club Commodores George Nichols and Junius S. Morgan). They currently are respectively at the Herreshoff Marine Museum and Mystic Seaport Museum. Unlike most of the class which had wishbone booms the front end of which protruded forward of the mast enabling it to be tensioned to change the draft of the mainsail, the booms for the mainsail and jib on the Herreshoff boats were half a wishbone in order to reduce weight and windage. The hulls resembled a lightly constructed whale boat with a square stern. C. Townsend Ludington, who was a co-founder of the first scheduled airline in the U.S. and also wintered in Coconut Grove, had Wirth Monroe, son of the Commodore, design and build him a Suicide in which he tested his theories of aerodynamics. In his words:

> *If one thinks of sailing as akin to soaring and of going fast in a planing boat as 'legalized low flying,' the relationship (between aviation and sailing) becomes clear.*

Notable Quotes of the Suicide Class cite L. Francis Herreshoff as saying:

> *These little boats are the most fun to sail of any that I have ever tried, not barring sailing canoes.*

VICTORY CLASS

The Victory, named in honor of the Allied Forces in World War I, was designed by William Gardner in 1919 whose chief draftsman was Francis Weisguth. Twenty were built at Henry B. Nevins Shipyard on City Island, Long Island Sound of which 15 out of 16 were still racing in 1942. Some of the boats had been brought back from places as far away as Maine, the Great Lakes and Houston, TX, where purportedly the Houston Yacht Club had as many as four at one time. A Manhasset Bay Yacht Club member writing to Will Hamilton, Commodore of the Houston Yacht Club, and owner of Victory No. 2, *Alerte*, was hortatory in his praise of the Victory:

> *Shall we say it is a dying class and not bother about adopting a modification of sail plan that might make the Victories, in the summer of 1943, the ablest one-design boats on the Sound?*[34]

Modification of the class rules "to make the boats faster with a modern rig and a larger loose-footed jib" was the topic of the annual dinner of the class feting builder Henry Nevins and Francis Weisguth and at which Cornelius Shields, who formerly owned a Victory, spoke.

In 1925 a team race was held between the Victories and the 'S' class which the latter won handily. Both classes were successful examples of one-designs that served the dual role of intra and inter club racing. Before the advent of such classes only a regatta format such as Larchmont Race Week provided a means of members of clubs to race outside of their home waters, and even so, it did not offer racing against members of other clubs in matched boats. For example, at Larchmont Race Week in 1901 there were Larchmont 15-footers, Seawanhaka Knockabouts, Seawanhaka Raceabouts, American Yacht Club one-designs and Manhasset Bay one-designs.

The first design on the Sound that provided inter-club racing was the Manhasset Bay Bug in 1906 which evolved into the Star class. The evolution was slow, however: at the 1925 Race Week there were only four such classes – Stars, Victories, 'R's and Six-Metres, and the latter two were restricted designs racing without handicaps rather than pure one-design. In the same year there was evidence that the intra-club concept was still popular inasmuch as Cox & Stevens was designing a 23-foot LOA fleet of one-designs for the Islip Yacht Club on Long Island's Great South Bay, which were very similar to the Indian class that the firm had created in 1920 for the West Hampton Yacht Squadron on Moriches Bay on the South shore. To cope with the body's shallow water it drew only 2 feet 3 inches with board up.

In the next decade two new classes provided additional opportunities for inter-club racing when almost simultaneously Charles D. Mower designed the Sound Interclub and Starling Burgess the Bermuda One-Design. So nearly identical were they that Larchmont and the Royal Bermuda Yacht Clubs initiated a home and home series in which each club transported its boats to the other's venue in alternate years. The series was perpetuated in later decades with the importation fleets of International One-Designs (IOD's) to both clubs thereby obviating transportation of boats.

ON CLASSES, RIGS AND DESIGNERS

CHARLES D. MOWER AND THE SOUND INTERCLUBS[55]

Histories about the sport of yachting have brought to the fore the names of designers in North America such as the Herreshoff's, Burgess's, Duggan, Kirby, Alden, Stephens, Douglass, Crane, Crowninshield and others but not so much so the name of Charles D. Mower. Yet Mower was a prolific designer whose yachts and classes turned up all across the continent. A friend once said:

His was always the artist's approach to his profession.

To quote William P. Stephens:

Mower always designed to the spirit, as well as to the letter, of the rules when turning out a yacht to a rating rule.

Charles Mower was born in Lynn, MA in 1876 and died there in 1942. While still in high school, he designed a 21-foot sloop that was astonishingly successful racing at Marblehead and other places in Massachusetts Bay. In the early 1900's he designed a Sonder Class boat that was the star of the US team that won the Kaiser's Cup at Marblehead in 1909. A 25-foot boat of his sailed across the Atlantic in 1911.

In that year he joined a naval architectural firm in Philadelphia and after WW I moved to New York. While there, he designed several fast 'R' boats, several of the earliest American Six-Metres, an Eight-Metre and in 1929 a large yacht for Junius Morgan, later Commodore of the New York Yacht Club. Perhaps his most outstanding one-design class was the Sound Interclub (28 feet 9 inches LOA) in 1926. Said William H. Taylor:

It was one of the most successful one-design classes that ever raced on Long Island Sound. It was the inspiration for two other of his one-design classes – the Vineyard Interclubs and the Great South Bay Interclubs.

The Sound Interclub happened to be evenly matched with the Bermuda One-Designs, turned out by Starling Burgess at the same time, so the Royal Bermuda and Larchmont Yacht Clubs until WW II engaged in home-and-home team races with them, each team bringing its own boats. Taylor observed that the above were only a few of Charles Mower's accomplishments.

THE INTERNATIONAL ONE-DESIGN (IOD)

The Six-Metre had become the glamour yacht of the 1930's because of team racing among the Bermudians, British and North Americans and because of fleet racing in European and Scandinavian waters for trophies such as the Seawanhaka Cup, Scandinavian Gold Cup and the One Ton Cup put up by the French.[56] It was the desire of Cornelius (Corny) Shields of the Larchmont Yacht Club to have a one-design that incorporated the best features of the Six-Metre in a somewhat smaller and more easily handled boat. The result was the IOD at 34 feet 5 inches LOA designed and built by Bjarne Aas of Norway. The first group were delivered to Larchmont in 1937; later they spread to Norway, to Marblehead, Northeast Harbor (ME), Chicago, San Francisco, Bermuda and Scotland. Although their numbers are reduced, the IOD continues to hold its world championship.

After WW II Shields, again in search of a smaller and more easily handled around-the-buoys racing sloop, turned to Olin Stephens to design the Shields Class. Their distribution was concentrated on Long Island Sound, San Francisco Bay, Narragansett Bay, Buzzards Bay with the additional fillip of fleets donated via a family foundation to the U.S. Naval Academy, SUNY at Fort Schuyler (NY), U.S. Coast Guard Academy and University of Southern California at Irvine.

RIGS: MASTS AND SAILS

The centennial history of the Royal Hamilton Amateur Dinghy Club[37] explains the likely origin of the masthead, or Bermudian rig. In the sixteenth century Holland fell under the rule of Spain resulting in the introduction of the Mediterranean lateen rig in Holland – 'lateen' being a corruption of the word 'Latin'. The rig consisted of two spars, a short mast and a long yard lashed to the mast near its top to support a triangular sail. The mast was unstayed, and the yard had controlling lines at either end. The Dutch simplified the rig by disposing of the mast itself and stepping the yard in a thwart and raking it aft thereby utilizing it as a mast.

A Governor of Bermuda, citing an early work – Capt. John Smith's *Virginia*, tells of a Dutch carpenter who was marooned in Bermuda and began building boats with a similar rig for the locals. The next step was to make the mast more erect and install a boom for the loose-footed sail. The boom extended forward of the mast so that it could be drawn aft to flatten the sail, as is done today with a wishbone boom; hence the term 'Bermuda' or 'Mudian' rig predating the term 'Marconi'. Dixon Kemp in 1866[38] shows a racing sail plan with a Marconi main laced along the mast to the top and a boom running through an eye in the mast with the forward end boused taut aft with a small tackle taken from the eye-bolt to a strop around the mast to flatten the sail.

Until some form of slides and track was devised to overcome the problem of the hoops, securing sails to the mast and not being able to be hoist the mainsail above the hounds, or the point of attachment of headstay and shrouds, a true masthead rig could be used only on smaller yachts. Early forms of tracks and sail slides were tried but poorly designed and often failed. According to N.G. Herreshoff, Babbitt of Taunton, RI in early 1860's originated mast tracks that carried slides for gaff and boom hangings as well as the luff of sails. After WW I the mainmast and topmast became continuous, but for yachts with well over 100 feet total height:

> *Spreaders were fitted between the hounds and the deck [former junction of topmast and mainmast], which to allow free passage of the mast hoops up the lower mast, had to be slotted into the mast and set up on deck after the main was hoisted [not a routine to be carried out in a pitching sea]. The [top of the mast] too, which formerly had been a separate topmast, needed additional staying, effected by the use of jumper spreaders at about a third of the way from the top.*[39]

The ultimate evolution of the rig was the Genoa jib. Around 1920 Sweden introduced the concept of the Square Metre under which the sail area of main and jib was limited to 20, 30 or 40 square meters without any other limits. The mainsail was measured according to the area of the sail, but the jib was measured according to the foretriangle bounded by mast, forestay and distance at the foot between the two. One of the great Swedish Six-Metre sailors, Sven Salen, while sailing in Genoa, Italy noticed a number of vessels, both commercial and pleasure, with jibs that overlapped the mast. Under the square metre rule the portion of the sail aft of the mast was unmeasured (untaxed). On returning home, he had one made and called it a Genoa jib. When he came to America in 1927, his genoa was the talk of the yachting press, and when he won every race, a trend was born.

Designer B. B. Crowninshield of Marblehead, however, was highly critical of overlapping jibs and of unmeasured sail area, i.e. yachts limited to 275 square feet of sail actually carrying 350 with the jib twice the size of the main. He commented:

> *The hulls of these boats are beautiful, and they sail fast; what a pity they cannot have a decent rig.*

Crowninshield mentioned the origin of the schooner. The rig was used extensively all along the coasts during the eighteenth century for fishing, shipping and carrying passengers – a time when towns and cities were connected by few, if any roads. A sloop upwards of 50 feet LOA took more men to hoist the mainsail than were required to sail her. By dividing the sail area fewer crew were needed, and in addition it provided a more versatile combination of sail plans.

The apocryphal story of the origin of the term 'schooner' concerns Andrew Robinson's boatyard at Gloucester in 1713. A man watching a vessel being launched cried out, as he observed it bouncing down the ways into the water, "Oh, see how she scoons!" Robinson is said to have replied, "Aye, let her a scooner be." Alexander Laing in American Heritage History of Seafaring America calls it, "A foolish but durable legend." Old records and pictures, however, show that the rig was in general use many decades before the launching. As mentioned earlier, La Salle and Father Hennepin built a ten-ton schooner near Kingston, Ontario in 1678. As to the word itself, etymologists differ; one attributes it to a Scottish verb used to describe what boys do with flat beach stones, whereas another believes it to be an early English and New England word for 'scud'.[10]

CAPT. NAT HERRESHOFF AND DR. STUART WALKER CONCUR

If there has been a discernible trend among racing sailors respecting open and restricted, vis-à-vis one-design classes, to prefer one over the other, it has been to gravitate towards one-design. This is evident in the spread of the Olympic and centerboard International Classes, in production classes and in match racing events such as the Congressional Cup which was launched in one-designs in 1965 and is currently copied worldwide. Yet it is the events held in open, or restricted classes, such as the America's Cup and international team racing held under a rating rule such as the Admiral's Cup, Onion Patch Trophy, and Southern Cross Cup that have provided the testing ground for innovations and developments in the sport. From a philosophical point of view the comments by one of North America's leading International Fourteen and Soling sailors, Dr. Stuart Walker most succinctly sums up the rationale for what Capt. Nat Herreshoff terms 'developmental' class:

> *I think the Fourteen demonstrated a principle that applies generally – that if you put top sailors into two classes, one open or restricted, the other one-design – the performance of the boats will be closer in the former than in the latter. Good sailors will more easily overcome the inherent differences in the construction when given wide latitude than when excessively limited by one-design rules and as a result boats in an open or restricted class, despite widely disparate hull forms, etc. will perform similarly. The top Fourteen's were always far closer together than are the top Solings, for instance.*

UNIVERSAL RULE
(typical boats)

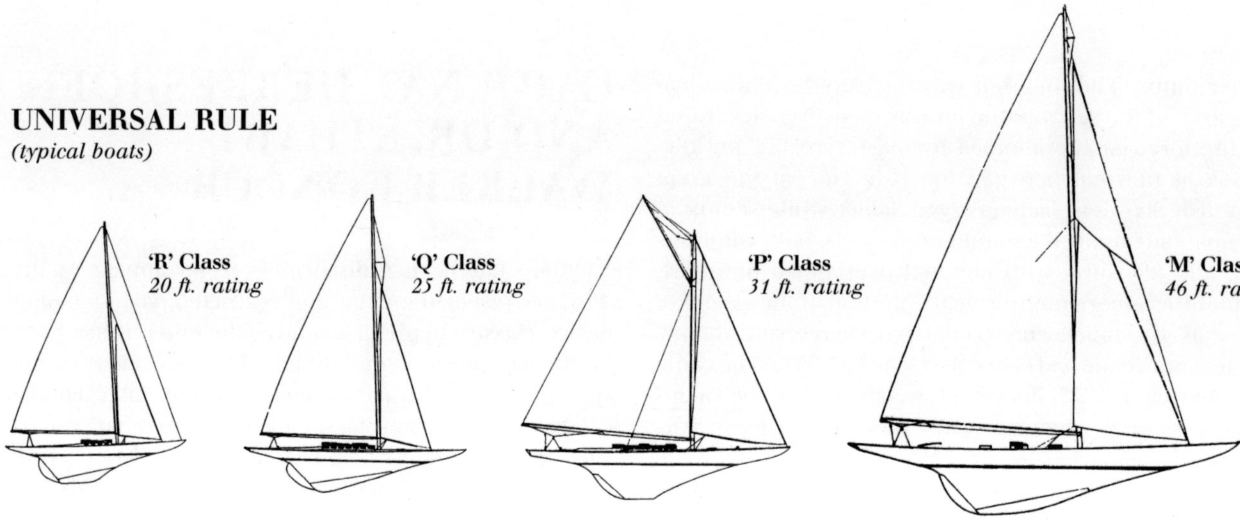

INTERNATIONAL RULE
(typical boats)

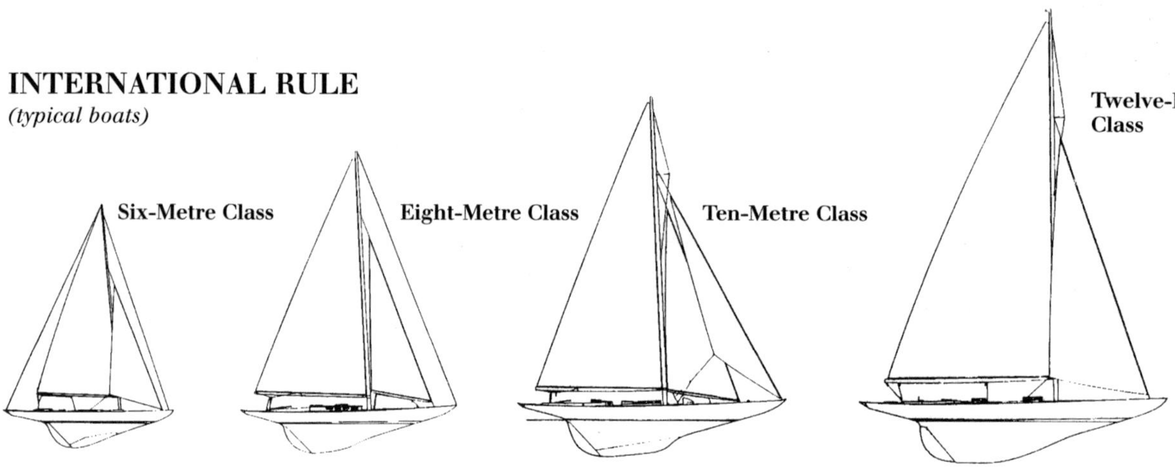

UNIVERSAL AND INTERNATIONAL RULE CLASSES EQUATED FOR PERFORMANCE[1]

Dimensions varied depending on designer and period. 'S's and 'T's raced as one-designs.

UNIVERSAL CLASS – RATING				RATING – INTERNATIONAL CLASS		
		LOA±	LWL±	LOA±	LWL±	
'J'	76 ft.	135 ft.	85 ft.	–	–	–
'K'	65 ft.	85 ft.	62 ft.	–	–	–
'L'	55 ft	74 ft.	53 ft.	72 ft.	50 ft.	New York Fifty
'M'	46 ft.	73 ft.	48 ft.	65 ft.	47 ft.	Twelve-Metre
'N'	38 ft.	66 ft.	44 ft.	–	–	–
'O'	35 ft.	52 ft.	38 ft.	–	–	–
'P'	31 ft.	53 ft.	35 ft.	59 ft.	36 ft.	Ten-Metre
'Q'	25 ft.	51 ft.	30 ft.	49 ft.	30 ft.	Eight-Metre
'R'	20 ft.	38 ft.	25 ft.	37.6 ft.	23 ft.	Six-Metre
'S'	17 ft.	27.5 ft.	20.6 ft.	31.9 ft.	21 ft.	San Diego PC
'T'	15 ft.	–	–	–	–	–

[1] Input from former 'P' owner and PHRF committeeman Royce Foley, Great Lakes.

CHAPTER IX

RATINGS, TIME ALLOWANCES AND YACHT CLASSIFICATION[1]

The motivating force behind the formation of regional yacht racing associations and a national governing body for yacht racing was the need for a uniform classification (classes) of yachts so that between clubs and between regions yacht owners could race similar types of boats in terms of size, rig and potential speed wherever they might be competing and under similar right of way rules. In the early days of yacht racing in North America, i.e. prior to the formation of NAYRU in 1897, by which time 13 such associations of yacht clubs were in existence, the consideration of uniform parameters for classification loomed more prominently than did the need for uniform racing rules. Since sailors experienced in commercial shipping and fishing were, by and large, familiar with the "Rules of the Road," with a few modifications a common code already existed adequate for conducting informal racing. Types of yachts, on the other hand, evolved locally primarily based on cargo and fishing craft peculiar to their home waters and consequently performed disparately. For example, the early catboats in Narragansett Bay, Cape Cod and New York differed markedly. Hence, the disparities militated a system of handicapping and/or classification to insure some sort of an equitable match among competitors. Both were essential for a yacht traveling to another region in order to avoid re-measurement and reasonably to expect to race in a 'class' with her peers. Further, both depended on a system of measuring and rating yachts – a subject that as late as 1897 proved too controversial to arrive at a consensus at the founding meeting of the North American Yacht Racing Union.

The usual parameter for classification was waterline length and rig, i.e. single or twin masts. An example was the earliest regatta held in North America for which a copy of the sailing instructions exists – the REGATTA held at Halifax, Nova Scotia on August 17, 1836, a year before the formation of the Halifax Yacht Club – which separated the "sailing boats" into classes approximately according to length.[2]

By way of comparison, three years earlier in England the Royal Yacht Club[3] in a regatta off Cherbourg, France used tonnage to determine classification which was a measure established by Customs to calculate the cargo capacity of commercial vessels (vis-à-vis tonnage representing the actual weight or displacement of a vessel), and a time allowance of 1¼ minutes per ton. Since the time allowance was applied at the start and extended nearly two hours, it led the French to ask when the race was to begin. By 1841 the allowance had been pro-rated to one second per ton per mile, and in 1843 George Holland Ackers (whose schooner was the largest yacht in the 1851 race for the RYS Hundred Pound Cup won by the yacht *America*[4]) produced a set of tables – *Graduated Time Tables* by G.H. Ackers, Esq. It contained scales applicable to Cutter Yachts, Fore-and-Aft Schooners and for all other Square-Rigged Yachts so that classes were determined by both rig and tonnage, e.g. cutters divided into classes of 30-to-50 tons, 50-to-75, 75-to-105 and over 105.

Universal and International Rule Classes Equated for Performance
Drawings by Maynard Bray for
The Evolution of the Rating Rules
by Michael Adams in issue no. 68 of
WoodenBoat, *January/February 1986*

Meanwhile, in the U.S. Congress had passed a Custom House Tonnage Act in 1792 for the same fee-collecting purpose as the British Act. It was very similar but produced a different figure for tonnage. For example, the yacht *America* rated at 170 tons when measured in America but 208 tons when later measured in England. Custom House tonnage was the measurement adopted by the New York Yacht Club in 1845; after a few years, however, it a adopted a rule of its own. There is no record of what that was, but it evidently did not lend itself to accuracy since most of the protests in those years were about measurement, and yacht's ratings changed markedly from year to year.

Evidence of the early use in North America of the English time allowance and tonnage system, albeit with modifications, appears in the report of a correspondent of the Boston *Daily Atlas* with a dateline from Newport, RI of August 12, 1844 relating to the first regatta ever held by the New York Yacht Club. Four yachts of the NYYC and one from Boston raced around Conanicut Island using the Royal Thames Yacht Club system of one minute a ton (presumably per mile). On another occasion yachts from Boston had brushes with the yachts from New York – notably Boston's renown *Northern Light* versus New York's *Cygnet*- that led to an argument conducted through the press over the proper application of the allowance system. A Boston yachtsman produced a copy of Acker's *Graduated Scale of Time According to Tonnage* claiming that the allowance is seldom more than half a minute a ton. When one recalls the complaints today by owners of similar boats which are rated differently in different parts of the continent, as sometimes occurs for example under PHRF, the Boston vs. New York argument sounds familiar. A further observation by the Boston yachtsman to the effect that the Royal Thames was dividing the fleet by tonnage and racing without time allowance was a harbinger of the system that the New York Yacht Club eventually adopted for a spell.

In 1853 the New York Yacht Club abandoned it and substituted a pure sail-area rule. It made much more sense except that owners were required to report which sails were being used at all times during the race. That was not only difficult to keep tract of and record, but it was a nightmare for the scorer. It lasted three years. The next attempt was its 'square-foot' rule which dropped sail area. That was fine with yachtsmen who believed that stability was a factor of crew skills and should not be a restricting element in a rating rule; at heart they were all sandbaggers. The new rule was LWL x Beam, producing a rating in square feet. Just as with the Thames Measurement, ratings could be reduced by reducing beam, and that is what happened. Each year new yachts became narrower and narrower. In 1871 the New York Yacht Club replaced it with another rule: the cube root of displacement times 100. That was an improvement, but the new allowance tables were so badly conceived that they killed the rule in one season. Races the next year to had be sailed on a one-on-one basis.

The Club's 1873 rule, called the 'cubic contents' rule, measured the volume of a hull "below a horizontal plane tangent to the lowest point of the sheer." That was a disaster. In ten years it produced some of the most ridiculous yachts ever built. If measurement downward began at the lowest point of the rail, a designer inevitably lowered freeboard. Then he reduced the volume of the hull below the horizontal tangent line, i.e. he reduced draft and fore and aft overhangs. Next, to overcome lost stability he increased beam. Then, since there was so little vertical space left below decks, even the largest yachts had to have raised cabin trunks. A yacht of 50 feet of waterline typically wound up with only 18 inches of freeboard so that, when she was at her optimum angle of heel, almost her entire lee deck was awash. Even more extreme, inasmuch as British physicist/yachtsman, William Froude, had recently pointed out the critical value of LWL as a parameter of how fast a hull could be driven, was the tendency for the LWL on some yachts to be greater than the LOA in order to take maximum advantage of the rule. Symptomatic of the extremes was the fatal capsize at anchor off Staten Island, NY in a sudden squall of the wide-beam shallow-draft schooner *Mohawk* with the loss of four lives.

RATING RULES AND CLASSIFICATION OF YACHTS – AN OVERVIEW

Rating (measurement) rules and a uniform system for classifying, i.e. dividing into yachts into classes, were the foremost (racing rules not withstanding), concern militating the formation of NAYRU in the 1890's and its reformation in the 1920's. Classification was the term originally used for setting up parameters for grouping yachts of similar dimensions in classes in which they competed with, or without, time allowances whether at home or away at other clubs or associations.

Chronologically the three rating rules (discussed in detail below) that dominated yacht racing in North America were:

(1) The Seawanhaka Rule which reputedly originated in Ireland or Scotland but remained isolated from mainstream yachting in the United Kingdom. It was a linear rule based on waterline length and later incorporating a sail area factor.

(2) The Universal Rule which stemmed from the Atlantic Coast Conference convened by the New York Yacht Club with representation from Clubs and YRA's in the northeast and the Yacht Racing Union of the Great Lakes. It became 'universal' in the northeast and eventually throughout North America after its adoption. It introduced a displacement factor in conjunction with waterline length and sail area as well as a quarter beam depth measurement.

(3) The International Rule which was the result of an international conference held in Paris in 1906 and combined in a linear rule both a displacement factor and sail area. All the 'Metre' classes were built to the Rule, except the 5.5 Metre the formula for which contained variances therefrom. The International Rule actually led to the formation of the International Yacht Racing Union the next near – absent North American participation where the Rule was not introduced until the next decade, initially in Canadian waters. It would not be until after World War II that the International Rule would virtually eclipse the Universal Rule in North America. As late as 1931 the tussle over the Universal Rule vs. the International Rule was the subject of discussion between the New York Yacht Club and the Royal Yachting Association resulting in a compromise that was academic respecting its effect on yachting on both sides of the Atlantic. New York adopted scantlings for the larger classes of 'J - K' (only the 'J's raced in North America and only for the America's Cup), and the British adopted the Universal Rule for the 14½ Metre Class (raced on a limited basis in the U.K).

Classes under the Universal Rule were determined by rating numbers to which a yacht's rating had to be less than, or in some instances not more than, the designated number for her class. In effect the system created an imprecise prototype for what today is termed on 'open' or 'restricted' class, and yachts raced either with or without time allowances (see illustration).

Distribution:

I Class: *rating 78 feet; raced on Long Island Sound.*
J Class: *predominately involved with America's Cup races.*
K Class: *raced in Long Island Sound.*
L Class: *rare in North America; the New York Fifty is comparable.*
M Class: *approximately five on east coast and some on west coast.*
N Class: *very few and only in California* and on Great Lakes.*
O Class: *known as Larchmont 'O' at Larchmont and Manhasset Bay Yacht Clubs.*
P Class: *a popular class across the continent; a few, restored, on the Great Lakes.*
Q Class: *also a popular class and a few, restored, sail on the Great Lakes.*
R Class: *from east coast to Honolulu; a few in GRP race on Lakes Ontario and Erie today.*
S Class: *first one-design built to the Universal Rule; from east coast to Honolulu; the San Diego PC rates almost the same under the Universal Rule.*
T Class: *designed by Frank Paine for Marblehead, MA, sailors.*

'P's, 'Q's and 'R's, like the 'S's, usually raced without time allowance.

*The 'N' boat, *Westward*, had a remarkable career. Commissioned by John R. Hanify of San Francisco, she was designed by William Gardner and Company of New York and built at the William F. Stone and Son Yard in Oakland, CA, for the 1915 Pacific International Exposition regatta. *Westward*, after several rig changes, wound up in Newport Harbor as a jib-headed sloop in the 1930's and in the post World War II decade won some major races, as well as finished third in the 1947 race to Honolulu. Finally in 1958 she was lost off the coast of El Salvador in transit to the east coast.

THE SEAWANHAKA RULE

Although the system of tonnage based on Custom House, or Thames, tonnage, which calculated cargo-carrying capacity and therefore penalized the interior volume of the hull and led to deep-draft, narrow-beam cutters prevailed for decades in the British Isles, English designer Dixon Kemp offered the idea that a balance between LWL and sail area would produce the "wholesome yacht" that everyone wanted but existed on neither side of the Atlantic. In North America the young and progressive Seawanhaka Corinthian Yacht Club (1871) picked up on Kemp's suggestion and, in concert with New York, produced a rule that was simply 'LWL plus the square root of sail area divided by two.' Both the Seawanhaka Corinthian and New York Yacht Clubs had appointed committees "to confer with other clubs with a view to the adoption of a uniform system of yacht measurement." The committees of the two clubs worked together and invited representatives from the Atlantic and Larchmont Yacht Clubs to their meetings.[5]

After two months the Committees, agreeing on all but one point, and both emphasizing that the goal was to produce a rule "which would be acceptable to all American Clubs," rather than only for home consumption, submitted a formula recognizing "that the ton as a unit of measurement in this country was less acceptable than the foot." It was this linear formula that was dubbed the 'Seawanhaka Rule'. The New York Yacht Club disagreed somewhat, believing that length should be taxed more heavily, and adopted a rule that doubled the tax on LWL and changed the divisor to three. It took only three years for the club to realize that it had been wrong, and it deferred to the Seawanhaka formula. Years later, Charles Lane Poor,[6] Chairman of the NYYC Measurement Committee, observed that if the Club felt that it needed to depart from the Seawanhaka Rule, it ought to have done just the opposite – placed the numeral '2' before the square root of sail area.

Usage of the Seawanhaka Rule spread quickly being adopted by the Eastern Yacht Club at Marblehead in 1885, New York Yacht Club in 1889 and eventually across North America and offshore to the Hawaiian Islands. Although the tendency was for clubs to look upon NYYC as natural leader whose direction they could emulate in the hope of finding a stable measurement system, the Boston Yacht Club, which is the oldest in New England (founded in 1866), took a different tack. Abandonment of the tonnage concept and replacing it with a waterline and area rule had been considered by a special committee of the New York Yacht Club in the 1850's, but a waterline rule did not come into effect in North America until Nathanael G. Herreshoff, a student at MIT in 1866, developed for the Boston Yacht Club a measurement rule based on just one element – length – which he defined as LOA plus LWL divided by two. In addition, he created a good time allowance table to go with it. Since he recognized that larger yachts require more wind to reach their maximum potential speed than smaller yachts, he made an adjustment in the table for yachts of more than 30-feet LWL. The rule worked very well for almost 30 years until Edward Burgess persuaded the clubs of Massachusetts Bay to adopt the Seawanhaka Rule. Burgess was soon to regret having recommended the switch, although in all probability Herreshoff's rule would have succumbed to some of the excesses terminal for the Seawanhaka Rule.

The Seawanhaka Rule has been described as "The ancestor of modern rules." It reputedly had its origin in Ireland or Scotland but, except for its adoption for a couple of years by the British Yacht Racing Association as the Kemp Rule (after its secretary, Dixon Kemp)[7] it remained isolated from mainstream yachting in the British Isles.

The impetus for a uniform rule in 1883 in North America was, as above-mentioned, the need of a rating system that would enable a yacht to move from port to port, from the seashore to the Lakes and to and fro across the US/Canadian border and compete without having to be re-measured and with the knowledge that she would be racing yachts of similar characteristics and performance.

Except for minor variations the Seawanhaka Rule dominated yachting on the continent for the rest of the century and formed the basis for a variety of offshoot rules. The cause of its ultimate demise was its failure to be comprehensive enough of all the parameters of boat speed and to restrain naval architects from exploiting the resulting loopholes.

Symptomatic of the century-long struggle to develop a formula capable of equitably equating disparities of hull and rig and of reconciling the British propensity to use displacement as the prime factor, vis-à-vis the American preference for waterline and sail area, were the seven or more rules used from 1851 until 1987 for the America's Cup matches. These fluctuated from the Waterline Area rule used in 1870 reflecting American practice; the complex Displacement Rule of 1871 emanating from England; the Cubic Contents rule used from 1876-1881 referred to as 'Chapman's Rule'; the New York Yacht Club version of the Seawanhaka Rule to which was added a multiplier of two to the waterline length and an overall divisor of three "deferring to the national prejudice for a tax on length and freedom in carrying unlimited sail;" switching for the period 1893 - 1903 to the basic Seawanhaka

Rule; adopting in 1920 the Universal Rule; and 1958 - 1987 the International Rule, i.e. Twelve-Metre Class.[8]

SAN FRANCISCO BAY

The fluctuations in rating rules reflected the attempt on both sides of the Atlantic to rate yachts and apply time allowances in order to produce 'fair' racing. In North America such efforts took various forms depending on the region, sailing conditions and types of boats. For example, in 1908 the San Francisco Yacht Club used the basic Seawanhaka Rule producing a Rating Length (RL) for a yacht and specified classes, such as: Class 'A' yachts as yachts with cabin, or open, not over 20 feet RL...Class 'H' yachts with RL greater than 75 feet, and applied a time allowance to schooners of 85 percent of RL, for yawls 93 percent, and for sloops and cutters 100 percent. Note that, even though a continent and ocean distant from Great Britain which was the cradle of the cutter – a sloop with narrow beam, deep draft and double head rig – the distinction between cutter and sloop was recognized in San Francisco Bay. The Club apparently also recognized that rating rules would inevitably remain in a state of flux when it adopted provision #2 of the Jan. 5, 1895 conditions for the San Francisco (Perpetual) Challenge Cup:

> *any recognized Yacht Club on the Pacific Coast having more than three yachts on its rolls... sailing length (RL) to be determined by the rules of the Seawanhaka Corinthian Yacht Club or any rule which may come into general use in its stead by a majority of the leading clubs of the U.S.*

By implication the provision likewise recognized the desirability of there being a consensus in North America on the rules.

LAKE MICHIGAN

Unlike San Francisco, on Lake Michigan in the first Mackinac Race held in 1898 two sloops and three schooners competed without handicaps. In the 1920's yachts built to the Universal Rule were competing with yachts built to the International (Metre) Rule, and the argument over which rule to use was settled in one instance by applying the Universal Rule and dividing the fleet into racing and cruising divisions. Near bedlam prevailed in 1933 when Chicago Yacht Club rules imposed equipment and accommodations limitations. Per the Club's *History*:

> *It was very confusing and when you consider that, in 1933, the Lake Michigan Yachting Asssociation Rule (adopted 1932) was used by the Jackson Park and Columbia Yacht Clubs in their races, the New York Yacht Club Rule was used by the Chicago Yacht Club in the Mackinac Race and the Chicago Yacht Club Measurement Rule (adopted in 1933) was used for all other CYC sponsored Cruising Races, one can appreciate the chaos figuring out the finishes after each race. The owners fumed over the situation, too, as every time the rules were revised (annually) they had to have their yachts re-measured in order to qualify to race.*[9]

Even after the LMYA in 1934 adopted the Wells Lippincott Rule, precursor to the CCA Rule, the Chicago Yacht Club continued to sail under the former LMYA rule until 1963.

PUGET SOUND

The lack of precise integration of rating rule, measurement and handicapping led to major controversies in other international events. On Puget Sound in celebration of the 1909 Alaska-Yukon-Pacific Exposition two weeks of racing were planned with the contest for the Alexandra's Cup being the highlight. Because of a dispute over the measurement of the Seattle yacht designed by Ted Geary, *Spirit II*, a half an hour before the start of the second race the Canadian fleet, including its challenger, *Alexandra*, pulled up stakes and went home. This led "to strained relations with good friends across the border which lasted four years." Ted Geary, by the way, later designed and campaigned the 'R' boat, *Sir Tom*, that racked up the most outstanding records of any boat in the class; he also designed numerous other boats and classes on Puget Sound. Geary's analysis of the state of the Seawanhaka Rule that led to the 1909 fracas was:

> *The prevailing measurement rule on this continent was the Seawanahaka Rule featuring waterline and sail area until the 1905 (when) Nat Herreshoff of America's Cup fame evolved the Universal Rule, taking into account the shape of hull and displacement. It gave promise of being the best rating rule ever and was adopted by all saltwater clubs and associations in the United States except here in the northwest where Canadian clubs insisted on the*

International Rule (the 'English' Rule to which the Metre classes were measured) as used in Europe. This (Universal10) Rule took in also girths and freeboard and seemed to need changing every year or so. In the interests of racing, we agreed to go along and it was adopted by the Northwest International Yacht Racing Association (in 1910).[11]

As a result of the controversy Ted vowed never again to race for the Alexandra's Cup, but paradoxically the ill will generated prompted Sir Thomas Lipton in 1912 to put up a $3,000 trophy for international match racing in the 20-raters of the 'R' class under the Universal Rule (the 'R' rated 20 under the Universal Rule) – perhaps an example of how sometimes the forces motivating the evolution and adoption of rating rules are neither logical nor scientific. Similar in one respect to the International Rule, the Universal Rule led to classes that were determined by rating numbers scaled from the America's Cup 'J' Class and the somewhat smaller 'M's and 'N's to the much smaller 'P's, 'Q's, 'R's and 'S's. The latter group raced without time allowances within their respective classes akin to one-designs today and gained widespread popularity across the continent – the 'R ' being the most prominent.

ROYAL ST. LAWRENCE YACHT CLUB AND SEAWANHAKA CUP

A few years before the controversy in Puget Sound a similar episode involving rating and measurement occurred with the Seawanhaka Cup at the Royal St. Lawrence Yacht Club in 1898. The extremes to which designers had exploited the Seawanhaka Rule, especially in the case of the Seawanhaka Cup yachts, is typified by Thomas Fleming Day's statement in *Rudder*:

I am glad to see that the Seawanhaka Yacht Club has come back to a common sense policy, and has started to do what it formerly did, encourage the building and racing of sensible boats. The one-raters or 20-footers that it fathered this year were certainly a lot of worthless boxes. It is curious to see a body of men who spent years denouncing and driving out the sandbaggers encouraging a type of craft more worthless and certainly as dangerous as the old gravel waggons.

Seawanhaka Cup yachts had become skimming dishes with a waterline of around 17 feet versus an overall length of 30 or more and drawing only 5 inches with centerboard raised. For the defending Royal St. Lawrence Yacht Club Herrick Duggan had designed *Dominion* a tunnel-hulled craft – virtually a catamaran – with a roof deck almost 36 feet in length connecting the two 17.5-foot cylindrical hulls. Clinton H. Crane as a young naval architect had designed the Seawanhaka's *Challenger* – a more conventional 'extreme' boat. Seawanhaka unsuccessfully challenged the legality of *Dominion* on the grounds of its being a catamaran (compare the 1988 America's Cup Match) and at the end of the series, which was handily won by the defender, the American team received a telegram from the SCYC Race Committee instructing them:

We advise you as our representatives and our other men to leave on the first train practicable after the deciding race. Also to preserve a very dignified attitude concerning this event and accept no public or formal hospitalities. We will address the Royal St. Lawrence Yacht Club saying that we will communicate with them regarding this contest as soon as we can gather our scattered committee.[12]

Unlike the four years hiatus in international racing that occurred on Puget Sound, it would be twenty-four years before Seawanhaka would again challenge for the Cup. By then the Seawanhaka Rule was history, and the popularity of the Universal Rule classes was facing competition from the introduction of the International Rule (metre) classes and burgeoning of one-designs.

NAYRU - 1897

As above recorded, the Seawanhaka Rule was generally adopted without furor or fanfare throughout North America and for a full decade worked well towards achieving the objective of creating 'wholesome' yachts. For more than a decade no yacht was built in which the square root of the sail area exceeded LWL by more than 12 percent. In 1891, however, N.G. Herreshoff upset the apple cart. The first designer on this side of the Atlantic to take a lesson from the experiments of designer, Professor Froude (see first section of this Chapter) was N. G. Herreshoff when he designed the 70-foot LOA *Gloriana.* The innovative feature of the yacht was the elimination of the knuckle on the traditional clipper bow which he determined was not worth its rating cost under the Seawanhaka Rule which then defined 'L' as LWL. The result was that the combined overhangs were two-thirds the length of LWL. While downwind she presented a minimum wetted surface, upwind when heeled her effective LWL became 50 feet. This startling departure, or end run around the rule, was widely emulated by other designers in order to take advantage of the enormous increase in sail area possible under the rule – 4,000 square feet compared to the 1,800 carried by the average Twelve-Metre. *Gloriana*, built for the NYYC's new 46-foot class, won every race against the other 46-footers in her first season with the result that the class never had a second season. In a single step Capt. Nat had gone from an excess of Sail Area over LWL of 12 percent to 41 percent thereby signaling the end of the Seawanhaka Rule. Other designers followed suit; Starling Burgess, for example, produced *Outlook*, a yacht of 52 feet 7 inches LOA, only 20 feet 10 inches LWL and sail area of 1,800 square feet.

As a further indication of the serious need for a uniform and universal rating rule, one of the foremost tasks of the North American Yacht Racing Union, following its formation in 1897, was the work of its Council. Its report adopted October 1, 1898 described:

> *That upon careful consideration of all the rules now in force the conclusion was arrived at, that the only additional rules needed by he Union would be those relating to Measurement, Classification (setting up of parameters for classes), Time Allowance and Crews. Of these the most important by far seemed to be the one relating to measurement.*

Members of the Council represented the principal areas of yachting in North America and were Louis M. Clark from Boston, Joseph M. Macdonough from San Francisco, Aemilius Jarvis from Toronto, A.F. Bancroft, A.J. Prime, Newbury D. Lawton and Frank Bowne Jones of New York. A sub-committee of the Council, including Jarvis, Macdonough and a third member, had visited England where it found itself in disagreement with most of the systems in use there except for the 'girth rule' known as the British Yacht Racing Association[13] linear rule.[14] It predicted:

> *The adoption of this rule would promote international uniformity, the benefits of which to this Union would be incalculable.*

– a uniformity that was not to come to fruition until the re-formation of NAYRU in 1925, and then only on an informal and temporary basis. Not until NAYRU joined the International Yacht Racing Union in 1957 and in 1969 co-sponsored with the Royal Ocean Racing Club the IOR Rule would there be a uniform international rule. As assurance to the Council the sub-committee concluded:

> *It would be quite unlikely that any change would be made in the rule anywhere without an international conference in which our Union would then have a prominent part.*[15]

Adoption of the Report was perhaps the most significant accomplishment of the nascent National Authority which shortly lapsed not to be revived until 1925, by which time both the Universal and International Rules were concurrently in use, with the latter on the verge of replacing the former, especially in the smaller classes. Nonetheless, prescient Cassandras, including W.P. Stephens, countered the prediction that the new rule "would unite two great nations" saying that it would not solve the measurement problems since the rule did not affect the smaller classes in which the majority of racing took place. It was really for this group that NAYRU was organized, inasmuch as the large yachts raced on a more selective basis in events organized by the larger clubs, such as the New York and Eastern Yacht Clubs, and tended to be self-sufficient in the conduct of their racing.

At the second annual meeting of NAYRU after the year of its formation further discussion concerning the measurement rule resulted in the decision to retain the 'girth rule' for another year. It was also resolved to appoint a committee of five to revise the racing rules. At the next annual meeting in October, 1900, held at the Yachtsmen's Club at 47 West 43d Street in New York City, it was resolved to rescind the measurement rule which had been incorporated in the NAYRU Racing Rules (the term 'racing rules' in earlier times included the subject matter of current 'sailing instructions') and that members use on a local basis such rule as they considered most desirable. This struck at the heart of the raison d'etre for NAYRU which most likely was why there is no record of any further annual meetings or proceedings of the Union. In retrospect it was unfortunate inasmuch as delegates to the meeting had come from yachting associations as far away as the Pacific Inter-Club Yachting Association, Corinthian Yacht Club of Philadelphia as well as the Yacht Racing Association of Long Island Sound, the New York Yacht Racing Association and the Atlantic Yacht Club of Brooklyn representing nine Associations comprising 113 clubs and 10 independent clubs. While this represented a modest increase over the 110 clubs attending the founding meeting, notably representation from the Great Lakes and New England was missing.[16]

UNIVERSAL RULE

By the turn-of-the-century the Seawanhaka Rule had led to extreme yachts built with long overhangs, skimming dish hulls and lofty rigs that made them both unmanageable and unseaworthy as exemplified in the Herreshoff America's Cup defenders, *Defender* (1895) and *Reliance* (1903) which, at 143 feet overall, 90 feet on the waterline and carrying 16,159 feet of measured sail area, were super scows and according to W.P. Stephens:

> *... open to all the objections of extreme costs, fragile construction, and limited utility...*

It was not until after the turn of the century, however, that order began to come out of the chaotic situation when the New York Yacht Club, after appointing a committee headed by Charles Lane Poor in 1902 to scout leading designers on both sides of the Atlantic concerning an improved rule, invited, among others, N.G. Herreshoff to a discussion with other New York and Boston Clubs. The group pressed him hard on his inadequate instructions for measuring L, which obviously was difficult to do accurately. Then they asked him a number of 'what if' questions. For example, what if designers hollowed bows to reduce L? What factor was in the rule that would prevent sail area from getting out of hand again? The group decided that only penalties could control these things, so they voted to adopt the following:

> *One half of any excess of L over 115 percent of LWL shall be added to the rating; and any excess of the square root of sail area over 135 percent of L shall be added to the rating.*

The latter was a far cry from Dixon Kemp's ideal of parity between LWL and the square root of SA, but to have made the penalty any stiffer would have rendered obsolete thousands of boats around the continent – an eternal dilemma for rule-making bodies. Before finishing, the group added one more penalty. To be sure, more draft was needed to overcome the shallow 'skimming dishes' that were flitting about, but Draft (D) was the divisor: the higher it was, the lower the quotient would be. There had to be a limit on draft, and that was worked out as .133 times rating plus 2' 8" with a penalty of twice any excess added to the rating. Finally, the 'D' measurement was multiplied by 5, simply to make the ratings come out approximately equal to 'L'.

So the job was done, and 1903 saw the advent of the Herreshoff Rule, soon to be called the Universal Rule. But Poor was not done. He realized how much was at stake with the new rule, not just for New York and Boston, but for the whole of North America. He appreciated that every club was poised to replace the Seawanhaka Rule as soon as possible so he kept his committee at work. He took it to Boston twice to gather input, and held annual meetings with the original group – the Atlantic Coast Conference – to appraise the effect of the rule.

Charles Lane Poor had long insisted that without the three penalties added at the outset the rule would have been an instant failure. Yet the Conference members found more changes needed as time went on. The limitation of 115 percent of L over LWL proved inadequate, so that was changed to .16 x rating plus 1' 6", with a penalty of three times the excess. That did not help much so a final change was made that put no limit on actual displacement but required that the cube root of 'D' could not exceed 20 percent of LWL. The effect of that as explained by Poor was:

> *While leaving the formula... intact, it completely changed the rule itself... reducing [it] to a single-factor rule with limits and drastic penalties. The rigid fixing of the upper limit of the cube root of displacement as a percentage of the waterline practically canceled those two factors... and left it, to all intents and purposes, a pure sail-area rule.*

Quoting from John Parkinson Jr.'s *The History of the New York Yacht Club*:

> *The feature of this [Universal] rule was the 'quarter beam length' measurement, which caused a yacht's displacement to be included as a factor, lack of adequate displacement being penalized. 'L' or the rated length of a yacht was the mean between overall and waterline length and this waterline length was measured at a point halfway between her centerline and her greatest beam, which was a quarter of her beam, a somewhat difficult measurement to make. Displacement was obtained by the areas of the cross sections of this load waterline measurement at five different points.*[17]

Further, Herman T. Van Mell in his *History of the 'R' Class Sailing Yacht 'Ardelle'* March 14, 1992 comments:

***Adelaide II*, a New York 30-class sloop of 1905**
Photo Herreshoff Marine Museum, Bristol RI

The Universal Rule was a complicated mathematical formula... intended to set parameters for the construction of fast, seaworthy sailing hulls, which within a given resulting 'number' could compete fairly, being both a handicapping and a limiting guide to variations in dimensions. The formula included overall length, water-line length, beam, draft, displacement, weight, sail area, and other elements which factored out to a single number. If that number was 20.0 the boat was identified as an 'R'. If the number turned out to be 30.0 it would be classed as a 'Q'. The designer was free to vary any or all the dimensions, just so that the total formula came out to 20.0 in order to produce an 'R' boat which could compete with any other 'R' without further handicapping. This encouraged yacht designers constantly to seek for just the right combination to produce maximum speed (without ever compromising safety and seaworthiness). 'R's varied in length from 36 to 44 feet, and certainly varied in beam, water-line, overhangs, bilge curves and other elements. The resulting hulls, however, were usually a beautiful combination of curves, enabling them to go through the water with minimum disturbance. The word 'sleek' certainly applied.

A dramatic example of how the Universal Rule reined in the extremities and excesses that had developed under the Linear Rule is the difference between the New York Seventies, which were not much smaller than a 'J' Class boat and designed in 1900 by Herreshoff as a one-design class for the New York Yacht Club (a.k.a. as Newport Seventies) and the New York Thirty's in 1905. The for-

1916 1979
NY40
NY40
ONE DESIGN

mer under the Linear Rule, because of their extreme overhangs and large sail area, were difficult to manage, were subject to wracking in heavy seas and were too expensive to become popular so that the class was short-lived. In contrast, the Thirty's, built to the Universal Rule without extremes, raced as a class until replaced in 1937 by the New York Thirty-Two (LWL still being the parameter for designating class size); after World War II the Thirty often outsailed the Thirty-Two boat-for-boat without benefit of handicap.[18]

The need for modifications to the Universal Rule in order to constrain innovative owners and designers and to insure their uniform application prompted the New York Yacht Club to convene the Atlantic Coast Conference in 1908 which included the Atlantic, Beverly, Brooklyn, Corinthian of Marblehead, Corinthian of Philadelphia, Eastern, Larchmont and New York Yacht Clubs, as well as the Narragansett Bay Yacht Racing Association, Yacht Racing Association of Long Island Sound, Yacht Racing Association of Massachusetts and Yacht Racing Union of the Great Lakes. Its chairman was Charles Lane Poor who later wrote a comprehensive analysis of rating rules and handicap systems the title of which, *Men Against the Rule,* epitomizes the ongoing struggle to maintain a level playing field. Minor changes were made in measurement, and major changes in the classification of Schooners and sloops and yawls. In the latter category classes such as the 'P' (not over 25 feet and over 20 feet of rating measurement), 'Q' (not over 25 and over 20), 'R' (not over 20 and over 17) and 'S' (not over 17) became widespread with the 'S' existing for a period as far west as Hawaii.

A submission made in October, 1912 to the Atlantic Conference titled *Proposed Amendments to Racing Rules* indicates that the New York Yacht Club continued its role in updating the Rule and supporting the Conference in its work. The submission includes detailed measurement procedures, covers idiosyncrasies such as "concave notches or jogs (curved or angular) at the plane of measurement of the quarter-beam length" – items familiar to today's measurers of International Rule and IOR yachts – time allowances, sailing instructions and racing rules.

Was the Universal Rule a good rule? It lasted for 40 years which suggests that it had some virtue. Another was the admission by L. Frances Herreshoff, who originally had complained loudly about its limitations, that:

> *The proof is in the pudding; it produced a great many sound and lovely yachts.*

On the other hand, Howard Chapelle, still a dissenter as late as 1935, said that the rule had created boats that were excessively heavy and slow, expensive to build and wasteful of good wood and lead. If they were as fast as boats at the end of the century, which he doubted, it was because of improvements in other areas: the masthead rig replacing the gaff rig and great advances in design and construction of sails, rigging and gear. Similar to what occurred under the Seawanhaka Rule, classes and clubs migrated to one-designs to enjoy a more level playing field at less expense which was an indication that the Universal Rule was not entirely successful as a panacea to the Seawanhaka Rule.

OTHER SYSTEMS OF HANDICAPPING

In the interim other types of handicapping had surfaced. For example, George P. Gronberg of the New Rochelle Yacht Club on Western Long Island Sound introduced a system of handicap racing based on performance during the season – a system which originated with Louis M. Clark of the Boston Yacht Club in 1906. Later versions of performance handicapping, under which a yacht's handicap was subject to continuous adjustment based on her finishing positions, were the Percentage (%) Handicap System used on Long Island Sound and after WW II the Performance Handicap Racing Fleet (originating in Southern California as the Pacific Handicap Racing Fleet.) The inaugural Transpac Race of 1906 adopted a handicap proposed by Commodore Harry Sinclair of the South Coast Yacht Club in San Pedro (predecessor to the Los Angeles Yacht Club) of 30 minutes times the length of the yacht; length was calculated as the load water line plus half of the overhangs. By 1923 a modification of the Seawanhaka Rule was in use, and after 1928, for which the Universal Rule was used, the Race reverted to the 1923 rule; and in 1932 back to the Seawanhaka Rule modified by a major change in the multiplier and finally to the Cruising Club of America Rule – a further indication of the ongoing struggle to find an equitable and universal rule. The appearance of light displacement and eventually ultra light displacement boats required modifications, first of the CCA Rule and later the IOR.

1916 NY 40 (LWL) vs. 1979 NY 40 (LOA)
Universal Rule NY 40 vs IOR Rule NY 40
Artwork by John L. Baringer for the 1979 Class.

WANE OF THE UNIVERSAL RULE

The wane of the Universal Rule occurred primarily as result of two factors. On the one hand, for around the buoys racing the popularity of the Universal Rule 'P' and 'Q' classes and eventually the 'R' and 'S' classes, which, although built to a rating were raced without time allowance, were being eclipsed by the emergence of native restricted one-designs, or rigidly one-designs, and by the introduction of the International Rule classes from British and European waters. Examples are the 'S' in Hawaii giving way to the 'PC's from San Diego, despite the fact that while team racing off Honolulu in 1931 the two classes were closely matched; the introduction of the Six-Metre in San Francisco in 1915 and by the Seawanhaka Corinthian Yacht Club in 1921; the adoption of one-design scow classes by the Inland Lake Yachting Association as early as 1897 and accelerating in the 1920's; and a plethora of one-designs coming off the boards at, and after the turn of the century, of designers such as Nathaniel Herreshoff, Clinton Crane, Charles Mower, the Burgesses, and so forth. Moreover, innovations by designers, just as was the case under the Seawanhaka rule, had outstripped the capacity of the Universal Rule equitably to assess their effect on boat speed. The result was the formulation of a more comprehensive rule for distance and offshore racing resulting in 1934 in the Cruising Club of America Rule which became virtually 'universal' in North America for over a quarter of a century. Its genesis was the Lippincott Rule named after its developer from Chicago and adopted by the Lake Michigan Yachting Association in 1934.

INTERNATIONAL RULE

Almost concurrently with the establishment of the Universal Rule there evolved the International Rule as a result of a meeting held January, 1906 in London attended by British and European delegates but none from America. Considered a linear rating rule it went into effect in 1907; in 1920 the formula was constrained by 'restrictions and limits' with heavy 'penalties' for exceeding the dimensions and allowed trade-offs among sail area, displacement and hull dimensions. Further changes became effective in January, 1936.

In the meanwhile, on the North American continent the Executive Committees of NAYRU and the Yacht Racing Association of Long Island Sound went on record November 1926, adopting "except for the Marblehead crowd", the International Rule for boats up to Class 'P', further eroding the use of the Universal Rule. Earlier, erosion had commenced in several areas when under the insistence of the Canadian Clubs the Northwest International Yacht Racing Association (now Pacific International Yachting Association) subscribe to the International Rule for certain events; when the International Rule Six-Metre competed in San Francisco Bay at the 1915 in the Panama-Pacific International Exposition; when in 1921 the Seawanhaka Corinthian Yacht Club built Six-Metres to compete in the British American Cup; and in 1928 when the Royal Canadian and Rochester Yacht Clubs amended the deed of gift for the Canada's Cup to permit competition under the International Rating Rule, i.e. the Eight-Metre Class.

In 1927 NAYRU delegates attended a conference held in February in London seeking to reconcile the dichotomy of there being two rules making it difficult to facilitate international racing. Clinton H. Crane was one of the delegates, and his paper about the conference was published by the *Boston Evening Transcript* excerpts from which follow:

> *I do not believe for a moment that these International classes should be our only classes. We have in existence too many fine racing boats built to the Universal Rule… and no doubt that the Universal Rule still presents a most interesting problem as to the largest yacht which may be driven with the smallest amount of sail.*

Seven of eight American suggestions were favorably received and adopted in principle.

> *… profound impression on the American delegates by their reception at the conference… Almost unanimous agreement on part of the technical advisors that our suggestions were for the benefit of the sport. It has been said many times that one of the greatest objections to joining an International Conference was the great difficulty of making any changes in a rule once adopted, the old argument against 'entangling alliances.' (Yet)… most extraordinary thing that we should have been able to go to London and criticize a rule which had been developed abroad and not be met with immediate antagonism.*

AT HOME AND OVERSEAS

The search for a solution to the rating question was a tortuous one in which input from NAYRU had an influence at the international level. In 1929 the Permanent Committee (in essence the governing body or board of directors) of the International Yacht Racing Union considered points submitted on the racing rules (the term being comprehensive of more than merely the racing rules). Previously in 1928 the Council of the British Yacht Racing Association (currently Royal Yachting Association), whose Vice-President chaired the IYRU meeting, had prepared a draft which it submitted to members of the Permanent Committee and to the American authorities, who compiled a further synopsis which was placed before the conference, and "proved to be a great assistance in the final framing of the rules".[19] Hence Americans, although not members of IYRU, nonetheless were more than mere observers.

Yachting also reported that "America has accepted our (Lloyd's) scantlings.[20] We understand cabin fittings (accommodations in today's rules) are to follow." The report comments that America has accepted the Universal Rule "either in its present form, or as... with such modifications as may be mutually acceptable." (Note that this is late in the era of the Universal Rule). "In either case, the end so greatly to be desired – the adoption of a rating rule common to both continents – will have been attained" (not until the adoption of the IOR in 1969 would both sides of the Atlantic again have a common rating rule, except for the International Rule applicable to the Metre classes). The impetus for the agreement was to refine the procedures for "effectively balancing length and sail area... and by putting a 'stop' on length." The carrot held out by Great Britain and Europe was the offer to scrap the present rule – International Rule – for yachts rating greater than 14½ metres, i.e. the larger classes extraneous to North America, in three years time. The conference was attended by Clifford Mallory and Sam Dauchy from NAYRU and George Cormack and W.A.W. Stewart of the New York Yacht Club.[21]

CRUISING CLUB OF AMERICA (CCA) RULE

While conferring was going on at the international level, the CCA for the 1928 and 1930 Bermuda Races – the only racing event regularly conducted by the Club – was attempting to distinguish between cruising and racing types in order to prevent the latter from relegating the former, which the Club characterized as 'healthy sea-going craft', to the sidelines. The earlier Bermuda Races had been handicapped on a simple length basis. The method used for the 1930 race was, "combined length of the fore and aft overhangs must not exceed one third of yacht's overall measurement." Also banned in order to prohibit 'lead mines' were yachts whose ratio of ballast to displacement is greater than 46 percent. One proposal devised in 1928 was a modification of the Universal Rule, but this was criticized on the basis that a rating rule for racing yachts cannot be satisfactory for cruising yachts – the aim of the CCA being to promote seaworthy types for offshore racing and cruising. Progression of rating rules under the Lake Yacht Racing Association, however, had taken a different tack: the sequence of rating rules employed went from the Seawanhaka Rule to the Universal Rule to the Royal Ocean Racing Club Rule before adopting the CCA Rule. The rationale for using the RORC Rule was that the Rule seeks to enable all types of yachts to compete together rather than having as its objective the development of certain salient features or type of yacht. This may have been the only instance of the use of the RORC in North America.

Evidence that the CCA's Special Committee was continuing working on a solution is a comment in the October, 1932 *Yachting* deploring the formulation of a new rule for ocean racing.

As later reported in a 1934 edition of *Yachting*:

> *Finally the Special Committee, composed of naval architects Clinton Crane, John Alden, Olin Stephens, Philip Rhodes, B. K. Sharpe and Gordon Munroe produced a rule that established 'normal ratios' for such parameters as beam, ballast ratio, displacement, draft, freeboard, etc. and taxes variations therefrom if less than normal, or gives a premium if greater than normal. To prevent undesirable features bow and stern overhangs were brought under control. Scantling tables were under preparation but until ready the previous restriction of entries to yachts having a ratio of ballast to displacement of not more than 46 percent is in effect. A propeller allowance to be decided separately to suit the condition of any particular race.*

The Rule had its genesis in the Wells Lippincott Rule (Lippincott being Commodore of the Chicago Yacht Club and a member of the Cruising Club) which was adopted by the Lake Michigan Yachting Association in 1934, although not by his club until 1963.

The thrust of the rule (which immediately put it at odds with the RORC's rule introduced for the 1931 Fastnet Race, especially respecting heavy deep-draft yachts) was to implement the mission of the CCA – promotion of seamanship and seaworthy craft – by creating a mold, or set of parameters, for the paradigm yacht and through a system of penalties, or deterrents, pressure owners and designers to hew the line. While the CCA, except for an occasional trans-ocean race conducts only the Bermuda Race and its concomitant Onion Patch Series on even years, the influence of its rule on yacht design in North America became continental in scope. It was first used, for example, for the Transpac Race in the late 1930's and spread up and down the west coast, to the Gulf of Mexico, Florida for the Southern Ocean Racing Circuit and on the Great Lakes. Worldwide, however, the RORC rule based on a different formula prevailed in the British Isles and European waters so that the goal of a uniform rule was not to be achieved for another quarter of a century.

By reason of both the CCA and the RORC rules being complex and entailing considerable expense for measuring a yacht to obtain a rating certificate, there developed simpler rules often relying on a few measurements and the plans of the designer. In North America some of these were the Storm Trysail and Offsoundings Rules used primarily in Long Island Sound, the Midget Ocean Racing Rule (MORC) for smaller yachts and Performance Handicap Rule (described below).

The situation whereby the larger clubs with large yachts developed racing formats and rules suitable for this segment of the yachting fraternity but not for the smaller yachts either at their own clubs, or other clubs in the area, tended to repeat itself across North America. The early and obvious instances were the New York and Eastern Yacht Clubs which catered to the large yachts and whose members could see no advantage in forming associations to meet the needs of smaller clubs which served as havens for the smaller yacht owners. A striking instance was San Francisco Bay where, despite the formation of the Yacht Racing Association of San Francisco Bay, which developed an excellent racing format and courses and sailing instructions for the Clubs on the Bay, the waters where the courses were located were not suited to the classes of boats sailed at many of the smaller clubs. To solve the problem the Small Boat Racing Association of Northern California was established in 1937.

PERFORMANCE HANDICAP RACING FLEET AND PORTSMOUTH NUMBERS

In Southern California, where in the late 1920's cruising and dual purpose boats were rated under the Universal Rule, the anomaly created the opportunity to develop a rule that probably has affected more yachts than any other rating rule used on the continent – the Performance Handicap Racing Fleet rule. As recounted by George D. Griffith[22] of Long Beach, California, in 1926 a group of Los Angeles Yacht Club owners formed the 45 Foot Sailing Association. They were the owners of cruising yachts not designed to any particular handicapping rule who needed a venue. Ratings were assigned by a Measurer – Joe Bitterland being one – based on performance and therefore always subject to review. By 1937 there were 66 active boats in the Fleet indicating the popularity of a rule not based strictly on a design formula. Shortly after World War II, when the Southern California Yachting Association became the principal representative of the clubs in the area (the Yacht Racing Union of California having served primarily the larger Clubs conducting the major offshore events), it assumed the administration of the 45 Foot Association for which Harold Adams was the handicapper. Frank Dair took over as handicapper in the 1950's and the Association became the Arbitrary Handicap Fleet of the SCYA.

Performance handicapping was not a novel concept at the time. In 1899 an official measurer was appointed by the Chicago Yacht Club to measure all yachts according to the rules of the Yacht Racing Union of the Great Lakes (est. 1896). Schooners raced as a separate class. By 1900 the handicap applied was based on a yacht's previous performance and each yacht had her own starting time based on her handicap.

It was an unwieldy system and difficult to keep the records accurate so in an era of large wagers and strong tempers the result was often chaotic and questionably gentlemanly conduct ensued.

Representing the larger yachts in Southern California was the Ocean Racing Fleet which was using the CCA rule, or modifications thereof, but no organization was serving the needs of yachts racing under arbitrary handicaps, other than the Arbitrary Handicap Fleet for its members. In 1959, therefore, representatives from various yacht clubs met at the Cabrillo Beach Yacht Club to adopt by-laws and form the Pacific Handicap Racing Fleet. Over the next couple of decades PHRF spread across the continent resulting in replacing 'Pacific' with 'Performance' in recognition of the proliferation of the use of the rule. Local PHRF chapters determined handicaps – a procedure that has the advantage of compensating for the phenomenon that the relative performance of the same type of yacht will vary by reason of variations in sailing conditions from region to region. Since this sometimes caused complaints on the grounds of lack of consistency, US Yacht Racing Union was eventually asked to serve as a clearing house and to maintain a data bank for use of local handicappers, although, unlike in the case of the CCA and IOR rules, it did not administer the system.

The data bank enables a local, or district, handicapping committee to compare a new boat with boats for which statistics are already in the bank. For example, a brand-new design of the same type and dimensions theoretically should be no faster than her five-year-old sister, but if there were changes in factors such as rig, rudder or displacement, the standard handicap for her class could be readily adjusted by changing the seconds-per-mile allowance. In arriving at an initial handicap the guiding philosophy is to err on the safe side by estimating a higher handicap than might be expected, i.e. if in error, only one skipper is upset instead of the entire fleet. Also, it is more politic to increase a handicap than it is to reduce it. The process of reviewing handicaps is a continuous one based on race results; the process contributes to upgrading the national data bank as well. In the end, it will be the local, or district, handicapping committee's judgment on how well a boat performs that determines its final handicap.

To its credit, PHRF, although not used for grand prix racing, has served by far the preponderance of yachts racing under handicapping systems.

A system also based on performance under which a mix of one-designs, whether monohull or multihull, are racing together around-the-buoys is the Portsmouth Numbers. Imported from the British and adapted to North American conditions, PN, which has been administered by Darlene Hobock of Tulsa, OK, and Joseph Spinnler of Doyleston, PA, handicaps classes, or one-of-kind boats, based on the submission of race results by clubs and fleets. NAYRU/USYRU formalized the Portsmouth Numbers Committee in the 1970's to coordinate the process of funneling race results into the computer program to provide periodic updates for the 'numbers' used for handicapping. Inasmuch as PN data historically has been processed on a central, or national basis, it differs from PHRF, but both systems depend on input of a volume of race results in order to filter out the 'skipper' effect, effect of new sails, etc. indigenous to a golfing type handicap.

CRUISING CLUB OF AMERICA RULE AND NAYRU

As the use of the CCA Rule by Clubs and YRAs became continental in scope, and as officials of the CCA and NAYRU/USYRU wore hats in both organizations, e.g. James Michael was President of NAYRU and Commodore of the CCA concurrently, the Cruising Club in 1969 turned over the administration of its rule to the NAYRU as the national authority. In this role NAYRU became the publisher of time allowance tables with features such as decimal hours, handled the certification of measurers and carried out other supportive functions for which the CCA without an office or headquarters found itself ill equipped. The officers and committees of the CCA continued, nonetheless, to be in the forefront of helping improve the Rule, setting standards for safety at sea and so forth, as it continues to do. The CCA Rule after World War II also set the pattern for a simpler versions requiring less expensive measurement system for organizations such as the Midget Ocean Racing Fleet and other groups.

EXPERIMENTS: PUGET SOUND AND BLUE HILL BAY

Other methods of leveling the playing field featured in different forms in different parts of North America. In Blue Hill Bay, ME, yachts were started at intervals separated by half their time allowance with the aim of all yachts sailing as long as possible in similar conditions of wind and current. The driving force for this was Commodore H. Irving Pratt who also led the fund raising campaign to set up a computer program at MIT to handle the International Offshore Rule (IOR) and the International Measurement System (IMS). This practice has been used elsewhere as well. In recognition of how different types and sizes of yachts sail to their maximum performance in different wind and sea conditions, in Puget Sound Walter Little worked up a system of plotted curves known as the Swiftsure Curves after the Swiftsure Lightship Races conducted initially by the Seattle Yacht Club and currently by the Royal Victoria Yacht Club. The curve selected to calculate corrected times was the one most closely fitting the conditions of the race. In some respects the system was a precursor to the introducting under the IMS rule a factor to reflect the conditions of the race.

INTERNATIONAL OFFSHORE RULE (IOR)

By the 1960's collaboration between the CCA and Royal Ocean Racing Club produced the International Offshore Rule (IOR) which was a feat tantamount to the discovery of, after a century and a half of searching, the Holy Grail – a chalice of the ingredients for a perfect rating cum time allowance system. This occurred in spite of the fact that the two clubs played quite different roles in the conduct and administration of the rating systems used by the preponderance of offshore yachts in their respective nations. As mentioned, the CCA had turned over the administration of its rule to NAYRU as the National Authority, whereas in Great Britain the major offshore races and rating rule were conducted and administrated by the Royal Ocean Racing Club, virtually independent of the Royal Yachting Association. Regardless, the two Clubs took the lead in negotiating a new and common rating rule.

How this occurred is best related by James Michael, who became Commodore of the CCA and President of NAYRU in 1972 and was an NAYRU delegate to, and vice-chairman of, the Offshore Racing Council – the international body formed to govern and administer the IOR rule, and by David Edwards who was Commodore of the RORC and became the first Chairman of the Offshore Racing Council (ORC) serving from 1970 to 1978. The accounts of the two bring into sharp relief the dichotomies that existed, and to an extent still do, between Europe and North America in the concept of the purpose of a rating rule and technically how to engineer a rule that would correlate divergent concepts.

According to the Offshore Racing Council Year Book, in 1961 delegates from four nations – Germany, Great Britain, Sweden and the United States met in London and formed the Offshore Rules Co-ordinating Committee (ORCC). It was chaired by Buster de Guingand and joined by delegates from the Antipodes, Lowlands, Scandinavia and Canada and worked for eight years. During 1966 the RORC and CCA were under pressure from the International Yacht Racing Union to frame a rule for possible use in the Olympic Games, and in response the ORCC formed an International Technical Committee (ITC) chaired by Olin J. Stephens, II and comprising American designer, Dick Carter, Gustav Plym of Sweden, Ricas van de Stadt of Holland, English measurers David Fayle and Robin Glover and in addition as non-voting secretary H. A. (Sandy) Haworth, U.K.

A quirk of fate, or perhaps diabolical planning, had perked the interests of Olin Stephens and Dick Carter on the subject of an international rule. When George Hinman was President of NAYRU, the speaker at an annual meeting of NAYRU held at the New York Yacht Club-suddenly canceled. On the spur of the moment Harry Anderson, Executive Director of NAYRU, dragooned Dick Carter to serve as a pinch hitter. Carter apocryphally projected a whole new system of rating yachts and a mass-production system of measuring that caught the ear of Stephens, who probably had not met Carter prior to the meeting. The appointment of Americans, Stephens and Carter, to the ITC was more than happenstance, however, since Carter further proved his perspicacity concerning the rules by winning the Fastnet Race in the One Ton Cup yacht, *Rabbit*, designed by himself.

In November, 1968 the ORCC accepted the results of the ITC's deliberations and decided to put the new International Offshore Rule in effect in 1969. In so doing it operated as an anomaly with respect to the role of the International Yacht Racing Union as the world authority for yacht racing inasmuch as this created a new organization outside of the aegis of the IYRU to monitor the offshore segment of international yacht racing. Albeit there was liaison between the two by reason of the latter's President, Beppe Croce, being a member of the Council of the Offshore Racing Council (the shortened title adopted for the ORCC), nonetheless, dual authorities became responsible for the administration of the sport of yachting globally thereby creating a jurisdictional problem that is still undergoing resolution.

PER DAVID EDWARDS

(a truncated version of his recollections)

What was the objective of those who set about running an international rating rule in the 60's? Was it to enable sailors around the world to race against each other in boats with differing characteristics whose effects were evened out by the rule? Was it to create a new sport? Nobody asked the question.

The Offshore Rules Co-ordinating Committee was a self-appointed body whose brief was to help owners faced, as they were then, with four different rules – CCA, RORC, KR in Germany and SHR in Sweden. The Committee's approach was to identify conflicts between the rules, such as sail measurement points, the length of battens and stability characteristics, and try to influence rule makers to bring these into line. When in 1966 the IYRU called on the CCA and RORC jointly to form a single rule for possible use in the Olympic Games, there was no discussion about philosophy or objectives, nor was there any review of the principles underlying the rules of the respective Clubs. The CCA was primarily a cruising club, and under its rule, which was the main rule in North and South America, comfortable and fast yachts had evolved from designers such as Olin Stephens and Philip Rhodes which were primarily intended for cruising. On the other hand the RORC was primarily concerned with racing, and its rule was used in much of the world outside of the America's, i.e. Europe, Mediterranean and the Antipodes.

The RORC was opposed to the use of any rating system in an arena so starkly competitive as the Olympic Games; it also did not want any major change and in March, 1967 Commodore Mike Vernon in a press release stated, "The RORC is convinced that the creation of an international rule will fail through lack of support." By then, however, the momentum for an international rule, controlled by an international body – not a club – was unstoppable. The big change was the arrival at the 1967 ORCC meetings of the Commodore of the CCA, Fred Adams, and his successor, Clayton Ewing, who issued a press release in April recording the establishment of the International Technical Committee (composed as above noted).[23]

The ITC began work on combining the two rules by using primarily the RORC hull measurement system and the CCA sail arrangements. Like the ORCC the ITC was originally free-standing, i.e. no direction was given whether it was to be a handicap or a development rule. There was a belief that such a distinguished representative body must inevitably succeed in producing a 'good' rule. The CCA rule was deliberately type forming, and the boats built to it were certainly dual purpose and made comfortable and fast cruisers. The RORC rule encouraged narrow, deep and stiff boats in order to optimize windward performance. The RORC had used various means of dividing the fleet including age allowance about which the CCA was not keen. There were thus large and important differences between the boats produced by each of the rules, and these differences tended to be a conscious reaction to local conditions. The CCA had traditionally changed the rule whenever the Club felt it necessary or when a designer had obtained an advantage over a boat's competitors. The RORC favoured stability, with a review every few years. Unfortunately the ORCC and then the ITC were given no guidance about resolving the fundamental differences before IOR Mk II was produced for the 1970 season.

The IOR rule very quickly became popular in Europe and elsewhere outside of the USA. As early as 1971 there were 17 nations sending three-boat teams to the Admiral's Cup and 19 in the years 1975-79. Level Racing for the Ton Cup classes also generated fierce competition and very close racing. At the peak in the 1970's there were more than 11,000 yachts in the world rated under IOR. In spite of worldwide success, leaders of the CCA soon became disillusioned and received complaints from US sailors involving both hull characteristics and measurement procedures. At about the same time work was started at MIT on a new measurement handicap system eventually originally titled MHS and later changed to IMS.

The ORC also affirmed that the IOR was a development rule and not the handicap rule for which many in North America hankered. Indeed, when MHS was republished in April, 1986 as IMS, it was described as a handicapping system "as opposed to a design rule." It was introduced as an alternative to IOR that was "designer proof" and aimed at achieving the Holy Grail of enabling good production yachts to compete with custom yachts. Sailors and journalists tended to blame the rule makers for every perceived problem in offshore racing. In fact two developments which probably sealed the fate of the IOR were very light new construction materials and allowing the crew members to sit on the rail with much of their body weight outside the lifelines. The additional power to weight ratio made all newly built boats extremely fast, especially downwind, and made most cruising type boats obsolete.

Ironically, while use of the IOR has severely declined worldwide, the by-product of the Rule, the Special Regulations specifying structural features of offshore yachts, equipment and personal safety of crew, which were first published in 1972, have been adopted as required standards by most National Authorities.

PER JAMES MICHAEL

(a truncated version from his files)

We should recollect that by 1969 the predominant rule for rating ocean racing yachts in North America (even when racing around the buoys) was the Measurement Rule of the Cruising Club of America (CCA Rule). Some 4,500 yachts then held measurement certificates under that rule. The rule was generally well regarded for two reasons: first, it encouraged a type of yacht, which not only could compete in racing, but also was an acceptable cruising boat; and, second, the rule was constantly adjusted to reflect design developments and correct any loopholes that avid designers discovered.

Also, it is well to mention the individuals, who were most active in bringing about the development of the IOR rule, and who played a significant role in getting it accepted in this country:

Fred Adams had been Commodore of the CCA in 1966-67 and had been part of the original international group that decided an international rule should be created. He pursued that effort and continued to support the new rule after its adoption.

Clayton Ewing's early contribution paralleled that of Fred Adams. In addition he was Commodore of the CCA and Vice Commodore of the New York Yacht Club in 1968-69 and Commodore of NYYC in 1970-71. He also was active in a number of ways in the North American Yacht Racing Union and ,as will be seen, played an important role in leading the adoption of the new IOR Rule.

Olin Stephens and Dick Carter, both experienced and well-known naval architects and designers of many successful ocean racing yachts, not only were major contributors to the content of the Rule, but also assisted in gaining its adoption, and later defending it.

Robert N. Bavier was President of NAYRU during 1966-67 and was a strong proponent of one international rule, a position he also advocated as Editor of Yachting *magazine. After adoption of the Rule, he was an outspoken authority both for the Rule and for changes he felt it needed.*

Arthur B. Homer was the long-time Chairman of the CCA Measurement Committee which reviewed and tested the proposed IOR Rule. He came to support it, and was one of the original U.S. delegates to the Offshore Racing Council. I wore quite a number of hats. I was Vice President of NAYRU in 1968-71, President in 1972-74, and also I had organized, and for several years, leading up to and including 1969, chaired the NAYRU Offshore Racing Committee. I served on the CCA Measurement Rule Committee in 1954-1970. I was Vice Commodore of CCA in 1970-71 and Commodore in 1972-73.

On January 16, 1969 the CCA Board of Governors adopted the recommendations of Commodore Ewing that: (l) CCA should request the International Technical Committee [of the Offshore Racing Council] to finalize the Rule as soon as possible; (2) that, when in final form, the Rule should be reviewed by the CCA Measurement Committee, which should test it for effect on various types of yachts and report its conclusions to the Board of Governors; (3) that the Board should then decide whether or not to administer it in this country, and (4) that only if the Rule was adopted and met its obligations to the yachtsmen of this country, should CCA phase out our rule making functions. In a position paper the CCA cited "that an internationally accepted measurement rule would be of great benefit to the sport of off-shore racing:" "Scantlings, previously a heavily weighted factor in the RORC Rule, and objectionable to American designers and yachtsmen, will appear in the new Rule only as a deterrent to dangerously light construction, if at all."; "The second unresolved matter of consequence, and still under study, is inclining (as a test of stability and righting moment) and the value given it… Sail area measurements will adhere closely to those of the present CCA Rule. Girth measurements will be similar to those used in the RORC Rule, although substantially modified to discourage pinched in ends." In conclusion, "Commodore Ewing stressed his concern for the Cruising Club's responsibility to the 1,500 or more yachtsmen now holding CCA Measurement Certificates."

Michael relates how, after expressing his reservations that "RORC boats did not have the combination of racing and cruising qualities that the CCA Rule produced", and his concerns over what type the IOR Rule favored and "about how flexible the administration of the proposed Rule would be in terms of meeting and adjusting for design developments and discovered loopholes," he was finally persuaded to join the team of Clayton Ewing, Fred Adams and Olin Stephens as an advocate of the Rule. Later when the Rule was adopted he served as Deputy Chairman of the Offshore Racing Council.

On May 22, 1969 the CCA adopted the IOR Rule for the 1970 Bermuda Race. With the concurrence of NAYRU it also nominated Arthur B. Homer and Robert L. Hall, former Offshore Director of NAYRU, as the U.S. representatives to the ORC, the first meeting of which occurred April 4, 1970. To deal with numerous complaints concerning the Rule, such as the Rule favoring light displacement unduly, Michael arranged on behalf of the St. Francis Yacht Club a meeting at Tinsley Island[24] September, 1971 at which thirteen countries were represented. The recommendations of the conference respecting hull depth measurement, an increase in the cost of the fore triangle area, a more accurate evaluation of swing keels and trim tabs and a method of measuring hull curvature to close the loophole benefit that bumps had been getting were adopted by the ORC in November in the form of IOR Mark III.

Nonetheless, complaints continued from American yachtsmen, and only after pressure from Commodore Ewing and Robert Symonette of Nassau, Bahamas was the Southern Ocean Racing Circuit dissuaded from abandoning the Rule. Both SORC and the Chicago Yacht Club adopted age allowances for the older boats. An example of taking advantage of a loophole in the rule was Jerry Milgram's cat ketch which resulted at the 1972 ORC annual meeting in the imposition of a 10 percent increase in rating on the cat ketch rig. At that meeting Gordon Curtis from Southern California was elected to the Council.

In 1973 Lynn Williams of Chicago prepared an extensive paper, pointing out that even if ratings of yachts were perfect, [but] the time allowance systems by which ratings were translated into handicaps were imperfect, the combined result might be imperfect (Note that this consideration became a major feature in the calculations of race results a decade or so later.)

During 1973-74 Michael and Edwards had frequent exchanges over problem areas with the Rule including:

Elimination of the practice of keeping the Rule effective for fixed periods of time

Trim at time of measurement;

Displacement, particularly ultra light displacement;

Use of micro balloons to alter hull shape at measurement points;

Propellor allowances;

Sail area in relation to waterline and evaluation of sail area;

Measurement of stability;

Measurement of after end of L.

Further input came from California yachtsman Allen Puckett via Jim Kilroy, and in January, 1974 the CCA Board of Governors adopted a resolution urging the ORC and its International Technical Committee to resolve promptly the items that had been submitted in 1973. In the interim, at Jim Michael's recommendation, Olin Stephens was made a 'Councillor of Honor,' a recognition well deserved for his untiring efforts in producing, defending and amending the Rule.

At the November, 1974 meeting failure of the ORC to implement many of the items in the CCA resolution widened "the dichotomy between the British and the Americans respecting amendments to the Rule." The CCA, for example, unilaterally adopted its own amendments to the IOR Rule for the 1976 Bermuda Race. Ironically, Michael a few years later relates:

> *I am somewhat amused to find in my file a memorandum in May, 1978 from David Edwards to members of the Council pointing out that there were complaints that the IOR Rule produced a type of yacht that was unsuitable for cruising, which was not in the long term interest of the sport; that the trend to very light displacement had led to safety problems; and the Council should be free to modify the Rule at frequent intervals to take into account the latest design trends. Almost a decade had passed and these were some of the same problems that we had faced almost from the outset of the Rule.*

INTERNATIONAL MEASUREMENT SYSTEM (IMS)

On the American side a major effort was under way in the 1970's aimed at providing a handicapping rule for the purpose of putting the older designs on a level footing with newer designs by providing multiple time allowances for each yacht, instead of a single number handicap, taking into account that certain sizes and types of boats do better than others in certain weather conditions and in different combinations of upwind and offwind courses. This concept, introduced by Lynn Williams at a meeting of NAYRU and with significant contributions by MIT, especially Professors Jake Kerwin and Nick Newman, eventually became known as the Pratt Project because of the interest and support provided by Commodore H. Irving Pratt. The Pratt Project produced not just a new rating rule, initially called the Measurement Handicapping System (MHS), but also a new system of measurement. Utilizing transits fitted with special heads linked to a tape recorder, multiple hull measurements could be taken and the data fed into the MIT computer program resulting in the complete lines of the boat and yielding such critical factors as displacement, righting moment when heeled to 100 degrees, etc. This represented a great improvement, although perhaps not perfection, in obviating, as Olin Stephens puts it, "the inconsistencies I saw as a designer between the weighed displacement and the floated water line." The component that became the keystone to the time allowance system was a speed predictor (VPP) for yacht's optimum performance. The VPP or Velocity Prediction Program was developed as a means to predict the speed of a yacht in various wind conditions and on different courses. The latest scientific data, including especially tank test data, was used to develop the VPP, and as more research results have become available, it has been further refined. Using the VPP, yachts racing under MHS would be scored against their own predicted speed potential. In 1985 the ORC adopted the rule renaming it the International Measurement System (IMS). IMS incorporated optional regulations for use by race committees governing a range of items affecting performance such as accommodations, bending and raking of masts, banning bloopers, crew weight limitations, sail inventory and so forth. For a while IOR was used for leading events and IMS for traditional yachts - a distinction that became more and more difficult to define. The status of the two rules is commented on below.

DAVID EDWARDS:

Is it possible or desirable to continue to organize racing on the basis of one international rule? Just as the USA soon became disillusioned with IOR, so some countries like Britain and France have not felt happy with IMS. After ten years there are still problems with hull measurement in practice, and the "scoring" system for producing results from ratings has been unpopular. Race Committees have found great difficulty in using the VIP program as intended by establishing the weather conditions for a race. Competitors dislike not knowing where they stand when part way round the course.[25]

Above all a development or design rule is seen as adding yet more to the expense of racing offshore at a time when the cost of grand prix racing has been escalating with the ever increasing role of professionals. These developments have almost driven out the private owner from the top class.

Is the day of an International development rule over? Will one design be seen as the future of top level racing? This seems to be what the professionals want anyway.

JAMES MICHAEL:

As I look back over the years, I am persuaded that in the beginning we on the American side were so anxious to bring about a single international rating rule, that we were beguiled into believing that such a rule, (a) while it would produce some differences from the type of yacht under the CCA Rule, still would allow a dual purpose racing/cruising yacht, and (b) that, like the administration of the of the CCA Rule, we could expect constant surveillance of the IOR Rule to assure that new developments in design and discovery of loopholes would not produce inequities in racing results. When it finally became apparent that neither of these objectives would be obtained, and that much of what was done to meet specific problems was only cosmetic, sponsoring organizations in the United States began deserting the IOR – in the first instance by writing their own amendments to the Rule and later by taking on the new MHS (later IMS) Rule or some other rule in its place.Today, the IOR Rule, as a single international rule, no longer truly exists. What started out with great objectives and broad and enthusiastic support, could not survive the strong underlying differences between the constituents on the two sides of the Atlantic Ocean.

The dilemma is epitomized in an observation in *A Century of Sailing, The History of the Royal Victoria Yacht Club*:

Fewer and fewer people were willing or able to make the commitments of time and money that serious racing required. New materials might make a boat faster and new equipment might give the skipper an added edge, but they did not come cheap. And somehow that took some of the fun out of competition.

Notwithstanding the euphoria in North American waters over its launching, IMS has not gained similar popularity in British and European waters where the Channel Handicap System (CHS) and the Scandinavian Rule, more akin to a handicapping system like PHRF in North America, are used for a much larger proportion of racing than IMS.

ROBERT SARTY FROM A CLUB'S VIEWPOINT

Chief Measurer in Nova Scotia, Robert Sarty's perception of the rating rule options for club sailing appeared in the Royal Nova Scotia Yacht Squadron newsletter, *Binnacle*, and typify the quandary of yacht clubs with fleets of small to medium yachts:

> *Our fleet is almost all old IOR designs with a few other boats that were not designed to any rule mixed in. For us the IMS works reasonably well... Our local performance handicap system... A.S.P.N. (Atlantic Speed Potential Number System) has been around... since before WW II. The principal differences between A.S.P.N. and PHRF are that A.S.P.N. has a well laid out manual describing exactly how the handicaps should be derived while the PHRF handicappers manual merely shows the resultant numbers of a large number of fleets, but not how each fleet derived those numbers. The other difference is that the A.S.P.N. handicaps are applied solely upon the duration of time it takes for a yacht to go around the course on a percentage basis; while the PHRF numbers are time allowances based upon the length of the course*[26]*... The A.S.P.N. is quick and easy (to calculate) and just as fair; multiply the yachts' elapsed time around the course by its handicap, express-ed as a percentage and you have its corrected time. PHRF has yet to prove itself under any great pressure because it has always had another rule to take the keen competitive racing pressure at the top... In conclusion I believe that it would be a great shame if the IMS were allowed to cease and leave us only with performance handicaps that we know to be flawed in other ways... In the 1980's our A.S.P.N. system became a contributing fleet to the USYRU national PHRF system.*

How to preserve IMS, which is generally recognized as doing a commendable job of enabling older and/or less extreme boats to remain competitive against the newer and popular, faster and more exciting 'IMS racing boat,' is the challenge currently being addressed by the ORC and numerous National Authorities – a goal that may be as perplexing and elusive as it has been for the past century. The objective, as Olin Stephens observes, is to dovetail the three parts that are integral to every rating rule, "the formula, the way measurements are taken and the time allowance formula." As he expressed in a recent letter:

> *I feel a terrible gap between the IMS as it is used and what it might be. I consider the principle so good that it must not be abandoned.*

Absent a solution, the trend towards level racing in one-designs may intensify.

That it has been this way from the beginning is quintessentialized by Daniel D. Strohmeier, past President of the Society of Naval Architects and Marine Engineers and past member of Cruising Club of America and NAYRU rating rules committees:

> *The complex laws of yacht behavior preclude the possibility of a perfect handicapping system under which skill alone will determine the winner among dissimilar yachts... Of all the technical disciplines in this world, yacht ratings and handicapping have probably the lowest coefficients of exactitude, and it is a Mexican stand-off as to which is lower... The typical rating rule is a stew consisting of theory, empiricism, practicality, vested interest, and emotion, all tossed in a pot and stirred together... Proof of this lies in the vast number of rules that have evolved over the years in a quest like that of the Holy Grail. This quest will continue as long as yacht racing continues.*

Star class fleet on the starting line off Barcelona. Inset: U.S. Sailing Team Star class gold medalists Hal Haenel and Mark Reynolds.

The U.S. Sailing Team. The Promise Fulfilled.

Deciphering the light shifting breezes off Barcelona as skillfully as they had navigated the gusting winds and high seas in Suyong Bay, South Korea, four years earlier, the members of the United States Sailing Team proved once again they are the most formidable sailors in the world.

The remarkable aspect of the Team's performance was not just its quality but its consistency. American sailors medaled in nine of ten events, more than any other sailing team in modern Olympic history. Then again, these results only extend a pattern established over the last four decades, during which the U.S. Sailing Team has dominated virtually every world championship and major international sailing event.

Steve Bourdow and Paul Foerster, silver medal winners in Flying Dutchman class.

To ensure that the Team continues its winning tradition over the next quadrennium, US SAILING, the Team's governing body, has increased the number of regattas and technical clinics it holds each year. These events attract more good young sailors each year and allow them to test and refine their technique.

Rolex is proud to support the efforts of US SAILING and its Team as they look forward to the 1996 Games in Georgia. There, they'll once again prove that endurance and performance under pressure are the key qualities in a championship sailor.

Not to mention a Rolex Oyster Perpetual timepiece.

ROLEX

Rolex Oyster Perpetual Yacht-Master Chronometer in 18kt gold with matching Oyster bracelet.
For more information about the U.S. Sailing Team write: US SAILING, P.O. Box 209, Newport, RI 02840.
Write for watch brochure. Rolex Watch U.S.A., Inc., Dept. RLX, Rolex Building, 665 Fifth Avenue, New York, N.Y. 10022-5383.
Rolex, ♛, Oyster Perpetual, Yacht-Master and Oyster are trademarks.

CHAPTER X

OLYMPIC SAILING[1]

For the 1924 Olympics in France IYRU stated that there would be only three events: Eight-Metre Class with crew of five; Six-Metre Class with crew of three; and a monotype less than five meters (16 feet) in length. They further stated that there could only be one entry from each nation and all crew members had to be from the country that they were representing.

The IYRU allowed the host country to designate the class to be used for the monotype but required the host country to furnish the boats so that even the poorer nations could compete in the yachting events of the Olympics.

The problem with the new arrangements was that the United States and Canada, who had participated in the track and field events of the previous Olympics, was not a member of IYRU. However, IYRU wanted to expand the Olympic yachting by attracting the other nations to participate.

Prior to 1924, only European countries had participated in the previous yachting events. For the 1924 Games 19 nations were represented. For the first time Spain, Argentina, Cuba, South Africa and Canada participated (Canada placed 18th).

1924 Olympic Yachting The Six and Eight-Metre Classes were sailed at Le Havre while the 17-boat monotype fleet was sailed on the Seine River at Meulan.

1928 Olympics in Holland The Six and Eight-Metre Classes were used again at Amsterdam sailing on the Zuider Zee off Muiden. This was the first time that the United States fielded an Olympic yachting team. In the Six-Metre Class the U.S. finished 6th out of 13. In the Eight-Metre Owen Churchill took 6th out of eight. One of his crew members was Manfred Curry who later gained fame for his books on yachting and aerodynamics. In the 12-foot dinghies the U.S. entry, Herman Whiton, ended up last in the ten-boat fleet.

1932 Los Angeles Olympics One-design racing was catching on throughout the world, and the Los Angeles organizers convinced the IYRU to add the dean of the one-design classes, the Star, which started in 1911. They furnished the Snowbird as the monotype, a boat 12 feet long with 102 square feet of sail.

In preparation for the Games the Canadians organized the Canadian Yachting Association in 1931 to help sailors participate in the Olympics. This was the first time that the Olympic yachting events had been held outside of Europe, and because of the worldwide depression only eleven nations participated. The races were sailed in Los Angeles Harbor; in the Eight-Metre Class; only the USA and Canada competed. Owen Churchill's Eight Metre, *Angelita* took a gold medal. *Angelita*, immaculately restored, featured at the 1984 Games where she led the sail pass at the opening ceremonies at Los Angeles. In the monotype only 11 countries competed of which Regional Dixon of Canada was 5th and Charles Lyon of the USA was 7th.

1936 German Olympics The yachting events were sailed in Kiel Fjord with 59 entries in the same four classes as in the 1932 Olympics except that the monotype was the new Olympia-Jolle.

Post World War II Olympics in 1948 in England The IYRU decided that the Eight-Metre Class was too expensive and replaced it with the three-man Dragon popular in Europe. They also added as a fifth event the two-man Swallow, a boat about the same size as the Star but with 30-percent less sail area.

At prior Olympics a standard high-point scoring system had been used with the boat getting credit for boats beaten in each race. The IYRU, however, came up with a new high-point, weighted system which gave more weight to the yachts which finished in the top positions – an incentive to take chances.

The Olympic yachting was held at Torquay on the southwest coast of England. Paul Smart, a 56-year-old lawyer from New York, and his 23-year-old son won the Star Class. Paul gained the distinction of being the oldest American ever to win an Olympic Gold Medal.

For the monotype the organizers furnished a newly-designed British boat, the Firefly. The dinghy is normally sailed by two persons so the skippers had their hands full trying to handle the mainsheet, jib, tiller and centerboard at the same time as well as bail. Ralph Evans, Jr, the USA entry, was leading going into the last race over Paul McLaughlin of Canada and only had to finish third to clinch the series. However, he finished second overall while a 20-year-old sailor from Denmark, Paul Elvström won the last race and the series.

1952 Enter the Finn. The Olympics were assigned to Helsinki, Finland and the IYRU decided one more time to keep the restricted-design Six-Metre, which had been in every Olympic yachting event from the beginning. Also retained were the two one-designs, the Star and Dragon, and the Swallow was replaced by the restricted-design 5.5 Metre. The Finnish Yachting Association was responsible for choosing the monotype and selected the Richard Sarby designed Finn which had outperformed the other prototypes.

The races were held in beautiful Helsinki Harbor. Paul Elvström won in the Finn because of the hiking technique which he had developed; most sailors were just sitting on the sidedeck instead of hiking on the sheer guard, as is customary today. NAYRU approved Ed Meliaka of Boston as the USA monotype entry. He had sailed well in dinghies and, most important, was willing to pay his own expenses to the Games. He, however, wound up 28th. Paul McLaughlin, who had represented Canada in the 1948 Games with a 5th, took 8th.

1956 The Antipodes With the exception of the two prior Olympics held in the United States all had been held in Europe making the 1956 Games at Melbourne the first in the southern hemisphere. The IYRU, because of their expense, dropped the Six-Metre and replaced it with the Sharpie, a 12-square-meter formula boat. The Dragon, Star and 5.5 Metre were retained, and because the Australians did not have a suitable dinghy and the Finn had proved to be such a great competitive boat, it also was retained as the monotype.

Unlike 1952, this was the first Olympic Yachting event in which shipping was free so competition in the trials was intense. The finals in the Finn were held at Point Claire Yacht Club, Pointe Claire, Montreal and won by John Marvin with George O'Day second thereby becoming the USA representative and alternate. Bruce Kirby, later to be the designer of the Laser and editor of *One Design Yachtsman* (now *Sailing World*) was selected as the Canadian representative.

Twenty-two countries sent entries for the monotype and again Elvström slaughtered the opposition gaining his third consecutive Gold Medal. Even though John Marvin had never sailed an international Finn regatta, he was just nosed out by Belgian Andre Nelis in the last race for second place.

Major changes Although NAYRU had finally become a full member of IYRU in 1952 and had adopted on its own the 'Vanderbilt Racing Rules' in 1948 in an attempt to simplify and clarify the rules, it was not until 1960 that the IYRU and NAYRU finally reunified the rules. Another problem was that the IYRU administered sailing through National Authorities, but NAYRU was a multinational organization. Canada had remedied this problem by establishing the Canadian Yachting Association. NAYRU, on the other hand, under the leadership of Henry S. Morgan assumed the role of the United States National Authority.

Recognizing that other nations, including Canada, were subsidizing their sailors to participate in the Olympics, whereas U.S. contestants were limited to those who could afford to pay their own expenses and the cost of shipping a boat, Henry S. Morgan formed the United States International Sailing Association to raise funds to defray such expenses. The result was that 454 sailors tried out for Olympic berths in 1960 compared to 199 in 1956.

1960 Naples, Italy The IYRU dropped the Sharpie and added the two-man Flying Dutchman retaining the 5.5 Metre, Dragon, Star, Flying Dutchman and Finn. The Finn Class was attracting young athletic sailors in the U.S. with 30 competing in the trials at Marblehead. A young Peter Barrett from the University of Wisconsin won and Ian Bruce was selected to represent Canada.

1964 Hayama, Japan The IYRU kept the same classes and approved the furnishing of Japanese-built GRP Finns instead of ones with wooden hulls. Peter Barrett won the USA trials with Henry Sprague selected as alternate. At the Games Peter Barrett fought it out for second place with Danish sailor, Henning Wind. In the last race Willy Kuhweide from the Republic of Germany eluded them, and they finished 7th and 10th respectively.

1968 Acapulco, Mexico The IYRU introduced the low-point scoring system which awards bonuses for the first six finishers. The classes remained the same, i.e. 5.5 Metre, Dragon, Star, Flying Dutchman and Finn. The USA entry in the latter was Carl Van Duyne. The 1964 Finn Silver Medal winner, Peter Barrett, crewed for Lowell North in the Star Class in which they won a Gold Medal.

1972 Kiel, Germany All the boats in future Olympics were to be one-design classes. The IYRU kept the Flying Dutchman and Finn and, since teams had prepared for the games in them, decided to allow the Stars and Dragons to compete one more time. The three-man keel boat, Soling, was chosen over the Etchells 22 to replace eventually the Dragon, and likewise the two-man keel boat, Tempest, to replace the Star; the 5.5 Metre was dropped.

Ed Bennett won the USA Finn trials on Buzzards Bay with Lou Nady as alternate, and John Clarke from Toronto represented Canada. In the Soling Class Buddy Melges with Bill Bentsen and Bill Allen as crew won a Gold Medal in the Soling for the USA and Glen Foster and Peter Dean won a Bronze in the Tempest.

In 1974 NAYRU established a U.S. Sailing Center at Association Island on Lake Ontario near Watertown, NY to provide a facility to promote and train Olympic sailors (it ceased operations in 1979). In January, 1975 NAYRU was dissolved and the U.S. Yacht Racing Union was established amicably severing ties with the Canadian Yachting Association. USYRU reorganized the U.S. Olympic Yachting Committee and took complete charge of preparation for the Games which had been partially in the hands of the Classes.

1976 Kingston, Ontario This was the first time that the Olympic yachting events were sailed on fresh water except for the monotype held on the Seine River in 1900 and 1924. In preparation for the Olympics the CYA established an annual Olympic classes regatta at Kingston, Ontario in 1969 known as CORK. Its purpose was to assist North American sailors to prepare, as well as give the organizers experience in conducting, an Olympic regatta, and it has became an annual fixture attracting competitors from many nations.

Peter Commette represented the USA in the Finn with Gus Miller as runner-up. Randy Riley represented Canada. IYRU dropped the Star and Dragon and added the two-man centerboarder, the 470, and the two-man Tornado as the first multihull in the Games.

Clinics In 1981 Pat Healy, a midwestern Finn sailor, who was a sailing coach at the U.S. Naval Academy, was hired by the Canadian Yachting Association as the Canadian Olympic yachting coach. He in conjunction with U.S. coach, Gus Miller, organized a clinic at the Ontario Sailng Center prior to the Olympics to help Finn sailors from the third world countries prepare for the Olympics. Likewise the U.S. Olympic Yachting Committee started providing clinics before major regattas to help improve the performance of sailors. Miller soon became a leading progenitor of clinics worldwide for the IYRU.

1984 California The USA trials in the Finn Class were marred by the infamous Russ Silvestri case in which he was protested by John Bertrand for harassing him while Silvestri was a PMS who had not re-started. The YMP for Bertrand put him ahead of Buzz Reynolds making him the USA representative. In the Canadian trials Terry Neilson beat out Lawrence Lemieux for the monotype berth, whereupon Lemieux won a berth in the Star. Bertrand won the Silver Medal and Neilson the Bronze. Owen Churchill and the Eight-Metre, *Angelita*, in which he competed in the 1932 Games were honored.

1988 Pusan, Korea Under the leadership of Andy Kostanecki the U.S. Olympic Yachting Committee arranged subsidizing for several Finn sailors to compete in regattas in Europe and sponsored clinics preceding many of the major regattas held in the USA.

In 1987 USYRU under the leadership of James M. Schoonmaker, II and Mario Bustamante established a sailing center in Coconut Grove, Miami to conduct regattas in the Olympic Classes and provide training for Olympic hopefuls. The site was leased from the City of Miami, and unlike Association Island, can be used the year around.

IYRU added a Women's 470 event bringing the number of events to eight. In the monotype Brian Ledbetter, USA, and Lawrence Lemieux, Canada. placed 10th and 11th. Lemieux became 'Olympic Finn Hero – 1988' and "Was awarded an Olympic Medal of Valor by the International Olympic Committee when he rescued a crew member of a capsized 470 who had become separated from his boat."

1992 Barcelona, Spain The IYRU increased the number of events to ten of which the US medaled in nine. One of the new events was a women's only Sailboard event and the other was the Europe Dinghy for women only.

1996 Savannah, Georgia The Flying Dutchman Class was dropped and the Laser added. While the event was successfully staged thanks to the Herculean efforts of the race management in overcoming extremely complex logistical and administrative conditions, the good sailing weather that marked the pre-Olympic regatta did not materialize for the Games, nor was the USA Team able to preserve its record as the predominant medal winner. In fact the geographic spread of medal winners was a new feature for yachting. 1996 also represented the final presence of the veteran Star Class.

(For a complete record of North American participation see *Appendix 'D'*; unfortunately space does not permit similar coverage of the Pan American Yachting Teams).

N·A·Y·R·U

Official Measurement and Racing Rules

NORTH AMERICAN YACHT RACING UNION
Maritime Exchange Building
80 BROAD STREET NEW YORK, N. Y.

Price to Non-members, $3.00 Members, free

CHAPTER XI

JOINS IYRU AND BECOMES U.S. NATIONAL AUTHORITY

The process of NAYRU joining the International Yacht Racing Union was long in incubation, and much of the credit for NAYRU finally becoming a member goes to Henry S. (Harry) Morgan who for many years attended the annual meetings of the international body as an unofficial observer. The reluctance to join stemmed from the same concerns that at the inception of NAYRU had restrained the large clubs, such as New York and Eastern, joining NAYRU, i.e. apprehension of being subjected to outside control and entangling alliances.

At the 1950 annual meeting of NAYRU, when Morgan was President, a motion was made that:

Serious consideration be given to NAYRU taking membership in IYRU and that the Executive Committee report (on the question). Further, that the Racing Rules Committee investigate the subject of the discrepancies existing between the racing rules of IYRU and NAYRU.

Peter Scott, a member of the Permanent Committee of IYRU (and later President) was an observer at the meeting and spoke on the desirability of joining and of conforming the rules.

At the 1951 meeting Walter Rowe, who represented the Eastern Connecticut Yacht Racing Association and who had both served in London in Navy Intelligence and been a co-founder of frostbiting at the Essex Yacht Club CT, spoke as a strong proponent for joining and expressed optimistically that NAYRU would get more than one vote as a member. Note that paradoxically the Canadian Yachting Association already was a member of IYRU.

Reservations over joining expressed at the meeting were primarily:

NAYRU might be compelled to things against its will

NAYRU racing rules might be affected

Only one vote would be disproportionate to the number of yachts in North America vis-à-vis those in Europe and the U.K.

There followed a motion that the Executive Committee:

Expedite its action and investigation of the IYRU affiliation and report as quickly as possible.

Commodore Morgan attended the IYRU annual meeting that year to research the subject of membership.

At the 1952 annual meeting of NAYRU Morgan, respecting the racing rules, stated that Herman S. Whiton, noted Six-Metre skipper from the Seawanhaka Corinthian Yacht Club and U.S. representative in the single-handed dinghy in the 1928 Olympics, reported that the British-American Cup – an international team race series in Six-Metres – will be raced in the United States under the NAYRU rules. He recommended that NAYRU have a non-voting representation on IYRU Committees and a motion was adopted to that effect. Actually, NAYRU wound up becoming a full-fledged member and of the three votes allocated to North America it was accorded two under an informal agreement with the Canadian Yachting Association.

The racing rules, however, were not conformed on an international basis until 1960 when at the annual meeting of IYRU its Racing Rules Committee co-opted F. Gregg Bemis to its meeting at which J. Amory Jeffries (President of NAYRU 1957-61 was an observer. In hindsight,

NAYRU/USYRU, rather than being inhibited by this 'entangling foreign alliance,' became one of IYRU's most influential members – witness its contribution of the 'Vanderbilt' racing rules, the International Offshore Rule and so forth.

JUDGES AND SILVER OAR OF THE ADMIRALTY[1]

The High Court of Admiralty of England came into existence about 1360. Sometime during the next two centuries the Court adopted as its mace, or staff of office, a silver oar with elaborate carving on the blade. It was carried by the marshal as evidence of his authority to arrest vessels or to preside at the execution of pirates. As time went on, it became the custom of the British Navy for a seaman holding an ordinary oar to stand behind the commanding officer while he was conducting courts martial. Later it became the custom for an Admiralty judge to have on a rack in front of the bench a symbol of his authority – a small silver oar – while hearing cases. The custom is still followed in the Admiralty Court of London.

Before the Revolutionary War the Admiralty Courts of the ports of Boston and New York had similar oars. As a judge entered his courtroom, he would be preceded by the clerk carrying an oar on a purple pillow which he would place on the rack to signify that the court was in session. Only two of these oars have survived. The Boston oar, found in the basement of a church many years ago, is in the Museum of Fine Arts, and the New York oar, found in the cellar of a Massachusetts jailhouse, is in the Museum of the City of New York. A replica of the English oar was recently presented to the Federal Court in Ottawa at a special ceremony. Today during an Admiralty proceeding in Federal Courts of the United States the custom is sometimes continued by standing a plain oar opposite the national colors behind the bench or placing a miniature on the bench.

During 1979, when a committee was at work creating the judge's program for USYRU, member Jack Feller of San Francisco, unaware of the existence of the silver oar of the Admiralty Courts, devised the pin affixed with an oar which is worn on the jackets of US SAILING judges – a most fitting symbol.

The Canadian Yachting Association and US SAILING have developed procedures for certifying officials such as judges, instructors, race officers and similar for conducting programs of service to sailors. The persons performing these services become the personification of the National Authority, especially since they are one of the few categories of representatives of National Authorities with whom sailors come in direct contact.

EMERGENCE OF USYRU AS THE UNITED STATES NATIONAL AUTHORITY

While the factors that militated the forming of a national sports governing body for the United States were inevitably building, two Vice Presidents of NAYRU became the catalysts for initiating the move – Paul J. (PJ) Phelan from Toronto and Lynn G. Stedman, Jr. from Detroit. During luncheon at the 1974 annual meeting of NAYRU, held at the New York Yacht Club, Phelan gave an off-the-cuff, or so it appeared to be, harangue concerning the status of yacht racing in Canada vis-à-vis in the United States which impressed Stedman as being more than a merely impromptu delivery. Later he counseled President James Michael that it was becoming evident that the Canadian Yachting Association was doing a much more effective job serving the needs of Canadian sailors than it was possible for the multi-national NAYRU to do for U.S. sailors; an inherent conflict of interest was built into the structure that was hamstringing the growth of yachting in the U.S. He recommended addressing the situation before it got out of hand. He made the point that the CYA, for example, had created a national system for certification of instructors, their own national championships for men, women and youth, integrated training programs for their Olympic yachting team and so forth.

The upshot was the appointment by the Executive Committee of an ad hoc committee:

> *... to study, evaluate and recommend to the Executive Committee in what form and function activities of NAYRU representing the respective interests of the CYA and US sailing in international yachting affairs could best be organized to expedite these activities. The Committee was directed to keep in mind that in many areas the CYA, especially with Federal funding[2] has moved ahead of the U.S. and that in other areas U.S. sailors have suffered for lack of a National Authority to concentrate on their needs.*

The Report of the Committee, presented by Stedman to the Executive Committee at the January meeting in 1975, was most illuminating and set the stage for a major transition in the administration of yachting in North America:

> *The Committee was of the opinion that the lack of a U.S. National Authority inhibits recognition and support of U.S. sailors by reason of NAYRU serving two masters – U.S. and Canada.*
>
> *It was agreed that the preponderance of the business of NAYRU Committees deals with U.S. sailing activity, but that too often the portion of the business of Committees dealing with multi-national affairs constitutes a block to full development and support of U.S. interests and needs.*
>
> *As a result of hypothesizing a U.S. [national authority] to administer all activities directly related to U.S. sailing, it was determined that the residue of business remaining for the existing NAYRU Committees would relate primarily to the North American Championships in which the CYA basically has little or no interest inasmuch as it already conducts its own National Championships. To the degree that coordination is needed for joint U.S.-Canada sailing activity conducted on contiguous waters, provision for this already exists in the Pacific International Yachting Association, Lake Yacht Racing Association, St. Lawrence Yacht Racing Association and would continue to function regardless of the existence of NAYRU.*
>
> *... the United States Olympic Committee has made drastic changes[3] in its organization, the essence of which is that the governing power will be transferred to the National Sports Governing Bodies concerned with sports on the Olympic and Pan American Games calendars. Under our present structure it might be claimed by the USOC that we are not a national organization, and we would thereby lose our position among the governing powers.[4]*
>
> *It is the recommendation of our Committee that we become national in nature, and authority. We suggest that our name be changed to United States Yacht Racing Union...*
>
> *It is further recommended that our championships be conducted by the USYRU on the present association basis. Thus, if a Canadian Club has an entry in a local association's quarter-finals, and is the winner, it will proceed to the semi-finals, etc. It is the suggestion that the names of these events be changed if they now imply 'North American Championship.' The Mallory activities should be handled...(according to) the procedure outlined in Dick (Richard S.) Latham's report...*
>
> *The Offshore activities should continue as at present with regards to the issuance of certificates, etc. There should be no need for Canada to duplicate our extensive facility. We can continue to serve all on a fee basis.*
>
> *Recognizing that the IYRU includes North America in Area 'G', it would be anticipated that Canada would continue to occupy one seat on the Permanent Committee (currently Council) and the United States two.[5]*
>
> *With these thoughts in mind, Harry Anderson and your Chairman met on the 7th of January in Toronto with Paul Phelan, Sicotte Hamilton Senior Vice-President of CYA, Terry Phillips Executive Director of CYA, Michael Clifford and David Uhl. We presented the thoughts as stated above as far as they pertained to our relationships with Canada, and received complete and enthusiastic agreement.*

Lynn G. Stedman, Jr., President NAYRU/USYRU, 1975 - 1977
Photo courtesy of Lynn G. Stedman, Jr.

Paul "P. J." Phelan, twice President of the Canadian Yachting Association and Vice President of NAYRU
Photo David Lee

> *It was then suggested by Michael Clifford that we establish a Joint Commission to act as liaison between the two national organizations. It was felt that three persons should be chosen by each authority, and that the first Chairman should be Paul Phelan...*

Stedman's Committee had laid the groundwork for the transition with the meticulous care that was to be characteristic of him when he assumed the Presidency of USYRU and subsequently orchestrated a major restructuring of the table of organization and modus operandi of the Union. The recommendations were adopted for action at the January 1975 annual meeting. It seems fitting that Paul Phelan, having 'broken the ice' on the subject at the 1974 meeting, set the stage at the 1975 meeting for implementation of the Stedman report with a memorable review of the historic relationship between the two nations – a joint relationship probably unique in the annals of an international sport. His long career devoted to the affairs of yachting in Canada included Presidency of CYA in 1960,[6] President again in 1990, past Commodore of the RCYC, a long-time delegate to the International Yacht Racing Union and Chairman of its Youth Sailing Committee, a competitor in classes including the International Fourteen, Dragon and Canada's Cup yachts as well as member of syndicates for America's Cup challengers and offshore racing. President James Michael, when inviting Phelan to speak, expressed his personal viewpoint:

> *... this action (adoption of the Report) has to be done, if it is to be done, with the complete blessing and support of our friends in Canada.*

Phelan responded:

> *For many years in our two countries sailors on contiguous waters carried on a close liaison through their mutually established area associations: Pacific International Yachting Association, Lake of the Woods Yacht Racing Union, Lake Yacht Racing Association, hundred-year-old Yacht Racing Union of the Great Lakes, St. Lawrence Valley Yacht Racing Association, Nova Scotia Yacht Racing Association, etc.*
>
> *In 1925 Canadians assisted in the formation of NAYRU to foster development of the sport on this Continent...*
>
> *In 1931 we formed the CYA to act as our national voice. (See George H. Gooderman's letter in Appendix G.)*
>
> *Sir Winston Churchill grumbled and growled to the effect that 'he did not become the Queen's First Minister to preside at the demise of the British Empire...'*
>
> *I feel as Sir Winston must have felt, grumbly and growly. The proposed change in our association is probably inevitable, and yet Canada will lose the privilege of sharing closely with so many great sailors in NAYRU.*
>
> *We, as Canadians, feel that we have never really contributed to the sport as much as our American cousins, and yet we have been honoured and privileged to share our mutual deliberations... It has become obvious that our sport will grow and prosper if we go our separate ways...*
>
> *One does not lightly put aside the comradeship we have built up over these past fifty years. Our sport gives to us, in a unique way; shared challenges draw us together, and yet it is probably inevitable that we go our separate ways.*
>
> *Our sport will be stronger if we do so.*
>
> *... Together, and in harmony, the United States Yacht Racing Union and the Canadian Yachting Association will be a source of strength for our sport in the World. Tonight, let us all toast – "Sailors Everywhere."*

The concept of the special Liaison Committee soon fizzled out, most likely because the severance had been so smooth and clean that there was lack of an agenda requiring joint action.

Paul Phelan had noted in an aside:

> *The replacement of the Vanderbilt rules with the IYRU rules made this day inevitable. The new rules freed the CYA to grow to its natural fulfillment.*

The need for a uniform code of racing rules, of course, had been one of the principal incentives for the formation of NAYRU, especially in waters where Canadian and U.S. clubs compete together. What he was referring to was the period from 1948, when the two countries adopted the rules that Harold S. Vanderbilt had forged and hammered out largely on his own initiative over a decade[7] and literally forced on NAYRU, to 1960 when they were adopted by IYRU. While they were far superior to the IYRU rules of 1948, it meant that for 12 years our two countries sailing under different rules from those of the rest of the world had become more inter-dependent than ever before. That situation was resolved by the indefatigable work of Gregg Bemis for NAYRU and Gerald Sambrooke-Sturgess of the U.K. at the IYRU committee level, and Henry S. Morgan and H.M. King Olav V of Norway at the ministerial level, in convincing National Authorities of the merits of the new rules. Their adoption by IYRU was one more loosening of the bands that had tied Canada and the U.S. together.

Paul Phelan, when he assumed the Presidency of CYA 15 years later, recapitulated:

> *... (Thirty years ago) they told me to go to New York and become a Vice President of the North American Yacht Racing Union and to make the Canadian Yachting Association as 'sister' organization of NAYRU. It took me ten years to do it, but it was done; we put NAYRU to bed and created the United States Yacht Racing Union, which brought new vitality to yachting in the United States, and yet our old trans-border associations are all still safely in place and both associations are now eligible for their respective national funding which we here in Canada so desperately need.*

JUNIOR OLYMPICS
1997
US SAILING
OFFICIAL USOC AND US SAILING LICENSED PRODUCT 36 USC

CHAPTER XII

USYRU TO THE PRESENT, A SUMMARY

It is as difficult to chronicle the developments of the last 20 years in a few pages as it is to chronicle the development of yacht clubs, classes, sailing associations, measurement rules, and their impact upon the sport in these few chapters. Nevertheless, some observations of the events of recent years is essential.

The enactment of the Amateur Sports Act of 1978 by the U.S. Congress, which empowered the United States Olympic Committee to appoint National Governing Bodies (NGBs) for each of the Olympic sports, had a profound effect upon our sport in the United States. The recently transformed USYRU became the NGB for sailing. Unlike some sports, whose NGBs concentrate solely upon Olympic participation, USYRU was already an "umbrella" organization (one which dealt with governance throughout the sport) at the time of its appointment. With that appointment came the responsibilities of compliance with the Congressional mandates, and the support of the United States Olympic Committee.

On the Olympic side, disappointment came first, with the U.S. boycott of the 1980 Olympic Games in Moscow, and the sailing venue in Talinn, Estonia. Four years later, however, at the 1984 Olympic Games in Los Angeles, the U.S. team, led by Olympic Yachting Committee Chairman Sam Merrick, medalled in every class. The 1984 Games also helped to ensure the continued success of the U.S. Olympic sailing team for years to come. Excess revenues from the 1984 Games were transferred to the USOC which, in turn, shared the financial windfall with the NGBs whose athletes had earned medals at the Games. The USOC then created the United States Olympic Foundation, which for most of the succeeding years under the guidance of former Secretary of the Treasury, William Simon, invested the moneys wisely for both the USOC and the member NGBs.

Over the past three Quadrennia, the USOC provided unprecedented support for each of the Olympic sports, most notably in the form of funding their NGBs' Olympic programs. In turn, incremental support was based upon performance of the sports' Olympic teams, and sailing benefited considerably in that support as a result of its Olympic performance. In the next three summer Olympic Games, the U.S. team won 16 medals (the 1988 team, led by OYC Chairman Andrew T. Kostanecki medalled in five of eight classes; the 1992 Team, led by OYC Chairman Michael B. Schoettle, medalled in nine of ten classes; only in 1996 did the team fail to achieve expectations, when the three returning medalists were unable to repeat. The two medals won were by new Olympians). The list of team members and results is contained in Appendix D.

At the same time, the Amateur Sports Act imposed obligations upon Olympic sports not only to govern, but to provide an infrastructure to support the sport over the longer term. While progress sometimes appeared to be agonizingly slow, given the history of the past 100 years we witnessed an invigorated effort to improve the quality of the sport over the past 20 years, an effort which may not have been possible absent the appointment of the association as a National Governing Body. Some indications:

US SAILING CENTERS

The US Sailing Center in Miami, FL, was designated as a U.S. Olympic Training Facility in 1996 – one of the few such sport-specific facilities in the nation. The effort was led by US SAILING President David H. Irish,

USOC delegate (later Secretary) Andrew T. Kostanecki, former US SAILING President William C. Martin, Vice President Mason Chrisman, board member James M. "Ding" Schoonmaker (a founder of the Miami center and 1989 recipient of US SAILING's Herreshoff Trophy), and former board member Beverly R. Carter.

Additional US Sailing Centers were established in Martin County, FL and Long Beach, CA.

TRAINING

In the early 1980's, USYRU initiated a program to train young sailors through a network of certified instructors. Initially developed to facilitate training in dinghies, particularly for yacht club junior programs, the program's structure consisted not only of instructors who teach at the local level, it also included Instructor-Trainers to qualify Instructors, and Master Instructor Trainers who train Instructor Trainers.

In 1988, the USYRU Training Committee developed an introductory handbook, *Start Sailing Right!*, which was adopted by the American Red Cross as its introductory sailing text, and became accepted as the standard for teaching beginning sailing throughout the United States. Other publications followed for the sport of windsurfing and various other aspects of training. By 1997, US SAILING's training materials had become the national standard for "learn to sail" and "learn to race" teaching and student curricula, and its Small Boat Sailor Certification Record Book (or "Little Red Book"), introduced in 1996, was adapted by the United States Navy in 1997.

In 1997, US SAILING Instructor-Trainers trained and certified more than 1,500 new instructors. Annually, those and previously certified instructors, in turn, taught thousands of new people how to sail, through commercial sailing schools, yacht clubs, community sailing programs, Boy Scout, Girl Scout, American Camping Association, American Red Cross, military MWR (Morale, Recreation and Welfare) programs, and other camps and associations.

It was the vision of Timothea ("Timmy") Larr, a noted sailor and tireless supporter of the development of a national training program (Mrs. Larr was awarded US SAILING's highest award, the Herreshoff Trophy, in 1992) to establish a National Faculty for the association. The National Faculty was to be responsible for creating national standards for training and certifying instructors and training students, and assisting other committees of US SAILING to develop training materials for their disciplines. Beginning with its first meeting at Oyster Bay, NY in November, 1992, the National Faculty and its parent Training Committee, guided US SAILING in the development of new instructional materials for students and instructors alike, and plans were underway for the development of a curriculum for a national Coaching College.

In 1993, representatives of a number of commercial sailing schools requested that US SAILING develop a comprehensive instructional program for adults who desire to learn to sail in keelboats. US SAILING, under the guidance of Training Committee Chair Susie Trotman and Vice President James P. Muldoon, and National Faculty Chair Timmy Larr undertook the development of the US SAILING Keelboat Certification System, directed at several levels of education ("learn-to-sail," basic and bareboat cruising, and coastal navigation). The first instructional level of the program (Basic Keelboat) was introduced in early 1995, and materials for three additional levels (through Coastal Navigation) were added in 1996 and 1997. By the summer of 1997, plans to complete the materials through offshore passagemaking were in development, and the National Association of State Boating Law Administrators had approved the contents of the introductory course as acceptable to the National Recreational Boating Safety Program.

Also in the early 1980's, USYRU initiated a National Junior Sailing Symposium to bring together junior program directors, instructors, and others involved with junior sailing to identify and resolve common issues. The NJSS attracted representatives from more than 130 camp, club, and community sailing programs each year.

RACE ADMINISTRATION

From its humble beginnings at NAYRU, where the chairman reported that no appeals had been received during its first year, the US SAILING Appeals Committee became the final arbiter of protest committee decisions and interpretation of the racing rules within the United States. Regional Sailing Association appeals committees issued intermediate decisions as a condition to appeal to the National Authority.

In the mid-1970's, USYRU began to recognize the need to improve the quality, consistency and fairness of decisions by protest committees who interpreted the racing rules at the local level. In 1977, USYRU created a program to certify judges, and invited experienced sailors to submit their qualifications for review. The Judges Program, administered regionally by Regional Administrative Judges, and nationally by the Judges Committee, certified 432 judges nationwide in 1997, and a national training and testing program was under development.

With the advent of on-the-water umpiring, created in 1987 and introduced nationally in 1988, the Judges Committee expanded its role to include certification of umpires. As of mid-1997, 51 umpires were certified by US SAILING.

Following the model developed for judges, USYRU instituted a national recognition program for experienced race officers in 1982. Certification of highly experienced race officers was adopted in 1994. As of mid-1997, US SAILING certified 34 race officers and recognized 447 others at two levels of expertise. As with the Judges Program, a national training program was being developed.

In the early 1980s, the Race Management Committee created the Race Management Handbook to assist local race officers in the procedures for conducting races. While it was initially a small text it accumulated a compilation of materials from various sources, and was revised in 1994. It became the definitive treatise on the management of sailboat races in the United States.

STRUCTURAL CHANGE

The change from a North American union to a national organization brought about the need to re-evaluate the structure of USYRU. A result was the development of the concept of Councils, representing various constituencies of the sport. From 1975 to 1997, the number of Councils increased to seven (one design classes, sailing associations, multihulls, offshore, and community sailing, and two independent organizations – the Intercollegiate Yacht Racing Association and the United States Windsurfing Association). The development of these Councils accommodated the expansion of USYRU, and later US SAILING, into other areas of the sport, some of which had not previously had direct representation on the Board of Directors.

Indicative of the desire to respond to the needs of a broader sailing constituency was the creation of the Community Sailing Council. Community sailing was originally a subset of USYRU's Training Committee. With the enthusiastic support of the Training Committee's Timmy Larr, representatives of community sailing conducted the first Community Sailing Conference in Boston in 1987 (during a blizzard). Recognizing the need to give the rapidly expanding community sailing programs a greater voice in US SAILING, and maintain the credibility of association with the NGB, US SAILING initiated an amendment to its by-laws in the spring of 1992, and passed it at the 1992 annual meeting in New Orleans, LA, creating the Community Sailing Council. The Council's by-laws were drawn during the winter of 1993, and ratified by the US SAILING Board at its Spring Meeting in 1993.

In addition to its annual Community Sailing Conference, the Council, the Training Committee, and the Commercial Sailing Committee, in cooperation with the US SAILING staff, began to publish a quarterly newsletter, *The Learning Curve*, directed specifically at issues of common interest to sailing schools, junior programs, and their instructors and students.

The development of councils as representative bodies gave rise to the development of divisional committees, responsible for the creation and implementation of programs within their specific disciplines (Inshore, Offshore, General Services, Olympic, Race Administration, and later Training). Over time, special committees and other associations have been formed as needed -- for example, the Sailors with Special Needs Committee, which addresses issues involving sailors with disabilities, and the Commercial Sailing Committee (now a subset of the Training Committee).

NAME CHANGE

As the role of USYRU expanded into areas outside of yacht racing, it became apparent to many that the name "United States Yacht Racing Union" no longer fully described the activities of the association. On March 24, 1991, the Board of Directors directed that an amendment to the USYRU by-laws, to change the name of the association to the United States Sailing Association, be initiated, circulated and placed on the agenda for the Fall 1991 Annual General Meeting. The Board separately directed that the Executive Committee investigate possible names under which the association would do business, which would include the word "sail" or "sailing."

Among the reasons given for the proposed amendment to the By Laws were: The word "yacht" was not clearly understood outside the sport; the word "racing" did not apply to every area in which the USYRU played a leadership role; the name United States Yacht Racing Union was long, sometimes confusing, and sometimes bore negative connotations; and communications with all sailing organizations and the sailing public, including participants in the sport and potential participants, was crucial to the organization's ability to lead and to govern the sport.

The amendment was considered on October 19, 1991, at the Annual General Meeting in Stamford, CT. President William C. Martin presided. Support for the amendment was by no means unanimous. A similar effort had failed the previous year. Of the 20 votes cast in opposition to the name change, 11 were by Yacht Racing Associations (23 YRAs supported the change). The Councils voted heavily in favor of the change. By a vote of 58 to 20, the amendment passed. On November 19, 1991, the Executive Committee resolved that US SAILING be used as the name of the organization, and the organization began conducting its business under that name.

It is interesting to note that the international federation for the sport later changed its name from the International Yacht Racing Union (IYRU) to the International Sailing Federation (ISAF). In the United States, many other organizations also followed suit, including at least one sailing association which had opposed the US SAILING name change, and the Yacht Racing Association Council (YRAC) soon changed its name to the Council of Sailing Associations.

ADDITIONAL EMPHASIS ON YOUTH

The Sears Cup (triple-handed) competition for junior sailors had been in existence for many years prior to the creation of the USYRU. The Bemis (double-handed) and Smythe (single-handed) trophy competitions had been added in 1975 and 1974, respectively. Like many US SAILING championships, these "ladder" events, required qualification through 36 regional associations and ten geographic Areas. Support by Rolex Watch, U.S.A., enhanced these events (and the Leiter event – see below) for many years. Although it later transferred its support to US SAILING's adult championships, Rolex left a lasting legacy for the benefit of these junior events.

A different format was introduced when the US Youth Championship was added in 1973. It soon became the nation's most elite youth sailing event. Applications to compete had traditionally been by resume only; however, in 1997, as the event became US SAILING's Junior Olympic National Championship, a change was allowed to accept a limited number of sailors by qualification from regional Junior Olympic pilot program events.

A third format, national women's open events, also proved to be popular. The Junior Women's Championship (for the Nancy Leiter Clagett trophy), a single-handed event, was introduced in 1980, and accepted as a US SAILING national championship in 1985. The Junior Women's Double-handed Championship (for the Ida Lewis Trophy) followed in 1996. In 1996 Mr. C. Thomas Clagett, a long time supporter of junior women's sailing, generously endowed both events in perpetuity.

Most recently, at its Annual General Meeting in October, 1996, the Board of Directors approved the implementation of the first stage of its Olympic Path program, designed to increase youth participation in sailing, better train sailors at a younger age, provide a coordinated nationwide opportunity for competition and recognition, and develop a clear path for the development of talented young sailors. The USOC endorsed US SAILING's proposed 1997 program as a Junior Olympic program, in March, 1997. The first stage, a series of regional Junior Olympic "pilot program" competitions and one youth sailing festival, took place during the summer of 1997.

MEMBER SERVICES

Perhaps the most significant development of the past 20 years was the ability of a National Governing Body to provide services and support for its members. In 1997, an individual US SAILING member enjoyed a number of benefits which were unheard of 20 years ago and were not generally available through membership in other sports organizations. Even so, most members still probably knew little of the programs and services which US SAILING was able to provide to sailors nationally because of those membership dues.

Nevertheless, the membership generally responded favorably to the individual attention and benefits which US SAILING increasingly provided. In 1982, the individual membership of USYRU was 15,080. It declined to 14,427 in 1983, and 13,882 in 1984. As of August, 1997, there are 36,972 individual members of US SAILING.

In 1989, President William C. Martin created the President's Club, which was comprised of members who made a commitment to pay substantially higher dues for a minimum of five years. In turn, a large percentage of those dues was earmarked for the support of worthy projects. President's Club membership rapidly grew to more than 100, and supported such projects as the development of simplified racing rules, scientific research, US observation of the selection trials for new Olympic boats, and creation of a film of sailing in the 1996 Olympic Games.

One of the primary needs of the increasing membership became better communication. The primary vehicle for communication for many years was a monthly magazine, *American Sailor*. While the magazine had taken various forms over time, in 1993 US SAILING formed an alliance with *Sailing World* Magazine to distribute both magazines to US SAILING members.

US SAILING also initiated a program in 1993 to increase visibility of the organization at various regattas throughout the United States by using representatives to staff booths at regatta sites. The primary purpose was to disseminate information about the NGB, but it proved equally effective at acquiring new members and was expanded to encompass several national and regional boat shows.

As communications technology increased, the use of personal computers and the Internet became important means of disseminating information. US SAILING adapted by creating an Internet website. The increase in youth membership spawned the creation of a new quarterly publication for youth, Junior Sailor in 1995. A proliferation of overlapping newsletters regarding various aspects of training, community sailing, commercial sailing, and information for sailing instructors was replaced in 1996 by *The Learning Curve*, a quarterly publication which addressed all of these aspects and was distributed to a constituency of over 5,000 sailing programs and instructors.

As US SAILING enters its second 100 years, it is a far different organization from that conceived to address common issues of rating and racing rules. The demands upon it come from many individual constituents, as well as member sailing associations and yacht clubs, sailing schools and other organizations. The demands for services have become far greater. The need for even better and more effective communication is paramount. The organization has continued to poise itself to meet future needs of the sport and its participants. If President Bavier's observation at the 1971 annual meeting continues to hold true for the next 100 years, we will make mistakes, even drop the ball occasionally, but seldom.

In the America's Cup, there is no second.
On this blue-water course, winner takes all.
Then, timing is priceless, if it makes the difference between winning and losing.
Which may explain why the superb Rolex Submariner has been the one
chronometer worn by all America's Cup defenders since 1958.
ROLEX
OFFICIALLY CERTIFIED SWISS CHRONOMETER
The Rolex Submariner Date, official America's Cup watch, self-winding
superlative chronometer, pressure-proof to 660 feet. In stainless steel with
matching bracelet, $725.* In 18kt. yellow gold, $5,300.*
For your free copy of the 64-page color Official Handbook, The America's Cup,
write Rolex Watch U.S.A., Inc., Rolex Building, 665 Fifth Avenue, New York, N.Y. 10022.
*Suggested retail price.

APPENDIX A

YACHT CLUBS PRE-1898 LISTED CHRONOLOGICALLY

1834 Boston #1 – lapsed 1837; reformed 1866 becoming oldest yacht club in New England

1836 Two 'Halifax Regattas' held in August; notices of race extant; earliest record of yacht races in North America.

1835 Boston Boat Club – lapsed 1837

1837 July 1 Halifax Yacht Club 1857 Royal; 1876 became Royal Nova Scotia Yacht Squadron and oldest yacht club in North America

1842 Detroit Boat Club first regatta; nee 1839 as rowing club; oldest yacht club extant in U.S.

1844 New York first regatta Newport, RI; oldest U.S. yacht club without a break since its founding

1846 Royal Bermuda Yacht Club never member NAYRU; Bermuda Isles source of Bermuda/Marconi rig

1847 Midshipmen Boat Club U.S. Naval Academy as rowing club; 1936 reorganized as sailing club

1849 Southern founded at Pass Christian; located Lake Ponchartrain New Orleans; nee 'Stingaree'

1850 Neptune - Highlands NJ

Mobile - AL

1852 Chesapeake - Baltimore

Pioneer - San Diego; lapsed

Royal Canadian - started as Toronto Boat Club; became Toronto Yacht Club; Royal 1854

Tarpon Springs - FL

1853 Carolina - Wilmington NC

1855 Pacific #1 - San Francisco short-lived; held two regattas 1856

Pioneer - San Francisco - aka #1 San Francisco Yacht Club; lapsed post 1859; #2 SFYC 1869

1856 Hoboken - NJ

1857 Brooklyn - NY second to New York Yacht Club in size and number of yachts

1858 Jersey City - NJ

1860 Buffalo - NY

Oakland #1 - San Francisco; lapsed

1861 Quebec

1864 Neenah -WI after 1894 joined Nodaway as Neenah-Nodaway

Union - Long Island NY 1872 became Long Island Yacht Club

1865 Atlantic in Brooklyn, NY founded by members of Brooklyn Yacht Club

Hudson Boat - Jersey City

Ione - NY

Raritan - NJ

Riverton - NJ

1867 Columbia - NY west side Manhattan

Detroit; 1882 split off from Michigan Yacht Club on Belle Isle

Savannah; 1869 Savannah Yacht and Country Club

Master Mariners Benevolent (aka Protective) Assn; inactive 1880-83 and 1886-90; long history of regattas

Inland - WI; lapsed 1875

1868 Lynn - MA

South Boston; second oldest in New England

1869 Bunker Hill - Boston tied with Portland Yacht Club as third oldest in New England

Delaware Yacht Navy

New Hamburg - NY

Oceanic City - NY

San Francisco #2 (see 1852 Pioneer); first permanent yacht club on West Coast

Pavonia - Bayonne NJ

Portland - ME tied with South Boston as third oldest in New England

Williamsburgh - NY

1870 Biloxi - MS -

Dorchester - MA

Eastern - Marblehead MA

Manhattan - NY (per W. P. Stephens)

Oskkosh - NY

Jeffries - East Boston

Stapleton - Staten Island

Yonkers - NY

1870/1 Daisy - WI
changed to Fond du Lac 1873

1871 New York Canoe Club

New Jersey - Hoboken

Milwaukee - WI

North Shore - Port Washington, Long Island Sound, NY

Seawanhaka Corinthian – Oyster Bay, Long Island Sound; merged with Oyster Bay Yacht Club 1892 as SCYC

St. Augustine - FL

Stevens - NY

Tom's River - NJ

Stuyvesant - NY

1872 Beverly - Beverly, MA
moved to Marion, Buzzards Bay

Old Club - Hansen's Island MD

Santa Barbara - Southern California; lapse until ca. 1920

Yale (University) - New Haven CT; 1893 became Yale Corinthian Yacht Club

Pensacola - FL;
per Hunt's Register; absent by 1900

1873 Albany - NY

Hudson River - NY

Sausalito - San Francisco; lapsed; reorganized 1910-1918

1874 Knickerbocker - Long Island Sound NY

Haverhill - MA

Quincy - MA

Lake Geneva - WI

Genesee - NY

Albany - NY

1875 Savin Hill - MA

Providence - RI
raced catamaran *Amaryllis* in New York City 1876 Centennial Regatta, (1877 Rhode Island Yacht Club?)

Chicago - IL

1876 Philadelphia; to Pennsylvania to Quaker City; lapsed 1980; then Philadelphia and split to Corinthian of Philadelphia

New Bedford - MA;
first yacht club on Buzzards Bay

Sippican - Buzzards Bay MA

Oconomowoc - La Belle Lake WI

Toledo - OH

Mantoloking - NJ

Monmouth Boat Club - NJ

Seattle - Puget Sound WA; reorganized 1890; merged with Elliott Bay 1909; second continuous on West Coast

Put in Bay - Lake Erie

Quaker City - Philadelphia lapsed 1980; then Philadelphia Yacht Club and split into Corinthian Yacht Club

Rochester - NY
became dormant and reactivated 1886

1877 Somerset - Dighton MA

Rhode Island Yacht Club - (nee Providence 1875?)

1878 Cleveland - OH

Pacific #2 - San Francisco; lapsed 1899

1879 Seattle - Puget Sound WA lapsed and reorganized 1892; merged with Elliott Bay 1909; 3d continuous West Coast yacht club

1880 Hull - MA

Lachmont - Long Island Sound NY

Lake Champlain - Burlington VT

American Canoe

pre-1881

Florida - Jacksonville

National - NJ

Pennsylvania - Philadelphia

Warwick - RI

1881 Oswego - NY

New Haven - CT

Michigan - formed by members of Detroit Yacht Club

Toronto - merged with Royal Canadian 1889

1882 Newark - NJ

Buffalo Canoe Club

1883 Harlem - NY

Carolina - Charleston SC

American - Long Island Sound NY

1884 Rochester - NY

Winthrop - MA
formerly Great Head

Yorkville - NY

Great Head - MA - later Winthrop

Salem Bay - MA

Bay of Quinte - Belleville ONT

Bohemia - Long Island Sound NY

East River - Manhattan NY

1885 American - Newburyport MA

Bar Harbor - ME

Bay Shore - Long Island Sound NY

Chesapeake Bay - MD

Glenada - Cold Spring Harbor, Long Island NY

Ohio - Presque Isle

Onondaga - upstate NY

New Rochelle - Long Island Sound NY

Corinthian - Marblehead MA

Hawaii Yachting and Rowing Association

Sandy Bay - Anisquam MA

1886 Corinthian - Tiburon, San Francisco Bay

Chelsea - MA

Corinthian - Staten Island NY

Shelter Island - east end Long Island NY

Essex - NJ

San Diego – combined with San Diego Rowing Club

Atlantic - Coney Island NY

Queen City - Toronto

1887 Burrard Inlet Sailing Club - Puget Sound; lapsed and 1891 became British Columbia YRA; lapsed 1894; 1897 became Vancouver Yacht Club #1; lapsed and 1903 became Vancouver Yacht Club #2; Royal in 1906

Houston - TX;
oldest yacht club in Texas

New Jersey Athletic

1887 Biscayne Bay - Coconut Grove FL; founded on Key Biscaye Lat. 25N; farthest south yacht club in North America

Douglaston Yacht Squadron - Long Island Sound NY

Carnarsie - Long Island NY

Port Moody - Puget Sound

Shattemuc Yacht and Canoe - NY

Pleon - Marblehead MA; first independently incorporated Junior Club

Tappan Zee - NY

1888 Mosquito Fleet - South Boston

Royal St. Lawrence - Lake St. Louis, Dorval (vic. Montreal)

Riverside - Long Island Sound CT

St. Johns - Quebec

Bay Head - NJ

Duluth - MN

Providence Corinthian - RI

Royal Hamilton - Toronto

Chula Vista - San Diego lapsed 1930's; reformed later

1889 Houston Launch Club - TX (might have been earlier and become Houston Yacht Club)

Yonkers Corinthian - NY

Corinthian Fleet - New Rochelle NY

Great South Bay - south shore Long Island NY

Indian Harbor - Long Island Sound CT

San Diego - CA

White Bear - MN

Minnetonka - MN

Queen City - Toronto

Excelsior - Brooklyn NY

Buffalo Canoe Club - Ontario NY

Horshoe Harbor - Long Island Sound CT

Tacoma - WA lapsed 1893; reorganized 1908

Corinthian Fleet - Long Island Sound, New Rochelle NY

Tower Ridge - Hudson River NY

1890 Fall River - MA

Encinal - Alameda CA

Squantum - MA

Stamford - Long Island Sound CT (may have been part of earlier Stamford Corinthian)

Chelsea - NY

Hempstead Bay - Long Island Sound NY

Lake Hopatcong - NJ

Inland American - Detroit MI

Weshampton - Eastern Long Island NY

Plymouth - MA

1891 Baltimore - MD

Hempstead Harbor - Long Island Sound NY

Lincoln Park - Chicago

Old Colony - MA

Piscataqua - ME

Searen Land and Water Club - NJ

Sea Cliff - Long Island Sound NY; was Seabird Yacht Club c. 1875 and lapsed

Staten Island - NY

1892 Anacorte - Puget Sound (or earlier)

Fairhaven - Puget Sound (or earlier)

Jamaica Bay - Long Island NY

Anahuac Boat Club - Lake Xochimilco, Mexico formed by American sailors

Manchester - MA

Bay-Waveland - MS

Corinthian - split off from Philadelphia Yacht Club

Delaware -DE

Victoria - British Columbia; Royal in 1911

Columbia - Chicago

Corinthian - Atlantic City NJ

Conanicut - RI

Greenville - NY

New Whatcomb - Puget Sound

1892 Port Townsend - Puget Sound

Hobe Sound - FL

Poughkeepsie - NY

1892 Green Lake - WI

Huntington - Long Island Sound NY

Norwalk - Long Island Sound CT

Harvard (University) - Cambridge MA

Nodaway - WI later joined Neenah Yacht Club as Neenah-Nodaway Yacht Club

Cohasset - MA

Sandusky - OH

Huguenot - Long Island Sound NY

Duxbury - MA

Baltimore Corinthian - MD

Weetamoe - MA

Bay City - MI

1894 Burgess (?) - Marblehead MA

Cedar Point - Long Island Sound CT

Eilliott Bay - Puget Sound WA; merged with Seattle Yacht Club 1909

Erie - NY

Thousand Islands - St. Lawrence River NY

1895 Hartford - CT

Hingham - MA

Taunton - MA

1896 Wood's Hole - Buzzards Bay MA

Columbia - Boston

Pass Christian - MS

Kingston - Ontario NY

South Bay - San Francisco

Vancouver Boating Club - BC

Halifax River - Nova Scotia

Jackson Park - Chicago

Sachem's Head - Long Island Sound CT

Bridgeport - Long Island Sound CT

Maumee River - Lake Erie OH

Tarantine - ME

1897 MIT (University) - Cambridge MA

Sag Harbor - Long Island NY

St. Regis - Adirondacks NY

Royal Vancouver - nee Burrard Inlet Sailing Club 1887; lapsed and #1 Vancouver Yacht Club

APPENDIX B

YACHT CLUBS PRE-1898 LISTED ALPHABETICALLY

Albany - NY	1873
Alpha - DE	1874
American - Long Island Sound	1883
American - Newburyport MA	1885
American Canoe Club - New York NY	1880
Anacorte - Puget Sound	1892 *or earlier*
Anahuac Boat - US in Mexico	1892
Atlantic - offshoot of Brooklyn	1865
Baltimore	1891
Baltimore Corinthian	1893
Bay City - MI	1894
Bar Harbor - ME	1885
Bay Head - NJ	1888
Bay of Quinte - Belleville ONT	1884
Bay Shore - NY	1885
Bay-Waveland - MS nee Bay St. Louis and Waveland Regatta Association	1892
Bayonne - NY	187-
Beverly - Nahant MA	1872
Biloxi - MI	1870
Biscayne Bay - FL	1887
Bohemia	1884
Boston #1 1834-37; #2 1866; oldest in New England	1834
Boston Boat Club - lapsed 1837	1835
Bridgeport - CT	1896
Brooklyn - NY	1857
Buffalo - NY	1860
Buffalo Canoe - NY	1882
Bunker Hill - MA; third New England	1869
Burgess (?) - Marblehead MA	1894
Burrard Inlet Sailing Club - Puget Sound - lapsed and 1891 BCYRA; lapsed 1894; 1897 #1 Vancouver Yacht Club; lapsed and 1903 #2 Vancouver Yacht Club	1887
California - San Francisco lapsed 1920	1893
Carnarsie - Long Island NY	1887
Carolina - Wilmington NC	1853
Carolina - Charleston SC	1883
Catalina - Avalon CA lapsed 1893; became Sophia 1903	
New Catalina - CA	1924
Cedar Point - CT	1886
Chelsea - NY	1890
Chelsea - MA	1886
Chesapeake - Baltimore	1852
Chesapeake Bay - MD	1885
Chicago	1875
Chula Vista - San Diego lapsed 1930's; re-formed later	1889
Cleveland - OH	1878
Cohasset - MA	1894
Columbia - Chicago	1892
Columbia - NYC west side	1867
Columbia - Boston	1896
Conanicut - RI; nee Jamestown	1892
Corinthian Fleet - New Rochelle	1889
Corinthian - nee Philadelphia	1876
Corinthian - San Francisco Tiburon third Pacific with Hawaii and San Diego	1886
Corinthian - Staten Island NY	1886
Corinthian - Atlantic City NJ	1892
Corinthian - Marblehead MA	1885
Corinthian Mosquito Fleet - New Rochelle, NY	1889
Crescent City - MS	18 -
Daisy to Fond du Lac 1873	1870/1
Delaware	1892
Delaware Yacht Navy	*circa* 1869
Detroit Boat Club - nee 1839 as a rowing club	1842
Detroit -	1867
Dorchester (MA) to Mass 1880	1870
Douglaston Yacht Squadron NY	1887
Duluth - MN	1888
Duxbury - MA	1894
Eastern - Marblehead	1870
East River - NY	1884
Elliot Bay - Puget Sound; merged with Seattle 1909	1894
Encinal - Alameda CA	1890
Erie - NY	1894
Essex - NJ	1886
Excelsior - Brooklyn NY	1889
Fair Haven - Puget Sound	1892 *or earlier*
Fall River - MA	1890

Florida - Jacksonville; lapsed by 1897	1881 or earlier
Genesee - NY; lapse 1876; reorganized; merged with Rochester 1927	1874
Glenada - Cold Spring Harbor NY	1885
Gravesend Bay - NY	1893
Great Head - MA; later Winthrop	1884
Great South Bay - Long Island NY	1889
Greenville - NY	1892
Green Lake - WI	1894
Halifax River	1896
Halifax - later RNSYS	1837
Harvard (University)	1894
Harlem - NY	1883
Hartford - CT	1895
Haverhill - MA	1874
Hawaii Yachting/Rowing Assn. third Pacific with SDYC and Corinthian Yacht Club (San Francisco)	1885
Hempstead Harbor - Long Island Sound NY	1891
Hempstead Bay - Queens NY	1890
Hingham - MA	1895
Hobe Sound - FL	1892
Hoboken - NJ	1856
Horseshoe Harbor - Long Island Sound CT	1889
Houston - 1st Texas - 1905 reorganized Houston Yacht and Power Boat Club; 1907 Houston Launch Club; 1923 HYC at Bayshore and 1927 Seabrook	1887
Hudson Boat Club - Jersey City NJ	1865
Hudson River - NY	1873
Huguenot - Weschester NY	1894
Hull - MA; 1898 merged Massachusetts Yacht Club; later Hull-Massachusetts Yacht Club	1880
Huntington - Long Island Sound NY	1894
Illini - St. Louis	1893
Inland - lapsed 1875	1867
Indian Harbor - Long Island Sound CT	1889
Ione - NY	1865
Jackson Park - Chicago	1896
Jamaica Bay - NY	1892
Jeffries - East Boston	1870
Jersey City - NJ	1858
Kennebunk River - ME	1888
Kingston - Ontario NY	1896
Knickerbocker - Long Island Sound NY	1874
Knickerbocker Boat Club - NY; lapsed 1812	1811
Lake Champlain - Burlington VT	1880
Lake Geneva - WI	1874
Lake Hopatcong - NJ	1890
Larchmont - Long Island Sound NY	1880
Lealani Boat Club - HI	?
Lincoln Park - reorganized 1913; merged with Chicago 1920	1890
Long Island NY - nee Union 1864	1872
Lynn - MA	1870
Madison - WI	1871
Machester - MA	1892
Manhasset Bay - Long Island Sound NY	1891
Manhattan - NY	1870
Mantoloking - NJ	1879
Master Mariners Benevolent Association aka Protective; inactive 1880-83, 1886-90	1867
Maumee River - OH	1896
Michigan - Detroit MI	1881
Middletown - CT	1896
Milwaukee	1894
M.I.T. - Cambridge	1897
Minnetonka - MN	1889
Mobile - AL (1893 per Coffin)	1850
Monmouth Boat - NJ	1879
Morrisania - Westchester NY	1896
Mosquito Fleet - South Boston	1888
National - Jersey City NJ	pre-1881
Neenah -WI; 1894 joined Nodaway	1864
Neptune - Highlands NJ	1850
New Bedford - MA	1877
Newburgh - NY	1885
New Hamburg	1869
New Haven - CT	1881
New Jersey - Hoboken NJ	1871
New Jersey Athletic	1887
New Rochelle - NY	1885
Newark - NJ	1882
Newburgh - NY	1885
Newport - RI	1894
New Whatcomb - Puget Sound	1892
New York Boat Club - briefly	1830
New York Canoe Club	1871
New York Yacht - NYC	1844
Nodaway - WI; joined Neenah	1894
Norfolk Boat Club - VA	1893
North Shore NY - later Port Washington	1871
Norwalk - Long Island Sound CT	1894
Oakland #1 - CA lapsed	1860
Oceanic City - NY	1869
Oconomowoc - WI	1878
Ohio	1885
Old Club - MD	1872
Old Colony - MA	1891
Olympia Boat Club - Puget Sound; later Yacht Club	1898
Onondaga - NY Finger Lakes	1885
Oshkosh - NY	1870
Oswego - NY	1881
Outrigger Canoe Club - HI	?
Oyster Bay - Long Island Sound NY; merged with Seawanhaka Corinthian 1892	1885
Pacific #1 - San Francisco CA; soon lapsed	1856
Pacific #2; lapsed 1899	1878
Palm Beach	1884
Panama - San Francisco - Alameda	1911
Park City - Bridgeport CT	1898
Pass Christian - MS	1896
Pavonia - Bayonne NJ	1869
Pennsylvania - Philadelphia; lapse pre 1897	1881

Pensacola #2 - nee Pensacola Yacht and Motor Boat; #1 1870 or 80's 1872
Philadelphia/Pennsylvania/ Quaker City; lapsed 1980; Philadelphia Yacht Club and split to current Corinthian Yacht Club 1876
Pioneer - aka #1 San Francisco Yacht Club; lapsed after 1859 1852
Pioneer - San Diego CA; lapsed 1852
Piscataqua - ME 1891
Pleon - Marblehead MA first independent junior club extant 1887
Plymouth - MA 1890
Portland - ME; third New England 1869
Portland - OR; lapsed and reorganized 1918 1910
Port Moody - Puget Sound 1887
Port Townsend - Puget Sound 1892
Providence - RI raced *Amaryllis* New York City 1876 Centennial; (1877 Rhode Island Yacht Club) 1875
Providence Corinthian - RI 1888
Poughkeepsie - NY 1892
Put in Bay - Lake Erie 1876
Quaker City; lapsed 1980 and Philadelphia Yacht Club and split to current Corinthian Yacht Club 1876
Queen City - Toronto 1886
Quebec 1861
Quincy 1874
Raritan - NJ 1865
Red Dragon Canoe - DE/NJ ??
Rhode Island - (nee Providence 1875?) 1877
Riverside - Long Island Sound CT 1888
Riverton - NJ 1865
Rochester - NY; reactivated 1886 1876
Royal Bermuda - 1864
Royal Canadian - nee Toronto Boat Club, Royal 1854 1852
Royal Cape Breton - Nova Scotia 1899
Royal Halifax - nee Halifax 1837 1857
Royal Hamilton - Lake Ontario 1888
Royal Nova Scotia Yacht Squadron nee Halifax 1837 1876
Royal St. Lawrence - vic. Montreal 1888
Royal Vancouver - Burrard Inlet Sailing Club 1887; lapsed and #1 Vancouver Yacht Club 1897 1897
Royal Victoria – lapsed; reorganized 1908; Royal 1911 1892
Sachem's Head - Long Island Sound CT 1896
Salem Bay - MA 1884
Sag Harbor - Long Island NY 1897
San Diego with San Diego Rowing Club; third Pacific with Corinthian and Hawaii 1886
San Francisco #1 as Pioneer; lapsed post 1859; #2 1869 first permanent west coast and third continuous in U.S. 1855
Sandusky - OH; Lake Erie 1894
Sandy Bay - Anisquam MA 1885
Santa Barbara - CA lapsed until 1920 1872
Sausalito - San Francisco; lapsed; reorganized 1910-1918 1873
Savannah or Savannah Yacht and Country Club 1867
Savin Hill - MA 1875
Sea Cliff - Long Island Sound; Seabird Yacht Club ca. 1875 and lapsed 1891
Seattle - second continuous Pacific; reorganized 1890; merged with Elliott Bay 1909 1879
Seawanhaka Corinthian - merged with Oyster Bay 1892 1871
Seawaren Land and Water Club - NJ 1891
Shattemuc Yacht and Canoe - NY 1887
Shelter Island - Long Island NY 1886
Sippican - Buzzards Bay MA 1877
Somerset - Dighton MA 1877
South Bay - San Francisco Bay 1896
South Boston - second New England 1868
Southern - New Orleans nee Stingaree 1849
Squantum - MA 1890
St. Augustine - FL 1871
St. Francis - San Francisco 1927
St. Johns - Quebec 1888
St. Regis - Adirondacks NY 1897
Stamford - Long Island Sound NY (included in earlier Stamford Corinthian ?) 1890
Stapleton - Staten Island NY 1870
Staten Island - NY 1891
Stevens - NY 1871
Stuyvesant - NY 1871
Tacoma - lapsed 1893; reorganized 1908 1889
Tappan Zee - NY 1887
Tarantine - ME 1896
Taunton - MA 1895
Tarpon Springs - FL 1852
Thousand Islands - NY 1894
Toledo - OH 1878
Toronto Boat Club became Yacht Club; Royal Canadian Yacht Club 1854 1852
Tom's River - NJ 1871
Tower Ridge - Hudson River NY 1890
Union - NY to Long Island 1872 1864
Vancouver Boating Club - lapsed 1896
Warwick - RI pre 1881
Weetamoe - Fall River MA 1893
West Hampton - Long Island NY 1890
White Bear - MN 1889
Williamsburg - NY 1869
Winthrop - MA nee Great Head 1884
Wood's Hole - MA 1896
Yale - Yale University; Yale Corinthian 1893 1872
Yonkers - NY 1870
Yorkville - NY 1884

APPENDIX C

COLLEGE SAILING HALL OF FAME MEMBERS

The following people have been honored for past performances as outstanding college sailors or for unusual contributions to intercollegiate sailing. This award is on display at the College Sailing Hall of Fame at the Robert Crown Sailing Center, U.S. Naval Academy, Annapolis, MD.

Robert M. Allan, Jr., Stanford '40
Henry H. Anderson, Jr., Yale '43
Peter J. Barrett, Univ. Wisconsin '57
Robert N. Bavier, Williams '40
Greg F. Bemis, Harvard '22
William Bentsen, Dennison '50
J. Gordon Bentley, Syracuse '50
Victor "Peter" Bethge, Webb '53
Maria Bozzuto, MIT '73
Harold "Hatch" Brown, Boston U. '59
William Buchan, Jr., Washington '54
Richard E. Carter, Yale '50
Jane Chalmers, Radcliffe '69
C. Runyon Colie, MIT '40
Dennis Conner, San Diego State '64
Robert E. Coulson, Yale '50
F. Gardner Cox, Princeton '41
William S. Cox, Sr., Princeton '35
William S. Cox, Jr., Princeton '63
Terry Cronberg, MIT '66
William B. Cudahy, Harvard '34
Alain J. DeBerc, MIT '55
Madeleine Disario
Carl M. Eichenlaub, Jr., San Diego State '53
Wallace A. Everest, Boston U. '59
John Fennessey, MIT '43
William P. Ficker, UC Berkeley '51
Carter Ford, Harvard '63
Glen S. Foster, II, Brown '52
Warren A. Foster, Ohio State '49
Leonard M. Fowle, Harvard '30
Nancy K. Fowle, Tufts '29
G. Shelby Friedrichs, Tulane '33
G. Shelby "Buddy" Friedrichs, Jr., Tulane '62
Cy Gillete, General Motors Inst. '35
Terrill F. Gloege, Coast Guard '57
Bruce G. Goldsmith, Michigan '58
James F. Googe, Jr., Navy '57
Barbara Grant, Radcliffe '73
David A. Grant, UCLA '54
Lt. Col. Leroy F. Grant, RMC, Canada '05
Edward A. Greenberg, Princeton '63
Heather Gregg, Tufts '86
George H. Griswold, College of Wooster '61
Prescott Gustafson, Brown '36
Graham H. Hall, USMMA KP '64
Thomas E. Hazelhurst, Brown '56
David E. Higginbotham, Northeastern '44
Robert H. Hobbs, MIT '64
Charles S. Hoppin, Harvard '53
Michael S. Horn, Harvard '63
Charles M. Hunt, MIT '48
Charles L. Ill, Brown '49
Kathleen Jones, MIT '71
Kathy Karlson, Navy '80
Arthur Knapp, Jr., Princeton '28
Charles M. Kober, Stanford '47
Timothea S. Larr, Michigan '62
Richard S. Latham
Frances A. Litchfield, USMMA KP '37
Theodore W. Livingston, San Diego State '49
Nance Lowe, Wilson '70
Alan "Doc" Lukens, MIT '38
Janet Lutz, Pembroke A.D.
Ronald E. Marshall, Ohio State '60
Steven C. Martin, USCGA '64
John Marvin, MIT '49
Oliver May, Yale '30
Robert W. McCullough, Brown '43
David S. Miller, U. British Col '67
David C. Minton, Navy '56
Robert E. Monetti, Yale '50
Admiral Hap Moore, USCGA '26
James B. Moore, Dartmouth '32
Capt. Peter A. Morrill, USCGA '52
Emil Mosbacher, Jr., Dartmouth '43
James E. Nathanson, Harvard '54
Nina Nielsen, Princeton '76
Lowell O. North, UC Berkeley '51
George D. O'Day, Harvard '45
Eric C. Olsen, MIT '39
Mary Paget, Radcliffe A.D.
S. Trevor Pardee, Princeton '43
Colin N. Park, U. British Col '64
LCDR. William C. Park, III, USCGA '60
Dennis C. Posey, MIT '59
Anne Preston, Princeton '77
Allan L. Priddy, Dartmouth '43
Charles A. "Capt. Joe" Prosser, RNC '43 (+USMMA)
Robert Purrington, Princeton '66
Augustus Putnam, Harvard '49
John C. Quinn, Brown '57
Hanson C. Robbins, Harvard '59
Leonard A. Romagna, Brown '42
Richard M. Rose, Princeton '60
William G. Saltonstall, Harvard '59
Otto J. Scherer, Jr., Michigan '61
Lawrence A. Shep, UC Berkeley '52
Cornelius Shields, Sr.
Cornelius Shields, Jr., Babson '56
Priscilla Storer, Radcliffe '70
Janice Stroud, Radcliffe '73
Patricia K. Sullivan, U Cincinnati '56
Richard B. Sweet, UC Santa Barbara '48
John A. "Jack" Taylor, UCLA, '56
E. Dexter Thede, Michigan '59
Richard L. Tillman, Navy '58
Robert E. "Ted" Turner, Brown '61
Charles R. Ulmer, Navy '61
Glen Waterhouse, UC Berkeley '18
Lawrence A. White, USCGA '51
Robert J. White, Ohio State '66
William S. Widnall, MIT '59
Frederick H. Wilson, Jr., Brown '43
Walter C. "Jack" Wood, MIT '17
John A. Wuestneck, USCGA '62

EVERETT B. MORRIS TROPHY

The Morris Trophy is awarded annually to the College Sailor of the Year. It is named in memory of a distinguished journalist who spent more than 30 years as a yachting writer and editor, most of them with the *New York Herald Tribune.* He was also actively involved in sailing programs and activities, including service as president of the Junior Yacht Racing Association of Long Island Sound.

1968 Scott H. Allan, USC
1969 Timothy P. Hogan, USC
1970 Richard T. Doyle, Notre Dame
1971 Jonathan Wright, USMMA Kings Point
1972 Gary A. Jobson, SUNY Maritime
1973 Gary A. Jobson, SUNY Maritime
1974 Augie Diaz, Tulane
1975 Sam Altreuter, Tufts
1976 Peter Isler, Yale
1977 Carl Buchan, Washington
1978 Steve Benjamin, Yale
1979 Alex Smigelski, USMMA Kings Point
1980 Stuart Johnston, Tufts
1981 Pede Dickey, Tufts
1982 Ken Read, Boston U.
1983 Morgan Reeser, USMMA Kings Point
1984 Morgan Reeser, USMMA Kings Point
1985 John M. Renehan, USMMA Kings Point
1986 Brad Read, Boston U.
1987 Rob Hallawell, Navy
1988 Chris Larson, Charleston
1989 Terry Hutchinson, Old Dominion
1990 Terry Hutchinson, Old Dominion
1991 Andy Lovell, Charleston
1992 Brad M. Rodi, Navy
1993 Brad M. Rodi, Navy
1994 Tyler Moore, Charleston
1995 Ryan Cox, Navy
1996 Senet Bischoff, Tufts

ALL-AMERICA TEAMS

The following is a list of college sailors who have been granted All-American status for outstanding intercollegiate sailing performances in the year indicated.

1967

Robert M. "Skip" Allan, Stanford
Scott H. Allan, USC
David A. Curtis, Tufts
Kim L. Desenberg, Stanford
J. Peter Doherty, Yale
Robert D. Fisch, Navy
James T. Ingham, USCGA
Robert L. Kuehlthau, Wisconsin
John J. Leonard, Ohio Wesleyan
Charles F. Loutrel, Jr., Tufts
Frederick V. Minson, USCGA
William B. Parker, Kent State
Henry G. Schofield, Long Beach
Carl I. Van Duyne, Princeton

1968

Edward O. Butler, San Diego State
Argyle Campbell, USC
Christopher C. Chatain, Michigan
David M. Coit, Yale
David A. Curtis, Tufts
Richard T. Doyle, Notre Dame
Timothy P. Hogan, USC
James T. Ingham, USCGA
Thomas W. McLaughlin, San Diego State
Arthur Messinger, SUNY Maritime
John F. Meyer, Michigan
Richard Meyerrose, Jr. SUNY Maritime
Frederick V. Minson, USCGA
G. Arthur Seaver, III, Tulane
Christopher T. Seaver, Yale

1969

Thomas E. Bernard, USCGA
Edward O. Butler, San Diego State
Argyle Campbell, USC
David M. Coit, Yale
John Dane, III, Tulane
Richard T. Doyle, Notre Dame
Robert E. Doyle, Harvard
Timothy P. Hogan, USC
R. DuBose Joslin, Navy
Andrew L. Johnston, Princeton
Thomas W. McLaughlin, San Diego State
Richard Meyerrose, Jr., SUNY Marit.
Stephen D. Milligan, MIT
Daniel M. Rugg, Navy
Christopher T. Seaver, Yale

1970

Thomas E. Bernard, USCGA
Edward O. Butler, San Diego State
Argyle Campbell, USC
John Dane, III, Tulane
Richard T. Doyle, Notre Dame
Robert E. Doyle, Harvard
Thomas M. Dykstra, URI
Timothy P. Hogan, USC
Paul G. Hunrichs, San Diego State
David W. McComb, MIT
Arthur L. Messinger, SUNY Maritime
John F. Meyers, Michigan
Richard Meyerrose, Jr., SUNY Maritime
Daniel M. Rugg, Navy
Christopher T. Seaver, Yale

1971

E. Louise Anstey, U. Victoria
Henry Bossett, URI
Edward O. Butler, San Diego State
Argyle Cambell, USC
William L. Campbell, Navy
Robert W. Crossley, U Brit. Col.
John Dane, III, Tulane
Robert E. Doyle, Harvard
Frederick G. Hanselman, Ohio Wes.
Paul G. Hunrichs, San Diego State
Gary A. Jobson, SUNY Maritime
Abbott L. Reeve, Harvard
Charles T. White, Michigan State
Rollin "Skip" Whyte, URI
Jonathan Wright, USMMA Kings Point

1972

William L. Campbell, Navy
Patrick Finnegan, U Brit. Col.
Jonathan Ford, Stevens Institute
Frederick Hanselman, Ohio Wes.
David Hodges, UC Irvine
Paul G. Hunrichs, San Diego State
Gary A. Jobson, SUNY Maritime
Robert Martus, SUNY Maritime
Jeff McDermaid, UC Irvine
Bruce D. Nelson, Michigan
David C. Noyes, Yale
Christopher W. Pollak, Tufts
Douglas P. Rastello, USC
Manton D. Scott, Tufts
Patrick T. Seaver, Yale

1973

Douglas Bull, Tulane
William L. Campbell, Navy
Stephen J. Cucchiaro, MIT
Augie Diaz, Tulane
Derrick Fries, Michigan State
Allen B. Hughes, Jr. USCGA
Gary A. Jobson, SUNY Maritime
Arthur Keefe, Yale
Mark Laura, Washington
William P. Leary, USCGA
Robert Martus, SUNY Maritime
Bruce D. Nelson, Michigan
Dan Thompson, UC Irvine
Peter Wilson, USC

1974
Roger "Sam" Altreuter, Tufts
Douglas Bull, Tulane
Thomas Darden, Tulane
Richard A. Davis, UC San Diego
Augie Diaz, Tulane
Derrick R. Fries, Michigan State
Allan B. Hughes, USCGA
Lawrence P. Klein, Miami-Ohio
Henry Krafft, Stevens Insitute
James S. Maltman, Tufts
Jeff McDermaid, UC Irvine
Christopher S. Middendorf, Harvard
Terry Neff, Harvard
Mark M. Wheeler, Stevens Instit.

1975
Sam Altreuter, Tufts
Augie Diaz, Tulane
Michael E. Crowley, USMMA KP
Greg B. Fisher, Miami-Ohio
Neal L. Fowler, Tufts
Thomas R. Gallagher, SUNY Maritime
Peter Isler, Yale
Mark Laura, Washington
Jeff McDermaid, UC Irvine
Ben Mitchell, USC
Bruce D. Nelson, Michigan
David B. Perry, Yale
Mark Reynolds, San Diego State
Hugh B. Schmidt, San Diego State
John Walton, Michigan State

1976
Alan Andrews, Stanford
Sam Altreuter, Tufts
Marvin "Buddy" Duncan, SUNY Maritime
Carl D. Fast, Webb
Matthew B. Fisher, Miami-Ohio
Neal L. Fowler, Tufts
Greg M. Griffin, Webb
Douglas W. Hart, Navy
Peter F. Isler, Yale
James B. McCreary, Tufts
Richard C. Sadler, SUNY Maritime
Hugo B. Schmidt, San Diego State
Alexander Smigelski, USMMA KP
Robert H. Wade, UC Santa Cruz
Kurt R. Wiese, Tulane

1977
Edward K. Adams, URI
Joseph K. Balconis, SUNY Maritime
W. Carl Buchan, Washington
Matthew B. Fisher, Miami-Ohio
Neal L. Fowler, Tufts
Maxwell R. Griffith, S. Carolina
Paul A. LaBossiere, Navy
Kenneth Legler, URI
James B. McCreary, Tufts
Terry McLaughlin, Queens
Terry Neff, Harvard
Mark G. Rastello, UCLA
James "Buzz" Reynolds, Notre Dame
David B. Perry, Yale
Peter G. Smith, Michigan
Brian C. Thomas, Washington
Kurt R. Wiese, Tulane
Garland P. Wright, Navy

1978
Edward K. Adams, URI
Donald B. Ayres, USC
Stephen D. Benjamin, Yale
Paul Clifford, Yale
Gerard T. Coleman, Navy
Kelson R. Elam, Texas
R. Kelly Gough, Texas
James K. Hammitt, Harvard
Allan L. Jewett, UCLA
Danforth "Gary" Knapp, URI
Timothy J. McGee, Navy
Nathaniel Philbrick, Brown
Mark G. Rastello, UCLA
Sandra L. Ray, Boston University
Alexander Smigelski, USMMA Kings Point
Peter G. Smith, Michigan
Paul M. VanCleve, Navy
J. Stewart Walker, Charleston

1979
James Buckingham, UC Berkeley
Gerard T. Coleman, Navy
Jasper Craig, Navy
John Duclos, USMMA Kings Point
Kelson R. Elam, Texas
Craig Gilbert, Yale
R. Kelly Gough, Texas
Stuart Johnstone, Tufts
Danforth "Gary" Knapp, URI
Terry McLaughlin, Queens Univ.
Kurt Miller, Orange Coast College
Phil Ramming, UCLA
Elliot Rossen, MIT
Alexander Smigelski, USMMA Kings Point
Peter G. Smith, Michigan
Monty Spindler, St. Mary's
Scott Steele, St. Mary's
Nell Taylor, Yale
Paul M. VanCleve, Navy
Scott Young, Texas

1980
Robert K. Anoll, Navy
Nicholas A. Burke, Boston Univ
Gerard T. Coleman, Navy
Milton T. "Jasper" Craig, Navy
Keith C. Dodson, Cal State Long Beach
John F. Duclos, USMMA Kings Point
John A. Eckart, USMMA Kings Point
Mark S. Golison, Cal State Long Beach
R. Stuart Johnstone, Tufts
Joseph W. Petrucci, Tufts
Christopher A. Raab, Orange Coast
F. Nevin Sayre, II, Tulane
John J. "Jack" Slattery, Boston U.
John G. Speer, Navy
Gary K. Sprague, Tulane
Stephen M. Strittmatter, Harvard
Tracy Usher, UC Irvine
Douglas Wefer, Michigan
Scott Young, Texas

1981
Robert K. Anoll, Navy
Mike Bello, Charleston
Mary Brigden, Navy
Paul "Pede" Dickey, Tufts
R. Kelly Gough, Texas
Jens P. Hookensen, Tulane
Ralph M. Kinder, Tulane
Tom Lihan, USMMA Kings Point
Nick Madigan, Navy
Jonathan McKee, Yale
Kurt Miller, Cal St. Long Beach
Ken Read, Boston University
Morgan Reeser, USMMA Kings Point
F. Nevin Sayre, II, Tufts
John J. "Jack" Slattery, Boston U.
Scott Steele, St. Mary's
Douglas Wefer, Michigan
Scott Young, Texas
Mike Zavell, Tufts

1982
Nicholas A. Burke, Boston Univ.
David Chapin, Texas
Keith Dodson, Cal St. Long Beach
Greg Eiffert, URI
Scott Ferguson, Michigan
Jens P. Hookensen, Tulane
Brian Keane, Harvard
Ralph M. Kinder, Tulane
Tom Lihan, USMMA Kings Point
Allen D. Lindsey, USMMA Kings Point
Jonathan McKee, Yale
Kurt Miller, Cal St. Long Beach
Ken Read, Boston Univ.
Morgan Reeser, USMMA Kings Point
F. Nevin Sayre, II, Tufts
John Shadden, Boston Univ.
Gary Stewart, USMMA Kings Point
Douglas Wefer, Michigan
Pede Dickey, Tufts
Paul Yost, Stanford

1983
Robert Brown, Navy
Bill Draheim, Texas
Scott Ferguson, Michigan
K.C. Fullmer, Old Dominion
Harold L. Gilreath, Jr., Navy
Brian Keane, Harvard
John Keane, Harvard
Brian Ledbetter, Navy
Allen D. Lindsey, USMMA Kings Point
William Lynn, Tufts
Scott J. MacLeod, Tulane
Jonathan McKee, Yale
Rick Merriman, Navy
Ken Read, Boston University
Morgan Reeser, USMMA Kings Point
F. Nevin Sayre, II, Tufts

1984

Robert Alexander, Boston Univ.
Brodie L. Cobb, Tulane
Scott Ferguson, Michigan
Paul J. Foerster, Texas
Harold L. Gilreath, Jr., Navy
Jay Golison, Cal St. Long Beach
Fred Hunger, Ohio Wesleyan
Brian Ledbetter, Navy
Allen D. Lindsey, USMMA KP
William Lynn, Tufts
Rick Merriman, Navy
G. Zachary Orlov, Tufts
Mike Pinckney, Charleston
Morgan Reeser, USMMA KP

1985

Stephen A. Bourdow, Tulane
Jack E. Christiansen, Washington
James J. Cummiskey, Brown
J.J. Fetter, Yale
Paul J. Foerster, Texas
Paul J. Grimes, Brown
Robert A. Hallawell, Navy
Brian Ledbetter, Navy
Allen D. Lindsey, USMMA KP
James Peter Melvin, Boston Univ.
Rick Merriman, Navy
Charles McKee, Washington
Scott J. MacLeod, Tulane
G. Zachary Orlov, Tufts
Bradford S. Read, Boston Univ.
John M. Renehan, USMMA KP
Michael Segerblom, USC
John Shadden, USC

1986

Stephen A. Bourdow, Tulane
Gordon M. Burnes, Harvard
Douglas Clark, URI
Alexander C. Cutler, Navy
Paul J. Foerster, Texas
Magnus Gravare, Tufts
Paul J. Grimes, Brown
Robert A. Hallawell, Navy
Allen L. Kruger, USMMA KP
Christopher B. Larson, Charleston
John C. Lovell, Charleston
Scott J. MacLeod, Tulane
Peter S. McChesney, St. Mary's
Jonathan Pinckney, UC Irvine
Michael Pinckney, Charleston
Bradford S. Read, Boston Univ.
Peter D. Renehan, USMMA KP
George Slook, Navy
Scott Sonnier, Spring Hill College
David Ullrich, Brown

1987

Stephen A. Bourdow, Tulane
Gordon M. Burnes, Harvard
Alexander C. Cutler, Navy
Edward A. Eckert, Navy
Matthew S. Fries, Tulane
Michael Funsch, Georgia Tech
Robert A. Hallawell, Navy
David J. Himmel, Tufts
Terry A. Hutchinson, Old Dominion
Alexander E. Jackson, Tufts
Allen L. Kruger, USMMA Kings Point
Christopher B. Larson, Charleston
Zachary N. Leonard, Yale
John C. Lovell, Charleston
John D. Pernick, Harvard
Peter D. Renehan, USMMA Kings Point
James B. Weber, Jr., Old Dominion
David F. Ullrich, Brown

1988

Stephen A. Bourdow, Tulane
Herbert Cole, Washington
Alexander C. Cutler, Navy
Keith B. Davids, Navy
Matthew S. Fries, Tulane
Lars Guck, URI
Kevin Hall, Brown
Terry A. Hutchinson, Old Dominion
Peter L. Johnstone, Conn. College
Allen L. Kruger, USMMA Kings Point
Thomas E. Kuhnle, Stanford
Christopher B. Larson, Charleston
Per Lovfald, Navy
Douglas McLean, URI
James C. Malm, UC Irvine
Christopher B. Moe, Charleston
John D. Pernick, Harvard
Jonathan Pinckney, UC Irvine
Nick Scandone, UC Irvine
James B. Weber, Jr., Old Dominion

1989

Charlie Allen, URI
Gordon Burnes, Harvard
Stephen A. Bourdow, Tulane
Chris Carroll, Michigan
Keith Davids, Navy
Chad Gould, Michigan
Lars Guck, URI
Kevin Hall, Brown
Terry A. Hutchinson, Old Dominion
Steve Kirkpatrick, Tufts
Bob Little, USC
John C. Lovell, Charleston
Per Lovfald, Navy
James C. Malm, UC Irvine
Mike Martin, Old Dominion
Charlie Ogletree, Old Dominion
Jonathan Pinckney, UC Irvine
Charlie Pucciarello, Navy
David Starck, SUNY Maritime
James B. Weber, Jr., Old Dominion

1990

Alex Ascencios, Tulane
Jim Bowers, Harvard
Keith Davids, Navy
Kristina Farrar, Brown
Lars Guck, URI
Rich Harries, Tufts
Terry A. Hutchinson, Old Dominion
Steve Kirkpatrick, Tufts
Marty Kullman, Old Dominion
Morgan Larson, Charleston
John C. Lovell, Charleston
James C. Malm, UC Irvine
William C. Park, IV, Tulane
Tony Rey, Connecticut College
Brad Rodi, Navy
David Starck, SUNY Maritime
Mike Sturman, UC Irvine
Charlie Ulmer, Tufts
James B. Weber, Jr., Old Dominion
Mike Zani, Brown

1991

Alex Ascencios, Tulane
Jim Bowers, Harvard
Kris Farrar, Brown
Willie Graves, Navy
Kevin Hall, Brown
Bill Healy, URI
Todd Hudgins, Old Dominion
Peter Katcha, Tulane
Marty Kullman, Old Dominion
Randy Lake, UC Irvine
Andy Lovell, Charleston
Susie Minton, Navy
Jeff Olson, Hawaii
Brad Rodi, Navy
Doug Schofield, USCGA
Mike Zani, Brown
Karl Ziegler, Conn. College

1992

Josh Adams, Tufts
Nick Adamson, UC Irvine
Geoff Becker, UC Irvine
Mike Breault, Yale
Geoff Ewenson, URI
John Fallon, Dartmouth
Rich Feeny, Brown
Willie Graves, Navy
Tim Healy, St. Mary's
Peter Katcha, Tulane
Marty Kullman, Old Dominion
Bryan Largay, Princeton
Andy Lovell, Charleston
Chris McDowell, Dartmouth
David Mendelblatt, Tufts
Susie Minton, Navy
Scott Nixon, St. Mary's
Mike O'Bryan, Navy
Jeff Olson, Hawaii
Brad Rodi, Navy

1993

Joshua C. Adams, Tufts
Geoffrey D. Becker, UC Irvine
Patrick R. Downey, Old Dominion
Geoffrey M. Ewenson, URI
David G. Fagen, Navy
Richard A. Feeny, Brown
Timothy P. Healy, St. Mary's
William J. Healy, St. Mary's
Randy A. Lake, UC Irvine
Morgan W. Larson, Hawaii
James C. "Chris" McDowell, Dartmouth
Mark Mendelblatt, Tufts
Robert M. Merrick, URI
Tyler W. Moore, Charleston
Michael G. O'Bryan, Navy
Jeffrey L. Olsen, Hawaii
Bradley M. Rodi, Navy
Nicholas G. Trotman, Tufts
Mike Zani, Brown
Karl Ziegler, Conn. College

1994

Josh Adams, Tufts
Ryan Cox, Navy
Patrick Downey, Old Dominion
Chad Demarest, Coast Guard
David Fagen, Navy
Bill Hardesty, Old Dominion
Mike Hare, St. Mary's
Tim Healy, St. Mary's
Morgan Larson, U. Hawaii
Chris McDowell, Dartmouth
Mark Mendelblatt, Tufts
James E. "Jay" Miles, Charleston
Mike Mills, Princeton
Tyler Moore, Charleston
John Myrdal, Hawaii
Eric Naranjo, Navy
Scott Sellers, Stanford
Nick Trotman, Tufts
Tim Wadlow, Boston U.
Peter Wells, UC Irvine

1995

Andy Beeckman, UC Irvine '96
Senet Bischoff, Tufts '96
R.D. Burley, Navy '96
Whitney Connor, Dartmouth '96
Ryan Cox, Navy '95
Brett Davis, Harvard '96
Patrick Downey, ODU '95
Bill Hardesty, USMMA Kings Point '97
Mike Hare, St. Mary's '96
Kevin Jewett, St. Mary's '96
Chris McDowell, Dartmouth '95
Charles Meade, Stanford '95
Mark Mendelblatt, Tufts '95
Tyler Moore, Charleston '95
Matt Reynolds, St. Mary's '96
Rob Richards, Tufts '95
John Torgerson, ODU '97
Tim Wadlow, Boston U. '96
Peter Wells, UC Irvine '96
Andy Zinn, UC Berkeley '96

1996

Senet Bischoff, Tufts '96
R.D. Burley, Navy '96
Tim Fallon, Tufts '97
Bill Hardesty, USMMA KP '98
Mike Hare, St. Mary's '97
Andrew Horton, Hobart '98
David Houser, UC Berkeley '97
Mark Ivey, St. Mary's '99
Kevin Jewett, St. Mary's '96
David Julian, USMMA Kings Point '96
Adam Lowry, Stanford '96
Dana Moore, Charleston '96
Matt Reynolds, St. Mary's '96
Mitchell Rogers, ODU '96
Harcourt Schutz, Charleston '97
Peter Spaulding, BC '98
Will Stout, Navy '98
James Wadsworth, Tufts '97
Peter Wells, UC Irvine '96
Graeme Woodworth, Tufts '97

WOMEN'S ALL-AMERICA TEAMS

1988

Mary Anne Boyer, Charleston
Kristina Farrar, Brown
M. Frances Fogelman, Brown
Jane A. Kirk, Tufts
Elizabeth A. Healey, Boston U.
Flurry Normann, Old Dominion
Theresa Parker, Boston U.
Gretchen C. Stage, Navy
Julia L. Trotman, Radcliffe
Nicole Ullrich, Brown
Merrill A. Ulmer, Dartmouth

1989

Mary Anne Boyer, Charleston
Julie Easom, Tufts
Jane A. Kirk, Tufts
Susie Minton, Navy
Julie Norman, UC Irvine
Flurry Normann, Old Dominion
Hannah Swett, Brown
Julia Trotman, Radcliffe
Nicole Ullrich, Brown
Cynthia Williams, Navy

1990

Holly Gregg, Tufts
Debbie Hopkins, Michigan
Jane A. Kirk, Tufts
Amy Lawser, Brown
Kim Logan, Old Dominion
Rosalind Meade, UC Irvine
Susie Minton, Navy
Melissa Purdy, Brown
Carolyn Ulander, Conn. College
Nicole Ullrich, Brown

1991

Jennifer Coolidge, Conn. College
Cara Harries, Tufts
Donna Kuhl, Old Dominion
Kim Logan, Old Dominion
Susie Minton, Navy
Melissa Purdy, Brown
Perry Reeves, St. Mary's
Hannah Swett, Brown
Carolyn Ulander, Conn. College
Cynthia Williams, Navy

1992

Nicole Breault, Yale
Whitney Conner, Dartmouth
Kristen Doyle, Dartmouth
Bell Hughes, St. Mary's
Paula Lewin, MIT
Susie Minton, Navy
Gately Ross, Charleston
Kara Shadwick, Charleston
Heidi Thoma, Old Dominion
Carolyn Ulander, Conn. College

1993

Whitney M. Conner, Dartmouth
Tracy Hayley, Conn. College
Cara Harries, Tufts
Carisa Harris, Tufts
Madeleine "Bell" Hughes, St. Mary's
Paula Lewin, MIT
Perry Reeves, St. Mary's
Gateley L. Ross, Charleston
Kara L. Shadwick, Charleston
Heidi Thoma, Old Dominion

1994

Christine Accetella, Old Dominion
Danielle Brennan, St. Mary's
Whitney Connor, Dartmouth
Lisa Flannery, Princeton
Tracy Haley, Conn. College
Carisa Harris, Tufts
Bell Hughes, St. Mary's
Kate McDowell, Tufts
Kara Shadwick, Charleston
Chelsie Wheeler, Brown

1995

Danielle Brennan, St. Mary's '98
Laura Dunn, Tufts '95
Lisa Flannery, Princeton '95
Elizabeth Graves, St. Mary's '95
Katherine McDowell, Tufts '97
Mallory Mestayer, Navy '97
Scotia Ryer, Northwestern '96
Kara Shadwick, Charleston '95
Chelsie Wheeler, Brown '95
Julie Younger, Navy '98

1996

Evangeline Callahan, ODU '96
Christin Feldman, Georgetown '98
Casey Hogan, Dartmouth '99
Caitlin Macallister, Tufts '99
Alice Maynard, Stanford '97
Katherine McDowell, Tufts '97
Mallory Mestayer, Navy '97
Scotia Ryer, Northwestern '96
Julie Younger, Navy '98

Suyong Bay, Pusan, South Korea, has a reputation for heavy weather. But the gusting winds and violent seas that confronted sailors at the last Olympic Regatta were extreme by any standard. In two of seven races, winds topped 40 knots and waves reached 12 feet, causing such havoc that, for many competitors, finishing became the only strategy.

John Kostecki and crew. Silver Medal winners for Soling.

But one group of athletes, the members of the United States Sailing Team, stood up to the rigors best, winning more medals than any other team.

It's a tradition they've established over the past four decades, as the U.S. Sailing Team has dominated virtually every world championship and major international sailing event.

To ensure that the Team continues its winning tradition, the United States Yacht Racing Union, the Team's governing body, has increased the number of regattas and technical clinics it holds each year. These events allow America's top sailors to refine and hone their technique.

Allison Jolly and Lynne Jewell sailing to Gold in the Women's 470 at Pusan.

The U.S. Sailing Team. The Promise Fulfilled.

Rolex is proud to support the efforts of the USYRU and its Team as they prepare for the 1992 Summer Games in Barcelona. There, they'll once again prove that consistency, endurance, and grace under pressure are the key qualities in a championship sailor.

Gold Medal winners Lynne Jewell and Allison Jolly.

Not to mention a Rolex Oyster Perpetual timepiece.

ROLEX

Rolex Oyster Perpetual Lady Datejust in stainless steel and 18kt gold with matching Jubilee bracelet.
Rolex Submariner Oyster Perpetual Date in stainless steel and 18kt gold with matching Fliplock Oyster bracelet.
For more information about the U.S. Sailing Team write: USYRU, P.O. Box 209, Newport, RI 02840.
Write for watch brochure. Rolex Watch U.S.A., Inc., Dept. 000, Rolex Building, 665 Fifth Avenue, New York, New York 10022-5383.

APPENDIX D

USA AND CANADIAN OLYMPIC PARTICIPATION AND RESULTS

Olympiad	*Gold Medal*	*Silver Medal*	*Bronze Medal*	*Representing USA*	*Representing Canada*
1924	**MEULAN ON THE SEINE, FRANCE**				
Five-Metre					
Six-Metre					
Eight-Metre					
Singlehanded					Norman Robertson *R Ham YC*
1928	**AMSTERDAM, HOLLAND**				
Six-Metre				Conway Olmstead (6)	
				Willets Outerbridge	
				Herman F. Whiton (WD) *Seawanhaka Corinthian YC*	
Eight-Metre				Owen Churchill (WD) *Los Angeles YC*	
				Manfred Curry *Beverly YC*	
				Frank Hekma *Huguenot YC*	
				Nicholas B. Hekma	
				James Thompson	
				Benjamin P. Weston	
12-ft. Monotype				Manfred Curry (10) *Beverly YC*	
1932	**LOS ANGELES, CALIFORNIA**				
Eight-Metre	USA Owen P. Churchill *LA YC*	CAN Ron Maitland			
	John E. Biby Jr. *Cal YC*	George Gyles			
	Alphonse A. Burnand, Jr. *Cal YC*	Ernest F. Cribb			
	Wm. H. Cooper *Cal YC*	Harry A. Jones			
	Pierpont Davis *Cal YC*	Peter D. Gordon			
	Karl J. Dorsey *Cal YC*	Herbert A. Wallace *Royal Vancouver YC*			
	Alan C. Morgan *Cal YC*				
	John E. Huettner *Cal YC*				
	Thomas C. Webster *LA YC*				
Six-Metre		USA Frederic W. Conant *LA YC*	CAN Philip T. Rogers		
		Temple W. Ashbrook *LA YC*	Gerald Wilson		
		Hal Carlson *LA YC*	Gardner Boltbee		
		Robert Carlson *LA YC*	Kenneth Glass *Royal Vancouver YC*		
		Emmet S. Davis *LA YC*			
		Donald W. Douglas, Jr. *LA YC*			
		Charles E. Smith *LA YC*			
Star	USA Gilbert T. Gray *Southern YC*				H.E. Wylie (4) *Vancouver*
	Andrew J. Libano *Southern YC*				H.H. Simmons *Vancouver*
Snowbird				Charles W. Lyon, Jr.(7) *Newport Hbr YC*	Reg. M. Dixon (4) *Toronto*

1936 KIEL, GERMANY

Olympiad	*Gold Medal*	*Silver Medal*	*Bronze Medal*	*Representing USA*	*Representing Canada*
Eight-Metre				Owen P. Churchill (10) *Los Angeles YC*	
				Karl J. Dorsey *California YC*	
				Fred W. Schick *Corinthian YC*	
				Antonia Churchill *Los Angeles YC*	
				William P. Keane, Jr. *Corinthian YC*	
Six-Metre				Wm. A. Bartholomae, Jr.(9) *Newport Harbor YC*	
				Jas. Harvey Adams, II	
				Morgan Adams	
				Morgan Adams, Jr.	
				Charles S. Garner *Newport Harbor YC*	
				Virginia Adams *Los Angeles YC*	
				Carl C. Paul *Newport Harbor YC*	
				John D. Wallace *Los Angeles YC*	
Star				Wm. Glenn Waterhouse(5) *Richmond YC*	
				Woodbridge Metcalf *Richmond YC*	
Olympia-Jolle				Frank Jewett, Jr. (9) *Vineyard Haven YC*	Reg. M. Dixon (16) *Toronto*

1948 TORQUAY, ENGLAND

Olympiad	*Gold Medal*	*Silver Medal*	*Bronze Medal*	*Representing USA*	*Representing Canada*
Six-Metre	USA Herman F. Whiton *Seawanhaka Corinthian YC*				
	Alfred L. Loomis, Jr. *Seawanhaka Corinthian YC*				
	Michael M. Mooney *Seawanhaka Corinthian YC*				
	James H. Smith, Jr. *Seawanhaka Corinthian YC*				
	James H. Weekes *Seawanhaka Corinthian YC*				
Dragon				Henry M. Duys (11) *Seawanhaka Corinthian YC*	
				Ralph C. Craig *Seawanhaka Corinthian YC*	
				Frederick Jackson, Jr. *Seawanhaka Corinthian YC*	
				Julian K. Roosevelt *Seawanhaka Corinthian YC*	
				Richard N. Jessup *Seawanhaka Corinthian YC*	
Star	USA Hilary H. Smart				W. Gooderham (8) *Toronto*
	Paul H. Smart *Noroton YC*				A. G. Fairhead *Toronto*
Swallow			USA Lockwood M. Pirie		J.N.F. Robertson (7)
			Owen C. Torrey, Jr. *American YC*		D. Townsend *Hamilton*
Firefly		USA Ralph L. Evans, Jr. *MIT Nautical*			Paul McLaughlin (5) *Toronto*

1952 HELSINKI, FINLAND

Olympiad	*Gold Medal*	*Silver Medal*	*Bronze Medal*	*Representing USA*	*Representing Canada*
Six-Metre	USA Herman F. Whiton *Seawanhaka Corinthian YC*				N.W. Gooderham (7) *Toronto*
	Everard C. Endt *New York YC*			R. MacDonald	
	John A. Morgan *New York YC*			D. Tytler	
	Eric Ridder *Seawanhaka Corinthian YC*				K. Bradfield
	Julian K. Roosevelt *New York YC*			W. Copeland	
					W. MacIntosh
5.5-Meter	USA Britton Chance, Jr. *Seawanhaka Corinthian YC*				
	Edgar P. E. White				
	Sumner W. White, III				
Dragon				Wm. L. Horton, Sr.(11) *LA YC*	J.N.F. Robertson (10)
				Meriel J. Horton	D. Hains
				Wm. L. Horton, Jr. *LA YC*	A. Howie *Hamilton*
Star		USA John W. Price			D. Woodward (10)
		John S. Reid			A. Hugessen *Montreal*
Finn				Edward Melaika (28)	Paul McLaughlin (8)

Olympiad	*Gold Medal*	*Silver Medal*	*Bronze Medal*	*Representing USA*	*Representing Canada*
1956	**MELBOURNE, AUSTRALIA**				
5.5 Metre				Victor F. Sheronas *Pine Orchard YC*	
				Ferdinad P. Schoettle, Jr (4)	
				Robert Stinson, Jr.	
Dragon				Eugene H. Walet, III (9) *Southern YC*	D.E. Howard (8)
				Carlos P. Echeverria, Jr.	C. Howard
					D. Tytler *Toronto*
Star	USA Herbert P. Williams *Chicago YC*				E. Pennell (10)
	Lawrence E. Low				G. Parsons *Montreal*
Sharpie	USA C. Eric Oslen, Jr. *Essex YC*				A.F. Cameron (11)
	W. Stan N. Renehan *Essex YC*				W.G. Thomas *Montreal*
Finn			USA John Marvin *Eastern YC*		Bruce Kirby (8) *Montreal*
1960	**NAPLES, ITALY**				
5.5 Metre	USA George D. O'Day *New York YC*				M. E. Gould (19)
	James H. Hunt				J. Conway
	David J. Smith *Boston YC*				B. Livingstone *Toronto*
Dragon				Eugene H. Walet, III (10) *South. YC*	S.A. MacDonald (5)
				Claude L. Kohler *Haveland YC*	L. Watters *Montreal*
				Alan W. McClure, Jr. *Southern YC*	G. Norton *Toronto*
Star			USA William W. Parks *Chicago YC*		W. Burgess (23)
			Robert S. Halperin *Chicago YC*		W. West *Vancouver*
Dutchman				Harry R. Sindle (20) *Lavallette YC*	P. Desjardins (22)
				Robert M. Wood *Monmouth Boat Club*	K. Wilson *Montreal*
Finn				Peter Barrett (11) *Alamitos Bay YC*	Ian Bruce (7) *Montreal*
1964	**SAGAMI BAY, JAPAN**				
5.5 Metre			USA J. Joseph McNamara *Boston YC*		S.A. MacDonald (7)
			Joseph L. Batchelder *Eastern YC*		D. Woodward
			Francis P. Scully, Jr. *Seawanhaka Corinthian YC*		B. Skinner *Montreal*
Dragon			USA Lowell O. North *San Diego YC*		E. Botterell (11)
			Richard B. Deaver *San Diego YC*		L. Watters
			Charles C. Rogers *San Diego YC*		J.J. MacBrien *Montreal*
Star		USA Richard I. Stearns, III *Chicago YC*			David Miller (7)
		Lynn A. Williams, III			W. West *Vancouver*
Dutchman			USA Harry C. Melges, Jr *Lake Geneva YC*		Paul Henderson (12) *Toronto*
			Wm. B. Bentsen *Lake Geneva YC*		R.A. Lennox *Toronto*
Finn		USA Peter Barrett *AlamitosBay YC*			Bruce Kirby (11) *Montreal*
1968	**ACAPULCO, MEXICO**				
5.5-Meter				F. Gardner Cox, Jr. (8) *Cor. YC (Phila.)*	Stan Leibel (6)
				Stuart H. Walker *Severn Sailing Assn.*	E. Weiss
				Stephen Colgate *New York YC*	J. Hasen
					G. Norton *Toronto*
Dragon	USA G. Shelby Friedrichs, Jr. *Southern YC*				Steve Tupper (4) *Vancouver*
	Barton W. B. Jahncke *Southern YC*				D. Miller *Vancouver*
	Gerald Click Schreck *Southern YC*				T. Irwin *Kingston*
Star	USA Lowell O. North *San Diego YC*				Bruce Kirby (15) *Chicago*
	Peter J. Barrett *Alamitos Bay YC*				O. Blouin *Ottawa*
Dutchman				David N. James *Yacht Haven YC*	Roger Green (7)
				Robert L. James, Jr. *Yacht Haven YC*	S. Green *Toronto*
Finn				Carl Van Duyne (13)	Paul Henderson (20) *Toronto*

Olympiad	*Gold Medal*	*Silver Medal*	*Bronze Medal*	*Representing USA*	*Representing Canada*
1972	**KIEL, GERMANY**				
Soling	USA Harry C. Melges *Lake Geneva YC*		CAN David Miller *Vancouver*		
	William Bentsen *Lake Geneva YC*		Paul Cote		
	William C. Allen *Lake Geneva YC*		John Ekels		
Dragon		USA Donald S. Cohan *Vineyard Haven YC*			A. Leibel (9) *Toronto*
		Charles J. Horter *Island Heights YC*			F. Hall
		John N. Marshall *Indian Hrbr YC*			N. Gunn *Toronto*
Star				Alan C. Holt (10) *Cor. YC (Seattle)*	Ian Bruce (12)
				Richard R.Gates *Cor. YC (Seattle)*	P. Bjorn *Montreal*
Tempest		USA Glen S. Foster *Noroton YC*			Ted Hains (15) *Oakville*
		Peter S. Dean *Beverly YC*			L. Scott *Hamilton*
Dutchman				Scott H. Allen (23) *Los Angeles YC*	P. Byrne (14) *Vancouver*
				Tim Stearn *Sturgeon Bay YC*	E. Bastet *Montreal*
Finn				Edward Bennett (22) *St.Francis YC*	John Clarke (23) *Toronto*
1976	**KINGSTON, ONTARIO**				
Soling		USA John W. Kolius *Houston YC*			Glen Dexter
		Walter M. Glasgow, Jr. *Texas Cor. YC*			Andreas Josephans
		Richard H. Hoepener *Texas Cor. YC*			Sandy McMillian
Tempest			USA Dennis W. Conner *San Diego YC*		Alan Leibel
			Francis C. Findlay *Lake Washington Rowing*		Lorne Leibel
Tornado		USA David R. McFaull *Wakiki YC*			Larry Woods
		Michael J. Rothwell *Wakiki YC*			Michael de la Roche
Dutchman				Norman Freeman (6) *Ithaca YC*	Hans Fogh
				John G. Mathias, Jr. *Buffalo Canoe Club*	Evert Bastet
470				Robert M. Whitehurst (9)	Colin Mark
				D. Thomas Whitehurst *Pensacola YC*	J. Cross
Finn				Peter Commette (11) *Mantoloking YC*	Sanford Reiley (8)
1980	**TALLINN, ESTONIA** (BOYCOTTED BY USA)				
Soling				Robert B. Haines, Jr.	Bill Abbott
				Roderick H. Davis	Bill Abbott, Jr.
				Edward N. Trevelyan	Phil Bisel
Star				William E. Buchan	Alan Leibel *Toronto*
				Ron Anderson	David Shaw
Tornado				Henry Bossett	Larry Woods
				Jeff Kent	John Burrows
Dutchman				Michael Loeb	Terry McLaughlin *Toronto*
				J. Marshall Duane	Evert Bastet *Montreal*
470				Stephen D. Benjamin	Tam Matthews
				Neal Fowler	J. Cross
Finn				John Bertrand	Rob Woodbury
1984	**LOS ANGELES, CALIFORNIA**				
Soling	USA Robert B. Haines, Jr. *Newport Beach YC*		CAN Hans Fogh *Toronto*		
	Roderick H. Davis *Coronado YC*		Steve Calder *Toronto*		
	Edward N. Trevelyan *San Diego YC*		John Kerr *Toronto*		
Star	USA William E. Buchan *Corinthian YC*				Lawrence Lemeur
	Steven R. Erickson				Wilton Gessing
Dutchman	USA Jonathan D. McKee *Seattle YC*	CAN Terry McLaughlan *Toronto*			
	William (Carl) Buchan *Seattle YC*	Evert Bastet *Montreal*			
Tornado		USA Randy L. Smith *Fort Walton YC*			Davis Sweeney
		Jay Glaser *Newport Harbor YC*			Brian Sweeney
470		USA Stephen D. Benjamin *Seawanhaka Corinthian YC*			Frank McLaughlin
		H. Chris Steinfeld			Martin Tenhove
Finn		USA John Bertrand	CAN Terry Nielsen *Canada*		
Windglider		USA R. Scott Steele			

Olympiad	*Gold Medal*	*Silver Medal*	*Bronze Medal*	*Representing USA*	*Representing Canada*
1988	**PUSAN, SOUTH KOREA**				
Soling		USA John P. Kostecki *Richmond YC*			Paul Thomason
		Robert I. C. Billingham *St. Francis YC*			Phil Gow
		William H. Baylis *St.Francis YC*			Stuart Flinn
Star		USA Mark J. Reynolds *San Diego YC*			Ross MacDonald
		Hal H. Haenel *Los Angeles YC*			Bruce MacDonald
Dutchman			CAN Frank McLaughlin *Tor.*	Paul J. Foerester (11) *Austin YC*	
			John Millen *Toronto*	Andrew D. Goldman *American YC*	
Tornado				J. H. (Pete) Melvin (14)	David Sweeney
				Patrick L. Muglia *Mission Bay YC*	Kevin Smith
470 - Men			USA John Shadden *Long Beach YC*		Nigel Cochrane
			Charles McKee *Seattle YC*		Gord Mcliquham
470 - Women	USA Allison Blair Jolly				Karen Johnson
	Lynne M. Jewell				Gail Johnson
Finn				Brian R.Ledbetter (10) *San Diego YC*	Lawrence Lemeux (9)
Sailboard Div II			USA Michael W. Gebhardt *Fort Walton YC*		Richard Myerscough
1992	**BARCELONA, SPAIN**				
Soling		USA Kevin P. Mahaney			Paul Thomason
		James H. Brady *New York YC*			Phil Gow
		Douglas J. Kern *Austin YC*			Stuart Flinn
Star	USA Mark J. Reynolds *San Diego YC*				Ross MacDonald
	Hal H. Haenel *Los Angeles YC*				Eric Jesperson
Dutchman		USA Paul J. Foerester *Austin YC*			Frank McLaughlin
		Stephen N. Bourdow *Southern YC*			John Millen
Tornado		USA Randy L. Smyth *Fort Walton YC*			David Sweeney
		Keith I. Notary			Kevin Smithy
470 - Men		USA Morgan I. Reeser *Coral Reef YC*			Nigel Cochrane
		Kevin Burnham *Key Biscayne YC*			Jeff Eckard
470 - Women			USA J. J. Fetter Isler *San Diego YC*		Penney Stamper
			Pamela K. Healy *St. Francis YC*		Sarah McLean
Finn		USA Brian R. Ledbetter *San Diego YC*			Hank Lammens
Europe			USA Julia L. Trotman		Shona Moss
Sailboard - Men		USA Michael W. Gebhardt *Fort Walton YC*			Murray McCaig
Sailboard - Women				Lanee Butler (5)	Carol-Ann Alie
1996	**SAVANNAH, GEORGIA**				
Soling			USA Jeff Madrigali		Bill Abbott, Jr. (4) *Sarnia YC*
			Kent Massey		Joanne Abbott *Sarnia YC*
			Jim Barton *St. Francis & San Francisco YCs*		Brad Boston *Sarnia YC*
Star				Mark Reynolds (8) *San Diego YC*	Ross Macdonald (14) *RV YC*
				Hal Haenel *California YC*	Eric Jespersen *RV YC*
Tornado				John Lovell (8) *Southern YC*	Marc Peers (11) *Wabamun SC*
				Charlie Ogletree *Houston YC*	Roy Janse *Wabamun SC*
470 - Men				Morgan Reeser (8) *Key Biscayne YC*	Paul Hannam (20) *RVYC*
				Kevin Burnham *Key Biscayne YC*	Brian Storey *RVYC*
470 - Women				Kristina F Stookey (4) *Belle Haven YC*	Penny Davis (9) *R YC*
				Louise Van Voorhis *Rochester YC*	Leigh Pearson *RVYC*
Finn				Will Martin (23) *Carolina YC*	Richard Clarke (9) *RCYC*
Laser				Nick Adamson (21) *Newport Beach YC*	Rod Davies (26) *RCYC & FBYC*
Europe			USA Courtenay Becker Dey *American YC*		Tina Moberg-Parker (13)
Mistral - Men				Mike Gebhart (6) *Ft. Walton YC*	Alain Bolduc (16) *CYSA*
Mistral - Women				Lanee Butler (11) *Dana Point YC*	Carroll-Ann Alie (12) *RSLYC*

APPENDIX E

EARLY RESTRICTED AND ONE-DESIGN CLASSES[1]

1840 (or earlier) Log canoe – development class vicinity of St. Michaels on Chesapeake Bay

1851 Whitehalls - single and double-masted; raced in San Francisco Bay (*Alta*, Oct. 23) J. L. Trimingham imported one from NY in 1883 to race in Bermuda

1870's 'Fitted' Dinghies in Bermuda

1880's Sailing canoe in San Francisco at Encinal Yacht Club, but for only a few years

1885 North Haven Dinghy – first truly one-design in North America; William Weld, North Haven MA

Sandbagger era (and earlier); NJ, New York Harbor, Long Island Sound, Narragansett Bay and Nantucket Sound

Sharpie with round bilge – Ralph Middleton Munroe in Biscayne Bay, FL and New Orleans

1888 40-foot development class designed for New York Yacht Club by Edward Burgess presaging concept of a controlled class for club sailing

New Haven Racing Sharpie by Lester Rowe for Lake Champlain

1890 Royal Nova Scotia Yacht Squadron 23-foot LOA, 18-foot LWL, gaff-rigged knockabout

1891 Catboat for Seawanhaka Corinthian Yacht Club, Oyster Bay NY

1892 (or earlier) Sailing canoe in Chesapeake Bay

First Knockabout *Jane* built and 1894 Massachusetts Knockabout Association formed. No detailed plans, but specs. for hull, sail area, materials and black bands on spars.

18-Foot Class – three boats at Corinthian Yacht Club (Philadelphia) under Seawanhaka Rule

1893 Mosquito Boat – Riverton Yacht Club DE

1894 Catyawl – 21-feet LOA, 5-foot 6-inch beam, 9-inch draft at Nodaway Yacht Club WI

1895 Herreshoff 21-foot fin-keel sloop

12-foot dinghy, Douglaston and Manhasset Bay

1896 Newport 30's – 42-foot LOA by Herreshoff

Newport 30's built by Herreshoff for owners at Newport RI

15-foot Class – 21 feet 9 inches LOA, 15 feet LWL for Yale University (CT) built at New Bedford MA

1897 15-foot centerboard sailboat racing as one-design at Pacific Yacht Club in San Francisco Bay

14-footer by I. Wilton Morse adopted by Lake Skiff Sailing Association for Toronto and Hamilton areas.

One-design 33-foot centerboarder with knockabout rig, Corinthian Yacht Club (Philadelphia)

1897/8 17-foot and 20-foot Scow classes adopted by Inland Lake Yachting Association to Seawanhaka Rule raced without handicap; similar to a design "used in the Northwest"

1898 One-design between a Knockabout and Raceabout (the latter had more sail area) for Seawanhaka Corinthian Yacht Club a.k.a. Leakabouts by Stearns & Mackay; fleets at Westchester Country Club and Corinthian Yacht Club (Philadelphia).

1898 Herreshoff 15 a.k.a. Buzzards Bay 15 and Watch Hill 15 (Fisher's Island Sound)

21-foot Dory by C.D. Mower for Swampscott Club (MA) and a dory for Riverside Yacht Club (CT)

Dinghy class at Royal Canadian Yacht Club (Toronto)

1899 Lark a.k.a. The Barn Doors for Corinthian Yacht Club (Philadelphia)

1900 Idem Class gaff-rigged centerboarder 32-feet LOA, 19-feet LWL for St. Regis Yacht Club, Adirondacks NY and Royal Bombay Yacht Club – original boats still racing on Upper St. Regis Lake

Redbank Knockabouts a.k.a. Red Bank 14's at Red Bank Yacht Club (NJ) and later Monmouth Boat Club (NJ)

1900 New York 70's a.k.a. Newport 70's by Herreshoff

1900's 'R' Class on East and West Coasts and Inland Lakes

1901 Manhasset Bay Knockabouts – used by several clubs

23-foot C. D. Mower Knockabout – Royal Victoria Yacht Club

22-Footers, Victoria Yacht Club; first one-designs in Pacific Northwest

1902 Buzzards Bay 30 – another successful Herreshoff design

Bar Harbor 31 – by Herreshoff for Maine Sonder – German design; first built in North America for Eastern Yacht Club for international team racing

1904 12-foot class, Corinthian Yacht Club, Philadelphia

1905 New York 30's – first of larger offshore one-designs to spread and sustain (a few extant)

1906 Bug – by William Gardner; design enlarged and became the Star Class

Sonder Class (restricted/development class) imported by Eastern Yacht Club (MA) from Germany; Herreshoff & Mower designs on Long Island Sound NY and Corinthian Yacht Club, Philadelphia

'R' Class – most popular Universal Rule class; first fleet Marblehead; spread to East and West coasts, Great Lakes and Hawaii; a few currently in GRP

Cotuit Skiff – Cape Cod

1907 Raceabouts – clubs on Long Island Sound

1908 or later Luedtke Catboat on Great Lakes

Dark Harbor 17½ a.k.a. Manchester (MA) or Bar Harbor (ME) 17½

1909 SS for South Shore of Long Island (NY)

1910 Chula Vista One-Design – 28-feet LOA by Clem Stose built in San Diego

1911 International Star Class

1912 Northeast Harbor (ME) 17-foot gaff-rigged a.k.a. Eastern Yacht Club 17-foot, Sloop Knockabout Class, Marblehead One-Designs et alia

1913 'R' by Ted Geary at Royal Vancouver Yacht Club with gaff rig; 1914 to Chicago Yacht Club; 1915 raced San Francisco Bay. Before 1913 on Long Island Sound and Marblehead ?

Wianno Senior on Cape Cod (MA)

1914 Herreshoff 12½, a.k.a. Buzzards Bay Boys Boats; a 15-footer; originals still sail; GRP version called Bullseye

1915 Six-Metre, first US-built in San Francisco for Panama-Pacific International Exposition; 1921

Seawanhaka Corinthian (Long Island Sound) fleet for British-American Cup

1918 18-foot Knockabout a.k.a. Cape Cod Baby

1919 Fish Class at Mississippi and Gulf Coast by J. Rathborne DeBuys

'S' Class – Herreshoff; 27 feet LOA; from Massachusetts to Hawaii; over 100 built of which 30 raced at Bristol, RI in class's 75th anniversary

1920's Barnegat Bay Sneakbox; first built in 1836 but no early record of its being a class

1920 Victory – 31-feet 6-inches LOA keel sloop by William Gardner for Larchmont Yacht Club; Great Lakes and Long Island Sound

Beetle Cat – Henry Beetle designer; currently in GRP

1922-27 Bay Bird on San Francisco Bay

1922 'O' Boat by Alden at Swampscott (MA) and St. Regis Lake, Adirondacks (NY)

1923 Class 'E' Scow adopted by Inland Lake Yachting Association – initially with single centerboard – Inland Lakes, NJ, SC, Midwest, St. Lawrence River

1924 Massachusetts Bay Hustler

1926 Sound Interclub by C.D. Mower; Long Island Sound and a few at Houston, Great Lakes

1928 Geary 18 a.k.a. Flattie 18-foot flat bottom for Seattle juniors by L. E. (Ted) Geary

Suicide at Huntington Yacht Club, Long Island Sound (NY) and Biscayne Bay Yacht Club, Coconut Grove (FL)

1929 Starlet – 16-foot keel sloop for juniors at San Diego; filled same role as Snipe, i.e. need for a smaller, less expensive version of the Star.

Atlantic – 30½-foot keel boat by Burgess and built in Germany; Long Island Sound NY and CT

1930 Junior Star – 17-foot keel sloop for juniors by John Linderman at Encinal Yacht Club, San Francisco Bay; served same function as San Diego Starlet but no connection.

1930 PC (Pacific Class)– keel sloops built by George Kettenburg, Jr. San Diego; raced as one-design but would have rated under Universal Rule similar to 'S' Class in size, rating and speed to Herreshoff 'S' Class.

1931 Snipe – 15½ foot keel boat by William F. Crosby; first boat built at Pass Christian MI

1932 Comet – 16-foot LOA centerboarder, first called Crabs & Star Junior, by C. Lowndes Johnson

1936 I.O.D. (International One Design) – 33-feet LOA by Bjane Aas (Norway) for Larchmont Yacht Club

1938 Lightning – 19-foot centerboarder by Sparkman & Stephens

Penguin – 11½-foot cat-rigged dinghy by Philip L. Rhodes

1939 110 – 11½-foot keel boat by Ray Hunt; distributed across continent

SAMPLING OF POST WORLD WAR II CLASSES

1945 Udell Class at Chicago Yacht Club by Dick Latham, Franz Wagner and George Jensen

Bluenose – Armdale Yacht Club, Halifax NS by William J. Roue designer of *Bluenose*

L-16 – keel boat by Alfred E. 'Bill' Luders, Jr. for Indian Harbor Yacht Club (CT); Long Island Sound, Chicago Yacht Club, Southern Yacht Club, San Diego, etc.

1950 Concordia – by C. Raymond Hunt; 103 of the yawls were built making it the largest in size and number in wood; many still sailing

1958 Thunderbird on Puget Sound by Ben Seaborn, Tacoma WA. Initially plywood, later GRP with fleets on Great Lakes, East Coast, California and Switzerland. Also popular for cruising.

The above is more a sampling, especially from 1920 onwards, than a definitive listing in order to provide an indication of the geographical spread and timespan of the development of the racing classes. Some of the sources relied upon: Sailing Craft *by Edwin J. Schoettle © The MacMillan Company 1937;* Early One-Design Sailboats *by Diana Eames Esterly © Charles Scribner's Sons 1979;* The Oldest West Coast One-Design Rediscovered *by Rusty White, Nautical Heritage Society 1991.*

APPENDIX F

CCA CLARIFIES ITS POSITION ON INTERNATIONAL MEASUREMENT

To clear up misunderstandings and conjectures concerning the status of the proposed International Measurement Rule, and the attitude of the Cruising Club of America towards its adoption, Commodore Ewing of the CCA has issued the following statement:

The Board of Governors of the CCA is unanimous in the belief that an internationally accepted measurement rule would be of great benefit to the sport of off-shore racing. Although the rule is not yet in final form, the International Technical Committee representing the U.S., Britain and ten other countries under the chairmanship of Olin Stephens has made great progress in bringing together the best features of the CCA and RORC rules.

Scantlings, previously a heavily weighted factor in the RORC Rule, and objectionable to American designers and yachtsmen, will appear in the new rule only as a deterrent to dangerously light construction, if at all. The subject is still under study, but the Technical Committee is agree that any new scantling factor will not affect the rating of a soundly constructed ocean racer, regardless of materials used. The second unresolved matter of consequence, and still under study, is inclining and the value given it.

Sail area measurements will adhere closely to those of the present CCA Rule. Girth measurements will be similar to those used in the RORC Rule, although substantially modified to discourage pinched in ends. Girth measurements are new to American yachtsmen and may seem complicated. However, the difficulty of taking them is exaggerated and they have the great advantage of enabling hull measurements to be taken with the boat out of water in the off-season and need be taken only once, unless hull changes are made.

Action by the CCA to adopt the new rule will not be taken until the Rule has been finalized, and put through a careful test to determine how it will affect the rating of a wide variety of American yachts. Such a test will take yachts of differing design, construction and size, calculate their ratings under the new rule, and then compare those with their CCA ratings and known performance. Any inequities or potential loopholes will be thoroughly explored. Neither will action be taken until the CCA is assured that machinery is set up to administer the rule internationally, and provision is made for continuing study and modification to keep the rule in step with new developments in design and construction. Finally, adoption will not be considered until a program for gradual and orderly transition from the CCA Rule to an International rule has been set. Such a program is now under consideration and will be ready should the CCA Governors be satisfied on all other points.

In concluding his statement, Commodore Ewing stressed his concern for the Cruising Club's responsibility to the 1,500 or more yachtsmen now holding CCA Measurement Certificates. He stated that the Board of Governors must have time for careful scrutiny of the new rule and the results of thorough testing; also, it must be assured that provision is made for orderly competition during any transition period.

THIRTY-SEVEN YEARS LATER ÆMILIUS JARVIS REFLECTS ON THE 1898 EXCHANGE

ÆMILIUS JARVIS
TORONTO, CAN.

July 15th, 1935.

Clifford D. Mallory, Esq.,
11 Broadway,
New York, N.Y.,
U.S.A.

My dear Mr. Mallory:-

In 1896 or 1897 the Yacht Racing Union of the Great Lakes was formed. This embraced both American and Canadian Clubs. It grew so fast that it was extended to the Atlantic Seaboard and was so well received that some of the Atlantic Seaboard Clubs became interested and the Clubs on the Lake and those on the Seaboard joined in forming the North American Yacht Racing Union.

We had many meetings in New York and in Boston. The late Louie Clarke of Boston, George Owen and Charlie Adams were the most active in that neighborhood. Frank B. Jones, Prof. Poor Joe McDonnough, Oliver Cromwell, Will Gardiner, W. P. Stephens, Hyslop Gillough (wrongly spelled I am afraid) and Duncan Butler were the most active about New York.

The dissatisfaction with the type of yacht being produced under the Length and Sail Area (Siwanica) led to a desired change in rules, and McDonnough and I and another whose name I forget but who did not come, were appointed a committee to go to England and study the yachts then being built under the girth rule. McDonnough and I went and presented out letters to the Y.R.A. Secretary, Dickson Kemp at that time, a very sick man, who shortly afterwards died owing to which a delay occurred, when Hextall Smith succeeded him and we had several meetings. Joe McDonnough went to France and left me to continu Through the introduction of the R.Y.A. I visited G.L.Watson, Will Fyfe Charlie Nicholson (then quite young), A. E. Payne the elder, Sybic, So and Linton Hope, and discussed the subject with them, and what amendmen and suggestions they had to make to bring about the desired end, as the Y.R.A. was at that time quite prepared to work in harmony with the new North American Yacht Racing Association.

One and all of these designers helped me in every way possible and I brought back lines of many of the most successful yachts. At that time Watson's BONA was cleaning up in the larger classes and the QUEEN MAB which ultimately came to this side, Fyfe's AILSA, Soper's SATANITA and a whole host of smaller and newer designs in the smaller classes.

ÆMILIUS JARVIS
TORONTO, CAN.

-2-

Clifford D. Mallory, Esq.-

These lines I brought out and McDonnough and I made a report to the Union, which must be on fyle among its early records. Living as I did, so remote from New York, and owing to the opposition of the New York Yacht Club, the organization languished, as you know, and, until you took hold, amounted to nothing, but we on the lakes, went on, and actually did adopt the British rule, but seeing that the salt water people were not in earnest and there being no use in a similar rule to the Y. R. A., we adopted for several years a rule that produced the IRONDEQUOIT, STRATHCONA and a number of similar craft which were a decided step ahead of those built under the Length and Sail Area rule. This rule was devised in collaboration with Will Gardiner George Owen, Hyslop, Crownanshields and one or two others on this side, with Fyfe, Watson, Soper and Nicholson on the other side. Then Nat Herreshoff showed interest but played a loan hand and brought out the Universal Rule which we promptly adopted, as in our opinion it produced what the others were after in a much more scientific manner.

I hope I have not wearied you with this tale, but I think it covers pretty well the request in your last paragraph. I know I have a copy of the report made by McDonnough and myself to the Union but cannot at the moment lay my hand on it - some day it will turn up unexpectedly. However, as I said before, there should be a copy on fyle, if friend Jones kept it. What has become of him, by the way? Last time I saw him, he was all crippled up with the rheumatism. No doubt, like so many of my old friends, he has passed on.

I dont suppose you ever come this way? If you do, I would consider it an unfriendly act if you did not let me know and come and stop with me. I live out in the country, where you can have plenty of fresh air, scenery and good fellowship, and have quite a model room in my library.

With kindest regards and best wishes, believe me to be,

Yours very faithfully,

A SUMMONS TO FORM A CANADIAN YACHTING ASSOCIATION

January 17, 1931.

Dear Sir:

The possible need for some distinctly Canadian Yachting Association that could be recognized as nationally representative, has been the subject for quite a lot of discussion among Yachtsmen here, largely as a result of developments in the yacht racing world during the last few years.

The matter becomes quite prominent from time to time when typically International yacht races are held and Canada is not represented by any National entry.

For example, when most of the Yachting nations competed on Long Island Sound for the Scandinavian Gold Cup - emblematic of the 6 Metre Yacht supremacy - our Public insistently asked through the Press, 'Why was Canada not represented?'

After the recent races for the 'America's Cup', a great movement appeared to be under way in the Press of Canada to organize some means whereby Canada might challenge for that Trophy in the near future.

And now we have to consider the International Yacht Races to be held in connection with the Olympic Games at Los Angeles in 1932.

The truth is that we have no Canadian Yachting body that is sufficiently representative to make a National entry in any such events.

Practically all of our Clubs are affiliated with Racing Associations composed of both Canadian and United States Clubs, and while this arrangement is a natural and most convenient one for the purposes of local or district racing, it does not provide for many aspects of the sport in a strictly National sense.

It has been urged also that the time has come to promote and develop a more distinctly National character in our Yacht Racing activities and to co-ordinate them through the medium of a National body preferably composed of our active Yacht Clubs from Coast to Coast.

We have been reminded of Canada's past record in Shipbuilding, when her sailing ships were to be found on every ocean; the fame of her Nova Scotia fishing fleets; the extent of her Merchant Marine; and her record past and present in building and racing Yachts; it is held that all these form a most proper background for the development of a national yachting spirit.

These and other considerations indicate the desire in many quarters to have some so-called "National Authority" to

- 2 -

be representative of Canada as occasion may require, and to provide means for acting in behalf of her Yacht Clubs. Such an Association presumably would be incorporated by Charter of the Dominion Government, and would seek recognition from the International Yacht Racing Union as Canada's representative body for National purposes.

It has been suggested that it should adopt as official the Racing Rules agreed to by both the N.A.Y.R.U. and the Y.R.A., so that these Rules should acquire a status in Canada that is now lacking because no sufficiently representative Canadian body is in existence to sponsor them.

It would not interfere in any way with existing Racing Associations, which already control local and district Yacht Racing. If it could succeed in fostering a Canadian yachting spirit; in establishing the status and authority of a uniform Racing Code; in sponsoring entries for International racing events and providing the machinery for selecting such entries; and in general serving as a medium for the Canadian Yacht Clubs to work and act together for the advancement of the sport, it should be well worth while.

The Royal Canadian Yacht Club is taking the liberty of bringing this matter to the attention of our Canadian Yacht Clubs in the hope that they will give it full consideration, and that they will favour the Club with their respective views.

Should the project meet with the wide-spread support necessary for its success, the R.C.Y.C. would gladly offer its services to initiate such further steps as may be required to get the movement under way.

Any suggestions as to the basis on which such an organization might best be formed would be most welcome. In the meantime, for the purpose of giving a lead to such suggestions, we attach a memorandum outlining a few features that have been proposed as a structure for a Constitution.

Respectfully submitted,

Geo. H. Gooderham

Commodore,
ROYAL CANADIAN YACHT CLUB.

APPENDIX G

CORRESPONDENCE – JARVIS, GOODERHAM ET ALIA

Letters relating to the trip by Æmilius Jarvis and J.M. Macdonough to London in 1898 to meet with officials of the Yacht Racing Association concerning measurement rules and other subjects. Letter from Commodore George H. Gooderham to 22 yacht clubs relative to formation of a Canadian Yachting Association.

To Sir George A. Leach, K.C.B.
Chairman, Y.R.A.
London, January 7th, 1898

My Dear Sir,

In your note of 2nd Dec. last you expressed a wish to be advised as to my movements, therefore, I write to say that business calls me to Scotland on Monday next where I shall be for at least a week.

From your note and from a conversation recently had with Mr. Newton-Robinson, I gather there has been a misconception of the object of our visit. Mr. Macdonough and myself were appointed a committee by the Council of the North American Yacht Racing Union to confer with your body upon the measurement rule question and other subjects of interest to yachtsmen, and to obtain authentic and practical information as to the working of your rule, – if it was satisfactory on the whole to yacht owners-and what type it was producing. I might say we had an impression it was not altogether popular, which impression no doubt arose from the recent proposed change.

Nothing in our instructions gave us power to bind our Union, therefore, it was not expected to commit yours, but merely bring about a state of affairs that should in the future prove beneficial to both bodies, it being very evident both are striving to bring about the same result.

Trusting to have the pleasure of meeting you again before my return to Canada,

Believe me to be,

Yours faithfully,

(Sgd.) Æmilius Jarvis

6 Wetherby Gardens
South Kensington
6th January, 1898
(Crossing my letter of 7th)

Dear Mr. Jarvis,

We are rather at sixes and sevens in the Y.R.A. matters in consequence of the resignation of our Secretary. I sent your note to Mr. Lake who is acting pro tem. and he was to call a meeting between the dates you names, the 3rd and 8th of January, but as I have no notice from him it seems probable he has forgotten amongst other pressing business, – for he is a very busy man, – to do so.

If you will send me a wire when you receive this I will get a few of the members to meet you on Saturday afternoon or Monday afternoon, if that will be convenient to you. Please give me your address in town so that I may communicate with you there, instead of through the Montreal Bank, as this will probably save time.

Yours faithfully,

(Sgd.) G. A. Leach

---

6 Wetherby Gardens,
South Kensington,
7th January 1898

Dear Mr. Jarvis,

I have called a meeting at the Royal London Yacht Club, 2 Savile Row, W., at 2.30 to-morrow afternoon, in response to your telegram. I hope this will suit you. I have not yet received your letter.

Yours faithfully,

(Sgd.) G. A. Leach

To Æmilius Jarvis, Esq.,
Yacht Racing Association
London West Kensington, W.
22nd January 1898

Dear Sir,

The Council of the Yacht Racing Association desires me to express to you the sincere satisfaction with which it welcomes the action of the North American Yacht Racing Association in deputing yourself and Mr. Macdonough to confer as to the possibility of bringing the British and American rules of yacht measurement into approximation, so that the yachts of either country may compete in the other without serious disadvantage.

The Council is conscious of the very great difficulty which would be experienced in any attempt to agree upon one and the same rule for both countries, and if such agreement were attained it is of opinion that differences of climate would cause the evolution of rather diverging types of yachts on the opposite sides of the Atlantic.

At the same time, the Council, understanding that the general desire of American yachtsmen, like that of our own is for a rule which will produce wholesome and roomy sea boats, feels confident that your Association will be able to assimilate British and American racing yachts in type, by adopting some formula conceived upon similar lines to our own, yet with such variations as the conditions of the American climate and racing courses may render necessary.

In reply to the particular questions which you have addressed to the Council, I am to say that the measurement rule

$$\frac{\text{L.} + \text{B.} + .75\,\text{G.} + .5\,\sqrt{\text{S. A.}}}{2} = \text{Lineal Rating}$$

which has now been in operation in British waters for two seasons to give general satisfaction at present.

It was adopted in order to correct the tendency of the former rule $\frac{L. \times S. A.}{6000}$ to produce yachts of very small displacement and sail area relatively to their hull dimensions.

The operation of the new formula has been decidedly such as was expected by its framer.

In conclusion the Council hopes that after your Association has thoroughly tested whatever rule it may finally adopt, another opportunity may be afforded for a conference between the representatives of the two organizations with a view to harmonizing such changes in the respective formulae as may ultimately appear to be desirable.

I am, dear sir,
Your obedient servant,
(Sgd.) B. Hechstall Smith, Secretary

To B. Hechstall Smith, Esq.
Sec'y Yacht Racing Association
31st January 1898

Dear Sir,

Your letter of 22nd inst., I beg to acknowledge its friendly expression, and the valuable information it contains I feel will be received and appreciated by the North American Yacht Racing Union in the warmest possible manner, and it will give me the greatest pleasure reading its contents and reporting to the Council the result of my observations, and the knowledge obtained through your Association and its individual members on the practical working and type of Racing Yacht being developed in G.B. under your present formula,

$$\frac{L. + B. + .75 G. + .5 \sqrt{S. A.}}{2}$$

Your suggestion for us to adopt a rule – if not identical – at least moulded on similar lines to yours and then after a few years experience, both organizations meet in conference to exchange ideas and experiences, appears to me to be a most practical way to bring about uniformity of rule and type of racing yacht on both sides of the Atlantic.

I am returning at an early date, and will at once make my report to the Council who in due course will, through our Hon. Sec'y, Mr. Jones, address to you our official acknowledgment of the courtesies extended to their Committee, Mr. Macdonough and myself, meanwhile kindly accept our sincere appreciation, and believe me to be,
Yours very faithfully,
(Sgd.) Æmilius Jarvis

Æmilius Jarvis, Esq.
London, Jany. 31, 1898

Dear Sir,

I am in due receipt of your favor of this date which it will give me much pleasure to read to the Council at their next meeting.

I am, dear sir,
Yours faithfully,
(Sgd.) B. Hechstall Smith, Secretary

Æmilius Jarvis, Esq.
Glasgow, 28th Jany. 1898

Dear Mr. Jarvis,

I have been at it night and day since I saw you and this must be my excuse for neglecting to write you before this. I, however, now enclose midship sections of two racing boats and a fast cruiser, which I trust may be of use and interest to your friends.

With regard to the centreboard question – I think our rule penalizes it out of existence, and that in framing any rule the clause regarding the board would have to be modified. As for American waters – I think it a very necessary adjunct. You have a lot of harbors accessible only for boats drawing under 10 feet, and you cannot get sufficient depth for weatherly purposes in a boat of any size without more draught than this. Were I making any alteration in our rule, I would suggest easing up the penalty on girth. As the rule acts at present, you can put $1^1/_2$ feet of beam or $1^1/_2$ feet of length for the same penalty as one foot of draught. My feeling is that this encourages too much curtailment of draught – a dimension which gives the best type of stability, and is also necessary of course for weatherly purposes. This I say is my feeling for the rule over here, but with the American Yachting ports, you want as moderate draught as possible, for there it might do very well as it stands.

Yours very truly,
(Sgd.) G. L. Watson

North Lodge, Alverstoke
Gosport, Feby. 3 1898

Dear Mr.Jarvis,

In my previous letter to you of this evening I had not time to say anything about the subject of your mission. As I said in the course of our conversation it seems very much to be desired that the experts on both sides of the Atlantic should confer and make use of each others experience when opportunity arrives, and in the meantime it is certainly desirable in order that our experiences may be mutually profitable that we should work on somewhat similar lines. If in America you could adopt our present rule or something similar to it, provisionally, the result would be very interesting and valuable, and not the less so if as you anticipate-and I think you are right – the same rule should lead to a somewhat different boat in the two countries owing to the difference in conditions. If our present rule were not adopted holus bolus it occurs to me to suggest that a very interest variation would be L. + B. + .75 G. simply, leaving the $.5 \sqrt{}$ S. A. out, and this would tend I think, to produce more nearly the popular kind of craft in America, viz., a craft of larger cross sections, and more power of cross section relatively to length that our present rule. For the course the power of taking more sail leads to increase in the hull qualities that make for sail carrying.

Personally I should greatly welcome the adoption of such a rule in America. For I strongly hope myself that if we make any change in our rule we should take the opportunity of abolishing the sail-tax, and the experience of the result of its abolition in America would be most valuable to us.

It seems to me that taking the L. + B. + .75 G. + $.5 \sqrt{}$S.A. as a starting point, dropping the $.5 \sqrt{}$S. A. out would be very closely equivalent to introducing K.$\sqrt{}$ M. S. with a negative sign in the division, and if so would be an immensely more simple way or producing the same effect. It would be doing away with one complicated measurement, instead of introducing another in addition.

Then again I think there is a pretty general feeling among even those – here – who approve of the present rule and approve of a sail-tax in principle that the present sail-tax – (i.e., in our present rule) – is too light to produce any effect worth having in the way of promoting snug sail plans, and that from the point of view we have all the bother of sail measurement for next to nothing. Yet if you keep the B. + .75 G. and increase the S. A. tax – i.e., put say $\sqrt{}$S.A., you will almost certainly get a longer and less powerful type of boat than is desired across the water.

For my own part, though I personally prefer a boat that neither requires not can carry a large press of sail relatively to length – I prefer an easily driven boat – it seems to me absurd for racing purposes that boats should not be allowed to take as much sail as they can utilize to advantage, and therefore I am against all sail-tax on principle.

Believe me. Yours very truly,
R.E. Froude

Hotel Victoria
Monte Carlo, Feby 3rd 1898

My Dear Jarvis,

Allow me to congratulate you heartily on the success of your efforts in England, and to thank you for your kindness in keeping my name forward in the negotiations. If I can be of any use later on, during the month of April, well and good. The final letter from the Council seems in my opinion to leave nothing to be desired. The basis for further negotiations being formed, it now only requires a little tact to keep both sides working in unison.

Yours sincerely,
(Sgd.) J.M. Macdonough

APPENDIX H

HAROLD S. VANDERBILT'S 41-YEAR STINT REVISING THE RULES

1920 As noted by Clinton H. Crane in his autobiography, Harold S. Vanderbilt had started work on the racing rules five years before the revival of NAYRU with the aim of simplifying them by defining "unmistakable right of way determinations."

1936 Vanderbilt publishes *A Suggested Revision of the International Yacht Racing Rules* in collaboration with Henry H. Anderson, Philip J. Roosevelt and Van S. Merle-Smith.[1] The three were asked by Vanderbilt to review and critique his work.

1944 His *Fundamental Right of Way Rules: New vs. Old Supplemental Rules Related to Right of Way vs. Old Operation of the New Rules* is a primer on the proposed rules. By this time the Lake George and Cincinnati Yacht Clubs had been testing them for a season or more .

1947 Clinton H. Crane, who was President of NAYRU and strongly in favor of the proposed revisions, leads the movement to introduce them as 'trial rules.'

1948 NAYRU adopts the new rules and Vanderbilt goes to London to try to sell them to the Royal Yachting Association. The President of the RYA, Sir Ralph G. Gore, and others, however, rebuff him.

1953 - 59 There were no major changes in the NAYRU rules. During this period Henry S. Morgan and Robert N. Bavier, Jr. represented NAYRU at the IYRU meetings, and IYRU adopted some of the features of the rules. Discussion continued: for example, in 1957 Sir Peter Scott, President of the International Yacht Racing Union, met with J. Amory Jeffries, President of NAYRU, at the Boston airport where the possibility of a universal set of racing rules was part of their agenda. By 1958 some of the Scandinavian countries had tried the NAYRU (Vanderbilt) rules. The initiative for this had come from discussions between Henry S. Morgan and Crown Prince Olav of Norway who had raced Six-Metres together in international competition. When Crown Prince Olav became King, he was succeeded as Chairman of the IYRU Racing rules Committee by Nils Benson of Denmark, who not only was well versed on the issues but also an able diplomat. At this juncture that Bavier and Gerald Sambrooke-Sturgess, leading authority of the Royal Yachting Association on the racing rules, maintained a continuing dialogue on the right-of-way content of the NAYRU rules which led, surprisingly, to the British initiating the move for a uniform universal code. As a sort of 'quid pro quo' the North Americans would accept the IYRU wording and arrangement and the IYRU the right-of-way content. This set the stage for F. Gregg Bemis, who served on the NAYRU/USYRU Racing Rules Committee from 1950-1989, working with, among others, Sambrooke-Sturgess, Lynn A. Watters of Canada and Nils Benson drafted a version for present-ation, but not adoption, at the 1959 annual meeting of the IYRU in London. During 1960 meetings were held almost weekly to refine the draft which then was reviewed almost daily during the Olympic Yachting Games at Naples by Bemis, Scott, Bavier, Beppe Croce of Italy, et alia.

35 YEARS LATER

1996 (IYRU now ISAF) at the November meetings adopts the first major – in terms of concept and philosophy – change to the IYRR. While it took fewer years to accomplish than in the case of the Vanderbilt rules, the process was almost as tortuous, and again it was North American input that provided the principal impetus for what was an evolution rather than a revolution. Vanderbilt's influence continued to play a part in the process as Dick Rose commented in the June 1997 issue of *Sailing World*:

The more we tried to simplify the rules, the more we came to respect the work of Harold Vanderbilt.

Rosenfeld

Which rule applies under the old concept?

Part I—Fundamental Right of Way Rules—New *vs.* Old

I HAVE a purpose in writing these articles. It is to have the North American Yacht Racing Union and, if possible, the Yacht Racing Association (representing the British Empire and Europe) adopt: (a) the four Fundamental Right of Way Rules quoted below to replace the seven existing ones; and (b) a new supplemental rule structure to cover all other meeting positions of two yachts. The four Fundamental Rules I advocate are —

1. If two yachts are on opposite tacks, the port tack yacht shall keep out of the way.
2. If two yachts on the same tack are clear ahead and clear astern, the yacht clear astern shall keep out of the way.
3. If two yachts on the same tack overlap, the windward yacht shall keep out of the way.
4. A yacht, while tacking or jibing, shall keep out of the way of a yacht on a tack.

The racing yachtsman needs these four rules. They are simple and unmistakable and can be applied without hesitation in an exciting race. Today but few yachtsmen have digested all the ramifications of existing rules. Even fewer can apply them in the complicated situations that frequently arise and require instant decision.

While I appreciate the difficulty of changing rules during the present emergency, I hope that rule committees will study the principles hereinafter set forth with a view to the adoption of the four Fundamental Rules at the earliest possible date. I also hope that yachtsmen who may be (or may have been) convinced of the soundness of the new rules will use their influence to that end. I say "may have been convinced," because the changes which I advocate (incorporated into a new set of Right of Way Rules) have been exhaustively tested throughout three racing seasons and have met with unanimous acclaim by all yachtsmen who have sailed under them.

When we are asked to consider whether we should substitute a new set of rules for an old set, one of the first questions we should ask is whether the new set has been tested under actual racing conditions and, if so, with what success. The adoption or rejection of the new set of rules should depend more on the answer to these questions than on any arguments that can be advanced in their favor. "The proof of the pudding is in the eating."

Results of New Rule Tests

The new rules have been used exclusively by the Lake George Yacht Club during the 1941, 1942 and 1943 seasons, and by the Cincinnati Sailing Club during the 1942 and 1943 seasons. They have also been used extensively in Havana. They have met with unanimous approval by those who have sailed under them. I quote a few excerpts from letters.

Dr. W. P. Barnes, Chairman of the Race Committee of the Cincinnati Sailing Club, wrote me in reference to his 1942 racing season, on June 4, 1942:

> "It has been quite a struggle to get all the members, especially the older ones, to acquiesce to using the new rules. Your book *On the Wind's Highway* was a great help in developing arguments in their favor. It was the reading of this book which first brought the rules to my attention.
>
> "They are well suited to the variable wind conditions here on the river inasmuch as you may be sailing within a few seconds from a broad reach to close-hauled all on the same leg. The resulting complications under the old rules were very puzzling.

A SUPPLEMENTAL NOTE ON THE ORIGIN OF THE TEAM RACING RULES

While the revision of the yacht racing rules was a singular effort, in both senses of the word, the team racing rules had their genesis in a committee so large and diversified across North America that it never ever met as one body. It arose from an incident that occurred in the 1949 team match for the British-American Cup held in the Six-Metre Class on the Solent off Cowes, Isle of Wight.

The American Team, coming from behind, had tied the series so that the final race would decide the match. Reaching to the final mark before the run to the finish, the Americans were in a losing combination as their lead team member, Emil (Bus) Mosbacher, Jr., in *Llanoria* rounded it. *Llanoria*, instead of heading for the finish, sailed back on the previous leg to luff two British boats that were holding up an American boat to let another British team mate through. The maneuver was successful in regaining for the Americans a winning combination thereby clinching the series.

After the racing a member of the British Team, James Howden Hume, hosted a cocktail party aboard his large ketch, *Vedura*, during which there was heated discussion over the legality of the move by *Llanoria*, her proper course once she lost her luffing rights, and so forth. There was a consensus that supplemental rules to the International Yacht Racing Rules were needed to cover tactical situations in team racing that do not normally occur in fleet racing.

Concurrently the Inter-Collegiate Yacht Racing Association, had found the same need for college team racing, and the Edgartown Yacht Club on Martha's Vineyard, MA, had been using some ad hoc supplements to the IYRR for team racing. As a result, Leonard M. Fowle, Executive Vice President of the Inter-Collegiate Yacht Racing Association, appointed a committee composed of: Herman F. (Swede) Whiton, Robert M. Allan, Jr., Robert N. Bavier, Jr., William S. Cox, Emil Mosbacher, Jr., George O'Day, Henry H. Anderson, Jr.,[3] to develop rules applicable to team racing.

An initial attempt to re-write the rules in their entirety was quickly abandoned inasmuch as the right-of-way rules are so inter-related that even a minor change in one part inevitably affects others. After extensive correspondence and re-drafts, a final session among the eastern members of the committee was held at the Cox home in Darien. By dawn the proposed supplements were put to bed, but not the committee members who downed cups of coffee and caught the commuting train to Manhattan.

The result was essentially the current Appendix - Team Racing Rules. Much of the credit for their incorporation in the IYRR goes to the Royal Yachting Association since more team racing was being conducted at that time in the United Kingdom than anywhere else in the world.

FOR SIMPLIFYING THE RULES

AN EDITORIAL IN THE APRIL 1944, ISSUE OF *YACHTING*

Mr. Vanderbilt's articles propose the simplification and clarification of the rules under which yachts are raced. That the present rules need simplification and revision has been long apparent to everyone who has raced under them. Many of the rules overlap; which take precedence and which apply in certain situations if often in doubt, and different rules may be interpreted differently not only by the helmsmen themselves, but by race committees and appeal boards as well.

As a case in point, a protest made in a race a few years ago was decided in three different ways by as many reviewing authorities and, after a lapse of two years, the final decision of the then highest authority was reversed by the new Appeals Committee of the NAYRU. If it takes two years and four reviews to get the right answer to a situation that the skippers of two boats have to decide in a flashing moment, something must be very wrong with the rules under which yachtsmen are asked to race.

The rules suggested by Mr. Harold S. Vanderbilt in the articles mentioned above have much to recommend them and should receive careful study with an open mind. They are based on four fundamental right of way rules that are easy to comprehend and to apply in any situation. In an earlier, and less complete, draft they were first suggested some seven years ago. Since then they have been tried out for several seasons, and such changes as seemed necessary were incorporated. As presented, they are the clearest and simplest we have yet seen. They commend themselves for this reason. In comparison with the ambiguities of the present rules, which frequently take a sea lawyer to interpret them, they shine like a masthead light on a dark night.

Faced with the task of making a change in anything that has the years of use and tradition behind it of the present rule, which is international in scope and is used in many yachting countries, their adoption will be difficult. Yachtsmen are a conservative bunch as a whole. Yet, after a lapse of years in which there has been no serious racing, and with many new men coming into the sport after the war, agitation for a change towards simplification is timely. An open mind will help in any approach to this most important subject. In recent years, navigational methods have been radically changed and greatly simplified in spite of the traditional conservatism of the seafaring class. Is it beyond reason that we may accomplish the same thing in our racing rules?

APPENDIX I

ASSISTS, SOURCES, HISTORIES AND CONTRIBUTORS

INDIVIDUALS AND ORGANIZATIONS

Thomas V. Allen, Jr., US SAILING coordinator for the History; Morton Bloom, Jr., expediter Los Angeles-Long Beach; William E. Bradshaw, Richard S. Marshall (author Corinthian Helmsman, 1945-1995 50th Anniversary Corinthian Yacht Club*), Dr. Robert Coe, Douglas Wilson (Historian) and Robert S. Carter, Seattle Yacht Club; Don McVittie and Richard M. Rose, Corinthian Yacht Club (Seattle); Margaret Brennan, Archivist, Frederick Brock, Nancy Shield, and Patrick Shield, past and present Hon. Archivists, Royal Canadian Yacht Club; Pat Healy, Canadian Yachting Association; Craig Arnold, Librarian and Editor, San Diego Maritime Museum; Maldwin Drummond, OBE JPDL, past Commodore Royal Yacht Squadron; Peter Evans, past Commodore, Royal Nova Scotia Yacht Squadron; Joseph Garland, editor* The Eastern Yacht Club*; Halsey C. Herreshoff and David Guertin, Herreshoff Marine Museum; Carlton Pinheiro,* Herreshoff of Bristol*; Becky Smith, Historical Association of South Florida; Joseph A. Jackson, Librarian New York Yacht Club, for his unearthing hard-to-find data; Matt Jones, Race Director St. Francis Yacht Club; Anne Russell, PhD (Historian) and Dr. Joseph M. James, Carolina (Wilmington) Yacht Club; Florence K. Scheib, author Richard Spangenberg and Oliver J. Counce (Co-Historians) and J. William Sherar, Southern Yacht Club; Jack Sutphen, San Diego Yacht Club; Roger Eldridge, San Francisco Yacht Club; David Hull, Librarian, and Bill Kooiman, Assistant Librarian, National Maritime Museum Library, San Francisco; Bertran Lippincott, III, Historian Conanicut Yacht Club; Ms. Vick Van Loo, Tred Avon Yacht Club; US SAILING: John W. Wright Offshore Director; Jonathan R. Harley, Olympic Director; Loren Barnett Appel, Director Marketing and Communications and Chip William Balch, Design Director; William M. Munroe and Lewis Oates, Jr., Biscayne Bay Yacht Club; David Mittel, Historian Duxbury Yacht Club; Joseph Muldoon, Director Library Services, Ransom-Everglades School; Mystic Seaport Museum: Deborah Digregorio, office assistant Rosenfeld Collection; Douglas Stein, Curator of Manuscripts; Lead Prescott, Oral History Librarian; Naval Institute Press; Ralph Roberts, past President Yachting New Zealand; P. James Roosevelt, Historian, and Ian A. McCurdy Seawanhaka Corinthian Yacht Club; Paul E. Shanabrook, Historian Boston Yacht Club; Irving C. Sheldon, Saunderstown, RI; Sir Peter Johnson, Bt., author* Yacht Rating *and other yachting books; Royce Foley, PHRF Committee, IL, re Universal Rule classes; Don L. Glasell and William W. Parks, Lake Michigan Yachting Association; George Griswold, Midwest Collegiate Sailing Association; C. Stanley Ogilvy, Yacht Racing Association of Long Island Sound, Star Class and Larchmont Yacht Club; Baird Tewskebury, III, Royal Vancouver Yacht Club; Jeremy P. Pudney and W. deForest Trimingham, International Fourteen Class; Jonathan Wilson, Editor,* Wooden Boat*; Robert M. Allan, Jr., Inter-Collegiate Yacht Racing Association; Lawrence A. White, Interscholastic Sailing Association;* Yachting *Magazine; Rudder Magazine; Don Lawler, Newport Computer Center; Gloria Melges and Carol Lothian, Lake Geneva Yacht Club; Tina McKinley, Secretary Southern California Yachting Association; Charles M. Kober, past President USYRU; Horace Benjamin, Commodore Newport Harbor Yacht Club; Jim Gladson, Los Angeles Maritime Institute/*Swift of Ipswich*; Michael J. Weir, Victoria, BC; Galen Crane and Howie Bond,* Adirondack Life *Magazine; Clifford D. Mallory, Jr.*

LIBRARIES

New York Yacht Club, New York Public Library, Herreshoff Maritime Museum, Ransom Everglades School, San Diego Yacht Club, San Diego Maritime Museum; St. Francis Yacht Club, Eastern Yacht Club, Mystic Seaport, National Maritime Museum Library (San Francisco), New York Historical Society, Nova Scotia Archives, Dalhousie University (Halifax), Redwood Library and Atheneaum (Newport, RI).

CONTRIBUTORS

Sam Ackerman, Houston Yacht Club; Professor Paul Alkon, Los Angeles Yacht Club Historical Committee; Robert M. Allan, Jr., James Rousmaniere, Tripp Alyn, Mortimer L. Downey, Janet C. Baxter, James O. Pease, Arthur Knapp, Jr. , Art Keefe, Gail Turlock, Robert W. McNitt, RAdm USN (Ret.) Inter-Collegiate Yacht Racing Association; Samuel A.I. Anderson, Interscholastic Sailing Association; Robert N. Bavier, Jr. and F. Gregg Bemis, NAYRU; Maynard Bray, Universal Rule drawings; William T. Dalessi, Long Beach Yacht Club; Rathbone deBuys, Fish Class, Southern Yacht Club; Ransom H. Duncan, Carl B.E. Shedd, John B. Trevor, Jr. and Michael Kahn, Idem Class; David Edwards, James Michael, Olin J. Stephens, II and Robert Sarty, IOR/IMS Rules; Cy Gillette, Hawaiian Islands; George D. Griffith, PHRF Rule; Anne W. Henry, Suicide Class; Joseph E. Jessop, San Diego Yacht Club; Robert C. Keefe, St. Francis Yacht Club; Albert Mallon, Hon. Historian Royal Canadian Yacht Club; Al Mastics and James M. Snodgrass, Inter-Lake Yacht Racing Association; Samuel V. Merrick, Inland Scows and Inland Lake Yachting Association; Lloyd Ryland, Historian Pacific Inter-Club Yachting Association; Jack Smock, Transpac Race; Dr. Albert Soiland, Los Angeles and Newport Harbor Yacht Clubs; John Willett, Bob Covarrubias and Rusty White Nautical Heritage Society; John W. Streeter, W. P. Stephens and N. G. Herreshoff letters; William U. Swan, sports writer, Boston Globe.

CLUB, CLASS AND YACHT RACING ASSOCIATION HISTORIES CONTRIBUTED OR LOANED

Bellport Bay Yacht Club; Biscayne Bay Yacht Club; Boston Yacht Club; Carolina Yacht Club (Wilmington); Chicago Yacht Club; Cleveland Yacht Club; Cold Spring Harbor Beach Club; Conanicut Yacht Club; Corinthian Yacht Club of San Francisco; Corinthian Yacht Club of Seattle; Cruising Club of America; Detroit Yacht Club; Duxbury Yacht Club; Eastern Yacht Club; Encinal Yacht Club; USA Finn Class Association; Fish Class; Indian Harbor Yacht Club; Inter-Lake Yachting Association; Lake Yacht Racing Association; International Fourteen Foot Dinghy Class Association; Interscholastic Sailing Association; Kaneohe Yacht Club; Lake Geneva Yacht Club; Larchmont Yacht Club; Los Angeles Yacht Club; Monmouth Boat Club; Neenah Nodaway Yacht Club; New York Yacht Club; Newport Harbor Yacht Club; Pacific Coast Yachting Association; Pacific Inter-Club Yacht Association; Richmond Yacht Club; Royal Canadian Yacht Club; Royal Nova Scotia Yacht Squadron; Royal St. Lawrence Yacht Club; Royal Vancouver Yacht Club; Royal Victoria Yacht Club; San Diego Yacht Club; San Francisco Yacht Club; Seattle Yacht Club; Seawanhaka Corinthian Yacht Club; Severn Sailing Association; South Boston Yacht Club; Southern Yacht Club; St. Petersburg Yacht Club; International Star Class Yacht Racing Association; Transpacific Yacht Club; Tred Avon Yacht Club; US Naval Academy; Yacht Racing Association of Long Island Sound; Yacht Racing Union of the Great Lakes.

APPENDIX J

NOTES

CHAPTER I - BEGINNINGS

1 By James Grant Wilson © 1892 New York History Company.

2 There is creditable evidence that in 1647 Governor Johan Printz of the Swedish colony in the Delaware Valley built a sailing vessel for the purpose of visiting friends in towns along the Delaware River; also that Governor William Penn in 1683 built a 30-40-foot pinnace for his personal use. The oft-cited *Onrust* constructed on Manhattan by Adrian Block, after his vessel was destroyed by fire, was used commercially to continue his commission of exploration thereby not qualifying as a 'yacht,' or as Queen Elizabeth I pronounced when she ordered the 80-ton *Rat of Wight* in 1855 a "pleasure ship".

3 Not quite accurate as Morrisania fronted on the Harlem River and Westchester Bay.

4 *American Yachts, Their Clubs and Races,* J. D. Jerrold Kelley, 1884.

5 From *Yachting, A History* by Peter Heaton, © Charles Scribner's Sons 1956. Double hulls, or catamarans, were not an American invention; for example, a twin-hull vessel was built for Charles II, and "in 1662 and 1663 Sir William Petty built two modest catamarans, which he called *Invention* and *Invention II*… a double-bottomed vessel designed for deep water…" Perry also recorded drawings for proposed towing tank tests. Over a century later N.G. Herreshoff refers to using a towing tank in 1879, and in the '80's was using a system of towing pairs of models from a balance yoke. Petty is mentioned by Samuel Pepys as racing his yacht against a "paquet boat" between Dublin and Holyhead, prior to the founding of the 'Water Club of the Harbour of Cork' in 1720 – two years after the Czar founded the 'Peterburg Yakht-Klub' on the Neva River. Peterburg's claim to being the earliest yacht club is substantiated in *Parkesnago Sporta, (A Guide for Fans of the Yachting Sport)* by G.V. Esh, 1895. The club survives despite hiatuses in activity, whereas the Water Club flourished only until 1765 and was not successfully revived until 1821.

6 Located in the Archives of the Royal Nova Scotia Yacht Squadron at Dalhousie University, Halifax, NS.

7 #6 of *The Last Letters from the Master – Annotated edition of correspondence, 1930-1937 between Nathanael Greene Herreshoff and William Pickard Stephens,* by John W. Streeter, awaiting publication.

8 *Capt. Nat Herreshoff – The Wizard of Bristol* by L. Francis Herreshoff.

9 #13 of *The Last Letters from the Master* (ibid. #6).

10 Ibid. #4

11 From *Schooner from Winard* by Mifflin Thomas

12 *New-York Gazette and General Advertiser* May 21, 1825 describes ca. 30,000 people witnessing rowing race in New York Harbor.

13 *Texas and the Gulf of Mexico or Yachting in the New World – Schooner Yacht* Dolphin *1845,* Mrs. Houston

14 *Origin of Yacht Racing in British Columbia and Washington 1870-1914* by James H. Hitchman in *The American Neptune,* Oct. 1976

15 *First in Class – The Story of the Royal Nova Scotia Yacht Squadron* by © Nancie Erhard, 1986, Numbus Pub. Co. Ltd.

16 Founded in 1815 as The Yacht Club and became Royal Yacht Squadron in 1834.

17 A variation of this system has been used by the New York Yacht Club for its Queen's Cup Race to enable smaller yachts to delay their starts and avoid being blanketed by larger yachts without the delay increasing their elapsed time.

18 Courtesy of James M. Snodgrass, Historian for Inter-Lake Yachting Association.

19 An example in the 1880's was the Oakland Canoe Club's Flying Scud with two masts, one at the bow and one at the stern, and the helmsman on a sliding board.

20 *The History of American Yachting* by Fred S. Cozzens and others (primarily Captain R.F. Coffin), 1887

21 *Time and Tide, A Centennial History 1892-1992* by Bertram Lippincott, III © Conanicut Yacht Club 1992.

Nathanael G. Herreshoff observing towing models, October 15, 1915
Photo Herreshoff Marine Museum, Bristol, RI

CHAPTER II - ORIGINAL BIRTH OF NAYRU

1 Primary sources: NAYRU records; *New York Herald, Boston Herald* and *San Francisco Chronicle.*

2 An historian best known for *Traditions and Memories of American Yachting – 1943,* reprinted by Wooden Boat Publishing, Inc. 1989 © Eleanor Stephens.

3 For which William Pickard Stephens covered sailing and yacht design.

4 Lake Yacht Racing Association 1884-1962 compiled by LeRoy F. Grant 1962.

5 He uses the term 'rules' to encompass measurement and classification as well as right of way rules.

6 Ibid.

7 Froude was not recommending retaining simply the LOA and LWL factors of the Seawanhaka Rule. Rather, per his letter of February 3 to Æmilius Jarvis (see *Appendix G*), he recommended using the girth rule, which featured a beam and girth measurement, without the sail area component.

8 Duggan also was a member of the Royal St. Lawrence Yacht Club which he represented in Seawanhaka Cup matches. Toronto Yacht Club later merged with the RCYC.

9 *Annals of the Royal Canadian Yacht Club 1852-1937* – a rare six-volume set a copy of which is in the Public Archives of Canada; compiled by C.H.J. Snider, 1937.

CHAPTER III - YACHT RACING ASSOCIATIONS

1 Sources: *1995 Centennial Regatta Book – Chronology of the Inter-Lake YA, 1885-1985* compiled from records of Commodore A. A. (Al) Mastics; *Inter-Lake YA 1995 Centennial Regatta Book Chronology* by I-LYA Historian, Commodore James M. Snodgrass; *The History of the Inter-Lake Yachting Association 1884 - 1908* by Robert E. Power.

2 *Lake Yacht Racing Association, 1884-1962* compiled by LeRoy F. Grant, 1962.

3 The club merged with the Royal Canadian Yacht Club in 1889, under the name of the latter.

4 Sources: *Pacific Inter-Club Yacht Association Centennial History* by Lloyd Ryland ©1996 and letters and clippings from publications furnished by him. In recognition of his work in this field he was the recipient in 1996 of the Robert Olson Memorial Poseidon award. He has established a collection of yacht club yearbooks and records of yachting at the John Porter Shaw Library – now part of the National Parks Service – at San Francisco.

5 *Rudder*, Sept. 2, 1896.

6 *A history of the development of yachts, yacht clubs, yacht racing and the racing rules* by Robert C. MacArthur 1991 © The Yacht Owner's Register, Inc.

7 *The Yacht Racing Association of Long Island Sound – A Centennial History – 1895-1994*, by C. Stanley Ogilvy, 1995.

8 As a measure of the respect in which the Sabbath was held, the New York Yacht Club used to substitute a light signal for the starting cannon on Sundays, and currently many yacht clubs use a whistle instead of a cannon to make colors on Sundays.

9 Yachting editor for *The Boston Globe*.

10 One of the all-time great Race Committee chairman, Theodore (Ted) E. Tolson, Jr. of the St. Petersburg Yacht Club, claimed that the gauge of the wind direction that he used to set the starting line was the attitude of the seagulls since they invariably float head to wind.

CHAPTER IV - REVIVAL OF NAYRU IN 1925

1 The actual speaker in the copy of the address in US SAILING files is not identified, but by process of elimination Robert N. Bavier, Jr. (President of NAYRU 1967-71) and H. H. Anderson, Jr. conclude that Stewart must have been the author.

2 *Clinton Crane's Yachting Memories* by Clinton H. Crane, © D. Van Nostrand Company, Inc. 1952.

3 It was Stewart as an ex-Commodore who proposed that NYYC join thus breaking a tradition of independence almost as old as the Club. Clinton Crane and Charles F. Adams persuaded the Eastern Yacht Club to follow suit in 1942.

4 Founder of the International Star Class Association and President for 25 years.

5 Members of the Appeals Committee, similar to Officers and Directors, were elected at the annual meeting.

6 Per his son, Clifford D. Mallory, Jr. in *Oral History Collections at Mystic Seaport* by Fred Calabretta.

7 N.G. Herreshoff also was pioneering in its development, esp. the single or half wishbone.

8 Concurrently in 1935 George Townsend launched a series of motor-sailers designed by Charles D. Mower named *Cheerio*.

9 Ibid #2.

10 He might have also noted that Jeffries was the only one who was not a member of the New York Yacht Club.

11 A foundation started by Henry S. Morgan to help fund U.S. Olympic sailors.

12 A prime cause of the unrest was it's rendering existing types of offshore boats non-competitive with those built to the new rule.

13 NAYRU delegates, however, had direct input in its development and without support from NAYRU and magazines such as *Yachting* it would never have become an international rule.

CHAPTER V - INTERCOLLEGIATE YACHT RACING

1 *Leonard M. Fowle Archive of the Intercollegiate Yacht Racing Association* and *Oral History Collections* at Mystic Seaport Museum, Inc. Also, materials sent from regional ICYRA Associations.

2 *A History of the Yale Corinthian Yacht Club – 1881-1971* by Mortimer L. Downey (Yale '58).

3 Rowing by comparison is one of the oldest college sports and started in Whitehalls at Yale in 1842 and at Harvard in the same craft the next year.

4 Frederick Coonley *The Yale Corinthian Yacht Club – Outing Magazine*, June 8, 1898.

5 Coonley is quoted in an unpublished treatise, *A Study of Collegiate Sailing in the United States*, by Lester Rhoads submitted in 1966 towards a degree at Teachers College, Columbia University.

6 *Sherman Hoyt's Memoirs* by C. Sherman Hoyt, © D. Van Nostrand & Co., Inc. 1950.

7 His paper, *The Foundation of the Intercollegiate Racing Association*, 1931 is the primary source.

8 Lost in a fire in the Princeton gym.

9 *Nowhere is Too Far* by Johns S. Parkinson, Jr. © Cruising Club of America.

10 *Oral History Collections* at Mystic Seaport Museum.

11 Much of the material that follows has been digested in mss. form in *A Brief History of Intercollegiate Yacht Racing* by James A. Rousmaniere (Harvard '40) under whose aegis the Leonard M. Fowle archives have been assembled.

12. Ibid. #5 & #9.

13 Partial source: *Women in College Sailing* by Julia Trotman.

14 Source: Art Keefe Yale '75 article in *Yale Alumni Magazine* ca. 1975.

15 Jewett two decades or more later would chair the U.S. Match Racing Championship Committee for the Prince of Wales Bowl presented in 1965 to NAYRU by the Vineyard Haven Yacht Club – his home club.

16 From *50 Golden Years of Great Sailing* by Gail Turlock, and MCSA records furnished by George Griswold, former MCSA graduate secretary.

17 From *Collegiate Sailing in the South* by Tripp Alyn, former Southeast ISA graduate secretary.

18 His daughter, Susie, achieved the further distinction in 1991 of being perhaps the only person ever to have competed at a Nationals and won in the Dinghy (Div. 'B'), Women's (Div. 'A') and Team Racing championships.

19 Each year's All America Team is included in the Inter-Collegiate Sailing Hall of Fame.

20 A digest of *Sailing at the U.S. Naval Academy – An Illustrated History* by Robert W. McNitt Rear Admiral U.S. Navy (Ret.), © 1996 Naval Institute Press.

21 James A. Rousmaniere notes that in 1938 he raced on a Harvard team against Navy in half-raters.

22 "The Naval Academy had previously had a boat club, believed to have been organized in 1947." Its claim to longevity as one of the oldest yacht clubs in North America has been questioned inasmuch as it has not been continually in existence, nor do there appear to be any records of yacht racing activity. The first Midshipmen Boat Club might have been simply a rowing club.

23 These were owned initially by undergraduates who turned them over the next year to the University.

24 Glass reinforced plastic.

25 *A History of the Yale Corinthian Yacht Club – 1881-1971* by Mortimer L. Downey, (Yale '58).

26 Grandfather of Henry H. Anderson, Jr.

27 One of the three founders of Mystic Seaport Museum.

CHAPTER VI - INTERSCHOLASTIC SAILING ASSOCIATION

1 Originally Interscholastic Yacht Racing Association.

2 *Interscholastic Yacht Racing Association, Sixtieth Anniversary, 1930-1990*, by Samuel A.I. Anderson.

3 By 1932 schools beyond New England were joining such as Hill School, PA, and Adirondack-Florida School, FL and NY.

4 *The Centennial History of the Seattle Yacht Club, 1892-1992* by James R. Warren ©1992 Seattle Yacht Club.

5 *The History of the Neenah-Nodaway Yacht Club – An Account of Yacht Racing on Lake Winnebago from 1859-1957* by James C. Kimberly, privately published 1957.

6 *Royal Canadian Yacht Club, Annals of 1852-1937* by C.H.J. Snider ©1937 Rous & Mann Ltd.

7 They were also renown for their gracious life style and gourmet tastes.

8 *Richmond Yacht Club, 1932-1982* ©1982 by nine members of the Club.

CHAPTER VII - YACHT CLUBS

1 Source: *100 Years at the Head of the Bay – Bay Head Yacht Club's First Century, 1888-1988* by Richard H. La Bonte, 1988.

2 From *One Hundred Years On Biscayne Bay, 1887-1987* by Stuart McIver, ©1987 BBYC.

3 Authors: Ralph Middleton Munroe and Vincent Gilpin, 1930.

4 *A History of The Boston Yacht Club – 1866-1879* by Paul E. Shanabrook © Boston Yacht Club.

5 The mystery of whether Capt Nat also designed her is cleared up by his affirmation in *The Last Letters from the Master* by John W. Streeter (awaiting publication).

6 Based on *Carolina Yacht Club Chronicles* by Anne Russell © 1993.

7 In NC as distinguished from the Carolina Yacht Club at Charleston, SC founded in 1883.

8 All four clubs were preceded by the Halifax Yacht Club, Nova Scotia, now the Royal Nova Scotia Yacht Squadron.

9 Bob Fish was a well-known and prolific builder of sandbaggers and catboats in New York waters.

10 See *Chapter I – Beginnings*.

11 Capt. Nat was named after his ancestor, General Nathanael Green of Revolutionary War fame, but mistakenly at birth his first name was spelt 'Nathaniel' (not 'Nathanial' as it appears in the Carolina Yacht Club history). In later life he paid a visit to the General's tomb and thereafter signed letters and documents using 'Nathanael.' Source: Halsey C. Herreshoff who heard this from his mother and whose brother, Nathanael, uses the same spelling.

12 The Inland Lake Yacht Racing Association differs from the other YRAs of the NAYRU which were composed of Clubs and Classes in contiguous geographical regions. While ILYRA was concentrated on the lakes in Wisconsin and Minnesota, it also included clubs in the regions of other YRAs where Scows are raced, e.g. Lake Murray, SC and Clubs in the south and even southwest. This sometimes opened up dual options for teams to compete in eliminations to qualify for national championships such as the Sears, Mallory and Adams, thereby creating consternation within NAYRU.

13 *Chicago Yacht Club, The First Years, 1875-1975* by Richard and Wendy Van Mell, 1975, Carl Gorr Printing Co.

14 From *The Yearbook of the Cruising Club of America* © CCA 1997.

15 Recently restored and sailing the Bras d'Or Lakes, Nova Scotia.

16 To enforce the Eighteenth Amendment (prohibition) Congress passed an Act sponsored by Senator Volstead that, in conjunction with the Tariff Act of 1922, authorized arrest of vessels within territorial waters, which were extended from three to 12 miles under the Tariff Act.

17 CCA, instead of a clubhouse, has stations extending from Bermuda to the Pacific Northwest.

18 His account is the source of this information.

19 From *Duxbury Yacht Club Story, 1875-1995* by David A. Mittel

20 Article in *Yachting* Feb., 1930 by William U. Swan, sports writer for the *Boston Globe*. His prose is left almost intact as an example of the journalistic writing of this and earlier periods.

21 From material supplied by Cy Gillette including newspaper articles from, e.g. *Pacific Commercial Advertiser*.

22 From a series of articles by Edna Whiting, "Yachting Enthusiast and Member of Pearl Harbor Yacht Club.

23 *Lake Geneva Yacht Club, 1874-1974* by Hal Hamilton, published 1974 by Lake Geneva Yacht Club.

24 From notes by William T. Dalessi, staff Commodore of the Long Beach Yacht Club and member of the syndicate composed of himself, Barney Flam, Mort Haskell, Stan Miller, Chuck Kober (past President of USYRU) and Jack Queen that purchased the New Zealand built, plywood sloop – a 'super Star – *Ragtime* to be first to finish in the Transpac Race, which they were.

25 A former Executive Director of NAYRU/ USYRU.

26 *Los Angeles Yacht Club History* from proofs furnished by Paul Alkon, Professor of English University of Southern California and member of the LAYC *Historical Committee*. *Transpacific Ocean Races and the Transpacific Yacht Club, 1937* by Dr. Albert Soiland. *Transpac 1906-1979 – A History of the Great Race to Honolulu* by Jack Smock © 1980 Maritime Museum Assn. of San Diego. *Newport Harbor Yacht Club, 75 Years* by Allan Farwell Trane © 1991 Newport Harbor Yacht Club.

27 *The Saga of Newport Bay and Newport Harbor Yacht Club* by Albert Soiland privately printed 1936.

28 More likely 1906 as that was the year of the P.E. branch to Newport Beach opened.

29 Excerpts with emendations from Chapter 12, *Room at the Mark* by Robert C. MacArthur © 1991, The Yacht Owners Register, Inc.; *Capt. Nat Herreshoff*, L. Francis Herreshoff © 1953, Sheridan House, Inc.; *History of the New York Yacht Club, Volume Two* by John Parkinson, Jr., © 1975, The New York Yacht Club.

30 A decade ago Congress when revising the Annotated Codes repealed, without explanation, Section 107 which had been the authority for displaying the yacht ensign thereby leaving only the national ensign as appropriate for yachts.

31 Throg's Neck marks the juncture of the East River and Long Island Sound.

32 While its origin is not recorded, it echoes the philosophy of Horace's *Epistula II* and may be a corruption of the line, "Non agimur tumidis velis" (not with swelling sails are we borne before a following North Wind [Augilone]).

33 Since *America*, failing in 1851 to land a wager for a match, raced against an entire fleet of British yachts, the club insisted that the challenger do the same. In the second defense the club used only one boat per race but retained the option of making substitutions. Thereafter, largely under the persuasion of George L. Schuyler, surviving member of the original America syndicate, the conditions were revised to require that only one boat be used throughout.

34 Explained in *Chapter I – Beginnings*.

35 *The History of American Yachting* by Fred S. Cozzens and others (primarily Capt. R.F. Coffin), © 1887.

36 The 'log' actually is a long letter with the signature of N.G. Herreshoff that Lewis sent, unbeknownst to Capt. Nat, to *The Spirit of the Times*. The Mr. Meigs referred to was a columnist for the *Spirit*.

37 Ibid. #35.

38 Who as Rear Admiral Alfred Thayer Mahan was renown for his *Influence of Sea Power on History* and many other works as a naval theoretician.

39 Full title: *Report of the Special Committee of the NYYC Relative to Certain Charges made by the Earl of Dunraven Concerning the Recent Match for the America's Cup* © 1896 NYYC.

40 Since publication of Froude's report to the Royal Navy defining LWL as being the parameter of speed, LWL has been the conventional way to express length instead of LOA, as was the case, for example, with the America. Concurrently the extreme overhangs of the skimming dishes built to the Seawanhaka Rule had rendered LOA meaningless as a measure of a boat's performance. The switchover to LOA was greatly influenced by the Cruising Club of America in the 1930's and stemmed from short overhang yachts such as the schooners *Nina* and *Mistress*. After WW II it became common practice to use LOA, especially with one-design classes.

41 The Eastern Yacht Club was a bit more hospitable. Its by-law read, "Ladies may be admitted to the Club House on such days and subject to such regulations as may be established by the House Committee." This would not change for many years, either.

42 *Rounding the Century Mark, One Hundred Years at Rochester Yacht Club, 1877-1977* by William J. Stolze © 1977 RYC.

43 Originally a Venetian term for a single race; today it connotes a series.

44 Whether Capt. Nat was also the designer has been a controversial question, but in the correspondence between himself and W.P. Stephens (vide *The Last Letters from the Master* by John W. Streeter, awaiting publication) he confirms that he did.

45 *Annals of The Royal Canadian Yacht Club 1852-1937* compiled by C.H.J. Snider © 1937, Rous & Mann, Ltd. and condensed by RCYC Hon. Historian, Albert Mallon; *History of the Lake Yacht Racing Association, 1884-1962* compiled by Colonel LeRoy F. Grant, 1962.

46 No connection with the Toronto Yacht Club formed in 1881 by younger members of RCYC, including G. Herrick Duggan and Hubert H. Macrae, which amalgamated with RCYC in 1889.

47 Source *Royal Nova Scotia Yacht Squadron – First In Its Class*, by Nancie Erhard © Nimbus Publishing.

48 Nova Scotia Archives at Dalhousie Univeristy, Halifax including archives of RNSYS.

49 Others are Royal Yacht Squadron, Cowes, England; Royal Sydney, Royal South Australian, Royal Melbourne, and Royal Queensland, Australia; and Royal New Zealand.

50 Notwithstanding, the Chicago-Mackinac Race in 1898 was held on 'an arm of the sea' as the Great Lakes were defined in a ruling by the Court in the next century.

51 Source: *The Royal St. Lawrence Yacht Club, 1888-1988* by George Hanson © 1988 RSLYC.

52 Source: *A Century of Sailing, 1892-1992 – A History of the Royal Victoria Yacht Club* © Terry Reksten 1992, Orca Book Pub.

53 Past Commodore Robert C. Keefe is author of the upcoming *History of the St. Francis Yacht Club* told through the medium of the famous yachts that have been enrolled in the Club.

54 The course was reversed in 1961 largely at the suggestion of C. Sherman Hoyt in order to entice yachts coming north in the spring to make the race a leg of their trip.

55 Offices held: Commodore St. Francis Yacht Club, Cruising Club of America and President of NAYRU.

56 *The Ships, The House, and The Men – A History of the San Diego Yacht Club* by Charles R. LaDow, 1917 Frazee Industries; *A History of Yachting in San Diego* by Linda M. Pearce Nolte, 1974; *Sailing in San Diego, A Pictorial History*, © 1991 Neva Griggs Sullaway, TSC Pub. Co.; *The History of Three Major Yacht Clubs of San Diego*; some courtesy of San Diego Maritime Museum; and verbal by the late Joseph E. Jessop.

57 *Oldest West Coast One-Design Rediscovered* by Rusty White, Nautical Heritage Society 1991.

58 *The First One Hundred Years of the San Francisco Yacht Club* Victor Jorgensen, editor, 1969.

59 *The Centennial History of the Seattle Yacht Club, 1892-1992*, by James R. Warren, © 1992 Seattle Yacht Club

60 *Seawanhaka Corinthian Yacht Club: Origins and Early History 1871-1896* by W.P. Stephens and Seawanhaka Corinthian Yacht Club and *The Early*

Twentieth Century, 1897-1940 by John Parkinson, Jr., © 1965 SCYC.

61 *The History of American Yachting* by Fred S. Cozzens and others (primarily Coffin).

62 Not to be confused with William U. Swan, a sportswriter for the *Boston Globe*.

63 The trophy was found after World War II by Walter C. 'Jack' Wood at the Royal Corinthian Yacht Club in Burnham, England. The engraving is on the underside, and he happened to turn it over which the RCYC member, who bought it at a pawn shop as a present for his mother-in-law, had failed to do. She, however, did so, and on finding that it was second-hand gave it back to him so he presented it for competition at the Club.

64 *Severn Sailing Association Club History 1954-1972* by Hugh C. Donald and articles and data furnished by Dr. H. Stuart Walker.

65 *History of the Southern Yacht Club* by Flora K. Scheib © 1986 Pelican Pub. Co.. She and her husband, J. Gilbert Scheib were known as "Mr. and Mrs. GYA"; he served as President of the Gulf Yachting Association and as secretary and treasurer for 40 years.

66 All located in Mississippi Sound between Lake Ponchartrain and Mobile, Alabama.

67 From an article in *Yachting* July, 1971 by William W. Robinson. See also Bay Head Yacht Club section in *Chapter VII*.

68 Sources: *The Tide* and misc. items from Club archives courtesy of the Commodore and Ms. Vick Van Loo. Also, first draft of a proposed history by W.J. Holt, Jr.

CHAPTER VIII CLASSES AND ONE-DESIGNS

1 His grandson, Michael Schoettle, served as Chairman of the US Olympic Yachting Committee 1988-92.

2 The first © 1904 Arthur H. Clark and published by G. P. Putnam's Sons; the second © 1937 The MacMillan Co.; the third © 1979 Diana Eames Esterly and published by Charles Scribner's Sons.

3 #14 in *The Last Letters from the Master* by John W. Streeter, awaiting publication and consisting of correspondence between N.G. Herreshoff and W. P. Stephens.

4 Inexplicably the club never joined either NAYRU nor Central New York Yacht Racing Association.

5 "The Unchallenged Idem," *Adirondack Life Magazine*, summer, 1972.

6 *History of Neenah-Nodaway Yacht Club – An Account of Yacht Racing on Lake Winnebago from 1859-1957* privately published in 1957 by James C. Kimberly. Founded in 1864, the Club later merged with the Nodaway Yacht Club.

7 Named for the former Custom House in lower Manhattan, NY. Although the precise origin of the design is not well documented, its antecedents may have been the English wherry or the gigs on naval vessels.

8 *The Whitehall Boat – Rudder*, Aug. 1943 by Capt. Charlton L. Smith.

9 Copies of the newspaper pre-dating the Gold Rush era are at the John Porter Shaw Library, part of the San Francisco Maritime National Historical Park at Fort Mason, San Francisco.

10 Ibid #9.

11 The first 'R' on the Bay was *Active* built by Lester Stone and raced in the Universal Rule 'N' class until the next year. Dimensions of the 'R' approximately 38 feet LOA, 25 feet LWL compared to approximately 37 feet 6 inches LOA, 23 feet LWL for a Six-Metre.

12 A Yacht Racing Association of San Francisco Bay yachting periodical.

13 *The First Hundred Years – A History of the Chicago Yacht Club – 1875-1975* Richard and Wendy Van Mell, 1975, published by Carl Gorr Printing, Co. and letters from Herbert T. Van Mell.

14 *Annals of the Royal Vancouver Yacht Club 1903-1970* by Norman Hacking © 1965 Evergreen Press .

15 *Annals of the Royal Canadian Yacht Club 1852-1937* compiled by C.H.J. Snider © 1937.

16 Sources: *The International Fourteen 1928-1989* © T.J.Vaughan 1964, publisher International. Fourteen Foot Dinghy Class Association. of Great Britain; article *The Leading Edge* by Robert Keeley; Dr. Stuart Walker and notes by de Forest (Shorty) W. Trimingham.

17 Mallory not only revived the North American Yacht Racing Union in 1925 but also imported the first Twelve-Metre and first Ten-Metre to the continent as well as the Fourteen that provided the stimulus to international team racing in the class.

18 *1995 Centennial Regatta Book – Chronology of the Inter-Lake Yacht Racing Association 1885-1995* compiled from records of Commodore A.A. (Al) Mastics.

19 A series devised by *Yachting* magazine for which Robert N. Bavier, Jr. was primarily responsible. It's purpose was to pit boats from various types of classes, ie. centerboarders, multihulls, keel boats, in a performance contest.

20 It was customary to change the single-handed class each Olympiad and leave the selection up to the host nation – a custom that the Finn put paid to.

21 Term for the four-year period running from the end of the previous Games through the next Games (now quadrennium).

22 Source: *The Fish Class – Origin and Growth* by Rathbone deBuys, alias 'Daddy of the Fish Class,' 1950.

23 The GYA became the successor to the Southern Gulf Yachting Association formed in 1901.

24 *Golden Age of Open Class Racing at Marblehead, 1906-40* by Evers Burtner, N.H. Wood Press 1968.

25 *The Small Yacht* by Edwin A. Boardman, 1909.

26 For more information see *A History of the 'S' Boats* by Kenneth B. Upton, 1994.

27 Sources: *Yachting*, Aug., 1961 & Mar., 1937; *The Western Boatman*, Feb., 1990; The *San Francisco Bay Yachtsman*, Sept., 1928; *Pacific Skipper*, Aug., 1935; and misc. material from Lloyd Ryland, Historian for Pacific Inter-Club Yacht Racing Association.

28 From a paper delivered by Samuel V. Merrick at the second Yachting History Symposium held at Mystic Seaport Museum in 1989. Material from Lloyd Ryland, Historian for Pacific Inter-Club Yacht Racing Association.

29 Sources: Hilary Smart in Star Class *Yearbook*, a Star sailor since age 11 and 1948 Olympic Gold Medalist; *A History of the Star Class*, C. Stanley Ogilvy © 1991, International. Star Class Yacht Racing Association; *Sailing Craft* by Edwin J. Schoettle © 1928 The MacMillan Company.

30 Letter Seventeen in *Annals of Yachting – The Last Letters of the Master and Notes* © John W. Streeter (awaiting publication).

31 Letters from Anne W. Henry, author of unpublished *Suicide – The Fastest Way To Go*.

32 W.P. Stephens had the same predilection.

33 *Herreshoff of Bristol* by Maynard Bray and Carlton Pinheiro © 1989 Woodenboat Publications. Also, recollections of Henry H. Anderson, Jr.

34 Letter sent by Sam Ackkerman, historian for the Houston Yacht Club (TX). It was written in 1942 on Manhasset Bay Yacht Club (NY) letterhead by Lingard Loud to Commodore Hamilton and given to Ackerman by Hamilton's family. Also, *A History of the Larchmont Yacht Club, Diamond Jubilee, 1889-1989* by C. Stanley Ogilvy © LYC 1993.

35 Source: article by William H. Taylor, *Yachting*, May, 1942.

36 Later it was put in competition in the 5.5 Metre Class and then for class racing under the Offshore Racing Committee.

37 *Sailing In Bermuda, Sail Racing in the Nineteenth Century* © J. C. Arnell 1982.

38 *A Manual of Yacht and Boat Sailing* (prior to 1866).

39 Source: article in Ocean Cruising Club *Flying Fish* by Roger Fothergill.

40 *Origins of Sea Terms* by John Rogers © 1984 Mystic Seaport Museum.

CHAPTER IX RATINGS, TIME ALLOWANCES AND YACHT CLASSIFICATIONS

1 For an in-depth study see *William Pickard Stephens, designer and chronicler*, in his *Traditions and Memoirs in American Yachting – 1943*, reprinted by Wooden Boat Publishing, Inc. 1989 © Eleanor Stephens and in publications of the Society of Naval Architects and Marine Engineers of which Stephens was a founding member. Also, *Yacht Rating – 170 years of speed, success and failure against competitors – and the clock* by Sir Peter Johnson, Bucksea Guides 1997.

2 See *Chapter VII - Royal Nova Scotia Yacht Squadron*.

3 The Royal Yacht Club became the Royal Yacht Squadron in 1834.

4 If time allowances had been applied to the 1851 race around the Isle of Wight, the *America* would have placed third or fourth [from records of RYS, courtesy past Commodore Maldwin Drummond, OBE JP DL].

5 The Atlantic Yacht Club started in 1865 as an off-shoot of the Brooklyn Yacht Club and next to the NYYC was the dominant player in terms of yachts and regattas held. It was followed by the Seawanhaka [1871] and Larchmont [1880] Yacht Clubs.

6 Poor was the author of *Men Against the Rule – A Century of Progress in Yacht Design* printed by Eugene V. Connett at the Derrydale Press © 1937.

7 See *Appendix G*.

8 For a more detailed review see W. P. Stephen's *Yacht Measurement – Origin and Development* in the Society of Naval Architects and Marine Engineers Proceedings - 1935 and *America's Cup Yacht Designs – 1851-1986* © F. Chevalier et Jacques Taglang.

9 *Chicago Yacht Club – The First Hundred Years 1875-1975* by Richard and Wendy Van Mell (1975 Carl Gorr Printing Co.

10 "Seawanhaka" in the text, but read in overall context is perforce "Universal".

11 Succeeded by Pacific International Yachting Association. *Centennial History of the Seattle Yacht Club 1892-1992* by James Warren © 1992 Seattle Yacht Club.

12 *The Seawanhaka Corinthian Yacht Club – Origins and Early History 1871-1896* by W. P. Stephens © 1963 SCYC

13 Later changed to Royal Yachting Association.

14 The formula was a more sophisticated form of the Seawanhaka Rule which determined a yacht's Racing Measurement (RM =rating) by adding together the load-water-line length, the beam, .75 of the girth and .5 of the square root of the sail area and dividing the sum by two. Yachts were divided into classes based on their RM and rig, e.g. Schooners lst Class all over 100 feet; Sloops, Cutters and Yawls lst class all over 65 feet. Time Allowance was calculated on RM; yawls rated at 93 percent of their RM. Crews were limited to one person to every two feet of RM.

15 See *Appendix G* for correspondence between Emilius Jarvis and the British Yacht Racing Association and later letter sent by Jarvis to Clifford Mallory in 1935.

16 As reported by W. P. Stephens.

17 Herreshoff earlier had designed a rule for the Boston Yacht Club, of which he was a member, which essentially was the Universal Rule without the quarter-beam length feature. He also had the rule in concept almost a decade earlier when he designed *Wasp* and in 1899 when he designed the New York Thirties. It was the impetus of the Atlantic Coast Conference that led him to formalize the rule to be used in conjunction with the table of time allowances that he had earlier created for the Boston Yacht Club.

18 In 1979 Lloyd Bergeson sailed New York Thirty No. 5, *Cockatoo II* transAtlantic to Norway singlehanded and en route home double-handed had to abandon her when she sprung a leak in a series of gales off Greenland (see *Cruising World*, June/July and August 1979).

19 *Yachting*, Feb., 1930.

20 N.G. Herreshoff had created a table of scantlings as well as a set of measurement rules well ahead of the times but apparently never adopted.

21 Reported by M. Heckstall-Smith, Secretary of the Yacht Racing Association of England and a pre-eminent British yachting editor who was a major influence in the development of the racing and measurement rules. The International Rule permitted a greater flexibility, or trading off, of sail area versus displacement than the Universal Rule. The 'carrot' mentioned was in expectation that a common rule would stimulate big class racing on both sides of the Atlantic.

22 His extensive research on the subject is the basis for this section of the *History*.

23 A later report on the position of the CCA respecting an international rule appears in *Appendix F*.

24 The Club has a station on an Island on the San Joaquin River below Stockton, Calif. where it holds an annual rendezvous to which members invite leading yachtsmen from around the globe.

25 A subject currently under intense review in order to make the procedure more user-friendly for both competitors and race committees.

26 Refers to the difference between the North American practice of calculating time allowances based on the length of the course vis-à-vis the RORC system of time-on-time based on the duration of the race.

CHAPTER X
OLYMPIC YACHTING

1 Primary source: *The Olympic Story - A Brief History of the Modern Olympics* from the *North American Finn Sailboat Racing Class 1992-1993 Directory*.

CHAPTER XI
JOINS IYRU AND BECOMES US NATIONAL AUTHORITY

1 *Courts of Admiralty in Colonial America* © 1995 David R. Owen & Michael C. Tolley. Also, the late Professor Julius Goebel of Columbia University Law School.

2 Under 'Sports Canada' federal support for the Canadian Olympic effort flows to the Provinces and is distributed to community and yacht club programs, whereas in the U.S. the only source of funding is from the U.S. Olympic Committee to the National Sports Governing bodies.

3 To conform to the requirements of the U.S. Amateur Athletic Sports Act.

4 Further, the USOC had all along been certifying U.S. Olympic yachting teams for the Olympics that had been selected by an international, rather than a national, sports governing body.

5 The IYRU elections in 1994 put paid to the complacent, but self-deluding, concept that North America is 'entitled' three Vice Presidents; the U.S. wound up with none and Canada with the Presidency.

6 CYA was founded in 1931, but the concept was proposed by G. Herrick Duggan of the Royal St. Lawrence and Royal Canadian Yacht Clubs at the 1884 meeting, which resulted instead in the formation of the Lake Yacht Racing Association.

7 An apocryphal story illustrating how seriously he tackled the task was told by some weekend guests who found him working at a table on the porch of his Carolina plantation. When they greeted him, he indicated that he was occupied but would be with them shortly; it was the last conversation they had with him the rest of the weekend.

APPENDIX E
EARLY RESTRICTED AND ONE-DESIGN CLASSES

1 For details about some of these classes see: *Early One-Design Sailboats* by Diana Eames Esterly, 1979; Rusty White's report of research with the Nautical Heritage Society of San Diego; *Herreshoff at Bristol* by Maynard Bray and Carlton Pinheiro; *Sailing Craft* by Edwin J. Schoettle, 1937; *Sailing in Bermuda* by J.C. Arnell; *The Sailboat Classes of North America* by Fessenden S. Blanchard; magazines including *Wooden Boat, Rudder, Yachting*, et alia; Sam Merrick's history of the Class 'E' Scow; and yacht club histories.

APPENDIX H
HAROLD S. VANDERBILT'S FORTY-ONE YEAR STINT REVISING THE YACHT RACING RULES

1 Three flag officers (Anderson being father of the co-author of this *History*) of the Seawanhaka Corinthian Yacht Club.

2 For most of this timetable we are indebted to notes recorded by F. Gregg Bemis whose influence on the process and final draft was enormous.

3 The authors were unable to locate any written records for the period so that the list of members of the committee may be incomplete.

APPENDIX K

INDEX